THE SMELL OF BOOKS

The Smell of Books

A Cultural-Historical Study of
Olfactory Perception in Literature

HANS J. RINDISBACHER

Ann Arbor

THE UNIVERSITY OF MICHIGAN PRESS

1995   1994   1993   1992   4   3   2   1

Library of Congress Cataloging-in-Publication Data

Rindisbacher, Hans J., 1955–
    The smell of books : a cultural-historical study of olfactory
perception in literature / Hans J. Rindisbacher.
        p.   cm.
    Includes bibliographical references and index.
    ISBN 0-472-10383-0 (alk. paper)
        1. European literature—History and criticism. 2. Smell in
literature. 3. Odors in literature.   I. Title.
PN761.R56   1922
809'.93355—dc20   92-30972
                                                              CIP

A CIP catalogue record for this book is available from the British Library.

Preface

The investigation of the olfactory is the investigation of everything else.

When I began this study of olfactory perception in literature, it seemed easy enough to select a few texts, look at descriptive passages, see if and how and to what purpose the olfactory element was used, and then come to some concluding generalizations about the matter. This concept has changed and become much more complex as my work has progressed. The selection of texts proved to be the first major methodological problem, a problem, in fact, that could be solved only by opting for an exemplary rather than a comprehensive treatment of the issue. What Dan Sperber points out for the phenomenon of smell itself holds true for the literary material from which I take my examples: it cannot be classified in terms of clearcut encyclopedic entries. Whereas we find "blue" or "red" or "green" in a paradigm for "colors," the "smell of coffee," the "scent of a rose," or the "stench of power" have no such superordinated paradigm. The very way we talk about smells—in metonymic language, denoting the origin of the phenomenon—sends us to as many places in the encyclopedia as there are "smelly" objects. This lack of a paradigmatic structure of the olfactory is reflected in my selection of texts. My research began with German bourgeois realist novels, and the emphasis has remained on nineteenth-century prose literature and on German cultural, historical, and literary developments. However, expansion beyond the German borders soon became necessary for the story of the sense of smell to be told meaningfully. Hence the inclusion of French and Russian material as an integral part of the account. If the selection of texts initially seems arbitrary, it begins to make sense and justify itself, I hope, in the unfolding of the story of the sense of smell itself. For there *is* a story to be told. The selected texts are meant to serve as exemplars around which the basic outlines of that narrative are drawn. A more detailed picture can then be painted as required.

Concepts such as *bürgerliches Trauerspiel* or symbolist poetry or realist narrative each comprise a relatively clear-cut and limited body of texts, limited because defined as a paradigm. In fact, such literary or literary-historical definitions tend to be circular from the outset: included in the category of *bürgerliches Trauerspiel* are all those plays that contain the features that beforehand have been extracted from a body of plays with a view to including them in the category. Such a hermeneutic circle is not possible for the literary (historical) study of a phenomenon that lies a priori outside literature, and is only loosely grounded in language in the first place. My selection therefore is inevitably incomplete for the very reason that completeness is impossible. It would mean including the whole encyclopedia. Contained in this admission is another one. The criteria applied in my selection of texts lie outside the phenomenon that I am studying. As my research is new, I decided to settle for a limited sample of texts based on traditional literary-historical criteria and thus refer to canonical works and well-known authors only. By this conservative measure I hope to ward off at least some of the objections that can be raised against a novel inquiry such as the present one.

There are more problems, however. I was hoping to be able to focus more exclusively on olfactory perception than it has turned out to be possible. Especially in my attempt to phrase the findings of the study in terms of an aesthetics, it became inevitable to refer to, in fact base myself on, other sensory modalities and their philosophical conceptualizations, above all the visual, which has furnished the major paradigms of practically all aesthetic theory. Aesthetic theory and the history of aesthetics simply do not deal with the olfactory. This sense is generally excluded even from cognitive-hermeneutic investigations, and it certainly has no corresponding art form; in fact there hardly exists a conscious production of olfactive objects with an aesthetic intention. Olfactory phenomena are accidental, are by-products of human activity and of the world we live in, but they can nevertheless help to characterize it. This view leaves out the one realm in which olfactive phenomena do play the role of intentionally produced objects: perfumery and fragrances. This strand of olfaction is well documented, both historically and in its scientific-technological and socioeconomic aspects. That it has an aesthetic dimension of its own is undeniable and would be well worth an in-depth investigation, but it is a realm, overall, that I can only touch upon within the framework of this study.

The accidental nature of smell is reflected in the absence of public education and learning about olfaction as well as in the fact that smell has no art form associated with it. In this respect it shares the fates of the other chemical sense, taste, and of touch, although the former, in the culinary, has long held a status approaching that of art. But it is above all the two senses of distance, vision and hearing, that are the leading senses in our culture both in terms of everyday perceptual functionality, that is, the absorbing and processing of information, and in terms of aesthetic production and theory. The consequences for the present study are two new challenges: to inquire into the possible historical and even anthropological reasons for this neglect of the olfactory (reasons that could also apply to the other senses of proximity), and to develop some aspects of an aesthetics of olfaction.

The first is an awesome task because the historical investigation opens up the literary study to social, political, technological, psychological, and physiological problems involved in (olfactory) perception as well as philosophical, hermeneutic, and epistemological questions. Just as olfactory phenomena are not contained in a manageable number of encyclopedic entries, the historical investigation of smells cannot be contained within one or two or even a reasonably small number of historical and scientific inquiries: the historical perspective really opens the Pandora's box of problems surrounding something as simple as the fact that we like the smell of a rose but find nauseating the stench of the dog litter we just stepped into.

This, however, is not yet all, for the historical investigation, as it deals with sensory perception, reaches the point where anthropological questions, the very development of the human species with its sensory capacities, have to be addressed. The historical inquiry then turns into outlining the larger process of civilization from its very beginning. All this, of course, cannot be accomplished in this study. I can only point to some crucial facts and phenomena.

The second challenge, the development of an olfactory aesthetic, is relatively easier. Once the civilizational and historical discussion has provided us with a number of findings, not lastly from aesthetic theory itself and its history, these may be used to establish a meaningful relation to the literary texts at hand and the olfactory references contained in them. It will emerge from the textual passages that the olfactory sense seems to have become a surplus sense, not really "necessary" in cultural patterning within our socio-semiotic systems. Historical evidence will corroborate these findings. Olfactory phenomena have been treated very differently under the sway of various guiding values at various times. As a perceptual phenomenon, however, olfaction is a physiological constant. It lies before, and is at the basis of, hermeneutic processes and thus can be seen as forming part of what Merleau-Ponty calls the "primacy of perception." It cannot be eradicated. It can only, in its social and psychological phenomenology, be factually eliminated, linguistically euphemized, psychologically repressed.

The introductory first chapter gives a short and inevitably sketchy overview of some basic scientific, sociohistorical, and aesthetic positions vis-à-vis the sense of smell as well as some instances of its poetic occurrence. Major euphemizing and repression seem to occur in the bourgeois age, the Biedermeier, the Victorian nineteenth century. The texts discussed in the second chapter are from this period and can be characterized as examples of olfactory repression. Russian literature and the contemporary developments in France, discussed more extensively in the second chapter, will help to modify this view somewhat. Against this epoch, which is posited as the empty and rather hostile environment for the olfactory at the dawn of the modern age, the following three chapters will present three periods of olfactory breakthrough, or at least of a surfacing of the olfactory.

Chapter 3 deals with literature from the late nineteenth century and from the first two decades of the twentieth century. In this period two contrary styles unite in reacting against the bourgeois repression of the olfactory. In naturalism, writers such as Zola go far beyond bourgeois realism and introduce olfaction as a new aesthetic element in literature. Decadence and fin-de-siècle, too, react to bourgeois realism with a vengeance in writers such as Huysmans, Wilde, Hofmannsthal, and Rilke. It is as if they felt a need to infuse the purged smells back into literary reality. Although the focus of this part of the study is on turn-of-the-century literature, it starts as far back in its historical outline as the preceding chapter and tries to uncover the birth of smells out of the spirit of the early French poetic modernism of Baudelaire, Rimbaud, and Verlaine, among others.

Chapter 4 will deal with the link of sensory perception and power structures through the example of fascism and its treatment of prisoners in death camps. The Nazi system demands individual suffering for the benefit of the *völkisch* community and in this process recognizes sensory experience only for the purpose of inflicting humiliation and pain on its victims. In this framework, the discussion of sensory experience in terms of aesthetics is taken to its extreme, and aesthetics emerges with its roots in basic sensory experience laid bare, an aesthetics that reaches to the limits of the physically as well as emotionally bearable.

The last area of investigation is the postmodernist present and recent past. Postmodernism has brought about, certainly in the realm of theory, a renewed awareness of the body and of sensory experience. Outside literature, the perfume industry is taking a more aggressive approach, and in literature itself a whole gamut of texts whose narrative structure relies at least partly on smells and scents, such as *Bitch, Jitterbug Perfume, Das Parfum,* and *Störfall,* has emerged in recent years. The superficial and inaccurate characterization of postmodernism as "anything goes" can, in my view, only partly be made responsible for this phenomenon. Other, more important, reasons are the effects of the new subjectivity of the 1970s and the powerful impact of feminism both in writing and in criticism and theory, with their interest in the body. Also in the air is a new, auratic perception of the object world, a trend toward aestheticization and beautification of the public and the private spheres that has begun to include the olfactory more and more openly.

One way of limiting the daunting vastness of the inquiry is to take a descriptive-phenomenological approach. This allows us to take some distance from the existing theoretical ballast and focus instead on the level of concrete examples. It also permits us to keep our own theoretical preconceptions phenomenological, by which I mean to say that each work or group of works dealt with in this study, together with the specific theoretical approach that we choose for it and the findings we may arrive at, forms first of all a paradigm of its own and is meant to be coherent in itself. The link between those paradigms will be provided as a sociohistorical, literary-categorical and theoretical-aesthetic continuum as we move along in our inquiry. There will not be—there cannot be at this point—an all-encompassing concept of olfactory aesthetics accounting for both historical developments and their phenomenological manifestations. To locate the present research more closely: perception is understood as "a sensory-motor *behavior* through which the world is constituted for man as the world of human consciousness prior to any explicit or reflexive thoughts about it," as James Edie has it in the introduction to Merleau-Ponty's *Primacy of Perception.* In terms of literature, however, or the limited selection thereof that will provide us with the data for analysis and the elements of theoretical reflection, perception must also be understood as the observation of re-presentation. Olfactory data as they appear in literature are no longer the "real-world" scents and stenches in Merleau-Ponty's sense but have been structured within a number of sociohistorically determined codes and conventions. That is, in fact, how they have acquired meaning. Meaning is structure. It lies, for instance, in language. The specific problem with the olfactory in this respect is that its linguistic structure of reference always throws us back into the dis-order of things. Thus in trying to make sense of the olfactory we must address it within a text not only on the level of reference to outside reality but also on the level of plot, description, and literary context. We cannot make sense on the real-object level but only on that of the textual, social, linguistic, and phenomenological data.

The direction of this study is not toward a perceptual reductionism of phenomena that are structured and meaningful on a higher level, but rather, while fully recognizing the overlying abstract and categorical thinking, to point out its very concrete sensory, perceptual basis. This is in tune with the general trend in Western enlightenment thought that has moved away from the body toward increasing cerebration—only to come back to it later; for the nonsensual, *unsinnlich,* is ultimately also that which is nonsensical, *unsinnig,* what does not make sense. Our inquiry focuses on one sense, the olfactory, and attempts to tell its fate as it is reflected in the limited amount of material over a limited expanse of time that we can cover here in depth. There will be a lot left to do.

Acknowledgments

It is impossible to mention everybody who contributed in one way or another to the gestation and completion of this book. Too numerous are all those who, usually after raising an eyebrow—if this is the right metaphor—and expressing some initial surprise at my outlandish topic, did not hold back with useful hints and suggestions.

I am very grateful to David Wellbery, whose enthusiastic support, as well as inspiring and critical guidance, have helped me see the project through. My thanks also go to Gerald Gillespie, whose help with the mechanics of writing has been invaluable. He has made me feel more at ease in the foreign tongue. I have received encouragement and feedback from Russell Berman and Christiaan L. Hart-Nibbrig. I owe special thanks to Jens Rieckmann for his careful reading and evaluation of the manuscript in one of its intermediate stages. I am grateful to Jürgen Trabant and James Rolleston for reading, and commenting on, individual chapters and to Sander Gilman for his interest in my work. Jeffrey Sammons contributed valuable details to the section on Wilhelm Raabe, and Ron LeBlanc's help on the Russian chapter is gratefully acknowledged here. I would also like to thank the graduate students at the German Studies Department at Stanford for their comments and suggestions in our "Work in Progress" meetings during a time when I was only just starting my research. Many detailed suggestions I owe to Michael Jakob, visiting from Geneva. Carl Hill and Barry Maxwell both referred me to theoretical texts that I might otherwise have overlooked.

For their deep and continuing friendship I am much indebted to Hans Jakob Werlen and Bernd Widdig. I would also like to thank Gertrud Pacheco. In addition to facilitating the initial administrative work, she has, through her unflagging support, been a true friend over the years. Lastly, my thanks go to my wife Larissa Rudova for bearing with me through the final stages of the manuscript, her invaluable help on the Russian chapter, and for her unfailing olfactory inspiration. To her this book is dedicated.

Needless to say, the errors and shortcomings that this study undoubtedly contains, despite the generous help from many sources, are all my own.

Foreign-language quotes have been left in the original in the text, but I have provided my own translations in the footnotes for the convenience of the reader. Multiple short foreign-language passages from the same work in one paragraph are usually gathered and translated together in the notes, with a single footnote reference in the text. Individual words or phrases are occasionally given in the text itself, either in direct translation or in a summarizing paraphrase. For important foreign-language titles, both literary and critical, that do have a readily available English translation, the reader will find bibliographical information in the first footnote. As the nature of the study requires rather frequent, though mostly short, quotations, I have placed page references in parentheses immediately following the quotes in the text itself. As the discussion generally focuses on one work at the time, this system is clear and concise. Occasionally, in order to avoid any ambiguity, the author's name has been added, such as (Süskind, 204) or (Canetti, 62). This way the footnotes can serve better their intended purpose of providing additional information, translations, and expansions or openings of the argument in directions that cannot be pursued in the text itself or indeed in the book as a whole.

Contents

CHAPTER I

Introduction

Western society has a history of distrust of the senses. As the suppliers of an experience that is unalienably personal, they contain an anarchic potential that cannot easily be yoked to social utility. On the other hand, as the providers of raw information about the object world they mark, of course, the essential first step along the complex route from perception to cognition. It is with cognitive data that we feel more comfortable. In the same way that immediate perception is not socially useful, it is also not communicable. It turns into social usefulness only by becoming communication first. Immediate perception, therefore, requires the mediation of language in order to enter the social contract and thus discourse, the regulated exchange of textualized experience.[1] Only in the form of a text can experience be investigated in social, historical, and linguistic terms. It is words, sentences, and paragraphs that form the net in which sensory perception is caught, but this net is never quite fine enough to retain it all. Whole chunks of experience escape. They remain dangling outside the structures of verbal communication in a world of unincorporated individuality. In some places, indeed, the net seems to have been woven deliberately loosely, and as a consequence the world of odors, for one, largely escapes its grasp.

Social, historical, and linguistic issues, then, form the general frame of reference for the present investigation. It is based primarily on literary

---

1. It is issues from this border realm that Merleau-Ponty addresses, even if from the perspective of the "primacy of perception." Maurice Merleau-Ponty, *The Primacy of Perception and Other Essays on Phenomenological Psychology, the Philosophy of Art, History and Politics,* ed. James M. Edie, trans. William Cobb (Evanston: Northwestern University Press, 1964).

manifestations of such experience.[2] However, it is essential for our understanding of olfactory perception to bear in mind scientific and technical aspects as well and to follow developments in fields as diverse as anatomy and neurology, city planning and public health, anthropology and sexology, and the production of perfumes and poison gas.

Our approach to the topic, through the social and the historical sciences on the one hand and the "hard sciences" on the other, is straddled by two relatively recent approaches, psychoanalysis and behaviorism. While in certain respects they are mutually exclusive—psychoanalysis attempting to construct the soul, the very inside of what behaviorism looks at from the outside as the black box of conditioned stimulus and response—they nevertheless both reckon on an inside that can be influenced by manipulations from without. Moreover, they both represent a *social* stand vis-à-vis the individual. Their basic concern is to produce a functional individual, to integrate him or her into accepted communicative and actional structures. Whereas in behaviorism the utilitarian aspect has been relatively dominant from the start, psychoanalysis, at least in the early days of Freud, started out from a position on the side of the individual, even if he or she was considered as somehow defective, as the "patient."[3] In the course of time, however, Freud's own views of the emancipatory potential of psychoanalysis turned more and more pessimistic, and psychoanalytic practice after Freud, especially in the United States, has taken a path toward servicing the soul with a view to its social functioning and the creation of the user-friendly personality.

In contrast to the dominant discourse on the individual in his or her communicative relation to, and functional integration in, society stands the complementary but somewhat marginalized inside perspective of sensory perception as a uniquely individual experience (body consciousness, consciousness of oneself as a psychophysical entity). In Western society this perspective has a long history as "alternative" culture and perception, from the early modernists' interest in alterity and "the primitive," in "being"

---

2. In our realm of linguistically mediated perception, then, perception must also be understood as "the observation of observation" as Allport calls it or, more specifically, the observation of textual re/presentation of observation. Floyd H. Allport, *Theories of Perception and the Concept of Structure: A Review and Critical Analysis with an Introduction to a Dynamic-Structural Theory of Behavior* (New York: John Wiley and Sons, 1955), 24.

3. For a contrastive overview of research approaches in perception see Dieter Hoffman-Axthelm, *Sinnesarbeit: Nachdenken über Wahrnehmung* (Frankfurt am Main: Campus Verlag, 1984), esp. chap. 2, "Wahrnehmungsfähigkeit," and chap. 4, "Der Untergang des Wahrnehmungsbegriffs."

versus Western "doing" or "having," to a literary fascination with Indian, Asian, and African cultures. In the 1960s this stance was renewed as a search for alternative lifestyles and has persisted in the practice of Eastern medicine, meditation, and so forth, as well as in the revival of old holistic health and healing practices. But in mainstream Western culture, the channeling of the senses in terms of their socioeconomic functionality, their harnessing to the yoke of social utility, and their blunting through overstimulation has deeply influenced our understanding of sensory experience, of "how we feel about ourselves." The reduction of experience at the workplace to the sensory stimuli strictly required for the performance of the task at hand, in the "ideology of concentrating" and in the name of the most efficient performance of a given task, is only the most prominent aspect of the ambivalent attitude toward sensory experience in general. Enforced sensory deprivation on the one hand is compensated by deliberate sensory overload on the other. This constellation has transformed the senses' inside-out perspective—the curiosity inherent in them as tools for the appropriation of the object world, as well as their fundamentally hedonistic side—into an anarchic potential that needs to be permanently checked and controlled. This need for social control meshes with the much older imperatives of acculturation through language and the establishment of linguistic norms and standards, themselves changing in the course of the civilizing process and as an essential part of it.[4] The most ancient roots of this process are shrouded in precivilizational and evolutionary darkness. Once it emerges into the light of human inquiry, it can be grasped in social and historical terms as (cultural) history. For the individual, its immediate reality is socialization and education. In all three contexts—evolutionary, historical, and educational—the body as the locus of sensory perception can be viewed as the provider of all that we can be sure about, of what Hegel calls "sinnliche Gewissheit," sensate certainty. Hegel's concept, however, marks in an exemplary fashion the very trend at issue here, the intellectualizing of the senses, which runs through practically all of Western thought. Sensate certainty is a highly abstract concept of dealing with both the act and the objects of perception after separating them from their concrete sensory

---

4. Norbert Elias, *Über den Prozess der Zivilisation: Soziogenetische und Psychogenetische Untersuchungen,* 2d ed., 2 vols. (Bern: Francke, 1969). (English: *The Civilizing Process: The Development of Manners,* trans. Edmund Jephcott [New York: Urizen Books: 1978].) For an account of the linguistic regulation of the senses at the stage of early childhood experience see Ernest G. Schachtel, *Metamorphosis: On the Development of Affects, Perception, Attention, and Memory* (New York: Basic Books, 1959).

content and recontextualizing them as cognitive data in a realm of intellectual rarification. One of the main problems with sensate certainty and sensory experience lies in their purely momentous nature, without past, without future. It is acculturation and particularly language that, while streamlining experience by molding it into its communicative structures, give it a temporal dimension, add past and future, loss and longing, hope and despair. The investigation of sensory phenomena in their literary rendering thus marks a crucial point of intersection of the physical and the intellectual, of the evolutionary and the cultural.

The mutual influence of immediate perception and communicative structures is a central issue. We are following two primacies, as it were: Merleau-Ponty's primacy of perception, which insists on a commonsensical base of perception, and the poststructuralist primacy of language, with its shift of meaning from the world of objects to the interplay of signifiers. The link between these two primacies and the cultural and historical unfolding over the past two hundred years of one sensory mode, the olfactory, is the focus of this study.[5]

Acculturation, the civilizing process, acts on sensory perception in two ways. In its *material* aspect, it changes the concrete sensory environment: neon, photography, and film have changed our way of seeing; new materials provide us with novel tactile experiences; the transistor has forever altered our aural environment by filling it with ubiquitous piped Muzak; our diet contains unnameable concoctions of artificial flavors; and the water toilet, the shower, sewage systems, and the products of the fragrance industry have improved hygiene and cleaned up our olfactory environment. All this, however, does not mean that our sensory capacities have changed physiologically. They take part in biological, evolutionary developments and react on different time schemes from sociohistorical trends and movements. For the time of less than two centuries covered here, they can safely be assumed as constant. Our senses are just as sharp and alert today or as imprecise and slow in their interaction with the object world as they were in antiquity, the Middle Ages, or in the eighteenth century.

---

5. For an introduction to phenomenological inquiry see Don Ihde, *Sense and Significance* (Pittsburgh: Duquesne University Press, 1973). Ihde, in the introduction, points out the specific link of experience and language. "Perception is seen here to have another side, inextricably bound to our sensory experience of the world in our 'linguistic' experience of the world. Ultimately phenomenology cannot speak of perception *and* of language, its 'unit' of meaning is perception-language, or better said, being-in-the-world" (18).

What is exposed to change, however, in addition to the sensory environment and the material "food for perception" (an increasing superabundance of it) is the *immaterial* semiotic or discursive dimension of sensory perception. It is in this realm more than anywhere else that certain phenomena emerge or disappear and the senses gain or lose acuteness. It is here that taboos of what may or may not be perceived are created or undone; that thresholds and norms are established or revoked; that sensitivity is honed or blunted. It is here that a general social *Über-Sinn* (a sort of sensory *Über-Ich,* a superego) is created that in turn leaves its marks on historiography, on social accounts, on literature. An individual's sensory perception is always social perception. The individual perceives what is socially permitted to be expressed in language. Although this study is based on textual sources and thus views perception as a discursive phenomenon, it attempts to cut through the strictures of these very discourses to the bottom line. More often than not, this bottom line is covered up: it is the body, the sensory mechanisms themselves. Before simply believing what we read in terms of (olfactory) perception, we need to question hidden or unconscious patterns and vested interests in each textual occurrence of olfactory phenomena. For what does appear in discourse is by no means the complete sensory realm; it is only the tip of the iceberg. The senses of proximity, above all the two chemical senses, the "lower sensory modalities" as Kant calls them, are by and large disfavored in our society.

The texts discussed in this study reach as far back as the middle of the nineteenth century. For epistemological concepts as well as for some scientific developments, however, we need to go further back, to notions and trends originating in the eighteenth-century Enlightenment. But we must not overlook that the epistemology of the senses has its origins in Plato and Aristotle. It is with Plato in particular and his forms that the emphasis in the dyad of perception and cognition is placed in favor of the latter and thus shifted from the concrete to the abstract; and it is in the opening lines of Aristotle's *Metaphysics* that the sense of sight is extolled in both its usefulness and its pleasure-giving function. It is Aristotle also who, by acknowledging the senses' potential for both knowledge and pleasure, places them at the beginning of a road that will soon bifurcate into the cognitive-scientific and the hedonistic-aesthetic realms. With the emergence of Christianity and its ambivalent attitude, to say the least, toward the world of the senses, this division is reinforced and undergoes a shift in emphasis: Augustine, after the agonizing struggle against the seductive powers of the sensory-sensual world described in the *Confessions,* redraws the line between the disembodied, spiritual, and transcendental realm on the one hand and the corporeal, sensual, and immanent on the other. Vision is his worst tempter. Smells never haunt him very much.[6]

In the emerging bourgeois *Zivilisationspropaganda*[7] in the eighteenth and the following centuries, the emphasis in sensory perception is clearly on the visual and the aural whereas "die Nahsinne sind gleich weit entfernt vom Glanz und vom Elend der Aufklärung."[8] Cultural historiography from the perspective of enlightenment has always given them short shrift.[9] In an inquiry less philosophical than Kant's but more medical and practical, Alain Corbin provides an extraordinary account of the discovery of olfactory phenomena as indices of unsanitary, unhygienic conditions to be corrected, sanitized, and eliminated.[10]

The present study of the smell of books investigates if, when, and how olfactory perception has been used—together with, or in opposition to, other sensory modalities—to create atmosphere, perspective, action, and meaning in literary texts. It addresses issues from at least four distinct areas of inquiry. The brief discussion of these fields will provide us with some reference points for the subsequent literary analyses. In addition to the interest of the humanities in perception, there exists a scientific and technical inquiry to be considered here. It aims at the "hardware" of perception, the body with its sensory surfaces and their chemicophysical and neurological functioning, as well as at the properties of the perceived objects.

Scientific Aspects

The first question, then, must be, just what is "olfactory perception"? The sense of smell forms, together with vision, hearing, taste, and touch, a part

---

6. See Saint Augustine, *Confessions,* trans R. S. Pine-Coffin (Harmondsworth: Penguin, 1961), esp. book 10. On the other hand it is noteworthy to what extent Augustine praises God in olfactory and gustatory terms. After the Christian injunction not to make "graven images" eliminated vision, and his own run-in with sensuality and sexuality has made suspect the senses in general, what seems left to him and most appropriate are the liminal senses of taste and smell for his description of divine qualities.

7. Dietmar Kamper and Christoph Wulf, *Das Schwinden der Sinne* (Franfurt am Main: Suhrkamp, 1984), 13.

8. Kamper and Wulf, *Das Schwinden der Sinne,* 14. "The senses of proximity are equidistant from both the glory and the misery of enlightenment."

9. On their ambiguous position Kant has more to say in his *Anthropologie,* below.

10. Alain Corbin, *Le miasme et la jonquille: L'odorat et l'imaginaire social XVIIIe–XIXe siècles* (Paris: Aubier Montaigne, 1982). (English: *The Foul and the Fragrant: Odor and the French Social Imagination* [Cambridge: Harvard University Press, 1986].)

of our five traditional sensory capacities, and it means the ability to perceive scents, smells, odors, or stenches and attribute meaning to them.[11] The realms of (sensory) perception (*Wahrnehmung*) and cognition (*Erkenntnis*) have undergone fundamental changes in their conceptualization and exploration over time. The "classical" modern understanding, which found its most clear-cut formulation in Descartes's thoroughly rationalized mechanical model of the human body and its interaction with the environment, assumed an unproblematic distinction between an object world "out there" and a perceiving subject, with the objects impressing themselves through the respective sensory channels on the subject. This is in many ways a more simplistic, certainly a more one-sided concept than, for instance, Augustine's. The latter reckons very much with an active, outward-directed element in the senses—and is afraid of it, as it threatens to contaminate and undermine pure spirituality through sensuous corruption. The study of the sensory channels in anatomy together with new findings in physics, however, began to raise doubts about the simplicity of Descartes's model.[12] Descartes's rationalist-mechanical setup of a receptive and perceptive *res cogitans* and a perceived outside world, the *res extensa*, had to be revised.[13]

---

11. Here we encounter a first obstacle, for there is disagreement on the very number of senses. Cf., e.g., Franz Brentano, *Untersuchungen zur Sinnesphysiologie,* ed. Roderick M. Chisholm and Reinhard Fabian (1907; Hamburg: Felix Meiner, 1979), esp. chap. 2, "Von der Zahl der Sinne." Brentano opts for three senses. Cf. also Hubert Tellenbach, *Geschmack und Atmosphäre: Medien menschlichen Elementarkontaktes* (Salzburg: Otto Müller Verlag, 1968). Tellenbach, basing himself on Ludwig Edinger, does not make a strict distinction between the senses of smell and taste. "In der Konzeption des Oralsinns als Einheit von Riechen, Schmecken und oralem Haut-Schleimhautgefühl hat Edinger morphologisch und funktional ursprünglich vereint gesehen, was Anatomie und Physiologie später, zum Nachteil für das Erfassen der natürlichen Gegebenheit, getrennt haben" (13). E. H. Weber in his 1846 treatise "Der Tastsinn und das Gemeingefühl" also talks about a common sensibility. A sense for weight and temperature is part of his broad understanding of tactile perception. See E. H. Weber, *The Sense of Touch,* trans. H. E. Ross and D. J. Murray (London: Academic Press, 1978).

12. Concerning the sense of smell and the various anatomical models of the olfactory apparatus, see, e.g., Jost Benedum, "Das Riechorgan in der antiken und mittelalterlichen Hirnforschung und die Rezeption durch S. Th. Soemmerring," in *Gehirn—Nerven—Seele: Anatomie und Physiologie im Umfeld S. T. Soemmerrings,* ed. Gunter Mann and Franz Dumont (Stuttgart: Gustav Fischer, 1988), 11–54. This essay sums up the olfactory medical and anatomical history from Aristotle to the late eighteenth and early nineteenth centuries. Soemmerring was considered the foremost anatomical and physiological eminence of his time.

13. For a popular scientific account of these matters see Hoimar von Ditfurth, *Der Geist fiel nicht vom Himmel: Die Evolution unseres Bewusstseins* (Hamburg: Hoffmann and Campe, 1976).

Problems connected with his view came under discussion not only in medicine, but equally in philosophy and religion. As the physiological seat of
the soul, the pituitary gland was posited; and in philosophical-speculative
terms Descartes himself, as well as Locke, among others, debated the notion of innate versus acquired ideas.[14] While the proposed systems of perception raised questions on the physical and physiological levels, psychology, especially psychoanalysis and behaviorism, finally all but destroyed the
notion of the subject as an a priori given. Moreover, research in chemistry
and physics into the nature of the objects of perception as well as the
human perceptual apparatus did away with many earlier models. With the
rise of experimental psychology the soul became a highly problematic issue
at the beginning of our century. It is noteworthy, though, that up to and
including Charcot, one of the teachers of the young Freud, the reasons for
psychological phenomena were still very much sought in physiological and
neurological causes. In more recent times neurological research, discovering the various parts of the brain to be of vastly differing evolutionary age
and performing distinct functions, has led to new insights into perception:
the older parts of the brain, developed on the basis of the austere evolutionary axiom of "as much interaction with the environment as necessary, but
as little as possible," are now understood to impose their a priori limitations on perception. In those parts are stored patterns of reactions to
certain environmental stimuli that can still be regularly triggered although
they may have become wholly inadequate in a modern environment.[15] In
this light, our sensory capacities have come under new scrutiny, and the
discovery of the limited scope of what we actually do perceive due to
preexisting neurological filters has led to new theoretical concepts, the
most revolutionary of which is the idea that models of the outside world
are already present within our neurological apparatus in the form of behavioral patterns before we even reach out into the world to appropriate it
deliberately. The image antedates the original.

As far as olfactory perception is concerned, it seems that in recent years,

---

14. For a critique of Descartes and even more so of his lingering influence on Pavlov's
behaviorist inquiries, see Erwin Straus, *The Primary World of Senses: A Vindication of
Sensory Experience,* trans. Jacob Needleman (London: Collier-Macmillan, 1963). Straus
rejects above all one of the implications of Pavlov's research, the conceptualization of
sensory perception as discontinuous, and thus the abolition of psychology altogether in
favor af a physical transcendentalism.

15. Even Soemmerring, in 1796, is still concerned with the question of the anatomical
location of the soul. Cf. his treatise "Über das Organ der Seele" and Kant's response to
it, as discussed in Benedum, "Das Riechorgan," 53.

the nose has gained in stature, if I may say so. This gain is reflected, for instance, in a more aggressive stance of the perfume industry and the exploding artificial fragrance and flavor business, both stepping up research in the hard sciences where olfactory perception and everything connected with odors has attracted considerable interest.[16] While the endeavor to structure the realm of olfactory perception is as old as that for other sensory modalities, it has been less consistently pursued and with less perseverance. In the late 1960s and through the 1970s and 1980s, however, research activity has been strong even if somewhat unfocused. Prior to that, starting around 1950, "a fleeting fascination had gripped many,"[17] as it had in decades and centuries before, but this fascination was generally short-lived and of a limited scope. Nevertheless, according to Carterette and Friedman,

> the degree of activity is astonishing, but it is also diffuse. Much of the vast modern literature deals with the analysis, preparation, and development of food products, and with perfumery, odor control, and other industrial endeavors. Nevertheless, there is also considerable basic research on physiological and psycho-physical properties of olfaction and on the role of smell in animal behavior and in physiological regulation. Even though the mechanisms of transduction, the physicochemical determinants of odor quality, and the neural code for quality are still largely mysteries, much has been learned in recent years. (198)

Generally speaking, "in no other modality has classification dominated research as it has in the case of the sense of smell."[18] The reasons for this

---

16. By way of illustration see, e.g., Kathleen Deveny, "As Lauder's Scent Battles Calvin Klein's, Cosmetic Whiz Finds Herself on the Spot," *Wall Street Journal*, 27 June 1991, sec. B. She announces "an aromatic summer" with the two perfume manufacturers running "a total of 80 million scent strips before Christmas." Regarding scent strips, cf. the scented keepsakes from an exhibit at the Museum of the City of New York, "Reflections of Fragrance and Society," 6 October 1987–7 February 1988. That the olfactory improvement of people's reading material and museum handouts cannot go undisputed is revealed in the following article: Doretta Zemp, "Scents of Trouble," *Los Angeles Times,* 18 September 1991, sec. E. Paul Raeburn reports on genetic olfactory research in "Found: Gene that Stops to Smell Rose," *San Francisco Examiner,* 5 April 1991, sec. A.

17. Edward C. Carterette and Morton P. Friedman, eds., *Tasting and Smelling,* vol. 6, A of *Handbook of Perception* (New York: Academic Press, 1978), 198. Their account has contributed more to my research than can be specifically referenced here.

18. Trygg Engen, *The Perception of Odors* (New York: Academic Press, 1982), 7. Engen, a specialist in sensorial psychology, has been one of the more persistent researchers in matters of olfaction in recent years. Trygg Engen, *Odor Sensation and Memory* (New York: Praeger, 1991) provides a recent readable overview of the field.

are manifold and interlinked. They lie on the one hand in the diverse physical and chemical properties of the objects of smell and on the other in the lack or at least the inadequacy of (verbal) classification and conceptualization. Olfactory perception lacks the scientific and linguistic models comparable to those for visual and aural phenomena. Whenever we compare two smells and say that one is more flowery or less sweet or that they are equally pleasant, we are on shaky ground. In terms of the object of perception, we lack classificatory models; in terms of the physiology of perception, there still remain a number of open questions; and in linguistic terms, we most frequently have to revert to similes to qualify smells—a method that has its inherent problems in creating a breach in the surface structure of the text. Although from the earliest beginnings of sensory and perceptual inquiry philosophers and researchers have agreed that there is some kind of emanation from an object reaching the nose of a subject, with air generally serving as the carrier medium, and that such emanations must be of distinct quality to produce different sensory experiences, even most recent physicochemical research is at a loss to explain why certain molecules of very similar structure produce sensory impressions of a completely diverse nature.[19] Already Plato, always in search of a typology, addressing the question from the reverse angle, notices that odors

> lack names because they do not consist of a definite number of simple types. The only clear distinction to be drawn here is twofold: the pleasant and the unpleasant. The unpleasant roughens and does violence to the whole cavity lying between the crown of the head and the navel; the pleasant soothes this region and restores it with contentment to its natural state.[20]

Lucretius, too, uses an early molecular concept:

> So that you may easily see that the things which are able to affect the senses pleasantly, consist of smooth and round elements; while all those on the other hand which are found to be bitter and harsh, are held in

---

19. The most recent classificatory approach generally accepted among scientists is J. E. Amoore's stereochemical theory of olfaction. For more details, see the bibliography in Carterette and Friedman, *Tasting and Smelling*, 225.

20. Francis. M. Cornford, *Plato's Cosmology: The "Timaeus" of Plato with a Running Commentary* (1937; London: Routledge and Kegan Paul, 1956), 273. Cf. esp. 273–75.

connexion by particles that are more hooked and for this reason are wont to tear open passages into our senses.[21]

The binary split between good and bad in the realm of olfaction, attributed both by Plato and by Lucretius to particulate causes in odoriferous matter itself, will be with us throughout this study. While our focus is on psychosocial and sociohistorical answers more than physicochemical ones, we still have to bear in mind the peculiarities that olfactory perception exhibits in the natural sciences. In this context it appears that earlier scientific categorizations are not much more than elaborations on the essential and somehow instinctual good/bad dichotomy of everyday life. But the problematic classification of smells marks only the beginning of the process of olfactory perception:

> The environmental information involved in olfaction is coded in the form of structural details of odorant molecules that are carried by the medium surrounding the organism. It is the task of the olfactory system to detect these details, to transplant their informational content into usable types of information, to process the latter, and to deliver the resulting pattern to the higher centers for comparison with memory contents, for interpretation, and for conversion into a terminal product such as an odor sensation, a verbal expression, or a behavioral effect.[22]

Carterette and Friedman provide us with a map to the trails that various sciences have followed in order to provide explanations for the multifarious aspects of perception. Their findings are as much part of the larger cultural, historical, and literary context as they are strictly scientific. And in literature a number of more recent texts, Dahl's *Bitch,* for instance, Robbin's *Jitterbug Perfume,* or Christa Wolf's *Störfall,* explore precisely such links between the natural sciences and the social and historical world.

---

21. Lucretius, quoted in Whitney J. Oates, ed., *The Stoic and Epicurean Philosophers: The Complete Extant Writings of Epicurus, Epictetes, Lucretius, Marcus Aurelius* (New York: Random House, 1940), 98–99. Oates's is a prose version of Lucretius's *De Rerum Natura.* For a concise overview of Lucretius's basic tenets, see also Copley's introduction to his verse translation of *De Rerum Natura* in Lucretius, *The Nature of Things,* trans. Frank O. Copley (New York: Norton, 1977). For the above-quoted passage in Copley see book 2, 28. Lucretius's theory of matter and perception is based on Epicure. It is a materialist, nontranscendental model with the soul—consisting of atoms just like the body and the object world—serving as the organ of reception and processing of sensory stimuli. For further explanations of olfactory perception, cf., e.g., 98–99.

22. Carterette and Friedman, *Tasting and Smelling,* 245.

However, the essential and innovative line of investigation for us to follow, more closely related to our inquiry than the findings of the natural sciences per se, originates in experimental psychology and psychoanalysis.[23] Experimental psychology made it clear that perception was by no means a one-way process from the external object to the isolated and fixed subject. Rather, the subject, at least to some extent a social construct and shaped by interaction with the world surrounding it, constitutes itself in the act of perception.[24] Thus memory and experience came to be understood as central elements in perceptual processes, together with subjective interests, drives, and emotions and with education—both theoretical and practical— in the senses. While we do offer classes in music and visual arts and cater to some degree even to the sense of taste in home economics, there is no learning process assigned to the sense of smell—and neither is there to touch, we should add.

The direction psychological inquiry took in psychoanalysis along the new track of discursive rather than physiological and neurological causation of mental symptoms had its effect on sensory perception, even if this did not become immediately clear. Indeed, for odors the dominant thrust almost up to the present has remained toward classification of odoriferous substances and the solution of questions pertaining to the physiology of the human olfactory apparatus.[25] This study applies, for the first time, the

23. An interesting interdisciplinary account is Lawrence E. Marks, *The Unity of the Senses: Interrelation Among the Modalities* (New York: Academic Press, 1978). Marks's inquiry, centered on perceptual psychology, includes a final chapter on synaesthetic phenomena in literature ("Synesthetic Metaphor in Poetry," 211–55). He discusses predominantly English Romanticists but sees in Baudelaire a father figure of modern synaesthetic representation.

24. For a classical account of the history of experimental psychology see Edward G. Boring, *A History of Experimental Psychology* (New York: Century, 1929). A similarly monumental work by him deals with sensations and perception, and contains a useful overview of nineteenth-century and early twentieth-century developments in olfactory research. E. G. Boring, *Sensations and Perception in the History of Experimental Psychology* (New York: Appleton-Century-Crofts, 1942).

25. For general introductory accounts of the olfactory sense and the problems associated with it, see Joan Steen Wilentz, *The Senses of Man* (New York: Crowell, 1968). Her approach is interesting as it has a strong literary and cultural bias besides furnishing basic anatomical and neurological information. See also Harvey Richard Schiffman, *Sensations and Perception: An Integrated Approach* (New York: Wiley, 1976). "The Chemical Sensory System II: Smell" provides a good outline of classificatory problems in Linnaeus, Henning, Zwaardemaker, and Amoore. See also Jacqueline Ludel, *Introduction to Sensory Processes* (San Francisco: Freeman, 1978). All three accounts stress the erratic nature of olfaction. Wilentz comments, "Smells just don't lend themselves to the neat analytic measurements that sound and light do" (118). Ludel remarks, "It is necessary for us to

close-reading and interpretative techniques emerging from dream analysis and psychoanalytic concepts such as repression to the interpretation of specific passages in literary texts with olfactory content.

Underlying this attempt is yet another track of investigation opened by psychoanalysis: the mental-evolutionary aspect of the species and of the individual, with the latter reproducing the former *in nuce*. Of particular interest in this context are Freud's far-reaching, even if speculative, remarks on the loss of the importance of the sense of smell brought about by man's upright posture,[26] and his comments to Fliess about this topic.[27] The drift of Freud's argument is to postulate a strong and direct link of olfaction and sexuality. This claim seems well-founded and can be supported with examples from the animal realm, from insects to mammals, whose reproductive cycles and behavior are largely based on olfactory stimuli. For man, according to Freud, the rise to an erect posture caused the fall of olfaction from its position of regulating sexual functions. Following this transition, the sense of smell was potentially free to assume other functions. However, it did not do so—either in the evolutionary terms of the development of the species, or in the shorter terms of the history of civilization. Smell seems to disappear altogether. The claim being made here, to the contrary, is that smell remains, even if repressed, strongly connected with sexuality, the forces of Eros.

---

discuss taste and smell in a somewhat hesitant way because taste and smell are poorly understood" (339). Schiffman attributes some aesthetic potential to olfactory perception: "Though the importance of smell for man . . . is much less than for most other animals, . . . it can aid in food selection, . . . maintenance of a clean environment, and in the case of certain odors, smell may provide some pleasant esthetic sensations" (140). The problems persist to this day, and most accounts of olfactory perception begin with the lament about such fundamental difficulties. Cf. also Stanley Coren and Lawrence M. Ward, *Sensation and Perception*, 3d ed. (San Diego: Harcourt, 1989), esp. chap. 8, "Taste and Smell." The book contains an extensive up-to-date bibliography of scientific research into the various aspects of sensory perception.

26. Sigmund Freud, *Das Unbehagen in der Kultur*, vol. 14 of *Gesammelte Werke. Chronologisch geordnet*, ed. Anna Freud et al. (1948; London: Imago Publishing, 1955). (English: "Civilization and its Discontents," vol. 21 of *The Standard Edition of the Complete Psychological Works of Sigmund Freud*, gen. ed. James Strachey [London: The Hogarth Press, 1953–74].)

27. Cf. Fliess's book-length study on the connection between the nose and the female genitalia. Wilhelm Fliess, *Die Beziehungen zwischen Nase und weiblichen Geschlechtsorganen in ihrer biologischen Bedeutung dargestellt* (Leipzig: Franz Deuticke, 1897). Cf. also Frank J. Sulloway, *Freud, Biologist of the Mind: Beyond the Psychoanalytic Legend* (New York: Basic Books, 1979). Sulloway makes it clear that Fliess in his time was not alone in his search for nasogenital connections; see esp. 147–52 and 198ff.

In connection with man's rise from the ground, an analogous paradigmatic shift is pointed out by Leroi-Gourhan.[28] The erect position that frees the nose from its immediate contact with the genitals also liberates the hand from its part in locomotion and allows it to take over functions of fabrication and tool-making. Similarly, both for vision and the oral and aural area, new horizons open up. The function of articulation is developed and thereby the potential for the eventual creation of symbols: language. Thus for Leroi-Gourhan, prehension (the hand), apprehension (vision, oral, and nasal sense), and comprehension (language) evolve as a consequence of man's erect position. Vision becomes the leading sense also in sexual matters. People fall in love at "first sight," not at "first smell"—or if so, they very rarely talk about this.

Literary and Linguistic Aspects

The second focal point of this investigation into olfactory elements in literature concerns, as we said before, the "textual creation of atmosphere, perspective, action, meaning," the semiotic and symbolic systems that for the sense of smell, with its linguistic peculiarities, require special attention. Vision, the leading sense in our (possibly in every) culture and the source of the dominant metaphoric reference system underlying language, will be seen to interfere time and again. Literature as an art form based on language is affected by the restrictions that language, its material, places on it. Barthes's "écrite, la merde ne sent pas" applies to all sensory modalities. It is in the nature of language as a reference system to allude to reality not to recreate "the thing itself," but to appeal to the imagination to trigger a representation of that thing. The olfactory with its virtual lack of recall potential for smell qua smell seems in its textual representation to be one step further removed from reality than other senses but, by the same token, especially close to memory. Olfactory perception is "percevoir un *context* plutôt qu'une *odeur*. . . . une odeur n'a aucune existence significante propre et n'a pas d'étiquette spéciale. La théorie courante de la perception ne convient donc pas à la perception olfactive" (emphasis added).[29] The lin-

---

28. André Leroi-Gourhan, *Le geste et la parole,* 2 vols. (Paris: Edition Albin Michel, 1964). Cf. chapter 2 of this study.

29. Trygg Engen, "La mémoire des odeurs," *La Recherche* February 1989, 176. "[Olfactory perception means] to perceive a context rather than an odor. . . . an odor has no proper existence or special label. Current theory of perception, therefore, does not fit olfactory perception."

guistic restrictions for the sense of smell are particularly dramatic insofar as language has not developed an abstract terminology for referring to smells. Smell is, with its storing and retrieving characteristics, an associative and expansive rather than an distributive and limiting sensory mode. The lack of terminological paradigms as they exist for colors necessitates a linguistic detour through the metaphoric, that is, a breach of reference level in the text each time we attempt to describe smells adjectivally. The same holds true for the common reference to smells in terms of their origins. "It smells like" or "the smell of" expresses relations of combination and contiguity rather than of selection and similarity. These two points may serve as a preliminary explanation of why the sense of smell is so often considered the most apt to trigger memory. Its very linguistic structure brings up an Other, a reference to the outside.

The main problem, then, seems to lie in the linguistic grounding of olfactory perception, in the way we talk about smells. Dan Sperber sums up this issue with admirable clarity:

Even though the human sense of smell can distinguish hundreds of thousands of smells and in this regard is comparable to sight or hearing, in none of the world's languages does there seem to be a classification of smells comparable, for example, to colour classification. Ethno-linguists systematically describe colour classifications, often containing several hundred terms ordered under a small number of basic categories. . . . We would search in vain for a similar work on smells; perhaps this is a sign of lack of imagination on the part of scholars, but more likely it is because there is nothing for such a work to be about. . . . There is no semantic field of smells. The notion of smells only has as lexical sub-categories general terms such as "stench" and "perfume." Our knowledge about different smells figures in the encyclopaedia not in an autonomous domain, but scattered among all the categories whose referents have olfactive qualities.[30]

It is the search for some such categories that I suggest to undertake here even if they should turn out to be lodged predominantly in the deep structures of the human psyche and not in literature itself. Literature never-

---

30. Dan Sperber, *Rethinking Symbolism* (Cambridge: Cambridge University Press, 1975), 115–16. On color universals—the reference is made by Sperber himself—see Brent Berlin and Paul Kay, *Basic Color Terms: Their Universality and Evolution* (Berkeley and Los Angeles: University of California Press, 1969).

theless retains and reveals their traces, consciously and unconsciously. Philosophy on the other hand puts hardly any concepts at our disposal. Following the direction that Plato and Aristotle gave it, philosophy may talk about the senses rather than indulging in them and aims in any case at converting their individual immediacy into the general and permanent. Aesthetics, the discipline within which the philosophical treatment of our material ought to take place, is in fact more revealing in its lack of olfactory concepts or theories, however loose, than in providing positive categories or even a model for such a discussion.

Philosophical and Aesthetic Aspects

The third focus in the initial statement of purpose for our study is thus the term *literature* itself, understood as an art form that rests on a number of aesthetic conventions. What emerges as the main task is to provide at least some conceptual outline of an aesthetics for the interpretation of olfactory perception in a literary context. The salient characteristics of such a concept ought to be a strong emphasis on the physical basis of the perceptual process; a phenomenological-descriptive approach to olfactory occurrences in plot or discourse; and an emphasis on the specific representational values of that sensory mode, its capacity for recalling and re-presenting experience thanks to the strong memory-triggering potential of smells. A tentative olfactory aesthetics is a general *desideratum* as well as a specific goal of this study.

In the first paragraph of his *Aesthetica* from 1750–58, Alexander Gottlieb Baumgarten defines aesthetics as "scientia cognitionis sensitivae."[31] Over the years, and not only in the German context, a shift has taken place from the sensate aspect of aesthetics, its grounding in the sensory and sensual dimension of the object world and its roots in the bodily realm of the subject, toward more abstract intellectual and theoretical concepts, that is, from *sensitivitas* to *scientia* with *cognitio* shifting uneasily between those two poles. This tendency reflects very much what Wulf and Kamper call the ambiguity of the "Glanz und Elend der Aufklärung," and it creates, in the shadow of intellectualized brilliance, the misery of the still—or again—repressed body. In the middle of the eighteenth century, Baumgarten, the "father of German aesthetics," stands at a turning point of perceptual-

---

31. A. G. Baumgarten, *Texte zur Grundlegung der Ästhetik,* trans. and ed. Hans Rudolf Schweizer (Hamburg: Felix Meiner, 1983), 79.

aesthetic development. On the one hand, he is preceded by Locke's and Leibniz's inquiries and writes as a contemporary of Hume's. All three of these philosophers are investigating the sensory, epistemological, and cognitive basis of human knowledge in general. Their respective thrusts, regardless of the differences among them, have a strong empiricist and sensualist component, but are not primarily aimed at an aesthetic. For Locke in particular there is nothing present in the intellect that did not before pass through the senses. Baumgarten is followed by such thinkers as Kant, Schiller, and Hegel, for whom the focus of philosophical, and more specifically aesthetic, concerns has shifted away from the concrete sensory toward the abstract intellectual. From Baumgarten to Kant, for whom aesthetics is the realm of the "disinterestedly beautiful," and on to Schiller's concept of "aesthetic education," where the aesthetic has become a mental state of equilibrium between the forces of individual drives and social norms, aesthetics is increasingly divorced from its sensual dimension and removed from its physical and corporeal grounding in sensory perception.[32] In this shift, the *sensitivitas* of Baumgarten's formulation of aesthetics disappears to a large extent and leaves the bourgeois nineteenth century with an aesthetics as *scientia cognitionis,* a concept within which only the two higher senses, vision and hearing, can survive and be conceptualized with a sufficient degree of abstraction.[33] Both Kant and Hegel explicitly exclude the lower senses, touch, taste, and smell, from the aesthetic realm.[34]

32. Eagleton sees that attempted equilibrium in an ideological-critical light and charges aesthetics with pandering to the social norms at the expense of individual drives: the "ideology of the aesthetic" is for him precisely the mapping of general standards onto the individual in the name of a project of aetheticization. See Terry Eagleton, *The Ideology of the Aesthetic,* (Oxford: Basil Blackwell, 1990). For a more specific discussion of Eagleton's concepts, see chapter 2, *Pfisters Mühle.* An article under the same title outlining some key ideas of Eagleton's book was published in 1988. Reference to it is made in the opening pages of chapter 2. I am indebted to Eagleton's concept of the sociohistorical unfolding of aesthetics beyond specific references made here.

33. Recently, Wolfgang Welsch has taken up this split, reconceptualized its two sides as "Ästhetik" and "Anästhetik," and connected the terms back to their Greek roots in *aisthesis.* This move allows him to discuss postmodern aesthetic issues in both their intellectual and sensory aspects. See Wolfgang Welsch, *Ästhetisches Denken* (Stuttgart: Reclam, 1990).

34. Kant actually counts touch among the higher senses, which contribute qua "empirische Anschauung mehr zur Erkenntnis des äußeren Gegenstandes . . . als sie das Bewußtsein des affizierten Organs rege machen." Immanuel Kant, *Anthropologie in pragmatischer Hinsicht,* ed. Karl Vorländer (Hamburg: Felix Meiner, 1980), 47. Cf. esp. the chapter "Anthropologische Didaktik," paragraphs 15–24, as well as Kant's *Die Kritik der Urteilskraft.* (English: *Critique of Judgment,* trans. Werner S. Pluhar [Indianapolis: Hackett, 1987].)

In his definition of the *Kunstschöne*, Hegel is quite explicit about the role of the sense of smell in "artistic beauty."[35] He concedes—and indeed it is a concession to, rather than a condition of, the materiality of the artwork—"daß das Sinnliche im Kunstwerk freilich vorhanden sein müsse, aber nur als Oberfläche und *Schein* des Sinnlichen erscheinen dürfe" (48). His conclusion as to the sensory modalities capable of art is that the "Sinnliche der Kunst [bezieht sich] nur auf die beiden *theoretischen* Sinne des *Gesichts* und *Gehörs*, während Geruch, Geschmack und Gefühl vom Kunstgenuß ausgeschlossen bleiben" (48). The latter senses have to do too directly "mit dem Materiellen als solchem und den unmittelbaren sinnlichen Qualitäten desselben" (48). Art objects do not allow for a "nur sinnliches Verhältnis" (49). Thus the senses of proximity fail to fulfill Hegel's demand that "das Sinnliche in der Kunst *vergeistigt*, da das *Geistige* in ihr als versinnlicht erscheint" (49). Art is intellectual production before it is sensual reality.

The question of an olfactory aesthetics has been broached occasionally—with inconclusive answers, generally tending, however, toward the negation of such a thing.[36] Osborne argues not directly in favor of the existence of olfactory art (in fact, he is skeptical, because it is not "a complexly structured organic unity" [46]) but believes that the olfactory permits "aesthetic acts" not unlike the higher senses.

> I have suggested that an aesthetic act takes place when attention is directed upon the sensory content of an experience without ulterior motive other than bringing that content more fully into awareness and that aesthetic judgement is concerned with the adequacy of any such sensory content to sustain attention at an enhanced level of awareness. (47)

---

35. G. W. F. Hegel, *Ästhetik*, ed. Friedrich Bassenge, 2 vols. (Berlin: Das europäische Buch, 1985) 1:48–49. Hegel concedes "that the sensual has to be present in the artwork, but ought to appear only as surface and semblance of the sensual." He goes on to say that "the sensual in art is limited to the two theoretical senses of vision and the ear whereas olfaction, taste, and touch are barred from aesthetic enjoyment" because they are too immediately linked "with the material and the unmediated sensual qualities of matter" (48). He postulates that in art "the sensual appears as intellectualized and the intellectual as sensualized" (49).

36. A relatively recent exchange on the subject was triggered by John Harris, "Oral and Olfactory Art," *Journal of Aesthetic Education* 13, no. 4 (October 1979): 5–15. The reply came from A. T. Winterbourne, "Is Oral and Olfactory Art Possible?" *Journal of Aesthetic Education* 15, no. 2 (April 1981): 95–102. Both authors refer to an earlier article by Harold Osborne, "Odours and Appreciation," *British Journal of Aesthetics* 17, no. 1 (1977): 37–48.

Aesthetic activity, for Osborne, is the "one path of escape still open to us," an escape from "a civilization which is already intellectualized beyond the reaches of apprehension and is therefore stultified" (47). Aesthetic experience can take us back to a more concrete, sense-based culture.

Harris, arguing directly for accepting food and smell as art, picks up on the complex structuring of the artistic object. "In an otherwise admirable . . . defense of odors and tastes, Harold Osborne seems to deny food and drink the ultimate accolade of *fine* works of art largely on the grounds that tastes and smells are not susceptible of elaborate structuring" (12). Harris is out to show—and he bases himself on Proust's incident with the madeleine—that food and drink fulfill at least part of the "gamut of functions performed by all the arts" (9). In the process, however, he ends up comparing apples and oranges, as Winterbourne remarks in his article, a direct criticism and rejection of Harris's. Winterbourne objects to what he sees as a confusion in the understanding of the crucial event in Proust. "The joy that Proust describes is *not* in the tastes, but in what the tastes evoke" (96). He criticizes the use of the same words in both their metaphorical and actual meaning; the equation of physical necessity (in the consumption of food) with intellectual necessity (in the "consumption" of artworks); and ultimately defends Osborne's hesitation about olfactory and gustatory art by pointing out that "the lack of such independently variable dimensions [as hue, brightness, and saturation of colors] may be part of the reason why it seems that with tastes, form and content collapse into one another" (99). The harmony between form and content features prominently in Hegel too, as an antagonism ultimately only to be resolved in the highest art form, the indissoluble harmony of religion. We will encounter it again later in the discussion of postmodernism.

When Adorno emphasizes the autonomous work of high art as opposed to the mass product of the culture industry, he too operates with form and content, working along "the great divide" that separates the intellectually demanding artistic work from the sensually and temporarily fulfilling product for the masses. Here, at the latest, is the moment where the aesthetic turns political. It becomes clear how in classical-idealist bourgeois understanding aesthetics develops more and more into a sociopolitical tool in the hands of the ruling elite, as Terry Eagleton points out, and becomes openly utilized in the aestheticization of politics. That is, the aesthetic now serves the purpose of marking as beautiful that which is to be made into and accepted as good, as the socially accepted standard prescribed from above. Within such an understanding of aesthetics, the simple binary division of olfactory phenomena into good and bad, both categories borrowed from outside aesthetics, makes sense. For in this way, smell, the liminal sense par excellence, can be instrumentalized in a project of the social encoding of (ethical) values in aesthetic terms without an explicit olfactory aesthetic ever having to be stated. In fact, as we have pointed out, there is strong theoretical evidence of evolutionary and anthropological developments that establish good and bad smells as an ancient classification, predating and underlying most sociohistorically grounded categories. And there is the simple pleasurable, hedonistic aspect of the olfactory that enlightenment philosophy has largely disregarded but that is nevertheless a real-life as well as a literary phenomenon. This is the

> characteristic that has figured explicitly or implicitly in accounts of olfaction through many centuries: Simple, unpatterned olfactory stimulation may be a source of great pleasure, even when the source of the stimulus (e.g., a flower) neither nourishes nor protects and when the stimulus contains minimal information. . . . Aristotle concluded that human beings alone could find pleasure in some odorants without regard to needs and appetites.[37]

At this point, with the question of good and bad in the air once again, the outline so far of scientific, linguistic, and aesthetic stakes in the literary investigation of olfactory perception needs to be integrated in the larger picture of sociohistorical developments.

Sociohistorical Aspects

Human interest in perception and cognition, necessitating first of all a model of the object world as well as a theory of the functioning of the neural apparatus of perception, is almost as old as civilization itself. In a sense, the issues addressed in the preceding sections all form part of social history in the wider sense of the term. In this section, however, this disparate list of investigative endeavors in the realm of olfaction is viewed specifically under the aspect of its historical unfolding, with the hope of integration in the larger context of cultural change. Shifting views and

---

37. Carterette and Friedman, *Tasting and Smelling,* 199.

emphases, developments and discoveries in various fields, and the general notion of progress form the parameters of this approach. The sum total of such changes is the process of civilization. For our purposes, this process can be seen as an ongoing shifting of threshold levels of perception. On the whole, it reflects an increasing awareness of smells, above all unpleasant ones, both in the domestic and the public realm. New standards emerge and are first practiced in the family realm as a limited public sphere and the center for the individual's socialization and education. It is the increasing preoccupation with olfaction in the social realm that is of particular interest to us. Numerous pieces of textual evidence emerging since the eighteenth century testify to these concerns among the rising bourgeois class. Not all such evidence is literary. Most accounts in fact form a new field of writing altogether, dealing with public health and sanitary issues, and assume a tone of increasing alarm and urgency in the course of the eighteenth and nineteenth centuries. The "big stink" is beginning to be raised in the eighteenth century, and what appeared normal to Liselotte von der Pfalz at that time became unacceptable by the end of the nineteenth.[38] It seems that in the eighteenth century, and certainly after the French Revolution established the bourgeoisie as the ruling class and its sensibilities and en-lightened (romantic) ideas as the dominant social discourse, olfactory phe-nomena undergo a slow process of revaluation. With hygienic, medical, and scientific progress as tributaries to the swelling stream of general knowledge, bad smells become an indicator of backwardness and their eradication adopted as a major social task.[39] These efforts occur in the public sphere as well as in the private realm down to the very body of each individual. Cultural history furnishes interesting details, such as the devel-opment of personal hygiene, the frequency or from our modern perspec-tive the shocking infrequency of baths or changes of clothing; the history of the water closet; and the slow growth of public sanitation and its reflec-tion in architecture and city planning. There are the unfolding scientific theories of miasma, contagion, flux and stagnation of air and their medical effects, as well as crude capitalist economic calculations of profits to be made from what nowadays would euphemistically be called waste manage-

---

38. Elborg Forster, trans., *A Woman's Life in the Court of the Sun King: Letters of Liselotte von der Pfalz, 1652–1722, Elizabeth Charlotte, Duchesse d'Orleans* (Baltimore: Johns Hopkins University Press, 1984).

39. Cf. Corbin, *Le miasme*.

ment.[40] In human interaction, smells begin to be increasingly perceived as criteria distinguishing social classes. Over time, the pressure to "clean up one's act" and to don "good" smells is growing. In this respect, the overall enlightenment project can be seen as one of deodorization and olfactory standardization of both the public and the private spheres in the name of cleanliness and hygiene. Growing out of this endeavor is a new line of demarcation between two social groups: the good-smelling and the bad-smelling ones.

The sociohistorical aspects suggested in the heading of this section form a uneasy category of investigation. Understood in a wider sense, *sociohistorical* simply is the umbrella term for all four aspects discussed here, from the history of the various sciences involved in perception to philosophical and literary ramifications. Everything is a social and cultural phenomenon unfolding in time. For the purpose of our inquiry, the term sociohistorical must initially be understood in this wider sense, because olfaction has indeed ramifications over a large spectrum of human activity. Moreover, the novelty of the present study requires an initial survey of the terrain and clearing of the ground for more narrowly focused follow-up work. At the same time, the term sociohistorical must also be understood in a more limited sense to help provide answers to the questions of when, how, and why olfactory perception rises to the surface of literary meaning. It is in this more restricted context that some of the most characteristic secrets of the olfactory sense are revealed at significant historical junctures. Its liminal as well as transgressive qualities emerge as something to be afraid of in the bourgeois period of the nineteenth century, especially its Victorian second half; as something very much appreciated and liberating in the shift of social and psychological paradigms around the turn of the century; and as a means of describing a time of barbarism from the perspective of survivors of the Shoah. On the other hand, the well-documented component of the history of the sense of smell as represented in the perfume industry only comes to light in the wider context of the sociohistorical spectrum. Its surge in the recent past, our own "liminal age" of cultural revaluation, makes perfumery an increasingly recognized player in aesthetic as well as

---

40. More information, as well as extensive bibliographical material about the eighteenth century from the perspective of social and medical developments can be found in Corbin, *Le miasme,* and for the German context in Stefan Winkle, *Johann Friedrich Struensee: Arzt, Aufklärer und Staatsmann: Beitrag zur Kultur-, Medizin- und Seuchengeschichte der Aufklärungszeit* (Stuttgart: Gustav Fischer Verlag, 1983). For the nineteenth century, see also Rudolf Virchow's essays, below.

ideological matters. With its high charge of eroticism and implication of forces of attraction, aromatic artifice helps to block out the other pole of the olfactory realm, the repulsive and thanatological. The modern fragrance industry leads the colonization of the last sensory realm, the olfactory, and fights its battles on the human body.[41] And it is again as a sociohistorical phenomenon in the wider sense that a new mysticism surfaces, clad in good smells and revealing a search for meaning outside the established channels, a postmodern quest for sense in the sensory at least as much as in the cognitive dimension.

If the goal of the discussion so far has been to place our literary inquiry in a larger context, let us now briefly address the specific literary questions, which are to take up the bulk of this book. My view of the role of literature within the general context is somewhat old-fashioned. While literature is understood as a primary phenomenon, not just a reflection of something other than itself, it is nevertheless necessary to emphasize its ties to, and links with, the social, historical, and cultural reality surrounding it. The problem arising from such a double vision is that the borders between "historical background" and "literary foreground" run the risk of becoming blurred. New Historicism, the line of thinking in which, I believe, this study finds its most appropriate place, is aware of that problem. The historical background cannot simply be used

> to limit and control the meanings of the text in the "foreground." Instead, the background itself becomes a task of interpretation, taking into account a myriad of written and other cultural representations. The background is neither a fixed entity nor a privileged authority located outside the text; it is, to a large degree, the critic's own construction.[42]

The awareness in New Historicism of the inevitable constructedness of historical backgrounds meshes well with our needs to do just this: to create a meaningful context within which to investigate the (literary) phenomenon of smell, in fact to establish first of all samples of texts of "primary" and "secondary" nature.

It is true that "new-historicist readings tend to look unsystematic, at

---

41. M. Jürgens et al., eds., *Ästhetik und Gewalt* (Gütersloh: Bertelsmann Kunstverlag, 1970), esp. Rüdiger Stiebitz, "Ästhetik und Erziehung zur Gewalt," 127–53.

42. Anton Kaes, "New Historicism and the Study of German Literature" *German Quarterly* 62, no. 2 (1989): 210–19.

times even arbitrary, playful, eclectic, and unabashedly personal" (Kaes, 212), but we have to accept such labels in dealing with a phenomenon as elusive as smell. It is extraliterary, has no linguistic register of its own, but a history that branches into many fields of human activity and intellectual inquiry. Yet to date there are few research findings to show for all this. If "playful," "eclectic," and "personal" are indeed qualities the reader perceives in this study, I would be very pleased. The New Historicist approach in the spirit of postmodernism also allows us to blur "the line between high art and mass culture, between past and present, between the canonized and the marginal, and between the 'simulated' and the 'real'" (Kaes, 216)—all helpful aspects for coming to terms with the phenomenon under investigation here.

My understanding of language is equally old-fashioned: language is still a reference system to a reality outside itself. Such a view is almost implied in a project that focuses on a sensory mode, the very physical and perceptual underpinning of language communication. I refuse to accept completely the current critical trend of a purely linguistic determinism of literature and texts in general and would like to emphasize instead some older determinisms: economic and political (above all in the chapter on the nineteenth century); cultural (dominant in the analysis of turn-of-the-century phenomena); ethicopolitical (important for the Shoah chapter); and, among other eclectic ingredients, libidinal-aesthetic forces seen at work in the last chapter on postmodern texts. Such a stance does not deny that there are discourse networks into which each individual author finds himself or herself tied. Indeed, "literary texts are understood as products of circumstance, as expressions of, and comments on, collectively shared fears, hopes, wishes, and anxieties, and as active agents within the social context of their time" (Kaes, 214). The general slant of this study is phenomenological and descriptive within the loose framework offered by New Historicism, adducing and referring to materials from diverse realms of the cultural spectrum.

The intellectual climate prevalent for a long time, where one almost had to be "out of one's senses" in order to be "in one's right mind," has recently begun to change. The body has become a fashionable object of literary inquiry. The time seems to have come to "tear open passages into our senses" in general (Lucretius), but first of all to open up a passage for the one of our five senses that so far has not received much attention in the realm of literary inquiry. This is the goal of this project. I hope to achieve this in the painless yet persuasive way suggested by Hegel:

Die Mittheilung der reinen Einsicht ist deßwegen einer ruhigen Aus-
dehnung oder dem Verbreiten wie eines Dufftes in der widerstandslosen
Atmosphäre zu vergleichen. Sie ist eine durchdringende Ansteckung,
welche sich nicht vorher gegen das gleichgültige Element, in das sie sich
insinuiert, als entgegengesetztes bemerkbar macht, und daher nicht
abgewehrt werden kann.[43]

---

43. G. W. F. Hegel, *Gesammelte Werke*, ed. Westfälische Akademie der Wissenschaften
(Hamburg: Felix Meiner, 1968–), 9:295. "The communication of pure knowledge is
comparable to the dispersion of a scent in a nonresisting atmosphere. It is an all-out
contagion that initially remains unnoticed by the uncaring element into which it spreads.
Therefore, there is no defense against it."

CHAPTER 2

The Nineteenth Century

THE GERMAN REALIST PROJECT OF DEODORIZATION

In 1775 Alexander Cummings of London took out the first patent for a water closet,[1] and according to Alain Corbin the late eighteenth and the early nineteenth centuries marked the beginning of serious attempts at "purifier l'espace publique" (103). Nevertheless, in 1887 Europe still stinks, if we can believe Nietzsche.[2] One of the concerns of the time around 1800 is with bad air and putrefaction and with the death resulting from them. Hygienic investigation, a booming field, takes aim at the air and its role in the metabolism of the individual as well as of society as a whole, the "social body." The separation of the healthy and the living from the sick and the dead, of clean air from stale and putrid air, is the obsession of the epoch; and a major concern is ventilation and flux versus stagnation. Along with these concerns, according to Corbin, an "abaissement du seuil de la tolérance olfactive constitue un fait historique très bien perçu, très bien décrit" (69).[3] A change of attitude above all among the educated city population is on the way, from the more passive "anxiété olfactive" to a more aggressive "vigilance olfactive" (134). Yet a hundred years later Europe apparently still stinks. But bad air, Nietzsche's "Schlechte Luft! Schlechte Luft!" (291), in the workshop where ideals are manufactured

---

1. Roy Palmer, *The Water Closet: A New History* (Newton Abbot: David and Charles, 1973), 22. Credit for this invention should also be given to Sir John Harington, born in 1561, for the first known valve closet. He was simply ahead of his time. Cf. Palmer, 26ff.

2. Friedrich Nietzsche, *Zur Genealogie der Moral,* vol. 2 of *Werke. Kritische Gesamtausgabe,* ed. Giorgio Colli and Mazzino Montinari (Berlin: De Gruyter, 1967–), 291. There are further references to smell on the following pages.

3. "[The] lowering of the threshold of olfactory tolerance constitutes a historically well documented phenomenon."

hints at a process of relocation, a transfer of smells from the literal to the figurative realm. As odors slowly diminish in their public place in city streets and open gutters, they move into the literary public sphere of books and pamphlets. From the actual marketplace they relocate to the market-place of ideas in a process of "redéfinir l'insupportable" (Corbin, 67), and the "unbearable" establishes itself in written accounts. The inverse, how-ever, holds true, too: as talking, reading, and writing about smells begins to form a scientific, a public, discourse in the field of health and hygiene, efforts are made to eradicate smells as indicators of unsanitary conditions in the world of everyday life. European (and American) society goes to work on their elimination.

For the epoch under discussion in this chapter, a balance has already been reached: the bourgeois, educated world of the city has become fairly clean, hygienic, odorless. Consequently, actual odors are no longer a prominent topic of discussion. The levels of an individual's olfactive toler-ance and of olfactory phenomena in the average middle-class citizen's daily experience generally match. This equilibrium may be attributed to two factors: one is the relative odorlessness of the bourgeois environment; the other is a code of public discourse that represses the olfactory as a "dirty" topic. Every remark, therefore, in the one segment of public discourse this study focuses on, literature, has a considerable revelatory function. It allows us to determine what is still, or not yet, acceptable.

One place where smells exist and are perceived is nature and the coun-tryside. Generally, these smells fall on the good side of the spectrum; they are idealized, romanticized, and thinned out to *Duft*.[4] Further areas for us to check for olfactory traces are the immediate human environment, the town, the house, its rooms; products and goods of daily usage; the whole gamut of human activities, the workplace and the working environment, as well as the realm of personal or private occupations, from eating and dressing to interacting in private meetings and relationships with other human beings.

It is of less importance for our purpose here just how we define the era that traditionally is called *bourgeois realism* in German literature, or just

---

4. Romanticism as the formative *weltanschauung* for nineteenth-century (and later) sensibilities would deserve its own investigation. A superficial look reveals that German romanticism seems to be relatively odorless. This is somewhat surprising as smell, the liminal sense par excellence, could potentially serve a role in the romanticists' push toward the progressive universal poetry suggested by Schlegel. One preliminary explanation might be that smells are historically loaded with too many averse associations and thus inherently not yet suited for anything sublime.

exactly what years it is supposed to cover.[5] It also matters less under what specific literary-historical label we study the texts at hand.[6] What *is* important, is to understand the texts discussed here against the background of nineteenth-century sociohistorical trends and to see them in turn influence ongoing developments and confirm emerging tendencies and concepts. The texts themselves set norms and values, establish or confirm models of behavior and discourse. The five novels discussed here form a composite voice of literature as an institution[7] in the babble of public discourse,[8] a discourse that, for the bourgeois age, is itself only emerging and developing, still searching for its channels, its institutions, its tones, and gauging its power and influence.

In the complex grid of interdependent cultural variables (*cultural* understood in its broadest sense) where the change of one factor, sudden or slow, has repercussions throughout the system, it is virtually impossible to focus fruitfully on just two aspects—sensory (olfactory) perception and aesthetics. Instead we need to uncover the characteristics of the interdependence of aesthetics with social norms and of the physical and sensory with the aesthetic. Neither of these branches can be neatly cut loose from the social

---

5. Fritz Martini in his *Deutsche Literaturgeschichte von den Anfängen bis zur Gegenwart,* 5th ed. (Stuttgart: A. Kröner, 1954), avoids the term altogether; in his *Deutsche Literatur im bürgerlichen Realismus,* 4th ed. (Stuttgart: Metzler, 1981), however, it spans the years from 1848–1898. Peter Uwe Hohendahl, on the other hand, in his *Literarische Kultur im Zeitalter des Liberalismus 1830–1870* (Munich: Beck, 1985), contains bourgeois realism within the boundaries of these forty years. He explains in the preface how his time frame shifted from the originally envisaged "Epoche des Realismus (1850–1890)" to the earlier period. See also Max Bucher et al., eds., *Realismus und Gründerzeit: Manifeste und Dokumente zur deutschen Literatur 1848–1880,* 2 vols. (Stuttgart: Metzler, 1975–76).

6. There is certainly no shortage of labels for the various movements during that epoch, from "Biedermeier," "Junges Deutschland," or "Vormärz" to the "Taming of Romanticism," and "Nationalliteratur." See, e.g., Friedrich Sengle, *Biedermeierzeit: Deutsche Literatur im Spannungsfeld zwischen Restauration und Revolution 1815–1848,* 2 vols. (Stuttgart: Metzler, 1971); Walter Dietze, *Junges Deutschland und deutsche Klassik: Zur Ästhetik und Literaturtheorie des Vormärz,* 3d ed. (Berlin: Rütten and Loening, 1962); Virgil Nemoianu, *The Taming of Romanticism: European Romanticism and the Age of Biedermeier* (Cambridge: Harvard University Press, 1984); G. G. Gervinus, *Geschichte der poetischen Nationalliteratur der Deutschen* (Leipzig: 1835–42).

7. Peter Bürger, *Theorie der Avantgarde* (Frankfurt am Main: Suhrkamp, 1974). (English: *Theory of the Avant-garde,* trans. Michael Shaw [Minneapolis: University of Minnesota Press, 1984].) See also Hohendahl, *Literarische Kultur.*

8. Jürgen Habermas, *Strukturwandel der Öffentlichkeit: Untersuchungen zu einer Kategorie der bürgerlichen Gesellschaft* (Neuwied: Luchterhand, 1962). (English: *The Structural Transformation of the Public Sphere: An Inquiry into a Category of Bourgeois Society,* trans. Thomas Burger and Frederick Lawrence [Cambridge: MIT Press, 1989].)

tree on which they grow. We will treat them as privileged aspects in a more comprehensive and interactive interpretative approach. In methodological terms, this means blurring the borderlines between "literature" on the one hand and "everything else" on the other. It means granting social, historical, and political findings an equal status with literary ones, and it clearly means an expansion of the notion of aesthetics. Aesthetics is then not a quality specifically pertaining to works of art and literature and the theoretical discourse about them, but rather, as Terry Eagleton understands it, a tool of the bourgeois epoch to link morals with hedonism, to define a nice, pleasant, and acceptable way of doing what *ought* to be done. Aesthetics is the lubricant in the jarring of theoretical social standards and actual social practice.[9] Its function is to mediate between the antinomic aspects of the bourgeois *comme il faut,* its implicit necessity and its implied beauty. This ideology of the aesthetic is clearly already known to both Kant and Schiller.[10] The latter openly admits in the *Ästhetische Erziehung* his indebtedness to the former and bases his arguments on "größtenteils Kantische Grundsätze."[11] It is again Schiller who spells out the general tendency in the aesthetic debate that emerges after the Baroque and through the Enlightenment: the shift of cognitive interests away from the material-perceptual base in the senses toward the intellectual-categorical superstructure.[12] This means an increasing cerebration of the sensory realm

9. Terry Eagleton, "The Ideology of the Aesthetic," *Times Literary Supplement,* 22 January 1988. 84.

10. In the *Kritik der Urteilskraft* (*Critique of Judgment*) Kant recognizes the link between aesthetics and power, and although he formulates this connection for visual art and within the context of religion, it can easily be generalized into the public need to harness and control the individual's sensual experience and imagination (*Einbildungskraft*) in order to facilitate social control. Governments, he says, have traditionally permitted religion to use imagery, "und so dem Untertan die Mühe, zugleich aber auch das Vermögen zu benehmen gesucht, seine Seelenkräfte über die Schranken auszudehnen, die man ihm willkürlich setzen, und wodurch man ihn, als bloß passiv, leichter behandeln kann." Immanuel Kant, *Die Kritik der Urteilskraft,* vol. 10 of *Werkausgabe in zwölf Bänden,* ed. Wilhelm Weischedel (Frankfurt am Main: Suhrkamp, 1974), 202.

11. Friedrich Schiller, "Die ästhetische Erziehung des Menschen in einer Reihe von Briefen," in *Philosophische Schriften,* vol. 20 of *Werke: Nationalausgabe,* ed. Lieselotte Blumenthal and Benno von Wiese (Weimar: Hermann Böhlaus Nachfolger, 1943–), 1. Brief.

12. Schiller sets up the state of classical antiquity as a model where the individual represents the potential totality of the community. In his time, however, society has become a clockwork "wo aus der Zusammenstückung unendlich vieler, aber lebloser Teile ein mechanisches Leben im ganzen sich bildet." The state is forced, "sich die Mannigfaltigkeit seiner Bürger durch Klassifizierung zu erleichtern und die Menschheit nie anders als durch Repräsentation aus der zweiten Hand zu empfangen. . . . " In this

in order to facilitate its structuring in terms of cognition. Schiller asks the reader's pardon for a development that is in fact beyond him and all-pervasive: "Lassen Sie daher auch mir diese Nachsicht zustatten kommen wenn die nachfolgenden Untersuchungen ihren Gegenstand, indem sie ihn dem *Verstande* zu *nähern* suchen, *den Sinnen entrücken* sollten" (emphasis added).[13] In the same letter of the *Ästhetische Erziehung,* in fact in its first paragraph, Schiller puts together the terms that will become crucial in the new century's intellectual-aesthetic debate: "Ich werde die Sache der *Schönheit* vor einem *Herzen* führen, das ihre ganze Macht empfindet und ausübt und bei einer Untersuchung, wo man ebensooft genötigt ist, sich auf *Gefühle* als auf *Grundsätze* zu berufen, den schwersten Teil meines *Geschäfts* auf sich nehmen wird" (emphasis added).[14]

Beauty, the aesthetic ("Schönheit"), is undergoing an investigation ("Untersuchung") that places it between the poles of feelings and emotions on the one hand ("Gefühle") and (intellectual and social) principles, norms, and standards ("Grundsätze") on the other. This investigation is carried out before the heart ("Herzen") as its witness and addressee. Schiller attributes to this complex organ the ambivalent position assigned to it throughout the dawning bourgeois epoch. The heart is the bourgeois organ of sensory perception par excellence, precisely in its ambiguity. The fact that Schiller calls his investigation a "business" ("Geschäft") adds an additional premonitory dimension, namely the question of the socioeconomic and political usefulness of the intellectual enterprise of *ästhetische Erziehung*—for instance in exercising control over the masses, as Kant pointed out. Our analysis of individual texts shows aesthetic education at work in the techniques of literary representation, specifically in the authors' structuring of references to various sensory modes. In literature—as in other strands of the public discourse—a subtle shaping of the reader's perception is taking place, based on the social patterning and linguistic

---

way "wird allmählich das einzelne konkrete Leben vertilgt, damit das Abstrakte des Ganzen sein dürftiges Dasein friste, und ewig bleibt der Staat seinen Bürgern fremd, weil ihn das Gefühl nirgends findet" ("Ästhetische Erziehung," 6. Brief). To overcome this modern alienation, which Schiller sees in a negative teleological perspective as the curse of a "Weltzweck," is the explicit purpose of the "Ästhetische Erziehung."

13. Schiller, "Ästhetische Erziehung," 1. Brief. "Grant me indulgence if the following investigation removes its object from the senses while attempting to bring it into closer contact with the intellect."

14. Schiller, "Ästhetische Erziehung," 1. Brief. "I will take beauty's part before a heart that fully senses and exercises beauty's power and that will take over the most difficult part of my investigation where one has to rely on emotions as often as on principles."

encoding of perceptual phenomena in the text. The "business of poetics" (or more generally, aesthetics) is thus by no means an idiosyncratic Schillerian spleen, and Gustav Freytag's "poetics of business," the *Poesie des Geschäfts,* hints at a broad trend.

Thus at the very end of the eighteenth century and leading the way into the nineteenth, Schiller refers to Kant—with a difference: by sentimentalizing the latter's concept of beauty ("Das Schöne . . . gefällt ohne alles Interesse").[15] He sentimentalizes it in the modern sense of the term, adding a sentimental, emotional dimension, but also in his own understanding of *sentimental,* developed in *Über naive und sentimentalische Dichtung,*[16] as aiming at or striving for a lost, naive immediacy and harmony. Kant's conceptualization of the beautiful (*das Schöne*) is itself by no means as free of interest as it might at first appear and is in fact close to that socially mediating position that Eagleton describes for the aesthetic. Kant is aware of this and sees inherent in the beautiful a "Neigung zur Gesellschaft" and therefore a certain "empirische[s] Interesse." The interest in taste (*Geschmack,* which Kant understands as the socially and educationally malleable element in his aesthetic system) tends to be connected with all the "Neigungen und Leidenschaften, die in der Gesellschaft ihre größte Mannigfaltigkeit und höchste Stufe erreichen." In taste, then, even in its socially impure, interested form, lies the nucleus of an "Übergang unseres Beurteilungsvermögens von dem Sinnengenuß zum Sittengefühl," the possibility of a transition "vom Angenehmen zum Guten."[17] While Schiller's aesthetics sentimentalizes Kant's concepts, it must not be overlooked that Kant himself represents a departure—even if in a different direction—from Baumgarten's earlier aesthetics,[18] which was understood as *scientia cognitionis sensitivue,* a concept that clearly recognizes the physical, bodily, sensory roots of (aesthetic) perception. Kant shifts the emphasis toward abstraction, thereby maneuvering the investigation into the mainstream of the enlightenment process. This means for the status of the human body that "Zivilisation als Transformation des Körpers ins Geistige war und

---

15. Kant, *Kritik,* 298.

16. Friedrich Schiller, "Über naive und sentimentalische Dichtung," in *Philosophische Schriften,* vol. 20 of *Werke: Nationalausgabe,* 413–503.

17. All quotes from paragraph 41 of the *Kritik,* 230–31. Kant understands beauty's "social inclination" and sees in taste a "transition of our capabilities of judgment from hedonism to morality," a transition "from the pleasant to the good."

18. For Baumgarten see chap. 1, footnote 31.

ist . . . Abstraktion vom Körper."[19] Schiller adds sentiment and brings back the—distorted—body, represented in its *one* central organ that unites both the physical and the intellectual aspects and is already turning into a metaphor, the heart. Hegel, finally, will add the historical-teleological superstructure promoting art to the transcendental status that ultimately implies its end.[20] Thus after the first third of the nineteenth century, the set of major parameters of bourgeois aesthetics is in place. It will unfold as the century wears on, interacting with concrete political events, technological developments, and social changes. Aesthetics appears as the sociopolitical category through which social norms are mapped onto the individual. The realist novel of the second half of the century represents a climax of such "role-modeling," of mediating that which is good, that is, socially desirable, with what is pleasurable, and shaping the latter to make it correspond to the former. The realist ideology of the aesthetic ties the individual, the body, and the senses to the social, the intellectual, and the legal.

The novels of Freytag, Stifter, Keller, and Fontane discussed here are overall strangely silent about the sensory and sensuous aspects of the lives they describe (less so Raabe). Nature, dwellings, objects and products, work and the workplace, people and their relationships: all are described, yet they seem to remain at a distance. They are seen, observed (usually from an omniscient narrator's perspective); they are overheard and commented on, but they do not become tangible. And they are largely inodorous. During this age the petit bourgeois maxim of education, the exhortation to children so often heard to this day—"Don't touch! Just look!"—begins to determine the general approach to the object world. For the olfactory this amounts to virtual disappearance, no surprise after the facts established so far. The enlightenment attitude toward the body and its functions as it unfolds in the eighteenth century and gains momentum in the nineteenth, fueled by technological progress, can be seen as one of sanitation, of hygiene, of deodorization. What is advertised as good and therefore as desirable is the developing social norm of the odorless or pleasantly scented public and private spheres. Smell is envisaged as the sense that is not (to be) talked about. Kant explicitly excludes the olfactory from the enlighten-

---

19. Kamper and Wulf, *Das Schwinden der Sinne,* 12. "Civilization as the transformation of the body into the intellectual realm was and still is . . . an abstraction from the body."

20. See Hegel, *Ästhetik,* esp. 1:48f. and 2:14f. for Hegel's arguments for the exclusion of smell from aesthetic considerations.

ment project, or rather, he includes it with a view to its ultimate eradication.[21]

Whereas Eulenspiegel in the sixteenth century could still shit and fart and raise a stink, and Simplicissimus would do the same in the seventeenth—although here, among the upper class, this already starts to turn heads—the eighteenth century begins to clean up its act, and odors are increasingly complained about, condemned, and more and more eliminated.[22] Excretory functions in particular are privatized and euphemized, from Swift's "plucking a rose" in the garden[23]—still viewed as a suitable place for such little business—to Cummings's patent in 1775, and generally by those measures described in detail and in their historical process by Corbin. The nineteenth century continues this trend with Chadwick's report from 1842 on the sanitary situation in Great Britain, a milestone on the road to the deodorized public sphere that begins to spread from city centers all over Europe at varying speed.[24] Odors are understood as signs of deplorable sanitary conditions but they are also—still—considered noxious and disease-causing in themselves. One important aspect in the movement that Chadwick both represents and pushes forward is its primary

21. Kant, *Anthropologie,* 53f. See also chapter 3, footnote 14 and Horkheimer and Adorno, chapter 3, footnote 17.

22. However, there is also Eulenspiegel's sophisticated play on the discrepancy between the indexical and material reality of sensory phenomena when in one of his pranks he pays a stingy innkeeper who wants to charge him for the aroma of a roast he has inhaled, with the mere chinking sound of a few coins.

23. On Swift, see Donald T. Siebert, "Swift's 'Fiat Odor': The Excremental Re-Vision," *Eighteenth Century Studies* 1 (1985): 21–38. Swift in his scatological poetry uses smell in human, especially marital, interaction as a (realistic) means to deflate stylized, (literary) romantic notions of love.

24. E. Chadwick, *Report to Her Majesty's Principal Secretary of State for the Home Department from the Poor Law Commission on an Inquiry into the Sanitary Condition of the Labouring Population of Great Britain,* ed. M. W. Flinn (1842; Edinburg: University Press, 1965). Cf. Corbin, *Le miasme,* for a detailed discussion of both the eighteenth- and nineteenth-century French city, especially Paris. For Prussia and the city of Berlin in particular, Rudolf Virchow becomes the leading advocate of public health and sanitation. Not only is he an outstanding medical researcher, but for him, a social and medical progressive, medical concerns are always social concerns, the medical science is a social science. Cf., e.g., his report on a typhoid fever epidemic in Upper Silesia (1849), a courageous political, as well as a vivid and naturalistically exact medical and social, document. Rudolf Virchow, *Die Not im Spessart—Mitteilungen über die in Oberschlesien herrschende Typhus-Epidemie* (Darmstadt: Wissenschaftliche Buchgesellschaft, 1968). For a brief account of his medical achievements and political efforts, see Arnold Bauer, *Rudolf Virchow—der politische Arzt.* Preußische Köpfe (Berlin: Stapp, 1982). A comprehensive survey of his activities and efforts can be found in his *Collected Essays on Public Health and Epidemiology,* 2 vols., ed. L. J. Rather, M.D. (Canton, Mass.: Science History Publications USA, 1985).

concern with public health and hygiene rather than with the elimination of odors. The movement has several roots. Following the *economic* argument, the ruling class begins to understand that public health care for the increasing number of poor in the rapidly growing cities (London at that time has about six million inhabitants and is the world's largest city) will ultimately be cheaper than picking up the tab of an unregulated laissez-faire development at a later point. The *philanthropic* undercurrent stresses the moral duty of the newly rich industrialists to care to some extent for those classes they exploit in their factories. And the undercurrent of *anxiety* carries the deep-seated fears of an already relatively clean upper class of the contamination, infection, and corruption by a growing class of people who lack the facilities and means of even minimal hygiene in their daily lives. The passing of the Public Health Act in 1848 marks the beginning of a new era in England. The British state recognizes officially a certain amount of responsibility for its citizens and counters Benthamite laissez-faire politics with some new social ethics. Progress is uneven in the big European cities. While the French have at least been talking—and complaining—about the deplorable sanitary state of Paris, it is the Londoners who are the first to begin work on a sewage and drainage system. Around the turn of the century, however, it is Berlin that emerges as a relatively well-sanitized place.[25]

Today—as in the nineteenth century—we are far past the stage of that hypothetical society where, as Eagleton puts it, "the three mighty regions of the cognitive, libidinal-aesthetic and ethico-political were still subtly interrelated."[26] Thoughts have dissociated themselves from feelings, and it has become "increasingly difficult to derive values from facts." The feeling of, or the need for, such interconnectedness, however, lives on, and one important driving force behind the modern tradition in thought, literature, and the arts has been precisely the search for such unity. As ideas, ideals, and ideology on the one hand and social practices on the other drift further and further apart, as ideas and ideals turn into ideology precisely to cover up the split, one of the major forces behind modernism is finding structures of mediation. In Eagleton's general outline of societal development, modernity is understood as a recurring phenomenon, rather similar to Bürger's historical and historicized avant-garde. However, our search for origins is

---

25. Cf. Virchow's references to French and British medical statistics and epidemiological findings in his report on Silesia. See also Corbin, *Le miasme*, and Bauer, *Rudolf Virchow*.

26. Eagleton, "The Ideology of the Aesthetic," *Times Literary Supplement*, 84.

frustrated from the start, for the subtle interrelation of the cognitive, the libidinal-aesthetic, and the ethicopolitical breaks down with its very first formulation in classical antiquity. The advent of Christian modernity with its new promise of wholeness only brings about the next disappointment and break. The wholeness barely held together—by *ideological* means, such as the medieval aestheticopolitical practice of *Minnesang*—is broken up again during the Renaissance with its emphasis on science and individuality. In search of *its* state of unity, the Renaissance rediscovers classical antiquity as a locus of wholeness and ideality, whereas romanticism later on projects its wish for harmony into the Middle Ages and combines it with Renaissance achievements into a new wholeness of its own. Classicism in turn looks once more toward antiquity. Inevitably, however, the historical position of modernity cannot leave out—in fact, it stands at the vanguard of—accumulated knowledge and cognitive advances. The modernist movement that becomes visible in the humanities and the arts in the second half of the nineteenth century, has its basis in socioeconomic and scientific-technological changes, and from there tries to find a new balance between the cognitive, libidinal-aesthetic, and ethicopolitical. This endeavor can be, and indeed is, itself subjected to ideological criticism from the vantage point of postmodernism. Postmodernism can thus be understood as the latest attempt at fusing Eagleton's three principle realms. In its "anything goes" variety, however, the frustration over the apparent impossibility of such a fusion surfaces and results in the movement's strong tendency to simply leave clashing values next to one another, without even an attempt at integration.[27] In nineteenth-century realism such endeavors at integration clearly exist, however bourgeois-centric they may be, but the century overall is marked by its own kind of strain between the three realms.

Soll und Haben (1855)[28] and *Der Nachsommer* (1857)[29] represent two different attempts to overcome the centrifugal powers in their contemporary society. Both are, to some extent, reactions to the recent political events

27. Andreas Huyssen, *After the Great Divide: Modernism, Mass Culture, Postmodernism* (Bloomington: Indiana University Press, 1986). The anything-goes variety is just one form of postmodernism, its worst, according to Huyssen. He stresses postmodernism's aspects of a continuation of modernism. For him it marks yet another attempt at integrating—rather than breaking apart—high art and low culture, the elite cognitive and the mass libidinal-aesthetic in a new ethicopolitical framework.

28. Gustav Freytag, *Soll und Haben* (Leipzig, 1855; Munich: Hanser, 1977). All references are to this edition.

29. Adalbert Stifter, *Der Nachsommer* (Frankfurt am Main: Insel, 1982). (Same as vol. 3 of Adalbert Stifter, *Werke,* ed. Uwe Japp and Hans Joachim Piechotta, Insel, 1978).

of the revolution of 1848. One keeps silent about those events and develops strongly nationalist ideas of colonialism; the other attempts a kind of retrospective and escapist aesthetic utopia. The protagonists of both novels come from similar petit bourgeois backgrounds: one's father is a lower-ranking public official, the other a self-employed merchant. They enter different careers, however. Despite the aspects of *bildungsroman* present in both novels, and their overall narrative stance typical for bourgeois realism, the texts suggest two distinct models for creating or, more accurately, regaining a lost social center.

Both Freytag's and Stifter's visions are based on the bourgeoisie as the carrier of the envisaged values. For both, the bourgeoisie is a well-defined social group that has, at least in its own self-understanding, managed to draw clear boundaries around itself. It has started to be exclusive toward ethnic and national otherness as well as class otherness (both the upper class, the nobility, and the lower class, the workers) and developed its own strong sense of identity, even if often based on nothing but self-righteousness. This bourgeoisie is under attack in 1848 by opponents demanding a share of the very *liberté, égalité, fraternité* that it itself embraced a good half century earlier as its own supreme trinity of values. Since then, however, the bourgeoisie has lost its taste for the earlier all-embracing emancipatory gestures and developed features of a ruling class. Although drawing the boundaries around it is still a major concern of both authors and principles of exclusion are vague, they appear as tacitly understood both by the members and the nonmembers of the class. Anton knows at the beginning of Freytag's novel that he does not belong in the "Vorderhaus" (67); but at the end he knows equally well that now he does. Gottfried Keller's Heinrich Lee also is instinctively aware of his outsider status, whereas Heinrich Drendorf in Stifter's novel *is* bourgeois from the start. The three authors only differ in the criteria of exclusion they apply.

Freytag heads toward exclusion, or at least the pronouncement of divisive social value judgments, on the basis of nationality, ethnicity, and class: the Poles, the Jews, the aristocracy. The groups thus marked are put in relation to each other and in contrast to the bourgeoisie mainly in their attitude toward work, which is almost exclusively characterized as business and trade. Freytag's main characters are not producers of goods, for production is considered essentially aristocratic. Schröter in talking to Fink calls "jede Tätigkeit, welche neue Werte schafft, . . . Tätigkeit des Fabrikanten; sie gilt überall in der Welt für die aristokratische. Wir Kaufleute sind dazu da, diese Werte populär zu machen" (Freytag, 309). This implied democratic claim is one of the gut feelings of the liberal bourgeoisie to this day.

Stifter's principles of exclusion have a concrete material and spatial base, the country estate, which ultimately curtails on social grounds the utopian potential that the novel builds up to its culmination in the protagonist's aesthetic education. The realm in which this process takes place is secluded from the "real" world in a fairy-tale manner by a thick hedge of roses.

Freytag's politics of national and ethnic exclusion, his rhetoric of *Pflichttreue,* of work ethics and duty, and his implicit notion that everybody, provided he or she (but mostly he) has enough willpower, can become a useful, essentially bourgeois member of society point toward what Russell Berman calls "Fascist modernism."[30] Throughout the text we hear the reverberations of the central notions of *ein Volk* and *ein Reich*— the bourgeois laissez-faire capitalist ideals. What is absent, and this saves the text from becoming totalitarian, is *ein Führer*. This, indeed, Freytag neither means nor foresees, and I want to make it clear that I do not understand him as a forerunner, a pre- or proto-Fascist. He is a liberal, but embodies all the problems and internal contradictions that engulfed both political and cultural liberalism during the nineteenth century. Such problems are explicitly issues of definitions, of borderlines, of inclusion and exclusion, and liberalism has been beset with them from its very beginning as a political force when it emerged as the ideal, soon the ideology, of its carrier class, the bourgeoisie.[31] The novel plays on the different value systems of the aristocracy—the Rothsattels—and the bourgeoisie—Schröter and Anton—including the mixed emotions that these two classes have for each other. Their values, but certainly their attitudes toward work and their economic views, are ultimately irreconcilable.

Stifter's vision, on the other hand, with his model of aesthetic education

---

30. Russell A. Berman, *The Rise of the Modern German Novel: Crisis and Charisma.* (Cambridge: Harvard University Press, 1986), 205. Berman's analysis informs my own account of nineteenth-century literature, esp. of *Soll und Haben,* far beyond the specific references made here.

31. For a more extensive historical analysis of the German bourgeoisie in the nineteenth century see James J. Sheehan, *Der deutsche Liberalismus: Von den Anfängen im 18. Jahrhundert bis zum Ersten Weltkrieg, 1770–1914,* trans. Karl Heinz Siber (Munich: C.H. Beck, 1983). (English original: *German Liberalism in the Nineteenth Century* [Chicago: University of Chicago Press, 1978].) Sheehan analyzes the emerging bourgeois discourse of just *who* is a bourgeois on the basis of the changing material and educational criteria that explicitly and implicitly decide about an individual's membership in that still fluctuating class. See also James J. Sheehan, *German History 1770–1866* (Oxford: Clarendon, 1989).

materially based on the country estate, does contain a truly utopian, emancipatory moment vis-à-vis a dominant and expanding capitalism—the very capitalism described in Freytag with so much gusto as essentially bourgeois. The novel describes a rapprochement between the bourgeois protagonist and his aristocratic host and provider of educational opportunity, Freiherr von Risach. Just as Freytag's story in its historical extension into the present takes at some point a turn toward fascist views, Stifter's semiaristocratic, aestheticist, and closed-off universe finds its historical extension in fin-de-siècle aestheticism and may be seen in connection with the decay of the Austro-Hungarian Empire as an overaged, rigid structure that has completed its life cycle.[32] Freytag's model is aggressive. Stifter's, although in its outlook utopian, is set in a nostalgic, essentially past and backward-looking, social context. "Stifter is closer to a fin-de-siècle décadent than to a Biedermeier stalwart."[33]

A trend common to both novels is to cut out a part of "reality" and posit it *pars pro toto* as an ideal, a model to be followed by the (bourgeois) community at large. This propagandistic feature turns both these realistic novels into ideological projects and reveals (literary) realism's true face: it is not a faithful description of what *is,* but a projection of what *should be.* This political dimension is open in *Soll und Haben,* from Julian Schmidt's motto to Freytag's dedication of the book to the Duke of Sachsen-Coburg-Gotha, and it permeates the whole novel itself.[34]

In structural and aesthetic terms, the realism of *Soll und Haben* appears as a sociopolitical project of marginalization and centering, of elevating and lowering aspects and qualities according to their ideological desirability. These shifts are represented in several realms. In nationality and geography: the Poles and the East versus the Germans and the West; in the body: the tall, slim, classical body versus the distorted, bent-over bodies of the marginal figures; in the realm of sensory perception: the marginalization of the senses of proximity, the "lower senses." For Stifter this will turn out

---

32. For a detailed discussion of Stifter's *Nachsommer* in terms of its aesthetic structure and the social implications of the model and its shortcomings see Herbert Kaiser, *Studien zum deutschen Roman nach* 1848. Duisburger Hochschulbeiträge 8, (Duisburg: Walter Braun Verlag, 1977).

33. Nemoianu, *Taming of Romanticism,* 217.

34. For a brief summary of contemporary comments and views of the novel, see Horst Denkler, ed., *Romane und Erzählungen des Bürgerlichen Realismus* (Stuttgart: Reclam, 1980). On *Soll und Haben* see Hartmut Steinecke, "Gustav Freytag: 'Soll und Haben' (1855): Weltbild und Wirkung eines deutschen Bestsellers," 138–52.

to mean the explicit exclusion of the olfactory.[35] The desensualization of the material world of *Soll und Haben* on the story level (the perception of their environment by the protagonists) as well as the discourse level (the narrator-as-mediator, directing the reader's attention to certain realms of sensory perception) must strike the modern reader. In *Effi Briest,* the absence of the physical is at least partially thematized: "'Nicht so wild, Effi, nicht so leidenschaftlich'" (9). It is *Der grüne Heinrich* that is not only the most olfactory, but the most sensual of the first four novels in this section.

Soll und Haben: The Poetics of Business

Beschreib das Aroma des Kaffees!—Warum geht es nicht? Fehlen uns die Worte? Und *wofür* fehlen sie uns?
—(Wittgenstein, italics original)

Soll und Haben is a novel of well over 800 pages. The values it presents are predominantly abstract: (Protestant) work ethic, law and order, industriousness, sense of duty, reliability, dedication, perseverance, willpower, and so forth. They can be subsumed under and amount to the sum total of *deutsche Bürgertugenden,* the traditional German civic virtues. For the story, of course, these abstract qualities need a material base on which they can be enacted and honed. This is the petit bourgeois household of the Wohlfarts in the beginning, and the bourgeois "Handelshaus Schröter" for most of the story. From this double base, the plot branches out into the lower and socially marginal classes, above all the Jews. Further lower-class elements, predominantly soldierly and rural, are brought into the narrative strand that deals with the colonial enterprise in Poland. Through Fink, the reader is offered a quick glance at America and its capitalist ruthlessness; and from the very opening of the novel the aristocracy forms another important social group, shown in its interaction both with the bourgeoisie and with the Jewish world of business and finance. This social spectrum seems relatively broad. But the perspective that the reader is offered is quite clearly and determinedly that of the bourgeoisie and its values. What this means in terms of sensory perception in general and olfaction in particular is the aim of the following inquiry.

---

35. For an extensive discussion of the contrast of the grotesque and the classical body (even if focusing on the eighteenth century), see Peter Stallybrass and Allon White, *The Politics and Poetics of Transgression* (Ithaca, New York: Cornell University Press, 1986).

The taste sensation at the beginning of the narrative is obviously de-signed to create a quaint, old-fashioned, in fact a fairy-tale-like atmosphere: "Ostrau ist eine kleine Kreisstadt unweit der Oder, bis nach Polen hinein berühmt durch ihr Gymnasium und *süße Pfefferkuchen.* . . . In diesem *altväterischen* Ort *lebte vor einer Reihe von Jahren* der *königliche Kalkulator* Wohlfart" (II, emphasis added).[36] But already earlier, in the opening lines of Freytag's dedication of the novel to Ernst II, Duke of Sachsen-Coburg-Gotha, we encounter a conspicuously charged setting: "Es war ein lachen-der Maiabend auf dem Kalenberg. Oben um das Schloß blühte und duftete der Frühling und die Blätter der roten Akazia warfen gezackte Schatten auf den tauigen Rasen" (9). The paragraph closes: "Seit diesem Abend habe ich den Wunsch, mit Eurer Hoheit Namen das Buch zu schmücken, dessen Plan ich damals mit mir herumtrug" (9).[37] In between we find a whole collection of Biedermeier genre elements, such as "tame deer," the "light figure of the lady," the "dusky distance," and the "golden words" of the duke. Twice, then, at the beginning of narrative sequences, in fact at the very outset of the work, taste and smell, the chemical senses of proximity, are invoked, constituting an apparent contradiction to my gen-eral claim above that the bourgeois age is one of sensory repression. In order to examine this question, let us focus on the story told by Anton's father, which opens the main plot of the novel.

Anton, the protagonist, son of the royal accountant, has been living under the influence of the Handelshaus Schröter since his early childhood. His involvement with the trading firm begins in fact with the Schröter's annual Christmas gift of sugar and coffee to his father for a document that the latter had found and duly returned to its legal owner, thereby enabling Schröter to win a lengthy lawsuit. "Sehr angenehm war das Selbstgefühl mit welchem der würdige Hausherr die erste Tasse dieses Kaffees trank. Das waren Stunden, wo ein poetischer Duft, der so oft durch die Seelen der Kinder zieht, das ganze Haus erfüllte" (13). This *poetischer Duft* that wafts through the beginning of the main plot even before Anton's arrival in the city, triggers narrative: "Der Vater erzählte dann gern seinem Sohne

---

36. "Ostrau is a small district capital near the Oder river. The fame of its college ["Gymnasium"] and its sweet gingerbread has spread far into Poland. . . . Many years ago in this old-fashioned place there lived the royal accountant Wohlfart."

37. "The May evening was smiling over the Kahlenberg [a hill]. Around the castle the lilacs were blossoming and scenting the air, and the leaves of the red acacias threw sharp shadows onto the dewy lawn. . . . Since that evening I have wanted to honor with your name the book whose idea I was harboring inside of me at that time."

die Geschichte dieser Sendungen" (13). Obviously, it is a narrative with a tradition, a narrative as tradition. Its antiquarian beginning stresses the temporal distance of the events and their remoteness from everyday life: "*Vor vielen Jahren* hatte der Kalkulator in einem *bestäubten* Aktenbündel, das von den Gerichten und der Menschheit *bereits aufgegeben* war, ein Dokument gefunden" (13, emphases added).[38]

The *poetischer Duft* associated with the Schröter gift is linked with the hero's childhood. It will disappear in the process of his growing up and maturing. As he decides to enter the business world himself, the poetics shift from past to present, from narrated story to action. The "Poesie dieser gemütlichen Beziehung," that is, the poetics that Anton's father perceives in his connection to the Schröter business and that originates in the gift of coffee will, dissociated from coffee and divorced from its childhood locus, be transformed into the "Poesie des Geschäfts" (326) and will pervade the whole book. This "poetics of business" is one of networks, of relations, of channels of trust, loyalty, and uprightness as well as of shrewd and tenacious negotiating. Trade is "diese lebhafte Unterhaltung mit der ganzen Welt" (66). Anton, as Fink predicts, finds himself very soon caught in the system, "als Rad eingefügt in die Maschine" (63). The opening pages of this long novel thus contain *in nuce* its central set of emotions and values, and the main narrative goal is precisely the depiction of the fundamental shift from a "gemütliche Beziehung," which for the protagonist is associated both with his childhood and with a concrete sensory experience, to the rational, nonsensory relations of the business world with its machine-like qualities. At times, "mitten in dem Rauschen des Geschäftslebens," Anton tires of the "ewige Gleichförmigkeit" of his days (64). This is the process of maturation, the *Erziehungsroman* aspect of the novel. In this regard Anton has a headstart, for his parents had trained him well in "Ordnung und regelmäßigem Fleiß" (64). Part of the process is the hero's finding his social place, enabling him to set up acceptable personal relationships within his class.

The *poetischer Duft* of coffee provides further connections, namely be-

---

38. The three preceding German passages translate as follows:

The worthy master of the house was filled with pleasant sensations when he drank the first cup of the coffee. These were the hours when a poetic scent, which so often wafts through the souls of children, filled the whole house. . . . Father then used to tell his son the story of these shipments. . . . Many years ago the accountant had found a document among a pile of old, dusty files that had long been abandoned by the law courts and mankind.

tween the colonial, foreign, exotic element on the one hand and narrative, storytelling, and history on the other. In an emotional, *gemütlich,* atmosphere, the sentiments of the father are passed on to the son, for whenever he asks Anton if he wants to become a *Kaufmann,* the "leise Sehnsucht" of the older, his longing for the wide wild world out there, filters through to the younger:

> Und in der Seele des Kleinen schoß augenblicklich ein schönes Bild zusammen, wie die Strahlen bunter Glasperlen im Kaleidoskop, zusammengesetzt aus großen Zuckerhüten, Rosinen und Mandeln und goldenen Apfelsinen, aus dem freundlichen Lächeln seiner Eltern und all dem geheimnisvollen Entzücken, welches ihm selbst die ankommende Kiste bereitet; bis er begeistert ausrief: "Ja, Vater, ich will!" (14)[39]

The aesthetic representation displayed here shifts from the olfactory to a visual configuration of images in the kaleidoscope. The common element lies in poiesis, the imaginative potential of both sensory modes. The visual, however, comes appended with an authorial warning:

> Man sage nicht, daß unser Leben arm ist an poetischen Stimmungen, noch beherrscht die Zauberin Poesie überall das Treiben der Erdgeborenen. Aber ein jeder achte wohl darauf, welche Träume er im heimlichsten Winkel seiner Seele hegt, denn wenn sie erst groß gewachsen sind, werden sie leicht seine Herren, strenge Herren! (14)[40]

This warning to cut one's dreams in order not to be overpowered by them is an appeal to leave the realm of the smell of coffee and the images of "Zuckerhüte, Rosinen und Mandeln" behind and replace this childish *Poesie* by the real *Poesie des Geschäfts,* to relinquish, in other words, the

---

39. When Anton is asked by his father whether he wants to become a merchant and feels his "gentle longing," the following happens:

> Immediately, a beautiful image coalesced in the child's soul, like the colorful rays in a kaleidoscope, consisting of large sugar cones, raisins, almonds, and golden oranges, his parents' friendly smile, and the mysterious rapture that the shipment [of coffee] had caused him, so that he exclaimed enthusiastically: "Yes father, I want to [i.e., become a merchant]!"

40. "Do not say that our lives are poor in poetic moods; the enchantress Poesia is still dominating the doings of the earthlings. But everyone ought to take care about the dreams he hides in the deepest recesses of his soul. For when they have grown, they may easily become his masters, his strict masters!"

concrete for the abstract poetics of links, networks, partnerships, and deals. The Handelshaus Schröter thus is not a realm of sensuous experience, as one might imagine when considering all the exotic goods in its cellars and warehouse, *Kolonialwaren* in the true sense of the term. The goods, rather, serve as objects of sensory temptation and as such have to be resisted. Young Karl Sturm for instance, the son of one of the shippers, is on one occasion subjected to a veritable temptation test when ordered to remain next to the almond and raisin containers and to see "wie lange du vor diesen Tonnen stehen kannst, ohne hineinzugreifen" (85). Things are not to be touched, only to be looked at, in accordance with a fundamental bourgeois maxim of education.

The project of aesthetic education in the novel can be understood as a process both of de-emphasizing the sensual aspects of reality and desensitizing the perceiving subject. This strategy leaves the olfactory with a mere thirty-some references in the whole book. Yet in the face of the veritable adjectival overkill reigning in this novel, our claim of desensualization of reality may seem inappropriate. It is only through a closer look at the adjectival or adverbial components in descriptive passages that their low specificity and their appeal to vague emotions or evocations is revealed.

Whenever a sensory mode is directly referred to, it is the visual. Consider the passage where old Wohlfart asks his son if he wants to become a *Kaufmann:* "Und in der Seele des Kleinen [adjectival noun] schoß augenblicklich [nonsensory, metaphorically referring to vision] ein schönes Bild zusammen [low specificity, subjective, not objective quality], wie die Strahlen bunter Glasperlen im Kaleidoskop [low specificity; combined with "Strahlen," "bunt" creates a vague association of something shining, brilliant, and indiscriminately colorful], zusammengesetzt aus großen Zuckerhüten [low specificity], Rosinen und Mandeln [no adjective of sensory reference] und goldenen Apfelsinen [visual-material, aiming at high emotional value], aus dem freundlichen Lächeln seiner Eltern [non-sensory, social attitude] und all dem geheimnisvollen Entzücken [explicitly low specificity], welches ihm selbst die ankommende Kiste [factual, non-sensory] bereitet; bis er begeistert ausrief [non-sensory, high emotional value]: 'Ja, Vater, ich will!'" (14). The enthusiastic "Ich will!" is thus the result of a vague, associative mode of description and perception. In this particular instance, the narrative procedure might even realistically capture the child's perspective and thus be appropriate; but the technique is all-pervasive. Indeed, the organ of sensory perception most frequently addressed is the *Herz, Gemüt, Seele,* or general *Inneres* interchangeably used and all rolled into one, *the* organ of (German) bourgeois perception. Unfortunately, this complex organ knows no aesthetic criteria. It is prone to falling victim to *kitsch,* sentimentality, and tear-jerking. In the heart are *emotionally* fused together, in a mixture of perception and sentiment, those elements of the social, economic, and cultural reality that the bourgeoisie is fully able to distinguish *intellectually.* It is in the heart where, metaphorically speaking, the wool is pulled over a society's eyes that is otherwise well capable of an analytically incisive vision.

Soll und Haben spells out first and foremost an ideology of ethics, an apology of one sociopolitical practice that it sets in contrast to other, objectionable ones. In terms of aesthetics almost anything goes as long as the propagated civil code of an aspiring lower-bourgeois merchant class appears in the right light. This aesthetics is opportunistic, ridiculing Jewish interior decoration for its ostentatiousness, secretly admiring aristocratic taste, but really only feeling at home in its own four walls. Nevertheless, a clear sense of good and bad, of right and wrong and, above all, of in-group and out-group emerges.

The scene where Anton, having been at Schröter's for some time, is introduced into the "Geheimnisse der Warenkunde,"[41] reveals how this

---

41. The complete passage to which the subsequent analysis refers reads as follows:

Herr Jordan gab sich redlich Mühe, den Lehrling in die Geheimnisse der Warenkunde einzuweihen, und die Stunde, in welcher Anton zuerst in das Magazin des Hauses trat und hundert verschiedene Stoffe und merkwürdige Bildungen persönlich mit allen Kunstausdrücken kennenlernte, wurde für seinen empfänglichen Sinn die Quelle einer eigentümlichen Poesie, die wenigstens ebensoviel wert war, als manche andere poetische Empfindung, welche auf dem märchenhaften Reiz beruht, den das Seltsame und Fremde in der Seele des Menschen hervorbringt.

Es war ein großes dämmriges Gewölbe im Parterre des Hauses, durch Fenster mit Eisenstäben notdürftig erhellt, in welchem die Warenproben und kleinen Vorräte für den täglichen Verkehr lagen. Tonnen, Kisten und Ballen standen auch hier massenhaft durcheinander, und nur schmale gewundene Pfade führten dazwischen durch. Fast alle Länder der Erde, alle Rassen des Menschengeschlechts hatten gearbeitet und eingesammelt, um Nützliches und Wertvolles vor den Augen unseres Helden zusammenzutürmen. Der schwimmende Palast der Ostindischen Kompagnie, die fliegende amerikanische Brigg, die altertümliche Arche der Niederländer hatten die Erde umkreist, starkrippige Walfischfänger hatten ihre Nasen an den Eisbergen des Süd- und Nordpols gerieben, schwarze Dampfschiffe, bunte chinesiche Dschunken, leichte malaiische Kähne mit einem Bambus als Mast, alle hatten ihre Flügel gerührt und mit Sturm und Wellen gekämpft, um dies Gewölbe zu füllen. Diese Bastmatten hatte eine Hindufrau geflochten, jene Kiste war von einem fleißigen Chinesen mit rot und schwarzen Hieroglyphen bemalt worden, dort das Rohrgeflecht hatte ein Neger aus Kongo im Dienst des virginischen Pflanzers über den Ballen geschnürt; dieser Stamm Färbeholz war an dem Sande herabgerollt, den die Wellen des mexikanischen Meer-

ideology of ethics functions in aesthetic terms. The secrets of the "hundert verschiedene Stoffe und merkwürdigen Bildungen" (all low-specificity adjectives and nouns) can only be expressed in "Kunstausdrücken." It is an art to be able to name them and memorize them, just as it is an art to find one's way through the warehouse and the amassed goods since there exist only "schmale gewundene Pfade" as in a labyrinth. Nevertheless, the goods

busens angeworfen haben, jener viereckige Block von Zebra- oder Jakarandaholz hatte in dem sumpfigen Urwald Brasiliens gestanden, und die Affen und bunte Papageien waren über seine Blätter gehüpft. In Säcken und Tonnen lag die grünliche Frucht des Kaffeebaumes fast aus allen Teilen der Erde, in rohen Bastkörben breiteten sich die gerollten Blätter der Tabakspflanze, das bräunliche Mark der Palme und die gelblichen Kristalle aus dem süßen Rohr der Plantagen. Hundert verschiedene Pflanzen hatten ihr Holz, ihre Rinde, ihre Knospen, ihre Früchte, das Mark und den Saft ihrer Stämme an dieser Stelle vereinigt. Auch abenteuerliche Gestalten ragten wie Ungetüme aus dem Chaos hervor, dort hinter dem offenen Faß, gefüllt mit oranger Masse—es ist Palmöl von der Ostküste Afrikas—ruht ein unförmiges Tier—es ist Talg aus Polen, der in die Haut einer ganzen Kuh eingelassen ist—, daneben liegen, zusammengedrückt in riesigem Ballen, gepreßt mit Stricken und eisernen Bändern, fünfhundert Stockfische, und in der Ecke gegenüber erheben sich über einem Haufen Elefantenzähne, die Barten eines riesigen Wals.

Anton stand noch stundenlang, nachdem die Erklärungen seines Lehrmeisters aufgehört hatten, neugierig und verwundert in der alten Halle, und die Gurte der Wölbung und die Pfeiler an der Wand verwandelten sich ihm in großblättrige Palmen, und das Summen und Geräusch auf der Straße erschien ihm wie das entfernte Rauschen der See, die er nur aus seinen Träumen kannte, und er hörte die Wogen des Meeres in gleichmäßigem Takt an die Küste schlagen, auf welcher er so sicher stand.

Diese Freude an der fremden Welt, in welche er so gefahrlos eingekehrt war, verließ ihn seit dem Tage nicht mehr. Wenn er sich Mühe gab, die Eigentümlichkeiten der vielen Waren zu verstehen, so versuchte er auch durch Lektüre deutliche Bilder von der Landschaft zu bekommen, aus welcher sie herkamen, und von den Menschen, die sie gesammelt hatten. (64–66)

Herr Jordan took great pains to introduce the apprentice to the secrets of the products. The moment when Anton entered the warehouse for the first time and personally learned to refer to hundreds of materials and exotic phenomena by their proper technical terms ["Kunstausdrücke"] became the source for a peculiar poetics for his receptive senses. It was at least as valuable as many other poetic sensations that rest on the fairy-tale impression that the unknown and foreign produces in the human soul. It was a huge, dusky space. . . . There were masses of barrels, boxes, and bales, with only narrow, winding paths between them. Nearly all the world's countries, and all the human races had been working and gathering in order to pile up all these useful and precious things in front of our hero's eyes. The floating palace of the East India Company, the flying American brig, the ancient Dutch ark had circled the globe; strong-ribbed whalers had rubbed their bows against the arctic and antarctic icebergs; black steamers; colorful Chinese junks; and light Malayan boats with their bamboo-masts had busied their wings and fought against storms and waves in order to fill this warehouse. This bast mat had been woven by a Hindu woman, that box painted with red and black hieroglyphs by a hard-working Chinese; the weaving over there had become for Anton and "seinen empfänglichen Sinn" the source of an "eigentümliche[] Poesie," a peculiar poetics at least as valuable as "manche andere poetische Empfindung, welche auf dem märchenhaften Reiz beruht, den das Seltsame und Fremde in der Seele des Menschen hervorbringt." The impression on Anton's receptive sensuality and impressionable intellect is specifically due to the foreignness, the exotic aura of the goods in the warehouse. The poetics is based on the fairy-tale-like attraction of those goods, which are but dimly perceived in the dusky space. The *Warenästhetik* presented here is nothing but the reified poetics of business, the commodities exchange clad in *Kunstausdrücke* and exoticism—an exoticism, however, that does not smell. Not its sensory aspects are foregrounded but the transactional ones.

This poetics, which ambiguously addresses both the senses and the intellect, "seinen empfänglichen Sinn," describes a form of perception whose organ is the heart, the soul. Intermingled in this poetics are also the psychological, emotional, educational, and other aspects, together with nostalgia, wishful thinking, daydreaming, and a strange kind of exhilarating fear. It is important that the young bourgeois hero partake "gefahrlos" and without risks in the strange, exotic world. His perception is authorially constructed toward emotional and intellectual, not sensuous effects. For the reader, too, the narrator has in mind specific emotional goals and the mediation of certain values.[42] Whether we focus on Herr Jordan as the

---

been wrapped around that bale by a Negro from Kongo at the order of a Virginia plantation owner. . . . Hundreds of different plants had united their wood, their bark, their buds, their fruit, their pulp, or the saps of their trunks in this place. . . .

Even hours after the explanations of his teacher had ended Anton remained in the old warehouse, curious and amazed, and the ribs of the vaulted ceiling and the pillars in the walls turned into large-leaved palm trees; the hum and noise in the street seemed to him like the distant roar of the sea that he only knew from his dreams, and he heard the waves run ashore in a regular rhythm, the shore on which he stood so securely.

The joy about the foreign world that he had entered without risk did not leave him after this day. While he was taking pains to learn about each particular good, he also tried to gain through reading a clearer picture of the land where these goods came from, and of the people who had collected them.

42. Berman is certainly right to say that

[a]uthor and reader confront each other on an equal footing as individual laissez-faire entrepreneurs. Meaning is passed back and forth between them through the sensuous textual details, the hallmark of realism, which constitute the commodified currency of the literary economy. (*Modern German Novel*, 104)

At our level of investigation, however, it turns out that this sensuous richness is itself highly restricted.

implied narrator of the passage under discussion or on the narrator of the whole novel or even on Freytag as its author, the perspective remains the same: the bourgeois. What is emphasized is the labor that goes into the products; the international ethnic nature of that labor; the far-away geographical origins of the goods; and above all the seeming teleology, expressed in the use of final clauses, which brings all this wealth to the European bourgeoisie. The goods thus described lose their sensory aspect and are seen as commodities, indeed exchangeable, in an international network of links and relations. There is something irresistible in such a convergence in which the producers—"alle Rassen des Menschengeschlechts," "eine Hindufrau," "ein fleißiger Chinese," "ein Neger aus Kongo"—as well as the animated, anthropomorphous means of transport—"die fliegende amerikanische Brigg," "der starkrippige Walfänger"—and even the goods themselves—"hundert verschiedene Pflanzen hatten ihr Harz . . . an dieser Stelle vereinigt"—take part and unite their efforts to end up in the Schröter warehouse. No wonder that Anton stands "neugierig und verdutzt" at this display in which so much world and so much concerted effort seems to be contained. He takes great pleasure in "der fremden Welt" and tries to increase his understanding of it and to gain, by reading, "deutliche Bilder" of the countries and the people that stand at the origin of the goods.

The educational aspect in *Soll und Haben* is as strong as in the other novels discussed in this chapter. Freytag uses the all-pervading business metaphor to describe important changes in education, namely the beginning shift of parameters from *perception* to *information*. Bourgeois society both creates this shift for the first time on a large scale and reacts to it in the perceived need for public education and the measures taken to institute it. After the mid-nineteenth century, education is, historically speaking, no longer close-up observation and imitation of a professional skill or a labor process. Education in the modern world, with increasing distance between the objects and the learner, rather means the acquisition of an understanding of, and insight into, a foreign world that one is thus enabled to enter by vicarious participation and without much risk. Narratives, mostly in printed form, become the medium of transferring somebody's original, concrete experience packaged as knowledge in the medium of language from its origin to the place of reception or consumption. In language, however, some of the proximity, the sensuous detail, is inevitably lost. The author's sensory appeal is made to the readers' imagination through the senses of distance, to their intellect through factual information. Analogically, in the medium of trade, too, the goods lose some of their original sensuous qualities while in transit. But they also gain: social and geographical information accrues around them, as well as trade and financial considerations of the very process that brings them to the consumer. The goods in transport, then, both in trade and in language undergo certain changes. As long as there existed more or less direct, personal, emotional contacts between producer and consumer, or between consuming subject and consumed objects, we may still talk about a relation built on knowledge. For the modern age, the second part of the nineteenth century marks the first stage of a dramatic shift away from this concrete relational system toward a more distanced and alienated one, which can no longer be characterized in terms of knowledge, but of information. Information is without experience on the recipient's side; it is abstract, public, and nonsensuous, whereas knowledge contains at least the desire for experience, a speck of personal engagement. Seen in this larger perspective, the business ideology as represented by Schröter in *Soll und Haben* either appears as already outmoded and old-fashioned, as it is no longer such a "lebhafte Unterhaltung mit der ganzen Welt" (66), or as a deliberate ideological practice that pretends to maintain a relational proximity that is no longer there. It is, for instance, noticeable that the capitalism represented by Schröter is far from the cutting edge of business. He does not speculate on exchange rates and borrowed money. Everything is accounted for in hard cash. The "sensuous detail," the "hallmark of realism," on the other hand reveals an effort to counter the trend toward a pure information society, but the absence of the senses of proximity from this effort can be taken as an indicator of the ideological nature of the project.

Narrative is trade, trade is narrative. For the novel, of course, all the transactions have to be encoded in language and therefore become analyzable in literary and linguistic terms. The trade process of production, transfer, and consumption is comparable to the narrative as an educational process of experience, transfer, and learning. Its main appeal is through the visual channel. Everything in transfer runs the risk of being divorced from its origin, as we have pointed out, and of missing its destination. This is the danger of straying from the faithful, objective image by giving in to the lure of the fantastic or imaginary, straying from the concrete to the abstract. Freytag, we recall, explicitly warns against it. Keller's Heinrich Lee we will find exposed to these dangers all the time.

It is significant that the goods in the Schröter warehouse do not smell, and only one instance refers to taste, the metonymical "süße Rohr" for sugar cane. The senses of proximity lose their importance in a world that shifts from perception with its inevitable bodily grounding and subjective component to information, the neutral, never-ending ticker tape of data, removed from anything physical. Information, far from causing even concern in our century where there is so much of it, is accessible to everybody and directed at nobody in particular.[43] This trend starts before the nineteenth century, of course, and is part of the process of civilization itself. In terms of the history of the senses it is antedated by far by the rise of vision to its dominant position, which is anthropologically based and historical only in its consequences. In its linguistic expression, this trend toward distance and abstraction is reflected in the all-pervasiveness of the visual metaphor, to the point that we barely notice it anymore.

Reality content, however, is precisely Anton's problem; the goods in the warehouse seem so fantastic that he needs to assure himself of their various aspects. As his medium of information is language and as the localization and concretization occurs largely in the semantics of vision, it is not surprising that Anton seeks to gain clear pictures, *deutliche Bilder,* of the goods, their origin, and their production process.[44] The verbal encoding of the sensory modes rests largely on the adjectival element: "Nützliches und Wertvolles" is presented "vor den Augen unseres Helden." The two substantivized adjectives hint at the general perspective: not objective, as describing a quality pertaining to an object, but rather functional, utilitarian, subjective considerations form the standard. Adjectival and adverbial clauses usually express social, geographical, and economic qualities or colors.

One of the characteristics of Freytag's adjectival guidance is its vagueness and its confirmation of already held concepts and stereotypes, such as "ein fleißiger Chinese" or "ein Neger aus Kongo." The dense adjectival network in *Soll und Haben* is a trap that captures what preexists in the reader's mind in the form of stereotypes and images and plays it back to him or her. It is in this sense that Freytag lives up to his claim made in the

---

43. In this sense it is significant that Keller changes the narrative perspective in his second version of *Der grüne Heinrich* from third person to first (1855; 1878–79). This is a move against the grain of his time. To phrase as individual concrete perception and experience and thereby forgo the third person authority of the omniscient narrator, the classical bourgeois narrative stance, constitutes a major shift toward a more individual and subjective anchoring of narrative responsibility.

44. The German term *Vor-stellung,* with its double meaning of re-presentation and imagination, captures both the concrete and the abstract dimension of the process at stake.

dedication, to be truthful, "wahr ... gegen seine Kunst und gegen sein Volk." He does not say anything that is not already present and true by virtue of its discursive confirmation. On the other hand he is probably also truthful in the sense of one of his warnings in the same dedication, that the writer, in the attempt to create "Poetisches" in these difficult times, often creates an "unschöne Mischung von plumper Wirklichkeit und gekünstelter Empfindung" (10).[45] Again, then, we have to take up this dichotomy of *Wirklichkeit* and *Empfindung;* the concrete-objective and the immaterial-subjective; the sensory and the emotional. Regardless of how we phrase the issue, it is the problem of perception and its linguistic encoding, ultimately the question of the social determination of perception.

The expansion of the realm that once was immediate sensory perception to a much larger sphere of intellectual penetration, however casual and oblique, brings with it both gain and loss. The newly added reach is brought under social control, partially through the very media that make the gain in distance possible in the first place, and partly by integrating the new in the expanding public sphere and subjecting it to an incessant critical discourse. The loss thus lies in the thinning out of individual experience down to its most immediate and intimate form, the experience of one's body.

The more perception and the body as its locus become a public domain, the less there is left for the individual subject as unique, inalienable, and authentic experience. The individual knowledge of one's body becomes a body of common knowledge in the realm of discourse. At the same time a dialectically correlated countertrend evolves, which unfortunately, however, curtails in its ultimate effect even further the sphere of the individual by cutting certain topics from public discourse. This concerns above all bodily functions and the sensory perception that goes with them, especially the olfactory. *Real,* therefore, is more and more only that which exists and is allowed to survive in public discourse. Paradoxically, both phenomena, the inclusion as well as the exclusion from public discourse, have the same effect on the phenomenological world dealt with and represented: they dilute it, and they standardize it. The sensory mode to be most watchful about in scrutinizing nineteenth-century fiction is the olfactory. *Non olet* becomes the iron doctrine, the unofficial decree of discourse and of aesthetic representation. The reason lies in the specific linguistic grounding of this sensory mode or rather its lack:

---

45. The attempt to create something "poetic" often brings forth an "ugly mixture of gross reality and fake emotions."

There is no semantic field of smells. The notion of smells only has as lexical sub-categories general terms such as "stench" and "perfume." Our knowledge about different smells figures in the encyclopaedia not in an autonomous domain, but scattered among all the categories whose referents have olfactive qualities.[46]

The last-mentioned aspect, the unpredictability of the categories and referents that an olfactive recognition is likely to bring to light, leads to the deep distrust of that sensory modality in an age that is bent on getting a grip on a rapidly changing reality. Cognitive processes are thus favored that allow easy and uniform recall in the absence of specific external stimuli. The latter, above all, is a desideratum in a cognitive situation that is turning from the sensory impression to information processing, as we have pointed out, skipping the level of external sensory stimulus altogether. Olfactory perception performs extremely poorly in this respect. One easily recognizes smells but one cannot recall them as smells. What one does recall, in fact, is generally a visual image of the situation in which a certain smell was encountered, of an object from which it emanated. Such a cognitive structure is ill suited to guarantee the object-value coordination that the bourgeois author/narrator is trying to establish. Smells, according to Sperber, do not even form part of a semiotic system, but rather of a symbolic structure of reference. Within such a structure there is no arguing about logic, about categories and hierarchies of phenomena. Whereas a semiotic structure, in order to be effective, has to aim at freedom from contradiction, logical coherence, and classificatory consistency, the concept of the symbolic order is much looser. The basically metonymic reference structure of smells ties the phenomena back into their objective origins in the unclassified object world rather than into a categorically structured hierarchy of semiotic reference. This referential backwardness leaves the realist author with a deep mistrust of that archaic sensory mode which appears as anarchic as the very object world itself that he is trying to structure and to make sense of. The olfactory is an ill-suited tool for describing a structural and hierarchical cohesion of reality in adjectival terms that would lead to the desired symbolic social order into which society's younger members must be introduced.

Perception is always already social perception and as such linguistically mediated. Therefore, what is left out of discourse as actualized language

---

46. Sperber, *Rethinking Symbolism*, 116.

and from language itself as a semiotic reference system either ceases to exist or, if it continues to be present in physical or perceptual terms, takes on the existence of the repressed that will break through to the surface occasionally and at psychologically revealing points.

Soll und Haben's thirty-some references to smell are all fairly innocuous. Is there really anything repressed? Historically speaking, the answer is a qualified "not yet." The nineteenth century is the period of instilling those very norms that will a short time later begin to be felt as repressive. The age itself is the heyday of mapping onto the individual the emerging norms of a rapidly changing society. Moreover, *Soll und Haben* is not a personal, emotional, erotic book (all fields with a high repression potential). It does not deal with some aspects of life that we suspect might be "smelly." One can therefore not realistically expect much in terms of olfaction. All the more interesting, then, are the olfactory comments at the beginning of narrative sequences already mentioned, even if they do not directly trigger the narrative, as will be the case later in Proust's famous incident of the madeleine.

On exploring the realms of human activity in terms of work as trade and exchange, and the products involved in the process, we noticed the parallelism of those activities with narrative structure and authorial aims. The institution of trade, the real marketplace, is duplicated in the public discourse, the figurative marketplace. We have also observed how, in initiating narrative, the chemical senses trace unpredictable connections between impressions and memory. There are other sensitive areas left to search for smells: the realm of nature as the primary human environment; the realm of human dwellings, houses, rooms, places; the realm of objects outside the trade network, such as interiors, personal belongings, crafts and artworks; and ultimately human beings themselves, bodies, clothes, as well as behavior and social interaction.

Nature is one of the few areas that do smell in bourgeois realism.[47] In *Soll und Haben* there are about a dozen instances, mostly neutral to positively connotated. Nature is a wholesome realm. Most of these passages are not specific in their olfactive reference; they simply hint at the fact that something emits scent, as for instance in the dedication: "[es] blühte und duftete der Frühling" (9). To the city dweller, "Waldesgrün und Wiesen-

---

47. The cultural construction of nature in the nineteenth century and in olfactory terms in particular would itself be a subject worth an in-depth study. Our present inquiry is of a more general character and, above all, leaves out the early and late romantic epoch that would be indispensable for such an enterprise.

duft" are "eine Erquickung des Herzens" (397). On the market in Rosmin, vendors sell "süße Backwaren, fremden Wein und wohlriechende Zitronen" (585), "good-smelling lemons." But even the plain air, the "frische Luft" (409), has a reviving effect on Baron Rothsattel; and the "reine Nachtluft" (703), after a day of fighting against the Polish insurgents who are besieging the run-down estate that Anton is trying to defend in Rothsattel's name, has something soothing to it. A few times the natural scents are more explicitly characterized. At the beginning, on his way to town and into his new life, in a scene of sensory richness not found again later in the novel, Anton "trank ... den berauschenden Wohlgeruch, der aus der blühenden Erde aufstieg." It is a good day; everybody greets the young hero, entering "ein Leben voll strahlender Träume und grüner Hoffnungen." "Alles um ihn glänzte, duftete, wogte wie ein elektrisches Feuer," and his heart "pochte heut ... zum erstenmal wieder in kräftigen Schlägen" (18). Later, after Bernhard Ehrenthal's death, upon leaving the death chamber, Anton notices a gust of wind that drives "balsamische Düfte" down the city streets (465). Nature is clean, stimulating, refreshing.[48]

In the absence of a systematic, "objective," classificatory grounding of smells in language, a simple, "subjective," second-order classification has evolved: the value judgments good and bad. On this binary scale, nature in bourgeois realism generally comes down on the good side. The only negative instance in *Soll und Haben* occurs in a simile, characterizing Löbel Pinkus, the Jewish innkeeper. He is described as one of those happy characters "welche Honig aus allen Blumen zu saugen wissen, auch aus übelriechenden" (52).[49] This example takes us into the realm of humans and man-made objects; it shows a more ambivalent tendency. Anton and Schröter, on their trip east to recover their goods encounter "viel Schnapsgeruch und glotzende Augen" (343); and the Polish innkeeper

---

48. Anton "drank ... the intoxicating, good smell rising from the blossoming ground." He is heading toward a "life full of radiant dreams and green hopes," and "everything around him was radiant, emitting scents, and billowed like an electric fire," so that "his heart was beating vigorously today for the first time in a while."

49. The translations for this paragraph read as follows: Löbel knows how "to suck honey from all kinds of flowers, even from bad-smelling ones." Anton and Schröter have met with "a lot of reek of booze and glazed eyes"; and they rest at an inn that is "a dirty room with blackened beams" and are led into "a stuffy room." In Karl's room there is "a smell of sickness," whereas the Rothsattels' rooms are "shiny and scented" and when heated, there is "a comfortable warmth" and the rooms "become filled with the powerful resinous odor of the wood branches." Soon, the "same perfume" as in the city apartment returns.

whose pub is "ein . . . schmutzige[r] Raum mit geschwärzten Decken-
balken" leads them into a "dumpfiges Zimmer" (352). In the room where
Anton happens to meet Karl, who has hit bottom at this point, "[riecht es]
so nach Krankheit" (377). In contrast to those lodgings, the bourgeois and
aristocratic rooms smell much more pleasantly, the room of the Baroness
Rothsattel "glänzte und duftete" (486), and even after the Rothsattels had
to give up their town apartment and move to their Polish estate, their
"behaglich erwärmte . . . Zimmer füllten sich mit dem kräftigen Harz-
geruch der Waldzweige" (532), a description linking nature and human
space. And as soon as they have settled in with Anton's and Karl's help, the
old smell comes back too, together with the furniture, carpets, and other
household items from the town apartment: "es waren dieselben Teppiche,
Stickereien, dasselbe Parfüm der Zimmer" (538).

Sabine's domain in the Schröter house is characterized by smell too:
"Sabine war in ihrer Schatzkammer" where linen, furniture, and table- and
kitchenware are stored. The place would be "für jede Hausfrau ein heim-
liches, herzerhebendes Zimmer. . . . Die Luft war mit einem kräftigen Duft
erfüllt, der aus uraltem Lavendel, Eau de Cologne und frischer Wäsche
aufstieg. Hier herrschte Sabine allein." Lavender and eau de cologne mark
off this exclusive realm of the young female. The scent is not Sabine's
personal scent, but rather the smell of tradition as it is passed on in the
female/housewife lineage. The mention of the heart as the affected organ,
just as in the passage above dealing with Anton, "makes sense" here, where
perception is both physical and emotional, both concrete and conceptual.
The room contains examples of the tastes of "mehr als drei Generationen"
(94), and the olfactory as a transgressive sensory mode provides the literary
representational connections.[50]

Perfume as personal scent is mentioned explicitly only on three occasions: Anton, up to this point unscented, is inspected by Fink before they
set out together for the first of a series of dancing events at the house of
one of the aristocratic families of the town. "'Zeige dein Taschentuch,'
sagte er. 'Bunte Seide? Schäm dich. Hier ist eines von meinen. Gieß dir
etwas Parfüm darauf'" (157). Both the color of Anton's handkerchief and
the lack of scent are criticized by Fink (whom we must assume to be a
regular user of eau de cologne), and it becomes obvious that the upper-class

---

50. The translations for this paragraph read as follows: Sabine's "treasury" is a "secret,
heart-lifting room" where "the air is filled with a strong perfume that rises from age-old
lavender, eau de cologne, and fresh linen. Here, Sabine reigns supreme."

world Anton is about to enter has different standards from the ones he has taken as his yardstick so far. A subtle social barrier, partly through scent, is erected, and Anton, ultimately, will stay on his side of it. The second mention of perfume occurs during that very evening, in a scene between Anton and Lenore, and it clearly has an erotic undertone. In fact, it is one of the very few erotic scenes in the novel, besides that one other, visual, instance where Lenore's dress, in Bernhard Ehrenthal's presence, turns see-through after her jump into the pond to save a child that has fallen in (cf. 304f.). The dance scene, in fact, refers to all sensory modalities, including temperature, except for taste:

> Das schöne blonde Haar, so nahe an seinem Haupt, daß er mit seinen Locken die ihren berühren konnte, ihr warmer Atem, der seine Wange streifte, der unsägliche Reiz des weißen Handschuhes, der ihre weiche Hand versteckte, das Parfüm ihres Taschentuches, die rote Blüte, welche vorn am Kleide befestigt war, das sah und empfand er, und sonst nichts. (166–67)[51]

Thus we find the good-smelling aristocracy in their pleasantly scented houses, forcing the inodorous but clean petit bourgeois to put on cologne before entering their world. Smells help to mark off territories, indicate transitions and warn of transgressions. In another border-crossing incident, a "heftige[r] Lampengeruch" is present when Anton is promoted from apprentice to clerk. The smell of the kerosene lamps, together with the "künstliche Dämmerung" and the "Lichterglanz" create a "fremdartiges und mysteriöses Aussehen" of the room (141), a "mysterious twilight" appropriate for such an event of transition and initiation.

Clearly marked as standing outside this system are the American Indians of whose ritual chants and dances Fink tells some anecdotes to Anton and Bernhard in a marginal but revealing incident: "'Aber die Frauen?' fragte Bernhard lächelnd. 'Wie es bei denen mit der Poesie steht, weiß ich nicht, mir rochen sie immer zu sehr nach Fett. Freilich, wenn man nichts anderes hat, gewöhnt man sich auch daran'" (246). The questionable reference of *man* in "wenn man nichts anders hat" places the olfactory in a murky realm of a sensuality that is not supposed to surface in language, but nevertheless

---

51. "Her beautiful blond hair so close to his head that he could touch her locks with his; her warm breath touching his cheek; the ineffable charm of the white glove covering her soft hand; the perfume of her handkerchief; the red flower stuck to the front of her dress: all this he saw and took in, and nothing else."

does.[52] The continuation reads: "Doch ist mit den Männern noch besser zu *verkehren*. So ein *nackter* Bursch auf seinem *halbwilden Pferd* ist kein übler Anblick" (emphasis added). The sexual overtones can hardly be missed. In terms of cultural politics, all this is presented as extraneous to the bourgeoisie.

Another incident concerning a marginal figure, Rosalie Ehrenthal, whose dark beauty and sexual attractiveness are mentioned on several occasions, once more implicates smell in sexual matters and again involves Fink. The letter she anonymously sends to Sabine to warn her of Fink's loose behavior toward women is scented with musk, the erotic fragrance par excellence: "Ein starker Moschusgeruch und die gekritzelten Züge verrieten, daß es [das Billett] von einer Dame kam" (274). The interesting cultural observation is not so much the use of scented paper, which is not uncommon in those days; more surprising is the fact that the scent is musk.[53] It is made to appear normal, however, in that Sabine concludes from this very fact that the letter must be from a woman.[54] Smell, *Poesie,* text, and sexuality are interrelated. Despite the scarcity of olfactory instances in the novel overall, a pattern emerges. Smell marks borders, of narrative at its inception, of text and its outside. It marks social and class lines, male and female realms. It is no accident that Fink is involved in both kinds of instances. He is a social border-crosser himself. He is linguistically by far the most versatile figure and the only one with some insight into social structures and forces. It is he who tells Anton up front what is in store for him in the course of his apprenticeship, that he will soon function like a cog in a machine. It is another marginal figure, Itzig, who speaks the truth in this respect and whose dreams of wealth and power are thereby revealed as much wilder and freer than those of the good bourgeois Anton, who indeed seems to curtail them at the narrator's warning.

---

52. "I don't know about women and poetics, they always smelled too much of grease for my taste" is Fink's answer to Berhard's question, and he continues: "However, if you have nothing else, you get used to it, too." The derogatory aspect lies in the ambiguity of the reference: is it the women who have nothing else but grease to adorn themselves with or is it Fink or the men who have no other (sexual) objects than those women? The ambiguity lingers: "The men are easier to deal with [literally: it is easier to have—social—intercourse with the men]. These naked guys on their untamed horses are not a bad sight."

53. Cf. Corbin, *Le miasme,* 78ff. The use of musk had become obsolete about a century earlier. Moreover, musk is, both in its zoological provenience and in its use in perfumery, strongly linked with the male.

54. On women and musk see the novella by Jakob Schaffner, "Die Geschichte vom Moschus," *Meisternovellen* (Berlin: Zsolnay, 1936).

The good-smelling upper class; the inodorous bourgeois middle class; the implicitly bad-smelling savages outside German culture; and the Jewish woman who is sexually attractive across class barriers:[55] where in such a system do the lower classes rank, the scum (indeed mostly Jewish, too) that form the dark background for the rising bourgeoisie? We mentioned the "Schnapsgeruch" associated with the Polish rabble (343), and the "dumpfiges Zimmer" (352). Associated with Karl is also a "schrecklicher Leimgeruch" (379) that Anton notices despite Karl's claim that it is "geruchloser Leim, den ich habe, eine neue Erfindung."[56] Karl's work of a handyman, in the nose of a bourgeois, stinks. Anton's work, in contrast, is clean. Just as modern comic heroes do not sweat, so Anton and his world do not smell, regardless of whether he is shown as as a clerk or farmer, warrior or lover. The outsiders, to whom Karl does not belong since he becomes Anton's important ally in the skirmishes in Poland, are the Jews. They form the objectionable subculture in more than one respect. They are not, however, explicitly described in terms of smell, but rather in the more general terms of the "grotesque body,"[57] the externalized Other of the bourgeoisie. This ranges from the actual physique—"Junker Itzig war keine auffallend schöne Erscheinung, hager, bleich" (24)—to the clothes they wear, their posture and the way they move, and to the general surroundings and places where they live. Thus Itzig wears "eine[] alte[] Jacke und defekte[] Beinkleider[]" (24); in his part of town there are "junge[] Burschen mit krummer Nase und runden Augen" (40); and the people generally loiter, "lungern herum" (40), and display "freche[s] Wesen" (236). There is a reference to Hippus as a "kleiner zusammengedrückter Mann" (780); and Itzig himself appears as a "gekrümmte Gestalt" (453) as

---

55. The Ehrenthal family: Mrs. Ehrenthal is complimented even by aristocrats on her good looks (although, maybe, with some business considerations in the background); Rosalie is "in der Tat eine Schönheit . . . mit . . . einer nur sehr wenig gebogenen Nase"; Bernhard, however, is "fast klein, mit einem bleichen, faltigen Gesicht und gebückter Haltung" (50).

56. Cf. a similar negative olfactory comment on glue in Keller, *Der grüne Heinrich*, 254 (For full bibliographical reference see footnote 68, below). *Leim*, etymologically, has the same root as *Schleim*, "phlegm." The process of making glue is historically associated with dullness, hence the expression *Leimsieder*, a "glue-maker," for a slow and dull-witted person.

57. Cf. Stallybrass and White, *Politics and Poetics of Transgression*, 9. The term is used throughout the book: "when the bourgeoisie consolidated itself as a respectable and conventional body by withdrawing itself from the popular, it constructed the popular as grotesque otherness" (193). For our purpose: it constructed the socially inferior and ethnically different as grotesque others.

opposed to Fink's elegant appearance as "ein schöner schlanker Mann, von mäßiger Größe" (43). We also note slender and blue-eyed Lenore's "schlanke Gestalt" with "strahlenden blauen Augen" (23). Itzig's, Pinkus's, Hippus's, and Ehrenthal's world is "wüst" and "verblichen"; "zerbroch-ene[s] Schnitzwerk" and "wurmstichige[] Balkenköpfe[]" are normal in the "verfallenen hölzernen Häusern," the "dilapidated wooden houses" in their part of town. Their world is "ein unheimlicher Aufenthalt für jedes Geschöpf, außer für Maler, Katzen oder arme Teufel" (52–53). Smell is only present here by association, especially toward the end of the story, when the very fog in which those murky figures operate, seems "poison-ous" and turns into "giftige[] Dünste" (780), and the very air gets thick ("dicke Luft," 818).

These instances account for about two thirds of the total of olfactory passages in the novel. The few that are left are either comparative or non-specific in terms of smell. For instance, Fink says of himself that he was like "ein Gaul in der Wüste, der eine Quelle riecht" (626), or purely factual such as a dog that "roch nach ihrer [Lenore's] Tasche" (635). But even those minor instances that are not so easily tied into a pattern capture some of the essence of olfactory perception. Thus when Tinkeles says to Anton that "eine Rede, die gesprochen ist, versiegt in der Luft wie ein Geruch, der eine fängt das auf, der andere jenes" (388), he is aware of the highly individual perception and unpredictable mnemonic associations that are characteristic of the olfactory in language.

Despite the scarcity of the phenomenon overall, certain patterns and clusters emerge. There is the fundamental underlying structure of develop-ment from *Poesie* steeped in the smell of coffee to the inodorous poetics of business; and there is the tendency of olfactory phenomena to mark border-lines, transitions, and social exchanges. The despised lower classes and outsiders, however, are not specifically and consistently marked by smell. When they are marked, it is only by allusion and implication rather than in explicit terms.

While certain detailed questions have to remain open in Freytag's case, his epoch appears as hostile to, but in any case not interested in, the olfactory, at least not in the medium of literature. Stifter is quite explicit and openly proclaims his repression of the phenomenon when he has Ri-sach pronounce that "der Geruch [of the roses] gehört nicht hierher" (133). With him, then, we are shifting our perspective from a poetics of business to the equally serious business of poetics or, in more general terms, the business of aesthetics.

Der Nachsommer: The Smell of the Rose

Und die Seele, den Duft, für den geselligen Kreis.

—(Gerhard Friedrich)

Der Nachsommer, like *Soll und Haben,* is a novel of considerable length. Its narrator, a young man of bourgeois background, only toward the end identified as Heinrich Drendorf, performs a lot of outdoor activities and is interested in the natural sciences in the widest sense of the term. He is an avid collector of all things natural. He lives for longer periods of time on two large agricultural estates or model farms concerned with both cattle-breeding and horticultural activities. In short, one could reasonably expect in this novel the description of a lot of smells and perfumes, scents and odors to emanate from all kinds of sources and in various degrees of pleasantness. The following description of the hero's room could therefore be very appropriate: "The studio was filled with the rich odor of roses, and when the light summer wind stirred amidst the trees of the garden there came through the open door the heavy scent of the lilac, or the more delicate perfume of the pink-flowering thorn." There is no such thing, however.[58] The fact is that there are hardly any smells in Stifter. One of the estates includes a building called the "Rosenhaus," completely overgrown with roses, which are the owner's, the Freiherr von Risach's, passion. They are kept in excellent condition, fertilized, cut back, and watered with ingenious devices; they blossom in abundance every year; and the "Rosenzeit" or "Zeit der Rosenblüte" serves as a time marker more precise than calendar dates—but not even these roses smell.

The question is whether one can reasonably expect a gamut of smells in Stifter's world in particular and in bourgeois realism in general. *Soll und Haben* left us with the impression of a certain reluctance, to say the least, vis-à-vis smells. Stifter takes this attitude into a different direction and to its extreme. The expectation of olfactory instances, based on the simple fact that so many things *do* smell in actual life, would mean to argue from a perspective beyond realism of the Stifterian variety, in fact beyond histori-

---

58. These are the opening lines of Wilde's *The Picture of Dorian Gray,* a novel briefly discussed in the next chapter. The question of how, in only just over thirty years from 1857 to 1890, the publication dates of *Der Nachsommer* and *The Picture of Dorian Gray,* such a significant change in perception, or rather in descriptive modes, could occur and whether, in fact, these two novels can be taken as exemplary representations of two different aesthetic worldviews, or whether they merely reflect two individuals' idiosyncratic tastes and whims will be discussed more fully in the next chapter.

cal (German) realism altogether, and closer to naturalism, fin-de-siècle, and decadence, that is, in terms of the main literary and artistic concepts of the epoch following realism. It would mean to argue from the perspective of an aesthetics of natural, mimetic representation. Stifter's, however, is closer to an aesthetics of a programmatic presentation, a sanitized hypermimesis. Yet even if we understand *reasonably* in terms of literary conventionality and the parameters of literary-historical concepts, we should still not expect much in terms of smells and scents. The eradication of smells and odors is precisely one of the reasonable hygienic projects, pursued openly or tacitly in Stifter's epoch. Cleanliness and order *are* the beautiful, at least its essential ingredients.

In the linguistic construction of representations of olfactory phenomena lies a possible explanation for Stifter's leaving them out. Olfactory phenomena do not behave reasonably in linguistic cognitive terms. Just as the olfactory nerves contain the only neurons in the human body directly exposed to the outside world, the linguistics of olfaction regularly breaks through the semiotic wall of closed intersignal reference and cuts, by means of the rhetorical devices of metonymy and contiguity, through to the level of the object world. Through this breach enters what bourgeois realists in general, but Stifter in particular, are afraid of: the unpredictable, the nonclassifiably individual, the repressed. This is the main reason Stifter has to exclude olfaction from the aesthetic realm established in the novel, a realm that is clearly constructed as a countermodel against the real, existing, and growing capitalism described by Freytag. This utopian element in Stifter's work centers around the autonomous artwork and an aesthetics of autonomy and proposes an aesthetic education leading toward these. In this respect Stifter can be fruitfully read in terms of Adornian aesthetics. The present inquiry, however, engages *Der Nachsommer* in terms of a sociohistorical discussion with some reference to Berman's *The Rise of the Modern German Novel* and Dan Sperber's sensory-taxonomical concepts outlined in *Rethinking Symbolism*.

Realism is not a description of what is, but much more an enterprise of establishing standards in values, behavior, and perception for the bourgeois capitalist class of the mid- and late nineteenth century. Berman sees three main attitudes operating in this age of bourgeois writing. One is the derision and marginalization of the aristocracy as the class dominant in setting taste and social values. It appears and is presented as on its way out and clinging to nonexchange values that are prebourgeois. At the same time, however, aristocratic social skills and aesthetic tastes are still admired by the bourgeoisie in quest of its own. A second trend is the marginalization and condemnation of hypercapitalism on the borderline of legality, as associated with Jewish trade and business practices. Thirdly, and in contrast to this, there is approval for the good bourgeois, capitalist way of laissez-faire. Moreover, there is exibited an attitude of superiority vis-à-vis the socially, ethnically, or nationally Other, who is cast as necessarily inferior. Bourgeois perceptions, bourgeois models, and bourgeois values in this age of transition need to be taught to a rising class. One way of doing this is through literature as *one* channel of discourse, and to present these values as already existing. "The presumption in realist literature [is of] a legible reality, the world as text, which presents itself passively to the hermeneutic subject anxious to appropriate and instrumentalize nature" (Berman, 105). Stifter, Berman goes on to say, stands in sharp contrast to Freytag and "presents the guilty conscience of that ideology [of laissez-faire]" (105). "The bourgeoisie constitutes the world as a text to be understood" in which "each detail fits into an universal pattern established by a basic law" (99). Whereas the "realist Freytag ... praises the bourgeois textualization of existence as a business ledger" (100), Stifter criticizes this attitude but runs into problems of his own with his utopian project of aesthetic education that generously overlooks its own material base. In the framework of the *bildungsroman* the subject is initiated into bourgeois, capitalist modes. Anton's education in Freytag's novel leads less to an independent individual position than, through imitation, to conformity and seamless integration into the mercantile bourgeoisie. Heinrich's education in *Der Nachsommer* runs on different tracks. He is taught and appropriates the value of objects in terms of their position on scales of material quality and usefulness for various intended purposes or their compatibility with already existing plans and projects. The exchange mechanisms he becomes involved in are less crudely commercial than Anton's. They occur in the area of education, language, and information, which, however, as we have shown for Freytag, also have a businesslike structure. While he himself is still learning, Heinrich starts passing on his knowledge to others, in particular to his sister. Learning and teaching the newly internalized values represent in themselves a pattern of exchange, vital within bourgeois society, which for the first time in history not only emphasizes but depends on general and comprehensive education of its active members.[59] This topic is foregrounded in Keller also, although in a different social

59. Earlier centuries, too, have aimed at a more general education, from the ideal of the all-around Renaissance man to the enlightened, scientifically complete and up-to-date eighteenth-century personality. New in the nineteenth century is the massive role played

milieu, namely the petit bourgeoisie and the *bohème,* one of whose problems is precisely its integration or at least participation in the bourgeois patterns of commodities exchange. For Stifter, however, this whole educational enterprise is a one-way street. Learning, communication, and exchange rest on a prestabilized harmony. There is never any disagreement, not even questioning of anything that is being passed on in the information exchange. There is not really any exchange in the first place, just a frictionless handing down of information. Discourse is authoritarian and always humbly, submissively received at the subordinate level. Questions, let alone criticism, are nonexistent. Behind this smooth surface, however, lurks imminent chaos, both natural and social, and Stifter's novel represents an attempt at keeping things in place, at stabilizing meaning, at making sense.

The gigantic positivist descriptive enterprise in the utopia of the two country estates of the novel testifies to his pessimism about the feasibility and durability of his own system. We cannot expect smells in Stifter's sensory universe, for his world, similar to Freytag's, is once again not real in terms of a "primacy of perception," but realist. It is a realism to which cultural and literary criteria, not raw sensory ones, must be applied. Stifter is aware that this epitome of realism is in fact a system of wishful thinking, a *fairy land.* Thus at the beginning, Heinrich's approach to von Risach's estate when he is seeking refuge from a threatening thunderstorm, is comparable to the prince's approach and perception of the castle in *Sleeping Beauty.*[60] "Das Haus war über und über mit Rosen bedeckt ... die Rück-

---

by state institutions in the establishment of a general school system, the sheer scale of the project, and the number of people affected. The literacy figures grow in proportion to the consolidation of the bourgeoisie and its self-understanding as both the ruling class and an all-encompassing social category that frequently, however, made its permeability from below dependent on a minimum education level of the lower classes. Cf. Alberto Martino, ed., *Literatur in der sozialen Bewegung: Aufsätze und Forschungsberichte zum 19.* Jahrhundert (Tübingen: Niemeyer, 1977), which contains statistics on the development of the public library system and its users; Rolf Engelsing, *Analphabetentum und Lektüre: Zur Sozialgeschichte des Lesers in Deutschland zwischen feudaler und industrieller Gesellschaft* (Stuttgart: Metzler, 1973), which gives literacy and readership figures; Susanne Godefroid et al., *Bürgerliche Ideologie und Bildungspolitik: Das Bildungswesen in Preußen vom Ausgang des 18. Jahrhunderts bis zur bürgerlichen Revolution 1848/49. Eine historisch-materialistische Analyse seiner Entstehungsbedingungen,* Edition 2000. Theorie und praktische Kritik 14 (Giessen: Andreas Achenbach, 1974).

60. The German title *Dornröschen* with its thematization of the roses that are so prominent in *Der Nachsommer* is thus doubly allusive to our topic. Here is the translation of the following quote: "The house was covered all over with roses ... the sole purpose of the design seemed to be the prevention of any gap in the wall of roses. ... I looked around for an entrance to the house, but could not find one."

sicht der Anpflanzung schien nur die zu sein, daß in der Rosenwand keine Unterbrechung statt finden möge. . . . Ich sah mich nach einem Eingange des Hauses um. Allein ich erblickte keinen" (44–45). He eventually does find the entrance, though, a door hardly distinguishable from the wrought-iron gate into which it is set. The man who appears after Heinrich rings the bell is "ein Mann mit schneeweißen Haaren" who addresses him with the words: "Was wollt Ihr, lieber Herr?" (46). This is fairyland, marked off from the rest of the world in one of the very few instances of smell in the whole novel: the anthropomorphic roses overgrowing the facade "schienen sich das Wort gegeben zu haben, alle zur selben Zeit aufzubrechen, um das Haus in einen Überwurf der reizendsten Farben und in eine Wolke der süßesten Gerüche zu hüllen" (44).[61] On the background of this instance the statement later in the novel that "smell does not belong here" must be understood as a deliberate and programmatic decision to restrict aesthetic representation to the cleanliness of the visual mode. Such a realism is on the defensive. In this opening scene it walls itself off from the dog-eat-dog outside world and attempts to establish an aesthetic realm of harmonious education in which the class conflict described in Freytag is sublated and the bourgeois hero Heinrich elevated and wedded to the higher principles of the aristocracy, the landed gentry. This utopian project, by its very setting, ignores its material preconditions, an oversight that both Freytag, with his meticulous bookkeeping, and Keller, who lets his Heinrich even suffer from hunger for a few days, keep us aware of. Stifter's world, held together by its creator's utmost efforts, cannot tolerate anything as subversive as smells. This will become clear as soon as we have established that very subversive, unpredictable quality of smells and olfactory perception as outlined by Sperber. He presents smell as the sense without a proper semiotic system, such as the aural/oral possesses in language or music, or vision in the perception of shapes and color. For colors there exists a semiotic system, a taxonomy by means of which it is possible to refer to objects in a patterned, almost one-to-one relation. In fact, color classification may have a universal basis.[62]

Not so for smells. Smells, Sperber argues, are processed by the nervous system in a more direct, archaic manner. In language they have no vocabulary of their own and are therefore most often paired metonymically with

---

61. The roses "seemed to have promised each other to blossom all at the same time and thus throw a cover of the most splendid colors and a cloud of the sweetest smells over the house."

62. Cf. Berlin and Kay, *Basic Color Terms*.

their origin or cause on the one hand or their effect on the other (the "smell of a rose," a "pungent," a "nauseating smell"). From their poor integration into language, our most elaborate, precise and all-encompassing semiotic system, and the unpredictable effects that olfactory experiences can have in triggering memory and hence text production, Sperber concludes that they best be investigated as forming, or being part of, a symbolic rather than a semiotic system. Sperber's symbols are individual concepts rather than communal ones, such as semiotic signs. Their encoding does not follow predictable and hence learnable rules; and they behave more irrationally and idiosyncratically than signs. Smell in his understanding appears as the subversive sense par excellence. There is no explaining or elaborating on what a smell means for an individual and his or her attempt at putting the experience into words.

The combination of Berman's and Sperber's arguments yields our own hypothesis: Stifter, despite his long descriptive passages, nature descriptions, and his "orderly," predictable, pedantic textual encoding, will hardly use smells. This holds true even though, in terms of the olfactory reality of the settings he describes, he should or at least might mention such phenomena. Smell has to be suppressed, as it would lead to all kinds of mischief, might conjure up images, memories, and thoughts that would break up the closely knit system of reality that Stifter creates and that serves as an ideal matrix for "real" reality. Such mischief can and does indeed happen in literature. The smell and taste of a madeleine produced hundreds of pages in its wake; Leopold Bloom's vagaries are at times rather smelly; and most recently in Patrick Süskind's novel *Das Parfum*, olfaction wreaks havoc on a whole city population. Stifter does not take any risks in this respect.

Smell Does Not Belong Here

For good reasons vision is the dominant sense in Stifter's text. It has the most extensive vocabulary; it can rely on an existing aesthetic code in, for instance, the visual arts; and it allows for a clear distance between perceiving subject and perceived object.[63] Moreover—and this is important in a

---

63. The eye and the ear are the only sense organs that allow for this; for tactile experience one has "to be in touch" with the object, and the aural, gustatory and olfactory stimuli literally penetrate, and are absorbed by, the perceiving subject. For the ear, this intake is immaterial, whereas the oral intake can be quite substantial. The nasal intake is

tradition-oriented world—visual objects can generally be collected. Thus we are treated to descriptions *ad nauseam* of houses, interiors, and all kinds of objects found there; of materials (wood, stone, cloth); of tools, implements, designs. Olfactory perception on the other hand, with hardly any linguistic anchoring pertaining to it and dependent on air as the medium to reach and penetrate the perceiving subject, is impure. But what is especially important for this novel of education and setting of standards and ideals is the absence of educational possibilities in the field of smells. Neither can they be collected and exhibited. They lack all potential of forming social tradition.

Stifter's awareness of this anticultural element inherent in smells leads to the extremely vision-oriented organizational patterns of the material universe of the novel and the active suppression of olfactory experience. The meals his characters eat are always both tasteless and odorless, even in cases where the reader is told in detail of what they consist. Thus on the first page: "Wir Kinder bekamen einfache Speisen, der Vater und die Mutter hatten zuweilen einen Braten und jedes Mal ein Glas guten Weines" (9). The following is a more elaborate example:

> Als wir [im Speisezimmer] angelangt waren, sah ich, daß in ausgezeichnet schönen weißen Linnen gedeckt sei, ... daß sich eingemachte Früchte, Wein, Wasser und Brod auf dem Tische befanden, und in einem Gefässe verkleinertes Eis war.... Mein Begleiter ... läutete. Sofort erschien eine Magd und brachte ein gebratenes Huhn und schönen rotgesprenkelten Kopfsalat.... ich war durch das Wandern wieder hungrig geworden. Ich genoß daher von dem Aufgesetzten. (55)[64]

---

much less so, a fact that locates the olfactory on the very border of materiality. This liminal quality, this atmospheric, not to say spiritual, dimension is drawn upon in many contexts.

64. The quote translates thus:

> When we had arrived in the dining room I noticed that the table was set in excellent white linen ... that there were canned fruit, wine, water and bread on the table, as well as crushed ice in a bucket.... My companion ... rang a bell. Immediately, a servant appeared and brought in a fried chicken and beautiful, red-flecked head lettuce.... I had become hungry from the hike and thus enjoyed the food.

The following passage deals with meals as time indicators: "As it is already past noon and we are wont to eat exactly at noon, after which meal nothing is served until dinner, we have to make special arrangements for your meal."

In general meals are treated even more cursorily, namely just as time references. The following instance shows a specifically punctilious one. "Da schon Mittag vorüber ist, wir aber genau mit der Mittagsstunde des Tages zu Mittag essen, und von da bis zu dem Abendessen nichts mehr aufgetragen wird, so muss für Euch . . . besonders aufgetragen werden" (54–55). The obsession with time is equalled only by an almost pathological concern with cleanliness, for even the fruit trees are washed down: "Man war damit beschäftigt, die Stämme der Obstbäume mit Wasser und Seife zu reinigen" (196); and naturally, apartments and linen are cleaned and washed regularly, however, odorlessly: "Alle Samstage prangte das Linnen 'weiss wie Kirschblüten' auf dem Aufhängeplatze im Garten, und Zimmer für Zimmer mußte unter ihrer Aufsicht gereinigt werden" (15). Not only is everything clean, almost sterile—the roses are "washed clean" by the rain (249), and even the birds in their nests dislike "verdorbene Luft" (156)—but the whole atmosphere is one of moderation, a climate of "angenehme Milde" (249), of avoidance at all cost of the least excess in every sensory and emotional aspect. The world literally moves on felt slippers (cf. 49, 75, 80).

The most fascinating case in point, however, are the roses, whose smell is almost completely suppressed. Roses in books other than horticultural ones have above all two qualities: they have color and smell sweetly; and they are not only roses, but symbols, often for very different concepts. Growing on literary rather than actual soil, their reference to something other than themselves is not a semiotic one (as a signifier standing for a signified) but rather truly symbolic in Sperber's sense. They are not the roses accounting for the splendor of a summer garden. Their roots are in literary tradition, in poetry, romance, and the novel. This is the environment they point to and only here are they real. They grow as symbols and are paper roses from the start, and as such the experienced reader understands them. However, in order to function like this they need to have at least a token element of reality about them, most often color but frequently smell. Thanks only to this topos do they function as symbols.[65]

Stifter's roses are different: they are treated first and foremost as horticultural objects. As such, however, they ought to have colors and smell. While the former is the case, the latter is not. By robbing them of their smell, by deliberately reducing them to a visual presence, and by presenting

---

65. For a cultural history of the rose with strong Germanic nationalist and anti-French undertones, see M. J. Schleiden, *Die Rose: Geschichte und Symbolik in ethnographischer und kulturhistorischer Beziehung* (Leipzig: Wilhelm Engelmann, 1873). Turgenev, below, provides two typical examples of "real" literary roses.

them in sheer abundance, Stifter undermines the credibility of his flowers. They gain a surreal quality, a symbolism by default. In the universe of the novel where models and ideals are established by means of semiotic principles, it is precisely the odorless roses that point to something outside themselves. With this minimal topos of reality removed, the roses open a significant gap, and the reader crashes through to the empty space in the reference structure. In the novel this space is ultimately filled with a different substitute object from another tradition of signification, marble.

The central incident where the smell of the roses beyond the elementary *Duft* is explicitly banned occurs at a fairly early point in the novel. It is worth quoting this passage in some detail; the speakers are Heinrich and von Risach:

"Ich wäre auch geneigt," sagte ich, "die Rose für die schönste Blume zu halten. Die Kamelie steht ihr nahe . . . [aber] das Weiche, . . . das Süsse der Rose hat sie nicht. Wir wollen von dem *Geruche* gar nicht einmal reden; denn der gehört nicht hieher."—"Nein," sagte er, "der gehört nicht hieher, wenn wir von der Schönheit sprechen; aber gehen wir *über die Schönheit hinaus* und sprechen wir von dem Geruche, so dürfte keiner sein, der dem Rosengeruche an Lieblichkeit gleichkömmt."—"Darüber könnte *nach einzelner Vorliebe* gestritten werden . . . [aber die Rose] wird sowohl jetzt geehrt, als sie in der Vergangenheit geehrt wurde. Ihr Bild ist zu Vergleichen das gebräuchlichste, mit ihrer Farbe wird die Jugend und Schönheit geschmückt, man *umringt* Wohnungen mit ihr, ihr Geruch wird für ein Kleinod gehalten und als etwas Köstliches versendet. . . . Besonders liebenswert ist sie, wenn sie so zur Anschauung gebracht wird wie hier, wenn sie durch eigentümliche Mannigfaltigkeit und Zusammenstellung erhöht und ihr gleichsam geschmeichelt wird. Erstens ist hier *eine wahre Gewalt* von Rosen, dann sind sie an der großen weißen Fläche des Hauses verteilt, von der sie sich abheben; vor ihnen ist die weiße Fläche des Sandes, und diese wird wieder durch das grüne Rasenband und die Hecke wie durch ein grünes Samtband und eine grüne Verzierung von dem Getreidefelde getrennt." (133, emphasis added)[66]

---

66. "'I am inclined' I said, 'to call the rose the most beautiful flower. The camelia comes close . . . but it lacks the softness, the sweetness of the rose. Let us not even talk about its smell; for it does not belong here.'—'No,' he said, 'it does not belong here when we talk about beauty; but if we go beyond beauty and actually talk about smell, then there is hardly a smell that matches the rose's in its loveliness.'—'About

This debate about the aesthetic merit of objects reveals a visual and aesthetic normative enterprise from which smells are to be banned. The argument is in terms of color and spatial arrangement, with some remarkable undertones, however. The roses as horticultural objects represent the effort, the hard work involved in setting them up as visual aesthetic objects in the visibly aestheticized world of the Asperhof. The "wahre Gewalt" hints at the sheer effort necessary to maintain this world. And Heinrich's words, "man umringt Wohnungen," recall the hedge of roses surrounding the estate, the closed-off, artificial universe. Heinrich's awareness of the extreme fragility of this world is what leads him to ban smells from it, as they include the threatening possibility of an argument "nach einzelner Vorliebe," based on individual, unpredictable standards. This must not be, for this would mean contact with the *real* world, not the Stifterian *realist* world. The same concern is reflected in the opening words, "gehen wir über die Schönheit hinaus," of Risach's more theoretical statement, which precedes Heinrich's. The *transcendence* beyond the (visual) beauty represented in the Asperhof world, can only mean *descent* into the real world of argument and individual predilection. In this real world, as Risach knows and admits, the *Lieblichkeit* of the smell of roses is acknowledged, is in fact perceived as a *Kleinod,* a precious object and a rare commodity. From Stifter's world, however, the smell of the rose is banned. Its role is taken on by something more sturdy and odorless, marble.

But if the smell "does not belong here," where does it belong? While it is ruled out in the *theoretical* underpinnings of the novel it does occur in the *material* world. There are few examples, additionally toned down by the use of the most standard and bland terms possible, such as *süss* and *duften.* Acceptable is the occurrence of smell where it can be linked to a scientific (meteorological) issue, the weather forecast:[67] "'In meinem Gar-

---

this we might argue according to our own preferences . . . but the rose is honored in the present as much as it has been in the past. Its image is very common in comparisons, its color decorates youth and beauty; one surrounds apartments with it; its perfume is thought of as a gem and sent out as something precious. . . . The rose is particularly lovely when presented, as it is here, enhanced and flattered as it were, through its abundance and composition. First, there is a veritable mass [literally, "violence"] of roses; then they are distributed over the large white facade of the house against which they are highlighted; in front of them is the white sandy area, which in turn is separated from the grain field by a green strip of lawn and the hedge as if by a ribbon of green velvet and a green lace.'"

67. "'In my garden and in my greenhouse there are plants,' he said, 'which show a striking connection to the atmosphere. . . . From their smell one can predict oncoming rain, in fact one can almost predict its intensity.'" The following passage is the only

ten und in meinem Gewächshause sind Pflanzen,' sagte er, 'welche einen auffallenden Zusammenhang mit dem Luftkreise zeigen.... Aus dem Geruche der Blumen kann man dem kommenden Regen entgegen sehen, ja sogar aus dem Grade riecht man ihn beinahe'" (117). Most interesting, however, is the only instance where smell is not just mentioned as *Duft* or *Geruch* or qualified as *süss* but is allowed to take its effect on the psyche of the hero:

> Ich ging in mein Schlafzimmer, öffnete die Fenster... und lehnte mich hinaus. Die Sterne begannen sachte zu glänzen, die Luft war mild und ruhig, und die Rosendüfte zogen zu mir herauf. Ich geriet in tiefes Sinnen. Es war mir wie im Traume, die Stille der Nacht und die Düfte der Rosen mahnten an Vergangenes; aber es war doch heute ganz anders. (256)

For the only time in the novel smell is here explicitly associated with emotion and remembrance. On another similar occasion, smell is absent. One evening the protagonist, looking out of his window, is "sehr traurig" and notices: "Es ging kein Duft der Rosen zu meiner Nachtherberge herauf, da sie noch in den Knospen waren, sondern es zog die einsame Luft kaum fühlbar durch die Fenster herein" (237–38). The association of smell and emotion is confirmed *ex negativo*. In another scene the roses function purely visually, in fact only as shadows.

> In der Nähe des Gartenhauses war eine Bank, auf welche von einem Rosengebüsche Schatten fiel. Ich lud sie ein, mit mir auf der Bank Platz zu nehmen.... Es war das erste Mal, dass wir ganz allein in den Garten gingen.... Sie barg ihr Angesicht in den Rosen vor ihr, und ihre glühende Wange war auch jetzt noch schöner als die Rosen. (718–22)

---

instance where smells and emotions are connected. "I went into my bedroom, opened the window... and leaned out. The stars began to glitter gently, the air was mild and still, and the perfume of the roses wafted up to me. I fell into a deep reverie. It was like a dream, the stillness of the night and the scents of the roses reminded me of the past; yet it was all different today." In contrast, there is the following instance: the protagonist is "very sad" and notices that "there was no rose scent rising up to my lodging, as they were still only buds; instead a lonesome air, hardly perceptible, entered through my windows."

The next example is purely visual: "Near the gazebo there was a bench, shaded by a rosebush. I invited her to sit down with me.... It was the first time that we were alone in the garden.... She hid her face in the roses in front of me, and her glowing cheeks were still more beautiful than the roses."

Der Nachsommer as a *bildungsroman* is an enterprise of collecting, ordering, systematizing, and establishing norms. It is characterized as such from the outset: "Der Vater pflegte zu sagen, ich müsste einmal ein Beschreiber der Dinge werden" (28). But the work can also be read as a story of love and courtship. There are actually two such stories contrasted with each other, but let us focus on the one in the present between the narrator and Natalie. As readers experienced in symbolic signification we would not be surprised if the roses played a role in these events, but we find ourselves disappointed. The declaration of love between the young people takes place in the grotto at the Sternenhof and is preceded by a lengthy dialogue on stones, precious, semiprecious, and otherwise. Marble is praised as the ultimate. Seen through marble the world appears "fast goldartig." Marble belongs "gewiss unter die Edelsteine," says Heinrich, who thinks it "ganz besonders schön" (570). Odorless stones, not scented roses, are the environment for the highest emotion. Art, not nature and cultural history, not natural time, are invoked by the lovers at the fountain. Stifter's roses serve as constant reminders of the artificiality of the world he creates. We cannot take them for real as symbols, nor truly symbolically in this programmatic reality. The "real stuff" Stifter's world is made of is *stone,* above all marble with its smooth, clean, cool, odorless surface.

It is revealing in more than one respect how the signifying context of marble is structured. Important is Heinrich's first encounter with the white marble statue in the stairwell on the day of his unexpected arrival at the Risach estate. He sees her, the "Gestalt aus weißem Marmor," on the landing of the staircase, illuminated by flashes of lightning that make her appear "noch röter" than does the light of the men's candles (75). While this description is physically wrong because lightning at night does not produce red but blue light, the vision is "correct" in literary terms—not in the realist, but in the romantic tradition, as represented, among others, in Eichendorff's or Mérimée's statues. The (marble) statue of a woman comes to life, expressed in the shift of color from white to red—on which Keller, below, has more—and symbolizes both the thingness of reality and its inherently destructive potential in coming alive. Setting the love relationship between Heinrich and Natalie in a context of stone, with the marble statue as its ultimate reference point, serves Stifter to combine the accidental with the necessary, the individual and emotional selection of each other by the two people with the aesthetic and structural necessity of their union. By this explicit reference to the romantic tradition, however, Stifter is conceding the return of the repressed through the unpredictable, potentially chaotic element inherent in the object world. The irony as it can be understood from the end of the novel thus lies in the potential eruption of the system that Stifter has so painstakingly erected and that altogether excludes the discourse on one sense, the sense of smell.

Stifter knows that his world, this epitome of realism, is in fact a system of wishful thinking, a well-guarded fairyland. Heinrich did find the entrance and ultimately, at the center of this hedged-off universe, his love is expressed in the ceremonial setting of the grotto. There is the "Anblick der Quellennymphe," and there are the two oak trees, standing like guardians, "wie Wächter." There is "das Weiss des Steins" in front of the "grüne Wand des Eppichs" that closes off the scene—another moment of closure, of shutting out (518–19). This scene, although set at the Sternenhof, not at the Asperhof with the roses, is part of the same universe. Flowers are absent here in the "stony" Sternenhof, whose buildings are just being restored to bring out their original natural stone surfaces after they had been rudely painted over in earlier times. Love petrifies in Stifter's world. At its climax not even the deodorized roses are allowed. Everything turns into statue and stone.

Der grüne Heinrich: Balsamic Breath

A main structural difference between *Der grüne Heinrich* and *Soll und Haben* and *Der Nachsommer* lies in the character of its first-person narrator.[68] It gives the novel a different perspective. The text does not speak for a class or a social group "from above" through writerly authority but proclaims first and foremost an individual truth.[69] The objective element of authorial bourgeois narrative is present to some extent in the fact that the first-person narrator is the older, more experienced Heinrich Lee, a public official who tells the younger Heinrich's life story up to his, the elder's, present. Part of this perspective is a much stronger emphasis on the hero's childhood.

68. Gottfried Keller, *Der grüne Heinrich,* vol. 2 of *Gesammelte Werke,* ed. Hans Schumacher (Zurich: Büchergilde Gutenberg, 1960). All subsequent references are to this edition. The first version of the novel from 1855 was only partly, the revised edition of 1878–79 throughout, a first-person narrative.

69. *Der Nachsommer* is, of course, also a first-person narrative. The way, however, that the older narrating voice looks back onto the younger hero is so distant, so objectifying that there is nothing left of the relativity and interpolated youthful perspective of Keller's stance. Stifter's narrator sounds virtually as distanced as any third-person narrator, characteristic for the narrative stance in bourgeois realism.

Whereas we meet Anton and Heinrich Drendorf at the moment of their leaving their homes, and learn about their childhood only in a number of minor instances or in general outline, Heinrich Lee's childhood, above all its educational aspects, takes up a considerable portion of the novel. This constellation allows us to gain insight into a child's perception, both in physical and sensory and, more and more, in intellectual and conceptual terms.

In material terms Heinrich Lee comes from the same social background, even if from its blue-collar, not white-collar segment, as Anton Wohlfart and Heinrich Drendorf, the lower middle class. It is the early and unexpected death of his father, whose enterprising life as a self-employed builder and stone-mason has left Heinrich and his mother with very little money, that puts him into a different social category from his two fictional brothers. Sitting on the fence between the "Bürgerkinder" and the "armen Kinder" (93) from an early age, Heinrich experiences social distinctions differently from Anton or Heinrich Drendorf. The latter, indeed, is never really exposed to them. The material setback allows Heinrich Lee only at the end of the narrative to reach a position in society comparable to that of his two peers, the rank of an accepted public official, a *Beamter*.[70]

The concern with school and education, together with its narrative stance and the emphasis on the hero's childhood, makes this novel a more typical *bildungsroman* than either of the other two. It is the most individually focused text and less conceptually preoccupied with the casting of social groups and the promotion of certain social values while denouncing others. Heinrich is not a success in career terms; his education is a more tortuous, less aimed process than it is for his two peers. In the case of Stifter's Heinrich for instance, the young man's sheer relentlessness, the absence of any of the fatigues and tantrums, the rejections and revolts of a child or young adult during his or her education, is almost frightening.[71] For Keller's Heinrich the world, in both its material and social aspects, is a much less structured place, and while those structures are a priori fixed in both Freytag and Stifter, part of Heinrich's education consists precisely in discovering their fluidity and coming to terms with them.[72] Heinrich is

---

70. As a *Beamter*, he now is what Anton's father was; and Heinrich Drendorf's father, in turn, already is what Anton is going to be, a *Kaufmann*, a merchant.

71. Cf. esp. *Nachsommer*, 23 and 27ff.

72. On education and especially the role of reading in Heinrich's socialization see Gail K. Hart, "The Functions of Fiction: Imagination and Socialization in Both Versions of Keller's *Der grüne Heinrich*," *German Quarterly* 4 (1986): 595–610.

the only one of the three heroes who shows imagination, *Einbildungskraft* (e.g., 53), and seems aware of the sensuous and sensual nature of his environment beyond the point of its economic usefulness or its classificatory-aesthetic potential. Despite this, however, his world is only marginally more "smelly" than Anton's and Heinrich Drendorf's. *Der grüne Heinrich* contains about forty-five instances, including some more marginal ones, of olfactory perception in just over 700 pages. Before analyzing them more closely to verify if the emerging patterns overlap with those found in the other novels, let us take a look at two passages that can be directly compared in terms of the sensory-sensual universe to *Soll und Haben* and *Der Nachsommer*.

The scene in *Soll und Haben* where Anton is introduced to the goods in the Schröter warehouse is explicitly one of initiation, and the information and associations, although narratively presented from Anton's perspective, must be assumed as originally coming from Herr Jordan.[73] The hero does not have to face the mass of unknown objects alone but receives some guidance, and the wealth of material is structured for him in the central terms of the novel, production, trade, and business. This is a different situation from the one Keller's Heinrich encounters when he strikes up his relationship with Frau Margret, the old woman from across the street who owns and operates an antique, bric-a-brac, and second-hand shop. She buys and sells all kinds of things to all types of people who come and go, "eine zahlreiche Menge, . . . welche fortwährend ab und zu ging" (42). The business takes place in an "offene[] dunkle[] Halle, ganz mit Trödelkram angefüllt" (41) and at the end of the day moves over into the "noch seltsamere[] Wohnstube" (43), which, in terms of the objects gathered there, can be considered an extension of the shop.[74] It is a world of strange objects

---

73. For the text of this passage and its translation, see footnote 41 of this chapter.

74. The whole passage reads as follows:

In dem Hause gegenüber befand sich eine offene dunkle Halle, ganz mit Trödelkram angefüllt. Die Wände waren mit alten Seidengewändern, gewirkten Stoffen und Teppichen aller Art behangen. Rostige Waffen und Gerätschaften, schwarze zerrissene Ölgemälde bekleideten die Eingangspfosten und verbreiteten sich zu beiden Seiten an der Außenseite des Hauses; auf einer Anzahl altmodiger Tische und Geräte stand wunderliches Glasgeschirr und Porzellan aufgetürmt, mit allerhand hölzernen und irdenen Figuren vermischt. In den tieferen Räumen waren Berge von Betten und Hausgeräten übereinander geschichtet, und auf den Hochebenen und Absätzen derselben, manchmal auf einem gefährlichen einsamen Grate, stand überall noch eine schnörkelhafte Uhr, ein Kruzifix oder ein wächserner Engel und dergleichen. . . . [I]n der noch seltsameren Wohnstube . . . hatte Frau Margret diejenigen Gegenstände

and strange characters who gather there in the evening when "das Feuer prasselte, die Töpfe dampften, der Tisch mit den soliden volkstümlichen Leckerein bedeckt wurde"; and the narrator asserts that those "arme Frauen und Männer" were, at least partly, attracted "durch den Duft des gastlichen Tisches," "the inviting smell of a well-stocked table" (45). The world emanating from those goods and people is radically different from that associated with the objects in Schröter's warehouse. Heinrich enters this warehouse world at a much younger age than Anton, and he enters it alone. The description soon turns away from the objects to the people, who after business hours talk and argue about matters stretching from religion to the occult, from black magic to ghosts. The narrator "weiß nicht, wie es kam, daß ich mich plötzlich am Tage oft in dem kurzweiligen Gewölbe mitten unter den Geschäftigen und am Abend zu Füßen der Frau sitzend fand" (49).[75]

The objects, as well as the room and the people, radiate with life and lore, imagination and conjecture, ghost stories and tall tales. This world vibrates with "wogende[] Phantasie" (44) and "lebendige[] Einbildungs-

---

zusammengehäuft und als Zierat angebracht, welche ihr in ihrem Handel und Wandel am besten gefallen, und sie nahm keinen Anstand, etwas für sich aufzubewahren, wenn es ihr Interesse erweckte. An den Wänden hingen alte Heiligenbilder auf Goldgrund und in den Fenstern gemalte Scheiben, und all diesen Dingen schrieb sie irgendeine merkwürdige Geschichte oder sogar geheime Kräfte zu, was ihr dieselben heilig und unveräußerlich machte. (41–42, 44)

The house across the street contained an open dark shed, full of second-hand things. The walls were decorated with old silk costumes, woven cloths, and all kinds of rugs. Rusty weapons and tools, black, torn oil paintings covered the doorposts and spilled over on both sides of the house. On a number of old-fashioned tables and machines was piled up bizarre glassware and China, interspersed with all kinds of wooden and earthenware figures. In the depths of the room there were mountains of beds and household equipment piled on top of each other, and on the higher plains and plateaus and sometimes even on a dangerous and lonely ledge there was sure to be a whimsical clock, a crucifix or a wax angel or something like that. . . . In the living room, which was even weirder, . . . Frau Margret had assembled those objects and set them up as decorations that pleased her most in her doings, and she did not hesitate to keep something for herself if it aroused her interest. On the walls there were old icons with gold backgrounds, and in the windows hung stained glass plates. To all these objects she attributed some strange story or even secret powers which made them indispensible for her.

75. The narrator "does not know how it happened that during the day [he] found himself all of a sudden in the fascinating shed among all the busy people and in the evening at the feet of Frau [Margret]." This world, as the following paragraph makes clear, is full of "surging fantasy" and "lively imagination," in the guise of the "sensually concrete forms of folklore." This makes Heinrich's own imagination somewhat "precocious and susceptible to strong impressions."

kraft" (49), and everything is clad in the "sinnlich greifbaren Formen der Volkstümlichkeit" (44) so that Heinrich's own "Einbildungskraft" becomes somewhat "frühreif und für starke Eindrücke empfänglich" (53). Indeed, he develops into a fantastic child, given to daydreaming and fabulations of his own, and the incident where he accuses four schoolmates of having taught him a bunch of execrable swearwords shows his difficulty in distinguishing between fact and fiction, between reality and daydream. For him, then, Freytag's warning to curtail one's dreams, which, unchecked, might grow into "strenge Herren" over one's life (Freytag, 14), would seem much more appropriate and necessary than for the prosaic Anton. Heinrich's world, although statistically not much richer in smells, is much more sensuous and palpable, much more determined by the senses of proximity than Anton's. In the debates at Frau Margret's the guests explicitly seek "more spicy food," a "gewürztere Nahrung . . . als die öffentlichen Kulturzustände ihnen darboten." They are driven by "unruhige . . . Triebe in der sinnlichen Welt" (45); indeed, it is the paucity of sensuous detail in the (religious) teachings of the time that drives them, together with the "Duft des gastlichen Tisches," into Frau Margret's universe.[76] This is an open criticism of the bourgeois world of the nineteenth century. Heinrich's own experience points in the same direction. He knows how "stoffbedürftig" children are and how his own "Phantasie und das Gemüt" remain empty as long as he is not enabled to satisfy his experience "with new food for thought," as it were.

The difference in realities represented in the "große[] dämmerige[] Gewölbe" (64) of Anton's world and the "offene dunkle Halle" (41) of Heinrich's is highlighted by Frau Margret's semiliterate bookkeeping method based on four Roman numerals, a piece of chalk, and the whole surface of the table. She generates "Zahlengruppen, deren Bedeutung und Benennung niemand kannte als sie" and that look like an "altheidnische Zauberschrift" (43). Such "ancient heathen magic" realism is not for the taxman. It is far from what Berman calls in Freytag's world the "existence as a business ledger" (Berman, 100). Margret's poetics of business has retained an old magic of its own, the magic of concreteness, of sensuousness, of palpability. The difference in the manner in which Heinrich and

---

76. Incidentally, cf. the depiction of the characters present, especially the admittedly few Jews in this novel (46–47; 549–50, 622) with the presentation of Jews in *Soll und Haben*. Although they appear in similar lowly and socially marginal positions, they are treated with much more sympathy and without the adjectival sneering of Freytag's narrator.

Anton fill out the spaces of the secret, the foreign, the unknown, is the difference between imagination and information. For Heinrich, the concrete often only serves as a base from which to start his imaginary constructions and conjectures; for Anton even the imaginary itself is reified.

That Keller's world is as different from Stifter's as it is from Freytag's is revealed when we read chapter 10 ("Das spielende Kind") against Stifter's chapter 2 ("Der Wanderer"). The fantastic attempts at collecting practiced by Keller's hero appear almost as a parody of the cold systematic methodology with which Stifter's hero begins to dedicate himself to the object world. The emphasis on rules and order points to the difference in their respective approaches. Heinrich Lee's attitude and ultimate frustration has a lot to do with his mediocre education. His drive to collect things arises from the already mentioned need for "sinnlichen Stoff, . . . welcher meiner Gestaltungslust anheimgegeben war" (70).[77] He has to create his own toys and thus starts a bizarre and eclectic collection of "Mineralien," "glänzende Schlacken," "Glasflüsse," "Marmorscherben," and so on. (70). He washes them, displays them "in Fächern und Behältern und legte ihnen wunderlich beschriebene Zettel bei" but in the end, when he realizes that other boys have "für jeden Stein einen bestimmten Namen . . . und zugleich viel Merkwürdiges, was mir unzugänglich war, . . . so starb mir das ganze Spiel ab und betrübte mich" (71). He does not fare much better with a butterfly and bug collection, and under his "mörderischen Händen" the creatures lose all their "Farbe und Duft" and end up as a "zerfetzte Gesellschaft erbarmungswürdiger Märtyrer" (71). Bigger animals are treated even worse, and his most fantastic and bizarre collection of embryo and fetuslike creatures of wax assembled in glass jars also ends in a massacre (74–75).

Stifter's Heinrich, in contrast, has immediate access to order and systematic organization; he was "schon als Knabe ein großer Freund der Wirklichkeit der Dinge gewesen, wie sie sich so in der Schöpfung oder in dem geregelten Gange des menschlichen Lebens darstellten" (27). It is the subclause that carries the emphasis. Heinrich is a friend of the object world

---

77. Following are the translations for this and the subsequent paragraph: Heinrich has a need for "sensuous material . . . to be subjected to my creative urge" (70). Such materials are, for instance, "minerals," "slags," "glass," "pieces of marble." He displays them "in compartments and containers and added curiously lettered notes" until he realizes that other kids have "a unique name for each stone." At this point "the whole game died for [him] and made [him] sad" (71). The butterflies too die in his "murderous hands," losing all "color and aura" ending as a "tattered bunch of pityful martyrs." Stifter's Heinrich on the other hand was "already as a boy a great friend of the reality of objects as they were present in [God's] creation or in the orderly flux of human life."

only insofar as it appears in the natural divine order of creation or can be included in the measured process of human life. In this vein, then, he begins to study systematically everything from domestic events, tools, and products to biology, zoology, and geology, that is, "alle Vorkommnisse des Hauses," "alle Werkzeuge," "Bodenerzeugnisse" (28), "Kunsterzeugnisse," and "Gegenstände des Gewerbefleißes" (29). Then he begins with "Naturgeschichte" and its first subcategory, "Pflanzenkunde" (30), followed by "Mineralien" (31), and on to the study of the landscape around his summer abode in the countryside, and lastly animals (36). In this process he switches from writing to drawing as his descriptive tool, and this opens up for him the highest level of integration in his nature studies, geology, which he pursues in an orderly way, "mit fortgesetztem Eifer und mit einer strengen Ordnung" (42). Later he begins a geological collection "mit viel mehr Ordnung als bisher" (215), and his "Kisten füllten sich, und stellten sich an einander" (216). The collection comprises the finds themselves, drawings and labels, as well as a description of each piece. Stifter's Heinrich is, admittedly, at this point older than Keller's, but his completely different approach to reality, his frantic drive to structure it, is noticeable from the first page in the very narrative stance and the methodical descriptions and accounts of events.

Beyond this comparison there exist further fundamental differences in the physical and objective reality and the social and institutional reality represented in the three novels. It cannot be overlooked that Freytag and Stifter describe an individual from the perspective of social structures, the "iron cage" of social norms, whereas Keller looks at social structures through the eyes of an individual who is not bent on a certain track from the outset, for instance on becoming a businessman or on carrying out a mission, such as a project of aesthetic education, but whose career choice is the very issue at stake. The social setting on the margins of bourgeois society rather than in its very heart reflects this different narrative project. Both these factors combined create some leeway for sensuous detail and sensory experience that is absent from both Freytag and Stifter.

There are several lines of argument to be taken up here. The first is that *Der grüne Heinrich*, as much as it is a *bildungsroman*, is also a *Künstlerroman* and as such is part of a tradition of novel-writing that traces its ancestry not so much to Goethe's *Wilhelm Meister* and classicism for its models but to Heinse's *Ardinghello* and (early) romanticism.[78] Against the background

---

78. Emil Utitz, *J. J. W. Heinse und die Ästhetik zur Zeit der deutschen Aufklärung: Eine problemgeschichtliche Studie* (Halle: Niemeyer, 1906), 16. In Emil Utitz's terms,

of this different heritage the relation between city and countryside, and between human creation and nature, appears in a different light. In Freytag it presents itself first and foremost in terms of colonization. The city, even the small town as the seat of (economic) power, subjugates the countryside. Anton, on his way to the provincial capital, the *Hauptstadt* in the opening pages of the novel, perceives the *Rittersitze*, the castles and manor houses situated next to the villages and small towns of the countryside, as performing a role of watchful supervision, "wie der Schäferhund neben der wolligen Herde" (18). Stifter phrases the relation of town and country in different terms. For him the city is the corrupt, crowded space, and the acquisition by Heinrich's father of a suburban house in the "Vorstadt," "wo wir freie Luft genießen, uns ergehen, und gleichsam das ganze Jahr hindurch auf dem Lande wohnen konnten" (12), appears as liberating. For the further spatial patterning of the novel, the country estate serves as Heinrich's base located in the countryside *and* in nature. The evolving activities are not primarily political but aesthetic. Stifter's point is not, as is Freytag's, the colonization of the countryside and exploitation of nature on strictly utilitarian principles (though there is an agricultural, even proto-ecological dimension to the workings of the two estates) but rather the ordering and structuring of natural phenomena in terms of both beauty and material appropriateness in every way. This ideal is ultimately reached in the symbol of the marble statue at the Asperhof. Stifter's aim is to highlight nature's beauty by means of civilizational processes. In this attempt, of course, the aesthetic component turns out to have social and political underpinnings: the aesthetic qua aestheticization is the political.[79]

In Keller the relation of city and countryside is the relation of city and nature. This view is rooted in both the romantic literary-historical heritage and in the hero's existence as a (visual) artist, in itself a romantic element. Romantic heroes do not work the land; they enjoy nature. Their countryside is not agricultural but aesthetic and spiritual terrain. Nature is, in olfactory terms, positively connotated. The contrast between nature and

---

Stifter would come down on the side of the empiricists, whose ideal is nature, improved and refined by man, as opposed to what he terms the classicists, whose ideal *in aestheticis* is Greece, and for whom nature has to be made to conform to classical ideals. Goethe defies such a binary categorization—and is for this very reason the implicit and admired model of both Stifter and Keller.

79. Cf. the outline of the conceptual and spatial setup of Stifter et al. and their extension into moral categories in Renate Obermeier, *Stadt und Natur: Studie zu Texten von Adalbert Stifter und Gottfried Keller,* Gießener Arbeiten zur neueren deutschen Literatur und Literaturwissenschaft (Frankfurt am Main: Peter Lang, 1985).

the city is sharper, the olfactory level is slightly higher, and the variation of smells in nature is greater than in the other two novels. The contrast between city and countryside qua nature is made quite explicit when Heinrich's sketches are subjected to serious criticism by his uncle as representing fantastic, "unmöglich[]" and "lächerlich[]" scenes that reflect the city dweller's "künstliche Krankhaftigkeit," which has to take flight "vor der einfachen Gesundheit dieses Hauses und der ländlichen Luft" (209). The "pure air of the countryside" is contrasted with the "hässliche[] Säuregeruch" that emanates from the factory of one of Heinrich's three guardians in town (196). The country air, however, is not merely pure. On the occasion of Heinrich's first visit to his uncle's after his expulsion from school, he revives from "Kummer" and "Niedergeschlagenheit" (130), describes his visit as a "Flucht zur Mutter Natur" (130), and breathes "die kühle erfrischende Luft . . . an der Brust der gewaltigen Natur" (134). He breathes the "balsamische Morgenluft" the next day; the air around the churchyard "duftete . . . gewaltig von tausend Blumen" (135), and when he meets his cousin Judith for the first time, she throws down an odoriferous bunch of flowers on the table "daß ein Gewirre von Form, Farbe und Duft sich auf der blanken Tafel verbreitete" (141). When he leaves her, she presents him with a bouquet of "Rosen, Nelken und starkduftenden Kräutern" (141). For Keller, the countryside *is* nature. It is full of sensuality, full of an erotic quality that is absent in both Freytag's and Stifter's countryside—and it has olfactive qualities. The media transmitting this impression of the erotic include the senses of proximity, smell, touch, and taste, expressing acts of incorporation, of imbibing, of appropriation through swallowing or breathing. Out in the countryside, the young boys on their paramilitary march to their host city "waren still geworden und schlürften den stillen, glanzvollen Tag ein" (98). A comment like this or the "lieblicher Speiseduft" already mentioned above and rising again from some fresh pieces of pork (674) are unimaginable in Stifter or Freytag.

With these examples we have begun to move from the first realm of olfactory interest to us, nature, into the second, the human environment of houses, rooms, personal spaces, and so forth. There is little of the latter in Keller. In fact, the "dumpfe dämmerige Luft des Kämmerchens" (695) in which Heinrich's mother lies dying as he returns from abroad is one of only two such instances. Here, too, nature serves as a positive contrast, in that the "reine Frühlingsluft" momentarily revives the woman's haggard face as Heinrich opens the window (695). Overall, Keller promotes no class distinction in terms of the gently perfumed rooms of the upper class versus the inodorous middle-class abodes we find hinted at in Freytag. There are also few instances of objects, other than natural ones such as flowers, that exude smell. One of them is the "duftende Schokolade" that consoles Agnes and her mother after Lys abandoned her (471). And another occurs at the Graf von W.'s estate, where the smell of incense serves to highlight the colors in the room, which thereby seemed "an Kraft und Tiefe zu gewinnen" (638).

The most innovative and daring use of smells is in the area of people themselves, above all their interaction, specifically in an erotic context. There was no such instance in Stifter, and only one in Freytag, when Anton is dancing with Lenore and has his moment of synaesthetic perception, discussed above (Freytag, 167). But there are several such instances in *Der grüne Heinrich,* most of them concerning Heinrich himself. They are graded in accordance with the intensity of his passion, and they tend to be coordinated with temperature sensation.

Anna, his somewhat ethereal first love, leads Heinrich "durch ein duftendes Rosen- und Nelkengärtchen" into the house that echoes "Reinlichkeit und Aufgeräumtheit" (159). Both flowers are among other things associated with the Virgin Mary in Christian iconography, a hint, together with the frequent diminutive forms in Anna's presence, that her love is not of the robust type of Judith's who, on their first meeting, presented Heinrich with the already mentioned "stark duftenden Kräutern" (141). On the occasion of Heinrich's and Anna's first kiss, or rather nonkiss, after a day that rises out of a "Morgenduft[]" (179),[80] there is barely a hint at smell in the statement: "wir küßten uns nicht und dachten gar nicht daran, nur unser Hauch vermischte sich" (184). Similarly, on Anna's death, a white odorless rose is put in her hands (372) about whose coldness Heinrich is shocked (374). This first love is noncorporeal, cool, and barely smelling. In contrast, a later erotic incident, much more robust, even if unconsummated, the meeting of Heinrich with Hulda, the working-class girl, is characterized in the following olfactory and gustatory terms: "ich ... suchte ... ihren Mund, der mir mit ambrosischer Frische entgegenkam, so rein und duftig wie eine aufgehende Rose" (577). This provokes such a turmoil in Heinrich that through all his veins "wogte und rauschte erst jetzt die erwachte Leidenschaft, wild und sanft, süß und frech zugleich ... " (579). The more physical and passionate nature of this en-

---

80. Cf. Stifter: *Duft* in terms of landscape description does not normally have an olfactive quality but means "mist" or the haze that is associated with heat and distance.

counter is represented through the senses of proximity, especially the chemical senses of smell and taste.[81] Dortchen Schönfund on the other hand, although Heinrich falls madly in love with her, is inodorous. Heinrich is so infatuated that it becomes impossible for him to act, let alone act reasonably—and their relationship goes nowhere.

Clearly the most odorous relationship and the most physical is the one between Heinrich and Judith. After the term *balsamic* has been introduced in the "balsamische Morgenluft" of the countryside (135), it receives a first explicitly erotic touch in the "balsamische Mailuft" (223) that envelopes the house of Heinrich's uncle, where the two young daughters receive nightly visits from their lovers, a rural custom of those days. Even Anna on one occasion had breathed "balsamische Luft" (297). Judith, however, has such balsamic air *inside* of her, and she emanates it, together with warmth, even heat, on that one nightly visit of Heinrich's to her house. He kisses "einen heißen, leibhaftigen Mund, und der geheimnisvolle balsamische Atem aus dem Inneren eines schönen und starken Weibes strömte in vollen Zügen in mich über" (316).[82] This is said explicitly in contrast to his recent experience with Anna on their ride home together a few pages previously in the novel. Then, Heinrich and Anna were riding on a path which was "kalt, feucht und schauerlich" (297), and after they kiss, an "eisige Kälte" (299) envelopes them, and the cup of innocent desire is emptied out over them "mit plötzlicher Kälte" (300). The coding of the erotic in Keller occurs in terms of the senses of proximity, not only smell, but also touch, often as temperature. Indeed, when Heinrich and Judith meet again after their return from abroad and decide to continue their relationship as friends rather than trying to be lovers, both touch and smell are absent. Eroticism is cut out.

These admittedly few instances in *Der grüne Heinrich* confirm a pattern in nineteenth-century fiction. Woman and (female) nature are perceived in terms of odor by the male. Remember the examples in *Soll und Haben:* Anton notices Lenore's perfume; Sabine comments on Rosalie's musked letter; Fink remarks on the greasy smell of the Indian women. The attitude

---

81. "I . . . sought . . . her mouth which was meeting mine with ambrosial freshness, pure and fragrant like an opening rose." Heinrich's blood then "gushed and rushed with the awakened passion, wild and gentle, sweet and fresh simultaneously." Cf. the English colloquial expression (in fact a romantic metaphor) used to describe a successful or unsuccessful romantic relationship: "the chemistry is / is not right."

82. He kisses "a hot, carnal mouth, and the mysterious balsamic breath from the depth of a beautiful and strong woman was rushing into me with full might."

toward nature (in Anton's and Karl's working on the Polish estate) is one of colonizing, of bringing nature, the land, under (male) control. In *Der Nachsommer* smell is banned almost completely and nature-as-female is vigorously structured, classified, categorized, and organized by the male agents. Heinrich's sister "mußte sich den Übungen unterziehen" (20), submit to the physical exercises that the fitness ideology of the day propagates. The ideal woman ultimately appears as the statue.[83]

Nature-as-female is brought under control by Keller not through colonization or categorical structuring as in collecting and naming, but by superimposing a grid of visual aesthetics. However, his supreme value is nature itself, not models of classical antiquity as for Stifter. The artist-elect Heinrich endeavors to represent nature faithfully and realistically in his sketches and paintings—and it is in this respect that he ultimately fails because his imagination runs away with him. In positing imagination as a force that threatens structures and norms, the bourgeois "law and order," the three authors resemble each other, despite the different valuation of the fact. It is no wonder, then, that the female is associated with nature and odor, the realms most resistant to classification, while standing most in need of it from the male perspective.

Recognizing this similarity among the three authors, let us not, however, overlook the differences. Freytag does not develop an explicit aesthetics on the plot level at all. His aesthetic evolves from the act of reading itself, the discourse of narrator and reader, who reach an understanding about the phenomenological world. Stifter reifies woman in the marble statue, and only Keller allows her some degree of freedom. She remains outside male control, desired but elusive, wanted, yet ultimately renounced, an object of eternal projection and imagination.

A revealing scene in terms of Keller's aesthetics is Judith's nightly bath in the lake. She appears to Heinrich "gleich einem überlebensgroßen alten Marmorbilde." But what a "Marmorbild" compared to Stifter's! A live one that turns "über und über rot"; one that kisses back (367).[84] This romantic scene—the narrator himself talks about their nightly strolls as of "roman-

---

83. Cf. Friedrich Ludwig Jahn (1778–1852), the "Turnvater." His ideas of the strengthening of the individual body as a strengthening of the (national) body politic are, at least for a time, gaining ground after 1848.

84. Love, eroticism, and emotion throughout Keller's work is color-coded, red and white. There are numerous instances in *Der grüne Heinrich,* such as this present scene, but also a much earlier one between the little boy Heinrich and the actress who plays Gretchen in the nightly empty theater (84–85). Cf. also *Das Sinngedicht.*

tische Gewohnheiten" (265)—reveals the woman as one with nature. "Es wurde mir zumute, wie wenn Judith sich aufgelöst hätte und still in die Natur verschwunden wäre, in welcher mich ihre Elemente geisterhaft neckend umrauschten." The reification of the vision in the marble statue "wie fabelhaft vergrößert und verschönt" is only momentary; then the statue moves, escapes, disappears (366).[85] It is this live quality that Keller grants nature, woman, even the marble statue, that distinguishes him most from Stifter. The latter just barely anthropomorphizes marble as a (female) statue. Keller, on this one occasion, imaginatively freezes a female figure into a marble statue—only to let her escape again. This vital aesthetics, however, has its price: (male) renunciation, resignation, melancholy. In Stifter this is ultimately not an issue, although thematized for the older couple, because his aesthetic aims at petrification from the start, at the *still life*.[86] The attitude is thus not one of renunciation as there is nothing to be renounced in the first place. Rather, the issue is control, even repression, from the outset.

The Judith scene, as we know, is cut out from the second version of *Der grüne Heinrich*. Is it a concession to conservative public taste as represented by the literary historian Emil Kuh, who recommended the cut? Or is it an admission that the price for the live quality, mobility, liquidity of the scene, the woman's escape, appears too high in retrospect, if not for Heinrich, then for Keller himself? To cut means to remove from discourse—because the experience is too painful (again not for Heinrich, but for Keller). Nonetheless, the second version of the novel cannot be called purged, more prudish or repressive than the first. It is shortened and streamlined, but there is no particular bias toward sensual reductionism and sensory deprivation. The more striking therefore is this cut here, together with another, the only one in the realm of the olfactory: at his uncle's home, young Heinrich, together with his male cousins, observes the girls on Sundays through "Schlüssellöcher" and "Türspalten" as they debate in their rooms over their outfits, with the doors of the wardrobes wide open, emitting alluring scents. "Ein starker Geruch verschiedener Spezereien verbreitete sich und bildete mit den neuen Stoffen und Siebensächelchen, welche in den Schränken lagen, jenen behaglichen Duft, der sich aus

---

85. It seems to Heinrich "as if Judith had dissolved and quietly disappeared into nature where her elements hovered around him, eerily and teasingly." For the (marble) statue as a romantic topos, cf., e.g., Joseph von Eichendorff's *Das Marmorbild* or Prosper Mérimée's *La Vénus d'Ille*.

86. The French term *nature morte* sounds even more appropriate in this context.

geöffneten Frauenschränken oder sonstigen Mobilien entwickelt" (156). Deleting scenes of woman and nature before, now woman and smell—"the cozy smell curling out of women's open wardrobes"—the elusive, the volatile, the transcending and transforming: is Keller, half-consciously, retreating from something he once knew better? His use of the olfactory compared to Freytag and Stifter is just barely more frequent. Much more obvious, however, is its function in coding nature and the female-erotic, and the parallel structuring of those two realms in terms of aliveness, wholesomeness, yet also unpredictability and elusiveness.

Another, more theoretical and aesthetic constant in Keller is the narrator's veneration for Schiller's (aesthetic) ideas. As a boy Heinrich already reads Schiller (215), educating himself, among other things, in aesthetics, while lacking resources, etchings, and other models for his practical artistic studies. Later on, disappointed over the fate of his first painting in an exhibition, he thinks of Schiller's as "ein wahres und vernünftiges Leben" (540). Heinrich admires the naive Schiller, himself always inclined to the sentimental in his flings of imagination. Truth and reason are precisely what he is searching for in his life and particularly in his religious instruction. But he experiences his catechism classes as too abstract, too nonsensual, and therefore as nonsensical. The concept of sin in particular is so vague and so revolting to him and yet so pervasive that in his imagination he equates it with a bad odor: "es hatte . . . einen widerlich technischen Geruch wie von einer Leimsiederei oder von dem säuerlich verdorbenen Schlichtebrei eines Leinewebers" (254).[87] The realm of (distorted) belief produces characters like Wurmlinger with his telling name, who contests the reality of the five senses as much as scientific findings and is such a notorious liar and critic that the contortions of his soul have completely twisted and bent his body, so "daß er aussah wie ein verbogener Wetterhahn" (259). The grotesque body is the result of both a reality concept that is not based on the five senses and an absurd and lifeless (religious) superstructure. Keller's realism lies somewhere in between. His acquaintance with Feuerbach's thought has robbed him of religious belief, but it has made his worldview brighter, richer, more sensual. But Keller's poetic mockery hits the opposite end of the scale, too, the itinerant Feuerbachian atheist Peter Gilgus, who is bumming his way around the country, and

---

87. Cf. the bad smell associated with *Leim* in *Soll und Haben,* footnote 56, above. *Schlichte* is used in a chemical process of smoothing woven natural fibers. See also chapter 3, footnote 51.

whom Heinrich meets at Graf von W.'s, carrying his belongings in a won-drously strange gunnysack. Among his possessions is a wax and glass model of the human eye that he stole from a school anatomy collection but does not want to give up despite the police warrants issued on his person, as it is "das wahre Auge Gottes!" (653). Sight or insight on the one hand and vision on the other represent the same dichotomy as reality and imagina-tion, and while Keller does not condemn the second, he grounds his real-ism more in the first.

In terms of representational aesthetics Keller's world is the most "realis-tically" and the least programmatically realist, whether in regard to social politics or aesthetic education. He makes fun of his characters, which Freytag and Stifter hardly do. Although a large part of the novel's vision is indeed visual and discusses representation in terms of painterly catego-ries, there is a relatively strong emphasis on other sensory modalities, an insistence, in any case, on the sensuous quality of life and the object world, an explicit condemnation of desensualized, regressive ideals. They appear as too abstract, if not absurd. This is the worldview of a bourgeois state official around 1880, well established and more self-assured than his literary projection Heinrich was, on his way from a petit bourgeois background to a comfortable white-collar position.

With *Effi Briest* we will follow things a step further into the 1890s and take a step up into the upper middle class. We will move from the more rural petite bourgeoisie of Swiss stamp to the more city-oriented Prussian upper crust.

Effi Briest: Daughter of the Air

With *Effi Briest,*[88] this "Roman der guten Gesellschaft" as Peter Demetz calls it,[89] we are taking leave of the century, "Abschied vom Jahrhun-

---

88. Theodor Fontane, *Effi Briest,* vol. 4 of *Sämtliche Werke,* ed. Walter Keitel (1st publ. serially 1894; 1st book ed. 1895; Munich: Hanser, 1962–). All references are to this edition.

89. Peter Demetz, "Formen des Realismus: Theodor Fontane. Kritische Unter-suchungen," quoted in *Theodor Fontane,* ed. Wolfgang Preisendanz, Wege der Forschung, vol. 381 (Darmstadt: Wissenschaftliche Buchgesellschaft, 1973), 233. The origi-nal version of this essay was published as part 3 of Peter Demetz, *Formen des Realismus: Theodor Fontane. Kritische Untersuchungen* (Munich: Hanser, 1964).

dert."[90] In comparison with the three novels discussed so far, a change of tone that is more than just another writer's voice cannot be missed. The different voice means more than a switch of locale from rural Upper Austria to the city of Berlin, a change of social class from the Swiss small-town petit bourgeoisie to Prussian ministers of state, or a shift of psychological focus from the busybody mercantilism of Schröter to Effi's ennui among the Kessin gentry. In an all-out comparative study of the four novels those aspects, and many more, would have to be isolated and weighed carefully. For our purpose it is sufficient to recognize that, in addition to being a unique work of art, *Effi Briest*, with its depiction of individual being and consciousness, as well as its mode of artistic representation, can help us mark a more general literary position in terms of historical and social development. We have observed the bourgeoisie "at work" in *Soll und Haben*, setting itself off from, while measuring up to, the aristocracy. We have seen its representative Heinrich Drendorf melt into this very aristocracy on the basis of a commonality of structural perception of the (social and aesthetic) world. And we have got to know its lower ranks and its more marginal figures in *Der grüne Heinrich*. This bourgeoisie now appears in Fontane at its most refined, most self-assured. It appears as a social class that has found its true destination in the repeated performance of its own social rites, indoors, at the dinner table, in the ballroom or the smoking lounge for the men, and in the salons for the women. This *haute bourgeoisie* laughs at Anton's demanding satisfaction from Fink—yet it has its own honor code with severe social implications for those who break it. This bourgeoisie, or at least those parts of it that Fontane presents in *Effi Briest*, would be scared of Heinrich Drendorf's strenuous excursions into nature: it dislikes nature and lives indoors instead. It would have no sympathy with Heinrich Lee either, the outsider, questioning, self-doubting, gloomy, for it is jovial and social. "Das Gesunde ist im heiteren und geselligen Kreise zu finden; das Einsame ist krank, grotesk, oder schwanger von Leid und Tod" (Demetz, 249).[91] Fontane's bourgeoisie is the jet set, in fact the train and coach set of the time. It is international and has its chroniclers every-

---

90. Walther Killy, "Abschied vom Jahrhundert: Wirklichkeit und Kunstcharakter," in *Theodor Fontane*, ed. Wolfgang Preisendanz, Wege der Forschung, vol. 381 (Darmstadt: Wissenschaftliche Buchgesellschaft, 1973), 265.

91. "Health is to be found in light-hearted, sociable circles; what is lonely is sick, grotesque, or pregnant with suffering and death." This "good society," as Demetz calls it in the following paragraph, is not "a fixed sociological, but rather a flexible aesthetic category" (241).

where: Balzac (1799–1850), Flaubert (1821–80), Zola (1840–1902), Proust (1871–1922) in France; Scott (1771–1832) and Thackeray (1811–63) in Great Britain; Fontane (1819–98) and Thomas Mann (1875–1955) in Germany. From America, Henry James (1843–1916) joins the chorus, though he mostly reports from the bourgeoisie's European centers, whereas in Russia the social border drawing resembles a trench warfare.

Historically speaking, the multilayered Western bourgeoisie of the 1880s and 1890s is a well-established class. It has passed its definitional stage. At the top it has happily merged with the remnants of an aristocracy that had long lost its social functionality in what Demetz calls the "gute Gesellschaft." This international conglomerate is less "eine starre soziologische als vielmehr eine bewegliche ästhetische Kategorie" (Demetz, 241) that has established itself as the new trendsetter. No longer does this class secretly admire the better taste of the aristocracy as we so clearly feel in *Soll und Haben.* Rather it buys out the aristocracy with its newly amassed industrial and commercial fortunes. And at the bottom it has shut out the workers, the emerging proletariat, Chadwick's "labouring population" in its factories, as well as the petit bourgeois craftsmen. According to Demetz, it looks down even on the intellectuals and is suspicious of artists, the *bohème*.[92] Anton, too, the representative of the aspiring merchant class of the 1850s and epitome of bourgeois middle-class ideology, is now looked down upon by Innstetten and his class. Innstetten belittles even "Konsuln," because they are nothing but "kleine, pfiffige Kaufleute; . . . [sie] begnügen sich damit, mit Zucker und Kaffee zu handeln oder eine Kiste mit Apfelsinen aufzubrechen und verkaufen dir dann das Stück pro zehn Pfennige" (57).[93]

This historically consolidated upper-crust bourgeoisie has created its

---

92. Significantly, Frau Jenny Treibel, the social upstart in Fontane's eponymous novel, characterizes the staircase in Professor Schmidt's house in olfactory terms, the only such instance in the whole narrative. There is a "schwere Luft, . . . die man füglich als eine Doppelluft bezeichnen konnte" lingering in the staircase (297); and the hallway leading up to Schmidt's apartment is permeated by a "sonderbarer Küchengeruch, . . . der, wenn nicht alles täuschte, nur auf Rührkartoffeln und Karbonade gedeutet werden konnte, beides mit Seifenwrasen untermischt" (298). This instance—beside some more general references to air—clearly has undertones of social distinction and, in Frau Treibel's case, is not without its irony, as she herself grew up "in der Molkenmarktluft" of a milieu she now looks down upon (331). Theodor Fontane, *Frau Jenny Treibel,* vol. 4 of *Sämtliche Werke,* ed. Walter Keitel (Munich: Hanser, 1962–).

93. They are "small, clever businessmen; . . . [they] are satisfied with dealing in sugar and coffee or with opening a crate of oranges which they then sell to you at a dime a piece."

own world with its own institutions, from the spa towns and the Grand Hotels to the municipal theaters and opera houses, together with the idea of the "Sommerfrische" to recover from them all, and the four-class train system to facilitate travel between the "happening" places and the "in" seasons. Upward, there is nowhere to go; they are at the top. The wealth of the emerging industrialists has allegedly even the Prussian king, Friedrich Wilhelm IV exclaim on the occasion of a visit to the Borsig factories and the owner's villa: "So wie Sie, mein lieber Borsig, möchte ich wohnen."[94] Distinctions have to be maintained toward the lower classes, and a lot of energy goes into the upkeep of the bourgeois *comme il faut,* that conglomerate of aesthetic order and sociomoral code. Its strictness, together with other factors of a "late" age, brings about a new type of person, the nervous, the high-strung, the aesthete.[95] This bourgeoisie that sees nature as an impressionist tableau (for instance in James's *The Ambassadors*) develops its subtle, in addition to its not-so-subtle, ways of expressing its newly acquired social powers—vis-à-vis both the working classes, the maids, servants, and craftsmen working for it, and the merchants and shopkeepers providing its daily necessities. *Kaffee* and *Zucker,* for instance, the proverbial *Kolonialwaren,* are the products of labor and trade with which the upper class has to do mainly insofar as it provides the financing. Accounting is its major hobby as well as part of its essential being, and Innstetten talks about money as well as do the Briests. Thomas Mann carefully and irreverently notices the fluctuations in the Buddenbrook family fortune.[96] In literature we ordinarily see this moneyed class on vacation rather than at work, more frequently in its salons and dining halls than in the office, although, here, too, Thomas Mann leaves the door open for the reader to get a glimpse and for Christian Buddenbrook to escape the regular hours that he is unable to keep. This class, represented in Jane Austen's novels—such as *Sense and Sensibility* (1811)—in its early manifestation, produces by the end of the century some quite delicate individual representatives, preoccupied more with the *senses* and *sensitivity* and with how to avoid too much of both. It is a class of "hochgebildete[], feinnervige[],

---

94. Herbert Roch, *Fontane, Berlin und das 19. Jahrhundert* (Düsseldorf: Droste, 1985), 266.

95. Historically speaking, this is a recycled type from romanticism. The differences arise from the historical context.

96. The role of money in Russian novels would be well worth a close study in itself. Generally, it is constrained circumstances, the ever-threatening pennilessness that is emphasized rather than the thrifty accumulation or sovereign possession of large fortunes.

nervöse[] Grafen, Baronen oder Gesellschaftsdamen" (Demetz, 242), a society of fragile health and delicate minds, and the nerves in their bodies
seem always too short on one side, as in Christian Buddenbrook's case. In
France and England this type has already emerged and left its aesthetic and
artistic mark. The romantic realism of a Balzac or Scott has been superseded by naturalism, and that in turn has been replaced; the nervous disease
has found an outlet in sensory and sensual indulgence, from Baudelaire and
Huysmans to Oscar Wilde. Germany and German literature lag behind by
a decade or two. Hofmannsthal and Rilke will represent the new type.

Thus the bourgeois realism of the last decade of the nineteenth century
is no longer that of the 1850s. The *literary-historical* category is changing,
because both *literature* and its aesthetic-representational principles change;
and because *history* is transforming the social, economic, and political structures. Bourgeois realism as an ideological project is fizzling out, not because the bourgeoisie is disappearing, but because its day-to-day experiential reality is changing, its tastes, its likes and dislikes. Naturalism has
barged in with its critical and scientific claim on realism and on its sentimental rearguards, symbolism and *Jugendstil*. The psychoanalytical movement, led most prominently by Freud, is, at the very beginning of the
twentieth century, starting to deconstruct the soul, that bourgeois trinity
of *Herz, Schmerz,* and *Kommerz*.[97] While Charcot is still longing for an
organic anchoring of that most delicate of bourgeois organs, Freud is
beginning radically to dissolve it into narrative, into a story. And Proust,
upon a mere sensation of taste and smell, gushes forth hundreds of pages,
spreading the soul on paper.

And yet, the object world still has its quirks and is far from perfect.
Fontane calls the toilets at his *Sommerfrischen* "eine ganz ernsthafte
Kalamität" (Roch, 171). The countryside, its inns and hotels, sadly lag
behind Berlin (and other cities) in terms of sanitary installations, and however much Fontane decries the "Erfindungsplunder, mit Ventilation und
Wasserwerk" of the city, he is an "an das WC gewohnte[r] Berliner
Bürger" (Roch, 171). As such he does not mention smells, but it is obvious
that the borderline between the upper-class bourgeois cleanliness and odorlessness as it is now found in their city homes, and the unsanitary, smelling
outhouses and similar installations in the countryside is still rather precari-

---

97. For further instances of the multitude of functions of the heart in the bourgeois
body politic, cf. *Frau Jenny Treibel*. For her "die rechte Vernunft [kommt] aus dem
Herzen" (468), or the juxtaposition of "Herz," "Glück," and "Erlösung" (415).

ous. Historically, these devices are by no means a long-gone memory. The account for the town of Windsor, given in Chadwick's report from 1842, may serve as an example. Despite

> the contiguity of the palace, the wealth of the inhabitants . . . Windsor is the worst beyond all comparison. . . . a double line of open, deep, black, and stagnant ditches extends to Clewer-lane. From these ditches an intolerable stench is perpetually rising, and produces fever of a severe character. (87–88)

It is true that since the date of this report considerable progress had been made, but the process of transforming the "technisch-hygienischen Fortschritt[] in Verwaltungs-, Polizei- und Baunormen"[98] and thereby assuring its widespread application is only slowly gaining momentum.

Effi Briest in just under 300 pages contains a mere half dozen references to smells, of which three are to nature, and three to the social sphere of dwellings and human beings themselves. That is fewer than we found in any of the other novels, except for Stifter's. What we do find instead is an elaborate, if somewhat submerged, discourse on air, its qualities and effects on the body. Breathing itself, for the nervous circle of the Berlin upper class, becomes problematic, and for Effi the epithet "Tochter der Luft" (8), given her on the second page of the novel, turns out to be prophetic as she gently and quietly wastes away. The bourgeois respiratory system at the end of the century is affected, and especially the upper class is threatened by consumption, tuberculosis, *Schwindsucht*. Not stench or odors, not smells or scents, are causing the phenomenon, it is the medium itself, the air, that seems to become too thin and too rarefied to sustain the nervous, high-strung bourgeois mind in its delicate body. A whole discourse on air is evolving, with *Effi Briest* at its inception. Thomas Mann's *Zauberberg* (1924) will represent its unsurpassed diagnosis and cure simultaneously in its retrospective account of the *haut-bourgeois* years before World War I.

In *Effi Briest* visual techniques form as much of the descriptive mainstay

---

98. Juan Rodrigues-Lores and Gerhard Fehl, eds., *Städtebaureform 1865–1900; Von Licht, Luft und Ordnung in der Stadt der Gründerzeit. Allgemeine Beiträge und Bebauungsplanung* (Hamburg: Christians Verlag, 1985), 20. In Rodrigues-Lores's and Fehl's formulation becomes visible the "Dialektik von Ordnung und Unordnung" in city planning and public hygiene (19) together with the double roots of public health care and social hygiene in both a stepped-up administrative control mechanism and a not wholly disinterested philantropism.

as they do in the other novels, in fact they are taken to an extreme. Time and again the scenery freezes into a light, airy impressionist tableau: of the garden, for instance, in the opening pages; or of Effi's and Crampas's November picnic at the stormy beach (138); or of Effi's view of the steam trains from the "Chaussee" near her Hohen-Cremmen home on her last outings (290–91). These carefully arranged views are intentional aesthetic insets, and they differ markedly from the utilitarian and scientific depiction of individual elements of nature as we find them in Stifter, or the painstaking attempts of Keller's Heinrich to represent nature truthfully. The more formal aestheticism of the class of people described by Fontane is reflected in the novel's own descriptive stance. Smell does not form part of either realm. Language has the capacity—itself being first and foremost an abstract system of signs, black on the white page and almost void of sensory qualities of its own—to appeal to all sensory modalities, from the purely visual, its most dominant category in narrative prose, to the purely aural in onomatopoeia and exclamations. In *Effi Briest* there are passages that are so predominantly visual that only a hint at other sensory modes saves, or prevents, them from congealing into a tableau. This sense may be touch (in its most general form, motion); it may be sound (as in the opening passage, conversation); it could be taste (which, however, is never used); or it may be smell, such as the *Duft* that the wind carries up to Effi and her mother from the heliotrope in another tableaulike garden scene at Hohen-Cremmen (29). Heliotrope is mentioned several times after that, but always without aroma. On the last page of the novel it grows around the white marble plaque that bears Effi's name.[99]

There are other plants occurring in this novel, dry, odorless ones, such as *Strandhafer* or *Immortellen,* chosen for their name rather than for any physical property (45, 241), as well as "blutrote Nelken" (241) for the explicit color association with the impending duel between Crampas and Innstetten. If the editor sees *Immortellen* as "Bilder eines *duftlosen,* wehmütig kargen Todes" (709, emphasis added), Effi's story too can be read as just that: the account of a slow dying, of suffocation in a stifling, physically and sensually deprived environment. In this sense it is appropriate, in fact inevitable, that the respiratory system should be the affected area. While we can exist, however poorly, without taste or touch, even

---

99. Cf. the connotation of white marble here and in Stifter. As regards the plants discussed in the following paragraph, Keitel, the editor, sees "Immortellen" as "Bilder eines *duftlosen,* wehmütig kargen Todes" (709, emphasis added).

without sight or hearing, breathe we must. Breathing is the primordial link with the environment. The novel as a story of deprivation proceeds very systematically. The *Tochter der Luft,* admonished from the very beginning to calm down, to integrate, to accept the norms—"Nicht so wild, Effi, nicht so leidenschaftlich" (9)—dies breathing pure air, the last physical element that is left her, unrestricted by others, and that brings her death. Effi's last days are described with more sensuous detail, and more sensory modalities are addressed jointly there, than anywhere in the novel, and indeed the last olfactory reference to nature occurs here: "Effi, der *freie Luft* noch mehr galt als landschaftliche Schönheit, . . . hielt meist . . . die große Straße. . . . An allem freute sie sich, atmete beglückt den *Duft* ein, der von den Raps- und Kleefeldern herüberkam. . . . Dabei *klang* ein leises *Läuten* zu ihr herüber" (emphasis added).[100] It seems to her that she only needs to close her eyes and simply could "in ein *süßes Vergessen* hinübergehen" (290, emphasis added). She also takes walks with her mother during those last days: "Frau von Briest *streichelte* ihr die Hand," and Effi breaks off "einen *Frühapfel*" and *bites into it* with her beautiful teeth (291, emphasis added). All the senses are alluded to here, and their combined synaesthetic impression is summed up in "Wie schön dieser Sommer!" (291). They form the physical base of Effi's last happy days. She is untiringly imbibing the beauty around her, for instance in the nights with the shooting stars. "[Sie hatte] . . . sich nicht müde sehen können" (292). Not through vision, not through sound or touch, rather through the air death approaches her. Indeed, while she gives herself up to vision, to the observation of those nocturnal "Himmelswunder[]," it is the "Nachtluft und die Nebel, die vom Teich her aufstiegen" (292) that bring her down. No smell is mentioned here. It is the humidity and the temperature of the air that trigger the last onslaught of Effi's illness.

The discourse on air centers as much on the metaphorical qualities of that medium as on its concrete physical properties. Air is atmosphere, it is a life element, foremost in the figurative sense, but, as the novel makes clear in the parallel discourse about health, also in its physiological aspects. This double characteristic of concrete and figurative meaning, in the following instance even with a hint at smell, is emphasized in the retrospective authorial comment about Effi's life between her rejection by Innstetten and

---

100. "Effi, who appreciated the open air even more than the beauty of the land-scape . . . stuck mostly . . . to the main road. . . . She enjoyed everything, happily inhaled the fragrance carried over from the fields of rape and clover. . . . A gentle tolling of bells reached her ear. . . . "

her finding an apartment in Berlin. She spends the first few weeks in a *Pensionat* but soon cannot stand anymore the "herrschende Gesamtatmosphäre, die physische wie die moralische" (261).[101] It is not, however, the "geistige Atmosphäre" but much rather "rein physisch und äußerlich, die sich hinzugesellende Pensionsluft" that are unbearable for her. "Woraus sich diese eigentlich zusammensetzte, war vielleicht überhaupt unerforschlich, aber daß sie der sehr empfindlichen Effi den Atem raubte, war nur zu gewiß" (261). One of the maids at the boarding house, a sickly person in her midthirties, carries "den hier lagernden Dunstkreis überallhin in ihren Falten" (262). "Gesamtatmosphäre," "sehr empfindliche Effi," "den Atem rauben": these are the characteristics that form the etiology of Effi's illness, which is foremost rooted in stifling social conventions that Fontane questions and reveals as obsolete. The upper-class honor code of that late nineteenth-century bourgeoisie is life-threatening, indeed, murderous.[102]

The amount of repression arising from the existing *comme il faut* does not, in terms of the novel's discourse, openly stink, but it takes one's breath away. It is more a dry rot, hardly visible to the untrained eye, unnoticeable to the ordinary nose, that undermines the upper class. Its literary representation in terms of atmosphere and the implicit, on occasion even explicit reference to its inhalation points to its all-pervasive damaging effects. Thus Effi suffers from "katharralischen Affektionen" and repeatedly has her lungs checked (223) during her marriage with Innstetten, but the disease persists (259). Old Dr. Rummschüttel, of whom rumor has it that in his younger days he might have "shaken up" quite a few ladies, in perfect accordance with his name, diagnoses a turn for the worse in Effi, "'ihre Nerven zehren sie auf'" (276). With this news, once again, he shakes somebody up, Effi's parents, who finally let her return home—a decision that

---

101. Following is the translation of this and subsequent passages in this paragraph: Effi cannot bear "the prevalent atmosphere, both physical and moral." She confirms this by saying that it is not the "spiritual atmosphere" but also, "purely physically and externally, the air at the boardinghouse" that are unbearable. "What exactly it consisted of was probably impossible to determine, but that it took delicate Effi's breath away, was only too clear."

102. It must be noted here that the honor code requiring dueling was essentially derived from the military caste of the aristocracy. The ordinary middle bourgeoisie ignored or rejected it. It is precisely the uneasy mixture of aristocratic and bourgeois standards in Innstetten that lets him act as he does. He is not aristocrat enough to reject the dueling convention (which he could do at that time), rather he is so much of a bourgeois bureaucratic pedant that he accepts it. (On dueling see also footnote 140 in the Russian section, below.)

in itself means a shakeup of the social code. Effi, the fallen woman, the outcast, is forgiven by her parents who in turn become social pariahs themselves. The old doctor is fully aware that his diagnosis and prescription, although phrased in terms of air, are much more comprehensive. He does say that "ein Luftwechsel," a "change of air," is necessary, but he also knows that it is "nicht Luft allein" that can cure Effi, and he sums it up with "Andere Luft, andere Menschen" (276).

Behind this dominant discourse on air let us not overlook the few concrete references to smell in a social context, to human interaction. They help set apart the lower and the upper classes in more concrete, corporeal terms than was the case in *Soll und Haben* or in the other two novels, where such overt class coding is virtually absent. For her trip from Kessin to Berlin Effi buys herself "eine Flasche Sal volatile. 'Man weiß nie, mit wem man reist,' sagte sie" (188). The train is, despite its four-class segregation system, a place of social mixing where one's airspace might become contaminated. "Ich habe mir eben ein Fläschchen mit Sal volatile gekauft," says Effi to her friend Gieshübler, "im Kupee sind mitunter so merkwürdige Menschen und wollen einen nicht mal erlauben, daß man ein Fenster aufmacht" (189).[103] Effi's hypersensitivity to air and to smell is stressed once more when she debates with Roswitha what she could do to alleviate the boredom and the uselessness of her life outside society and family in her little apartment in Berlin. "'Ich kann nicht mal armen Kindern eine Nachhilfestunde geben . . .'—'Das wäre auch nichts für Sie'" counters Roswitha, "'die Kinder haben immer so fettige Stiefel an, und wenn es nasses Wetter ist—das ist dann solch Dunst und Schmook, das halten die gnädige Frau gar nicht aus'" (266). In both instances the emphasis is on the bad smell of the lower class as well as on Effi's extraordinary olfactory and pneumatic sensitivity. In one instance only in the novel does a clearly defined smell have a positive effect on her: on the occasion of an invitation to Gieshübler's, the Kessin friend and pharmacist, Effi gets "beinah

---

103. Following is the translation of this, the preceding, and subsequent passages in this paragraph: she buys a bottle of smelling salts, saying, "One never knows who one is travelling with. . . . In the [train] compartment there sometimes are such strange people who don't even allow that the windows are opened" (189). To Roswitha she complains that she "'cannot even give private lessons to children . . .'—'That wouldn't be for you anyway . . . children always wear such muddy boots, and in wet weather there would be such humidity and smell that mylady couldn't bear it'" (266). Earlier on, the odors of Gieshübler's pharmacy had made her "nearly giddy" (89).

übermütig... wozu die das Haus durchziehende Baldrian- und Veil-chenwurzelluft das ihrige beitragen mochte" (89).

In terms of the social encoding of sensory-sensual phenomena, one last aspect of Fontane's art seems noteworthy. It is the attribution of eroticism and sexuality—without an olfactory element—to the lower classes of the maids and servants and its almost complete absence in the nervous upper class. Among the *Gesellschaft,* only Dr. Rummschüttel is allowed an erotic history. "Früher war er ein Damenmann, aber in den richtigen Grenzen," says Effi's mother of him. But then Dr. Rummschüttel is not really "one of them," and he proves his disregard for upper-class codes by visiting the outcast Effi and taking her side, even if he does so under the convenient cover of medical duty. Generally, the body is something to be ashamed of, and thus, "ein junger Doktor ist immer genant" (199). Sexuality, morally reproachable sexuality, is present in Roswitha's tragic story as an affair among servants, far removed from the pampered bourgeoisie. Closer to home is the physical attractiveness of Johanna, the Innstetten servant, com-mented on several times (e.g., 250) and Roswitha's allegation that she is in love with Innstetten (248). It is also among servants that the explicit link of career and lack of time for passion and sexuality is made and commented on (72), whereas, on the other hand, it is among the upper class, between Geheimrätin Zwicker and Effi—"etwas frei, wahrscheinlich sogar mit einer Vergangenheit" is Effi's comment on her—that the sexual threat posed by the female servants to the master of the bourgeois household is discussed (250).

Effi Briest undoubtedly is "ein Roman der guten Gesellschaft." But our investigation into the sensual aspects of the life of this society and the structure of sensory perception among its members has revealed that this class at the turn of the century is seriously ill. While it became obvious that the bourgeois age as it represents itself in its realist narrative literature has never been very sensual and certainly does not characterize itself in terms of the olfactory, it seems that by 1900 an aggravation of its health has occurred. Both its body and its mind are affected. One of the main causes of the disease can be located in the repressive tendencies dominating its sensual life. While Freud begins a careful and cautious, but nevertheless alarmingly radical process of unveiling the repressive mechanisms that op-erate on the psyche, Pasteur, among others, takes up successfully the fight against the newly discovered world of germs and bacteria and thus contrib-utes to the improvement of the physical side, of the bourgeois body in the context of medicine and public health.[104] It is with Pasteur, Semmelweis, Jenner, and others, for the respiratory system above all with Robert Koch, the discoverer of the tuberculosis bacillus, that after the middle of the nineteenth century the realm of putrefaction, of disease, of organic decay in all its forms—up to then viewed and inhaled with revulsion and treated with awe in science—takes on a more concrete shape.[105] It can now be understood as the somewhat graspable, but still elusive world of microbes. Thus the enemy, long viewed with mythic fascination, eventually has a face and can be opposed. This is more than a figure of speech, for the last major outbreak of cholera in the Europe of growing, crowded, and unsanitary cities of 1832 is still within living memory of the oldest. And yet it *is* a figure of speech whose referent lies somewhere else, in the social and the aesthetic. While the concrete enemy, once spotted, is left to the special troops to fight, to medicine, chemistry, physics, and the growing technology of hygiene and sanitation, this enemy becomes useful and cherished in other places to justify scientifically behaviors that affect morality. And while on the scientific front major battles are won and the bourgeois body emerges cleaned and purified, other fronts open up, running right through the body politic, and new territories turn into battlefields, not of hygiene and health so much as of social distinction and aesthetic differentiation in terms of the body.

In *Effi Briest* there is just a hint of this, and indeed literature is not the sole or even the main area to look for the expression of such concerns. For equally characteristic of the epoch is the increasing separation and specialization of the various discourses: health, hygiene, smell, and the body are treated outside literature qua *belles lettres*. It is in accounts of city planning, debates over sewage systems, advertisements for *Kneippkuren* and *Luftbäder* that the body is present down to its liquid and solid excretions. *Belles lettres* at the turn of the century are only *belles* because they exclude so much.

---

104. Cf. esp. Freud's essay "Die 'kulturelle' Sexualmoral und die moderne Nervosität" from 1909. He refers to a number of earlier accounts of the emerging phenomenon of nervousness. His explanatory model, which posits repressed sexuality as the major causal agent, could be applied to *Effi Briest,* although (or precisely, because) the novel, as we have shown, phrases Effi's problems in terms of a discourse largely free from—open—sexuality.

105. For a connection between the scientific and the philosophical and literary discourse of the time, cf. Michel Serres, "Corruption—*The Antichrist:* A Chemistry of Sensations and Ideas," *Stanford Italian Review* 6, no. 1–2 (1986): 31–52. Serres talks about the switch in linguistic code from religion to microbiology, religion *as* microbiology.

Within literature we only find traces, between the repressive lines of the bourgeois moral and aesthetic *comme il faut*. But bourgeois realism itself is splintering under the influence of the sociohistorical changes of the times. Naturalism has emerged as its critical heir, less prim and prude, and with a distinct social message. Decadence, its other offspring, has risen too, conveying the languor of the fin-de-siècle. And while naturalism at least looks at the workers, even if its perspective is one of looking down on them, decadence and its companion, aestheticism, turn the other way. Ensconced in their beautiful salons, "with the rich odor of roses" wafting in from their lush gardens, the new leisure class gives itself up to the pleasures of the senses, with its chroniclers focusing on just that. Decadence does not suffer directly from the harsh realities, the speed, the noise, and the stench of the workplace, the actual experience of the working classes, which *its* chroniclers, the naturalists, tend to focus on. Rather, the agony of decadence springs from the tension between having seen it all and the impossibility of making sense of it all.

We will focus on the turn of the century as a new epoch in the history of olfaction in the next chapter when we trace the epoch's French roots, as far back as Baudelaire. Before this, however, the literary and olfactory picture of the nineteenth century itself requires some touching up. Wilhelm Raabe's *Pfisters Mühle* serves us as an example of a literary text that actually takes into account the industrial and technological progress that is the hallmark of the second half of the century not only in Germany. In its open thematization of smell, in fact stench, not only in separate instances but as part of its central theme, this short novel marks a clear departure from the realist texts discussed so far. This is not yet, however, a departure toward aestheticism as we will encounter it in the following chapter. Rather, Raabe's text remains realist in its essential parameters, even if showing the flipside and the unpleasant consequences of the programmatic realist model propounded by Freytag. The Rothsattels' sugar refinery, in *Soll und Haben* a failed aristocratic, capitalist venture, is now becoming an ecological problem. It stinks. Raabe applies realist values and realist narrative techniques to a critique of realism itself.

The nineteenth-century spectrum needs amplification in yet another direction—a term here to be understood quite literally. A brief survey of Russian literature will provide us with the Eastern counterpart of what we will add for the West in chapter 3. Eventually, the French developments will be the ones leading the way into the twentieth century, while the Russian findings confirm and complement and vastly enrich our view of the nineteenth by taking the old-fashioned, realist literary use of smells to its limits, to places where the German authors never quite dared to tread.

Pfisters Mühle: "L'Odeur de Pfister"

Pfisters Mühle from 1884 with its quasi-documentary elements is an exceptional text within Wilhelm Raabe's oeuvre. Although Raabe does use actual places, occurrences, or accounts of events as models for plot or setting in others of his writings, in *Pfisters Mühle* he uses for the first and only time contemporary scientific and legal material in detail. He deals with a topic not only of immediate but indeed of great future importance; and he employs a representational strategy unique not only for his own writing but exceptional in the contemporary German literary landscape. The novel relies on the sense of smell to convey how Pfister is forced out of business by the operation of a sugar refinery and its ecological impact on the stream that turns the miller's wheel. It is the very ghastly stench that emerges each fall with the beginning of the sugar-producing season that first drives Pfister's customers away from the public house and beer garden that is part of his business and in fact the socially and emotionally relevant part for the old man. The role of olfactory perception not only as a descriptive but indeed as a plot-driving element is unusual in realist prose.

This becomes clear as we compare *Pfisters Mühle* with *Soll und Haben*, that quintessential programmatic realist novel of the age. It is linked through its motto to the important theorist and critic of bourgeois realism, Julian Schmidt, and, through both Freytag and Schmidt, to the *Grenzboten*, the very voice of bourgeois realist ideas and ideals.[106] *Soll und Haben* represents the poetic embodiment of a theory that is not only literary but political, moral, and cultural and has fused within one horizon the demands of art and those of life praxis, with the former adjusted to the latter.[107] For Hebbel, it was a horrifying thought to imagine that "Kunst und Gesellschaft verhalten sich jetzt zueinander wie Gewissen und Tun. Welch eine Zeit, wenn sie sich dereinst decken, wenn die Kunst gar nicht schöner

---

106. For a brief overview of some of these connections and for further reading, see Hans-Joachim Ruckhäberle and Helmut Widhammer, *Romane und Romantheorie des deutschen Realismus: Darstellung und Dokumente* (Kronberg: Athenäum, 1977), esp. 3–33. See also Denkler, *Romane und Erzählungen des bürgerlichen Realismus*, esp. 138–52.

107. Cf. Ruckhäberle and Widhammer, *Romane und Romantheorie des deutschen Realismus*, 40ff.

träumen kann, als die Gesellschaft lebt."[108] The implicit connection between ethics, *Gewissen,* and aesthetics, *Kunst,* and their relation to social
practice, *Gesellschaft,* which Hebbel still postulated for his time, at least as
a desideratum, once again links the three focal areas discussed by Eagleton.[109] Hebbel's horrific vision of a complete overlap of aesthetic values
and social practice, which is the inherent doctrine of 1850s programmatic
realism, rephrases the problem already underlying Kant's concept of the
aesthetic judgment, that strange compromise to get out of an intellectual
tight spot where ethical values, which can no longer be derived from social
practice, become, as Eagleton claims, de facto mediated in aesthetics.[110]

In the context of German bourgeois realism as outlined so far, *Pfisters
Mühle* is a subtly "subversive" text. Jeffrey Sammons has neatly summed
up the unobtrusive contents:

> an honest, hard-working miller and country tavern-keeper finds himself
> beset by the effluent of a sugar-beet refinery, which pollutes his mill-
> stream, clogs his wheel and drives off his employees and customers with
> its stench. He goes to law against the refiner, obtaining evidentiary
> material from a young chemist whom the miller had supported through
> his orphaned youth. The miller wins the case and is awarded an indem-
> nity, but this victory cannot save the mill, and he dies in the ruin of his
> way of life. The young chemist goes on to become a dry-cleaning entre-
> preneur. The story is told in reminiscence by the miller's son, who pays
> a summer vacation visit to the mill with his young bride just before it
> is torn down to make room for industrial expansion.[111]

"Described in this way," Sammons continues, "the novel does not make
an overwhelming impression." Indeed, Raabe's plots are generally not
characterized by extraordinary thrill, high drama, or adventure. Rather, his

---

108. Fr. Hebbel, *Tagebücher* 3, 5011 (1851); quoted in Ruckhäberle and Widhammer,
Romane und Romantheorie des deutschen Realismus, 42. "Art and society now stand to each
other in the same relationship as conscience and action. What a time that will be, when
one day they fully overlap, when art will be unable to dream more beautifully than society
lives."

109. *Ideology of the Aesthetic.* Eagleton's thought-provoking account informs my argument beyond the specific references made here.

110. Cf. Eagleton, *Ideology of the Aesthetic,* chap. 3.

111. Jeffrey L. Sammons, *Raabe: Pfisters Mühle,* Critical Guides to German Texts
(London: Grant and Cutler, 1988), 38.

narrative skills lie more in the subtle and varied handling of his narrator figures and multiple perspectives. It is the recognition of this fact, slow in coming, that has led to an increased interest in Raabe in the recent past and a thorough reappreciation of his work.[112]

We have referred to Eagleton's discussion of aesthetics on several occasions so far, and this novel, too, can be approached in terms of his thesis that "aesthetics is born as a discourse of the body" (13). On the one hand, the *body* is an evolutionary given that for our present purpose can be assumed to be beyond the influence of historical developments and changes; but on the other, as a type of *discourse,* it both drives and reflects sociohistorical changes. Let us deal with the latter aspect first. In the course of its historical unfolding, Eagleton sees "the law," the abstract sum total of the social and political power structures of the absolutist state of the sixteenth and seventeenth centuries, being padded and clad in the less obviously coercive and increasingly internalized structures of "habits, pieties, sentiments and affections" (20) of the emerging bourgeois society of the eighteenth and nineteenth centuries. This trend is understood as the aestheticization of the discourse of power, as a logical accompaniment of the unfolding teleology of reason and rationality and as the latter's attempt at reassuring itself of the bodies of its subjects, which in their concrete individuality threaten to elude its totalizing and abstract grip. For Eagleton, "at the very root of social relations lies the aesthetic, source of all human bonding" (24), and an important upshot of this claim in the course of the historical development of society is the harnessing of human sympathies to a formal articulation, "the law." If the aesthetic is indeed the realm in which human consent is elicited from the members of society, then the historical trend toward the aestheticization of power structures can be understood as a shift in the "ratio of coercion and consent" (23). Through

---

112. For an overview of these issues, see Leo A. Lensing and Hans-Werner Peter, eds., *Wilhelm Raabe: Studien zu seinem Leben und Werk* (Braunschweig: pp-Verlag, 1981), which contains accounts of Raabe research up to 1981 in various countries; Stanley Radcliffe, "Raabe—und kein Ende," *German Life and Letters,* July 1989, 384–93, a review article of Jeffrey Sammons's *Wilhelm Raabe: The Fiction of the Alternative Community* that draws some useful historical connections; Horst Denkler, *Wilhelm Raabe: Legende—Leben—Literatur* (Tübingen: Niemeyer, 1989); as well as the various publications by Jeffrey L. Sammons. It is not my aim here to give an outline or a critique of recent Raabe research. However, the result of our investigation of Raabe's representational aesthetic strategies is in line with the more general re-evaluation of his work as essentially modern, critical, and less *gemütvoll* and idyllic than earlier scholarship, up to about the fifties, has tended to depict it. See also Denkler, *Romane und Erzählungen des bürgerlichen Realismus,* esp. 293–309.

the linchpin of *habits,* society's members have come to internalize and individualize the demands of "the law" through and as "beautiful action." This is the historical telos of aesthetics as a discourse of the body.

In *Pfisters Mühle,* where Raabe presents us with a piece of apparent historical and technological inevitability, the question has to be asked whether the novel, from the perspective of its protagonists, indeed reflects a kind of gracious acquiescence on their part in the ongoing changes. Are these figures colluding *in aestheticis,* through their ways of thinking, talking, behaving, with the very forces of the inexorably unfolding law of the land which, at this historical juncture, is that of an "Übergang[] der deutschen Nation aus einem Bauernvolk in einen Industriestaat," as Ebert has it in his diary?[113]

Before answering the question whether Raabe characterizes his figures' behavior as aesthetic in Eagleton's general sense of the term, in fact in partial answer to it, let us focus for a moment on the other component of Eagleton's claim for aesthetics as a discourse of the body, the body itself with its sensory surfaces and capabilities. This body, essentially unchanged in historical time and with its associated concept of the five senses largely unchallenged since its inception in classical antiquity, represents the inalienably particular and individual in the face of totalizing, generalizing reason and rationality. This body is tied into a debate of aesthetics in two ways: first insofar as aesthetics is understood as a kind of prosthetic device of reason in its desire to get a grip on the body, which, in its particularity, threatens to elude it. In this theoretical conceptualization aesthetics emerges as an important category of cognition in the historical phase of bourgeois self-constitution since the late eighteenth century. It is not accidental that the origins of aesthetic discourse in the German context with Baumgarten's *Aesthetica* from the 1750–58, date from this historical moment of coexistence of still largely absolutist political systems in the numerous principalities of the German territory and an emerging discourse of an enlightened intellectual elite. Almost from the start of this discourse the two chemical senses, taste and smell, are virtually barred from further consideration.[114] Touch as the short-range basis of long-range vision as-

---

113. Wilhelm Raabe, *Pfisters Mühle,* vol. 16 of *Sämtliche Werke,* ed. Karl Hoppe (Freiburg: Klemm, 1951–60; Göttingen: Vandenhoeck and Ruprecht, 1960–), 114. All subsequent references are to this edition.

114. Esp. by Kant, *Anthropologie,* and Hegel. For a full understanding of our discussion so far and esp. of Kant's endeavors in the concept of the aesthetic judgment to derive a claim to generality from subjective, individual acts of judgment, see Eagleton, *Ideology of the Aesthetic,* particularly chaps. 1–3.

sumes a kind of middle position; but it is clearly the senses of hearing and vision, as we have pointed out, that have dominated all efforts in the emerging discipline of aesthetics.

The second conceptual element in our analysis of *Pfisters Mühle* is Freud's footnote in *Das Unbehagen in der Kultur* already referred to, in combination with the fundamental concept of *Eros* and *Thanatos*:[115] bad smells signify repulsion, corruption, decay, and ultimately death. The underlying forces and the fear associated with them is of disintegration, of the dissolution of (both concrete, biochemical as well as figurative) bonds, which sets free odors. Our modern obsession with body odor and its commercial presentation as destructive of the individual's social life if not counteracted, is only a recent manifestation of this primordial nexus. Good smells, on the other hand, mean attraction, eroticism, sexuality, birth, life; they mean the creation of bonds. The modern perfume industry is explicitly marketing (erotic) attraction, irresistibility, charisma. The mythical force involved is Eros.[116]

If the aesthetic is a discourse of the body and the senses as Eagleton claims and if it is understood as the locus of ideology, in fact *is* ideological in its essence, then the fact that since the very beginning of an aesthetic debate in Germany the olfactory has been excluded can be seen as a reflection of ideology. As an exception to the rule, *Pfisters Mühle,* by thematizing smell in the literary environment of largely odorless prose in the second half of the nineteenth century, exemplifies this claim, and the publication and reception history of the novel provides confirmation in historical reality of what we have been arguing and developing in the realm of fiction and aesthetic theory so far. In effect, *Pfisters Mühle* in its contemporary literary surrounding reveals olfactory silencing as an ideological program

---

115. Freud's remark concerns the vastly diminished importance of the sense of smell brought about in man's dim evolutionary past by his assuming of an upright posture. Olfaction, Freud postulates, was once strongly linked with sexuality. Man's rise to an erect posture caused the downfall of olfaction from its sexual regulatory functions now that the (male) nose was no longer at the same level as the (female) genitals. In connection with man's rise from the ground see also Leroi-Gourhan. Prehension (the hand), apprehension (vision, oral, and nasal sense), comprehension (language) evolve as a consequence of man's erect position at an early evolutionary stage. The sense of smell could potentially develop into other realms of perceptual activity with a high degree of indeterminacy. However, it did not—neither in anthropological terms, nor in terms of the history of civilization. It remains, even if repressed, strongly connected with the erotic and the sexual. See esp. *Le geste et la parole* 1:76ff.

116. Thanatos and Eros are used here, if not identically, at least analogically to Freud's usage of these two figures of thought in *Das Unbehagen in der Kultur.*

quietly at work in the literature of bourgeois realism. Raabe puts the cards on the table: the stench of modern industry, both directly and indirectly, contributes to the disappearance of the romantic preindustrial past and is the hallmark of the future. At the same time, for an opportunist such as Asche, there is something positive and exhilarating in the stenches of modern industry. They are the very milieu in which he thrives. It may well be that it was the implied critique of the laissez-faire capitalism of the *Gründerjahre* through the medium of stench that, coupled with the bourgeois reading public's inherently negative valorization of smell, led to Raabe's difficulties in publishing *Pfisters Mühle*. The issue of smell, in any case, features explicitly in the exchange with his prospective publishers.

The manuscript is first rejected by Westermann, a rejection that, as Raabe sums it up, is due to the fact that "das Publikum behaupte, meine Bücher glichen einander zu sehr."[117] The second rejection, by Julius Rodenberg, publisher of the *Neue Rundschau,* occurs because the story stinks too much for his taste. Both publishers are right. Westermann (through Glaser) focuses on the nostalgic, "wehmütig" element that indeed appears on the surface of many of Raabe's works including *Pfisters Mühle* and rejects the text on this ground. Rodenberg is the more perceptive reader; he immediately picks up the olfactory as the new mimetic strategy and, deeply troubled, both personally and on behalf of his readership, refuses to publish the book.

Revealing for us is the letter accompanying Rodenberg's rejection of the manuscript, and it is worth quoting in full:

Zu meinem großen Bedauern muß ich mich nun freilich doch entschließen, Ihre Novelle zurückzugeben. Bis dahin, wo es in Pfister's Mühle übel zu riechen beginnt, war alles gut gegangen; aber über diesen Punkt konnte ich nicht fortkommen, so viel Schönes auch gerade noch die späteren Capitel enthalten. Es mag ein Vorurteil sein; aber es erging mir beinah ebenso, wie dem alten, braven Müller, dessen Figur so trefflich gelungen ist—ich spürte zuletzt nur noch diesen fatalen Geruch, der mir die Freude an Pfisters Mühle verdarb. Es soll damit nicht gesagt sein, daß jeder so denken und fühlen wird, wie ich; andere mögen anders empfinden, da das, was Sie darstellen, unzweifelhaft eine Tatsache des wirklichen Lebens ist und als solche vielleicht das Recht

---

117. The details of the events surrounding publication, see *Pfisters Mühle,* 520–22. Cf. on this issue also Sammons, *Pfisters Mühle,* 70f. According to Raabe, "the audience claims that my books resemble each other too much."

hat, dargestellt zu werden. Aber in Sachen des Geschmacks ebenso wie in denen der Moral, darf, nach meiner Meinung, der verantwortliche Herausgeber einer Zeitschrift so wenig wie möglich riskieren; umso weniger, als in dieser Art der Publikation der unangenehme oder zweifelhafte Eindruck nicht durch die rasche Folge neuer Eindrücke ausgeglichen, sondern durch den Zwischenraum von Wochen noch gesteigert wird. Diese Gründe haben mich bestimmt, Ihre Novelle abzulehnen, die mir im übrigen viele hübsche Bilder in der Erinnerung hinterlassen hat. (521)[118]

Rodenberg admits that what Raabe describes is "unzweifelhaft eine Tat-sache des wirklichen Lebens" but grants this fact only "vielleicht das Recht" to be represented in a literary text. This position goes beyond the programmatic realist doctrine of limiting literature to a horizon of social representation; it attempts to restrict this very horizon. First, Rodenberg admits the personal, even idiosyncratic nature of his decision: "Es soll damit nicht gesagt sein, daß jeder so denken und fühlen wird, wie ich." In so doing he also broaches the topic—which we cannot fully discuss here—of whether indeed judgments made in olfactory matters can be called aesthetic judgments in the first place.[119] This hesitation both on Roden-berg's and our own part to understand his decision as an aesthetic judg-ment finds justification in one alarming adjective, *fatal*. Rodenberg is prob-ably unaware that with this term he has hit on the original, primordial association of stench with death. His alarm at and rejection of the phe-nomenon may be the preconscious instinctual reaction that (not only) nineteenth-century bourgeois society draws on for its banning of the olfac-tory from aesthetic theory in general and from a role in literary mimetic practice in particular. The olfactory as the state of the radically uncivilized

---

118. To my great regret I had to decide to reject your novella. Up to the point where the bad odor starts in Pfister's mill everything had gone well. But beyond this point I could not go, despite the many beautiful moments in the following chapters. It may be my prejudice, but I felt almost like the good old miller whose character is so admirably drawn: I only smelled that fatal odor, which spoiled my whole joy in *Pfisters Mühle*. I don't mean to say that everybody thinks and feels as I do; others may feel differently, as what you represent is undoubtedly a fact of real life and as such has perhaps a right to be depicted. But in matters of taste as much as in those of morals the responsible editor of a journal must, in my opinion, run as little risk as possible, the more so as in this type of publication an unpleasant or dubious impression cannot be counterbalanced by a rapid sequence of new impressions. On the contrary, it is enhanced by the interval of weeks. These reasons have led me to reject your novella, which, apart from this, has left me with many nice memories.

119. See the discussion briefly outlined above in chapter 1, esp. footnote 34.

can be seen as a last hermeneutic niche free from aesthetic theory. As such, it constitutes both a potential and a threat. Due to its very nature, it allows us thus a glimpse at the mechanism of the Kantian aesthetic judgment, that individual pronouncement with its claim to universality. The olfactory judgment resembles the aesthetic judgment structurally so closely that we have to suspect this to be the very reason for Kant's exclusion of the former from aesthetics. For in the olfactory is revealed too directly and uncomfortably the irrational, primordial skeleton in the enlightenment closet so neatly cleaned out to make room for pure reason and rational judgment.

Rodenberg's decision does contain a general element, namely the aesthetic norms of the dominant realist doctrine of the time, which, while being silent about olfaction, casts it as negative by this very silence. The *vielleicht* with which he curtails the right of stench, this undeniable fact of real life, to be represented, can be read speculatively as a tentative opening toward a new mode of representation, the naturalist.[120] A second general aspect emerges in Rodenberg's assuming both aesthetic and moral responsibility vis-à-vis his readers and arguing that "in Sachen des Geschmacks ebenso wie in denen der Moral, darf, nach meiner Meinung, der verantwortliche Herausgeber einer Zeitschrift so wenig wie möglich riskieren." This juxtaposition of aesthetic and ethical concerns ties in with and confirms Eagleton's concept of manners as the ideological overlap between the two. What the bourgeois subject ought to do (i.e., what is right) comes down on it no longer with the brute force of the categorical imperative (Kant's or the Christian Bible's) but rather has, in the realm of taste, found its milder expression and arrives now as elegance, style, decorum, good taste, in short, as the bourgeois *comme il faut* (see Eagleton, 40ff.). Eventually, to strengthen his aesthetic and moral decision on behalf of his readership, Rodenberg turns, fully aware this time, to another quality of olfactory perception, its lasting memory component, by saying that in the serialization of a story such as Raabe's, "der unangenehme oder zweifelhafte Eindruck nicht durch die rasche Folge neuer Eindrücke ausgeglichen, sondern durch den Zwischenraum von Wochen noch gesteigert wird." To have his readers exposed for weeks, metaphorically speaking, to that horrible stench at Pfister's mill, is a thought unbearable for Rodenberg, who evidently knows of the haunting, lingering impression that a sensation of smell, even in the medium of the printed text, can leave. In concluding, he returns to

---

120. Cf., however, Sammons, *Pfisters Mühle*, chap. 6, 70ff., who raises this very issue of Raabe's naturalism, albeit from a different perspective from Rodenberg's.

the much safer mode of representation, safer both in aesthetic theory and in mnemonic actuality, visual images. In doing so, he also harks back to the leitmotiv of the novel itself, the question "Wo bleiben alle die Bilder?" raised for the first time as the opening line of chapter 6 (30). "Diese Gründe haben mich bestimmt, Ihre Novelle abzulehnen, die mir im übrigen viele hübsche Bilder in der Erinnerung hinterlassen hat." The noncommittal *hübsch* can be read both as a derogatory comment on the slightness of Raabe's writing as it appears to Rodenberg or, indeed, on the ease with which readers absorb and forget images—in contrast to odors.

Eventually Johann Grunow, publisher of the *Grenzboten*, accepts the novel. By the end of 1884, it is available in the journal and as a book.

A number of motives in the story reveal the kind of painful historical experience it deals with. *Pfisters Mühle* is a profoundly nostalgic text on at least three levels: it is nostalgic in its subject matter, the water mill.[121] By the 1880s the water mill is becoming technologically obsolete, which has profound effects on how it is perceived culturally. As long as the mill with its water wheel was the only technology available, it was culturally infused with and surrounded by magic, the uncanny; it was associated with the devil and appeared as the locus of strange and dubious events. The location of the mill, often outside the village or town, frequently somewhat secluded, according to the requirements of its water-dependent technology, undoubtedly contributed to this accretion of myths. Its location also explains the not infrequent existence of at least minimal accommodation and tavern facilities. As the mill was overtaken technologically by larger industrial enterprises, often steam-operated or later electric, the old water mill became, in a process of romantic retrojection, the locus of the "good old times"; an idyll (again, often due to its location in nature), a technological *locus amoenus*.

The novel is nostalgic in its technique of leitmotiv, the reiterated question "Wo bleiben alle die Bilder?" (e.g., 30, 63, 75). Images are emphasized throughout, and Ebert's diary, his "Sommerferienheft," can be understood as just such an attempt at recapturing past impressions, tightly interwoven with and abruptly interrupted by the events of the present.[122] It is "eine

---

121. Cf. on this point Günter Bayerl, "Herrn Pfisters und anderer Leute Mühlen: Das Verhältnis von Mensch, Technik und Umwelt im Spiegel eines literarischen Topos," in *Technik in der Literatur: Ein Forschungsüberblick und zwölf Aufsätze,* ed. Harro Segeberg, (Frankfurt am Main: Suhrkamp, 1987), 51–101.

122. This technique of cutting and pasting, reminiscent of film editing, is one of the more saliently modern features of Raabe's prose.

Täuschung des Menschen" to believe that "die Bilder der Welt um ihn her stehenbleiben" (42). Part of this painterly leitmotiv is also the metaphor of "Schönfärberei" (e.g., 40, "Schönfärber") that is used by Asche both as metaphor and reality in referring to his father, who is a dyer, but also has a tendency to paint things (too) nicely.

Pfisters Mühle is nostalgic on yet a third, the lexical and temporal, level: it is a *noch*-novel. In its whole verbal stance the text looks backward, situating itself at a breaking point in time from which the past is *still*—or indeed *no longer*—visible. The examples are legion, beginning with the very opening sentence: "Ach, *noch einmal* ein frischer Atemzug im letzten Viertel dieses neunzehnten Jahrhunderts!" (7, emphasis added; see also 10, 13, 80, and 81, 83, in connection with *Bilder*). This sentence, of course, also initiates the theme of air, breathing, and (absence of) stench that, in addition to the explicitly thematized issue of the foul odor, runs throughout the text in its verbal underground.

This quintessentially rural, idyllic world that is seen from a somewhat nostalgic viewpoint clashes with and indeed is destroyed by modern industry, narratively located in the Krickerode sugar refinery; the expanding city of Berlin; and the general economic and technological euphoria of the *Gründerjahre*. This modern world, "die Wissenschaft in ihrer Verbindung mit der Industrie," stinks, as Asche has it (60), and the visual and odorless world of realist (even if not realistic) aesthetics is beginning to reek. Raabe commits a double crime in associating stench with modern industry. He goes first against the dominant social trends and moods, the technological enthusiasm of the time, the ruthless money-making by the owners of the emerging industrial plants. Second he challenges the aesthetic taboo that surrounds the olfactory in his age. Raabe's critique, without being overtly political, hits a sensitive spot in the ideological underbelly of realist literary representation. His view is neither socialist, materialist, nor Marxist;[123] it is not based on class issues, nor does it require documentary efforts on the scale of a Zola to make its point. Raabe's critique is located in individual subjectivity and emotions, and it is expressed aesthetically in the novel medium of olfactory perception.[124]

---

123. The view of the factories as medieval fortresses, for instance, is politically not "enlightening" or critical (see below).

124. The novelty applies only within the German context. In contemporary French literature it is precisely the naturalists such as Zola who use the sense of smell as an essential tool for, above all, social characterization.

The stench caused by modern industry is tied to it with the inevitability of an indexical sign as smoke is to a fire. Water and air pollution are seen as the unavoidable consequences of progress.[125] The way of life associated with Pfister's mill is becoming a thing of the past. Raabe's text is not a rational critique of capitalist industry and its environmental and human costs; and the narrator's description of the refinery at Krickerode in terms of a medieval castle, "hoch aufgetürmt, zinnengekrönt, gigantisch beschornsteint" (99) and, explicitly as "das phantastischer als irgendeine Ritterburg der Vergangenheit mit seinen Dächern und Zinnen, seinen Türmen und Schornsteinen . . . aufragende große Industriewerk," (100) reveals more of a personal and emotional than an analytical attitude. The very fact that the miller's legal victory against the refinery is not able to reverse the tide makes it clear that legal, technical, and quantifiable issues are not at stake but rather psychological and elusive ones. This is corroborated by Raabe's finishing and publishing the novel before the legal proceedings in the case of Müller and Lüderitz versus the refinery at Rautheim, said to have served as the model for Pfister's, Asche's, and Riechei's efforts against Krickerode, were finally concluded. To show this outcome was evidently not Raabe's point. His point is the disappearance of a way of life whether or not there are legal, rational, and technological arguments in its favor. This is the resignative aspect of Raabe's tale; but at closer view there appear also positive, even if ambivalent, reactions in the protagonists. It is true: the old world, represented in Pfister and even in the poet Lippoldes, does not adjust to and does not want to accommodate itself with the new world. But the younger generation, above all Adam Asche (who carries the new beginning in his very name, as well as the ashes of the old order from which he rises like a phoenix) adapts remarkably well to the changing reality. (It is also Asche who will receive the miller's ax and thus become the symbolic heir of Pfister's old values.) The same holds true for Ebert for whom it turns out to be a blessing that his father let him find his own way outside the family tradition of the miller's profession. Together with his young wife Emmy, an urbanite, he establishes himself in the city as a teacher. Albertine, too, the poet's daughter, proves to be more resilient than one would at first imagine. We leave her as Asche's wife, expecting her fourth child (120), and it is not she, but rather her father who drowns

---

125. There is a contemporary debate taking place focusing on the former; cf. Bayerl, "Herrn Pfisters," esp. 80–85.

and floats down the mill creek (although Asche, in a Freudian slip, comes close to calling her Ophelia, 96).[126]

Asche emerges as the quintessential entrepreneur, not without a conscience, but with a conscience that has become detached from his actions. While he voluntarily helps Pfister to investigate the pollution of his mill stream, Asche admits freely his wish to go out and pollute a river of his own (67), and from early on in the story, he is associated with bad odors that are not a jot easier to bear by their emerging from a cleaning process (e.g., 51, 58). Asche appears as a tinkerer, an experimenter, a man of trial and error (e.g., 59–61), yet he also exudes the "Ruhe und Gelassenheit des Mannes der Wissenschaft" (89). His booming business in Berlin, where he resides in noise and stench (126–27), although at the cutting edge of technological innovation is, just like the refinery at Krickerode, explicitly associated with the Middle Ages and medieval architecture; and Ebert, the narrator, finds himself "grade wie bei Krickerode, vor gotischen Toren und Mauern" (126). Life continues, and the new generation finds itself in a new and changing environment in whose stench is intermingled the sweet smell of success.

Asche is also the quintessential modernist, unable to derive his values from his social practice. Appropriately, Raabe represents this ambiguous new situation in the new and ambiguous aesthetic medium, the olfactory. Asche's is a world of huffing and puffing, of "husten," "prusten," and "keuchen"; a cloudy atmosphere of "Gewölk" and "entsetzliche[m] Dunst" that takes one's breath away (57–58); it is a world of "Atemnot" (e.g., 170). While moral ambiguity is thus permeating the atmosphere, the spirit of capitalism is corrupting the soil, the very base of the new generation that finds no harm in the idea, repeatedly expressed by Asche, by Riechei (to old Pfister, 117), and even by Emmy (118), of investing in the sugar refinery, in order to get at least something out of the destruction of one world by joining forces with its very destroyer.

The medium of the olfactory lends itself like no other to the representation of transgression and the blurring of borders that is thematized in the proverbial *non olet* (Asche referring to his dry-cleaning business, 141). This shortest of formulas for obliterating the link of cause and effect, for erasing the traces from raw material to finished product, points to an essentially aesthetic process. *Non olet* puts a fine point on the capitalist transformation

---

126. Cf. the allusions to Shakespeare and the play on the letters *A* and *O*, Albertine and Ophelia, alpha and omega, the beginning and the end, 96.

of matter—any matter, indeed excrement will do—into money, the transmogrification of the concrete good with all its sensory qualities, pleasant or unpleasant, into the universal, nonsensory, abstract means of exchange, money.[127] Money is the ultimate sanitized commodity—and money laundering a term that in its metaphoric concreteness is particularly apropos for Asche's enterprise. "Making money" can be read as a process of aestheticization and money itself as the ultimate aesthetic object. As an empty signifier, it is the tempting place for power to reaffirm itself in its personification of kings, queens, and statesmen, and to imprint itself on coins and bills in lieu of the lost sensory qualities of the goods that once warranted the contract of exchange.

The new world is one of mixing and mingling where the smells of "Schwefelwasserstoff" and "Gänsebraten" (76, 77–78) combine to form the new atmosphere, where indeed the leitmotiv question for the images needs expansion to include odors: "Wo bleiben alle die Bilder und—die Gerüche in dieser Welt?" (76). Among Pfister's last words is the exhortation to his son to take care of his inheritance and of the two remaining servants who stood by him for better or for worse and "durch Wohlduft und Gestänke" (172) in this hopelessly mixed-up world.

Raabe adds to this cacophony of odors a mixture of opposite elements in the other chemical sensory modality, taste. Not only is the new age represented as a mixture of stench and perfumes, it is also a mixture of the bitter and the sweet. There is too much sugar in the world (65), and the very product of the Krickerode factory creates "Bitterkeit" (99) in its wake. Just a little prior to this, Adam snatches a forgotten "Zuckerherz" from the otherwise already empty Christmas tree, but then instead of eating it, launches into a tirade on the "Bitterkeit . . . auf dieser Lumpenerde" (92). Old Pfister himself, eventually, has nothing but a "sauersüßes Lächeln" left for his legal victory (143).

Life continues, and so does the story; its protagonists suggest collusion with the forces against which they are powerless, but to which they ingen-

---

127. Cf. the origin of the saying *non olet*, attributed by Suetonius to the Emperor Vespasian after the latter's introduction of a new tax on public latrines in Rome. He is referring to the first proceeds, odorless as they are. For a literary account of the explicit link between excrement and money contemporary with Raabe's writing, see the "Leviathan" chapter in Victor Hugo's *Les Misérables,* below. For a modern historical discussion and sources from the French context, see Corbin, *Le miasme.* See also Norman O. Brown, *Life against Death: The Psychoanalytical Meaning of History* (New York: Vintage, 1959). In chap. 15 he discusses the "filthy lucre" of money, its excremental connection, in capitalist society from a psychoanalytical perspective.

iously adapt. They reveal their mechanisms of coping essentially as the ideological invocation of *non olet* in an atmosphere that increasingly stinks. It is on the discourse level that Raabe challenges the reader with the resistances of the text and forces on him or her a new discourse couched in a new medium, the chemical senses, above all the olfactory; it is here that his modernity is confirmed.

"MOTHER RUSSIA, THE VERY SCENT AND SMELL OF HER"

Narrative literature, especially the realist literature of the nineetenth century, has its underlying geographical map that is rarely just geographical but reflects a host of other information as well. This is pointed out and exemplified by Russell Berman;[128] and Clifford Geertz uses the map metaphor explicitly as a model for the description of ideology as a structure of partial truths.[129] A combination of both these aspects, the literary geographical and the ideological, can serve us here to connect what has been said about German literature in the nineteenth century with what is to be said about a selection of Russian literature of the same time.

The European cultural and literary geography of the eighteenth, nineteenth, and even early twentieth centuries reveals major tensions along the two main axes of the compass: west-east and north-south. The former is the one relevant for us here. The enlightened Western nations England and France face the more backward German states of central Europe and the straggling countries further east on a scale of decreasing enlightenment. We have had a glimpse of this notion, translated into its nationalist and chauvinist form, in the attitude of Freytag's colonizing Germans and their disdain for their Polish neigbors to the east. We may add to this the midcentury expression of similar feelings by the writer Wilhelm Jordan, one of the Prussian delegates to the Frankfurt Parliament, who points out in a public address that "the superiority of the German peoples over the Slavs—with the possible exception of Russia—is a fact" and continues that "against such, I would say, facts of natural history, decrees issued in the

---

128. Berman, *Modern German Novel*, esp. chap. 1, "The Geography of Wilhelmine Culture."

129. Clifford Geertz, *The Interpretation of Cultures: Selected Essays,* (New York: Basic Books, 1973), 216, 220.

name of cosmopolitan righteousness will have little impact."[130] In the later years of the century—as Berman illustrates for Thomas Mann, and as can be shown for such twentieth-century authors as Gottfried Benn, among others—the tension builds increasingly along the north-south axis where a taciturn, inward-looking north is juxtaposed with a lively and outgoing south. Hölderlin represents an earlier version of this view, and so does Nietzsche. That the issues lined up along these geographical axes are different—largely social, cultural, political, economic in the west-east direction; more psychological, temperamental, artistic, philosophical on the north-south tack—does not matter for our purposes, as we are interested in one direction only and in one phenomenon, the olfactory in its literary manifestations and its ties to cultural parameters at large.

A first tentative hypothesis, then, leads us to posit the existence of an abundance of smells in Russian nineteenth-century realist prose. In the following we will test this hypothesis by examining some major Russian texts from the second half of the century and the first years of the twentieth, thus leading up to the following chapter, the investigation of turn-of-the-century literature.

There is a point on the west-east axis where Western and Eastern perspectives intersect, in Poland. In the Western, specifically the German view as we have developed it so far, Poland appears as a backward country, beyond which little is worth knowing. Jordan is inclined to give the Russians at least the benefit of the doubt, probably more on the strength of their military than their cultural forces. However, from the perspective of the East, that is, the Russian elite looking west, Poland appears in the sixties and seventies of the nineteenth century as an advanced place. It seems westernized, with all the negative consequences of decadence and nihilism.[131]

---

130. Wilhelm Jordan, quoted in Sheehan, *German History 1770–1866*, 688. For details, see Günter Wollstein, *Das "Grossdeutschland" der Paulskirche: Nationale Ziele in der bürgerlichen Revolution 1848/49* (Düsseldorf: Droste, 1977). Chap. 2, "Posen," contains excerpts from Jordan's speech and gives an immediate impression of the geographical-nationalist-ideological complex.

131. See for instance D. S. Mirsky, *A History of Russian Literature,* ed. Francis J. Whitfield (1926; rev. 1949; New York: Knopf, 1960), 282. See also the characterization of the Poles in *The Brothers Karamazov* as affected, snobbish, and pompous frauds. Fyodor Dostoevsky, *The Brothers Karamazov,* ed. Ralph E. Matlaw, trans. Constance Garnett, A Norton Critical Edition (New York: Norton, 1976), esp. part 3, where the Poles are shown during the events at Mokroe. All references to *The Brothers Karamazov* will be to this edition. On the East-West theme, Gogol has his own views, too. See chap. 5 of *Dead Souls* (1842). A more comprehensive study than ours would certainly have to

The theme of East versus West is of course itself the dominant parameter in the Russian cultural discourse of the time, both in literature and criticism and in social and political thought. It finds expression in virtually every major Russian novel in symbolic details as well as in the structural setup. Turgenev's Bazarov in *Fathers and Sons,* for one, cannot be thought outside the East-West theme on which is superimposed in this novel the account of a generation gap; the clash of realism and radicalism with romanticism; of progress and stagnation; of science and poetry; of old and new. Conceived by the first Russian writer to find widespread acceptance in the West as the account of a second-order observer who reports in fictional form, with just touches of hyperbole and irony, the novel stages a debate that is taking place in actual reality among such participants as Chernyshevsky, Dobrolyubov, Belinsky, and others, the modernizers, the radicals. It is a detail, but as such highly significant, that Arkady replaces Pushkin, the first modern Russian poet, with Ludwig Büchner, the popular German scientist, on his father's reading list. It is equally significant and testifies to the validity of the East-West dichotomic model—in fact, it points out a subtle historical and geographical detail in it—that there are tensions even among the older generation. In the brothers Nikolai and Pavel Petrovich a "Westerner" is facing an "Easterner." Pavel, however, in contrast to Bazarov, is an Anglophile; taste, style, class are English (or French, as the reader is made aware of in the numerous French language inserts) but not German. German is science, scholarship, and medicine, as so many doctors' names in Russian novels will confirm.

The attempts at westernization, begun programmatically and on a large scale under Peter the Great in the early eighteenth century, aggravate and perpetuate the distance between government and bureaucracy on the one hand and the still largely illiterate and medieval peasantry on the other, with only an exceedingly thin and now increasingly Western-oriented middle class in between. Westernization—the only intellectual game in town—finds its ideologically coherent opposition only in nineteenth-century Slavophilism, which in turn owes its existence at least partially to the influence of Western romanticism and the emerging nationalism in its wake. Both movements, westernization as well as Slavophilism, unfold with the emergence and consolidation of a social group not found in this form in other

---

include Gogol. His omission here can only be justified by limitations of space and the fact that his work was written just before the period focused on in this study.

European states, the Russian intelligentsia. In the broader sense, this group is composed of the small, educated, and professional class regardless of political convictions. In a narrower sense, the intelligentsia is the westernizing segment of this group, with the Slavophiles in opposition. To describe this group as similar in its role to the German liberal-critical bourgeoisie, minus its economic and financial base and its aspirations as a social class is, of course, to simplify matters dangerously (precisely because the question of a third estate is a crucial factor in the political and cultural developments of the time). And yet, it is with the intelligentsia that nineteenth-century Russian society finally begins to show features traditionally associated with enlightened bourgeois thinking—even if it is still largely lacking a bourgeoisie as such. In any case, the intelligentsia as a group is based on education and knowledge rather than on economic and property interests. For the German bourgeoisie both these aspects are constitutive—together with a third: the class's relative independence from the government bureaucratic apparatus, a criterion that does not apply to the Russian intelligentsia, at least not for its early stage.[132]

To return to geography: the different nature of the country's two capitals, Moscow and St. Petersburg, and what they symbolically represent, can also be associated with Eastern and Western attitudes respectively, as Sidney Monas shows.[133] Let us not strain the geographical metaphor, however, but rather complement it with findings more directly pertinent to our inquiry. We may safely assume a generally lower level of enlightenment penetration in the East (by which is meant the state of social and political structures and institutions; levels of urbanization and education; scientific, technological, and industrial achievement; economic, "capitalist" developments, etc.); there is no doubt about the backwardness of the "societal hardware," a huge gap in the middle of the social spectrum and thus between the living standards of the nobility and their peasants; there is a different sensitivity in social interactions (lord-peasant); there is a wide-

---

132. For this issue, see Nicholas Riasanovsky, "Notes on the Emergence and Nature of the Russian Intelligentsia," in *Art and Culture in Nineteenth-Century Russia*, ed. Theophanis George Stavrou, (Bloomington: Indiana University Press, 1983), 3–25.

133. For the symbolic roles of the two cities, see Sidney Monas, "St. Petersburg and Moscow as Cultural Symbols," in Stavrou, *Art and Culture*, 26–39. For a discussion of the intelligentsia from the point of view of its intellectual psychology, see also Isaiah Berlin, *Russian Thinkers*, ed. Henry Hardy and Aileen Kelly (Harmondsworth: Penguin, 1978), esp. "The Birth of the Russian Intelligentsia," 114–35.

spread mood of hopeless resignation among the latter, a situation that hardly changes even with the freeing of the serfs in 1861. Our inquiry, however, is concerned with these matters only insofar as they provide the raw material for narratives, and our focus is on the specifically literary-historical and aesthetic aspects of this situation, and in particular on the issue of olfactory representation.

We have pointed out that the olfactory undergoes a twofold development in the period under discussion in this study: insofar as it is tied to the material world of everyday reality, it is on its way to be purged in the overall unfolding of enlightenment progress. This progress appears as a "project of deodorization." Against this background the postulated higher incidence of olfactory phenomena in the East can simply be read as the immediate reflection of the material conditions of everyday public and private life, a reflection of the historical place of each country. On the other hand, in a more strictly literary and aesthetic sense, we will notice an increase in olfactory instances as the century draws to a close. This is the expression of opposite trends: of an artistic, aesthetic sensitivity; of decadent, sensualist concerns that deliberately draw on olfaction as a modern means of literary expression and creation. Both these aspects, mimesis as well as poiesis, operate simultaneously.

If our basic hypothesis, based in geographical distinctions in the advance of enlightenment, is correct, we may expect a fair number of olfactory instances of the old-fashioned, realistic type, used for the physical description of places and characters, social demarcation, and for the creation of atmosphere and milieu. This use may well extend into the realm of metaphor and thus help to characterize moral issues. Smells may emanate from places of physical as well as moral corruption, may accompany individual psychological decay as well as the decay of vegetable matter, and illustrate spiritual rot as well as people's rotten dwellings. Although this use of olfactory characterization takes the device from the mimetic to the metaphoric realm, it is still part of the older type of olfactory reference, tied to an essentially realist, mimetic mode of writing. Nietzsche's *Genealogy of Morals* is a good illustration of such a metaphoric use of the medium. It is, however, still worlds away from Baudelaire's or Huysman's handling of olfaction as a new, explicitly modernist aesthetic tool: not for the purposes of representation, but for those of presentation; not for description of something existing, but for the creation of something new.

First Love and *Fathers and Sons:* Fresh and Fragrant

Turgenev's *First Love* (1860) is a story that could easily be analyzed within the discourse that evolved in nineteenth-century German literature around the novella; in fact, *First Love* could serve as a perfect and sophisticated example of a frame novella fulfilling most of the demands, of structure as well as content, that have been made in that venerable generic discussion in German literature during the nineteenth and twentieth centuries.[134] The story's structural setup features a retrospective and reflective narrator who recounts in the first person (thus guaranteeing the authenticity of the material) a formative experience he had when he was a youth of sixteen. The events told are all part of that one "unerhörte Begebenheit," the "unheard-of event" that Goethe postulated as the nucleus of novella writing, and thus provide the story with a clear and limited focal area that is easily overseeable. Moreover, these events are crowned by a sharp turning point toward the end, followed by a short epilogue that serves to complete the frame even if it does not actually take the reader back into the narrative present but relates events that occur three or four years after the main story. The narrator learns in these last pages about his former love's presence in the same city and eventually about her premature death. *First Love* is a masterpiece—in the Western tradition. It is written by the first Russian writer who finds full recognition in the literary circles of the West. Turgenev had himself received an education in Western culture, spent a large part of his life outside Russia, and spoke French as easily as his native Russian. In *First Love* experiential realities (growing up, initiation, first love) are interwoven with narrative characteristics (the novella form, romantic nature elements, impressionistic touches) that are fully in tune with the essentially bourgeois sensibilities of the European readership of the time. The social classes represented are the landed gentry of the narrator's own family; the Zasyekins from the lower nobility, impoverished and a little disreputable; the soldier (Byelovzorov); the doctor (Looshin); the poet (Maidanov). They are all familiar to the Western reader of the 1860s, and so are the marital problems between the narrator's parents, the agonies of growing up, and the passions, both reciprocated and frustrated, that Turgenev describes. While *First Love* is undoubtedly a passionate story,

---

134. For an overview and a selection of exemplary statements on the German novella, see Josef Kunz, ed., *Novelle,* Wege der Forschung, vol. 55 (Darmstadt: Wissenschaftliche Buchgesellschaft, 1973).

passion is shown as individual and universal at the same time, which is part of Turgenev's achievement here. But it is a passion remote from anything Dostoevsky creates in this regard, the irresistible elemental force that appears as the characteristic of a whole nation, that passionate "Russian soul," which is much harder to feel at ease with, much more foreign and alienating for the European public (although no less fascinating) than anything Turgenev ever wrote. In many respects, then, Turgenev is the perfect Russian literary emissary to the West, a foreigner for Europe's reading public—yet not too much so.[135]

After these comments it is no longer much of a surprise to note that *First Love* contains few olfactory instances, three to be exact, and about half a dozen if we include the more atmospheric and metaphoric ones. This number in a text of eighty-five loosely printed pages is comparable with German texts from the period, and so is the thematic context of their occurrence, although a tendency seems to emerge (which, however, cannot be borne out statistically on this small data base) toward an impressionistic, psychological, erotic use of olfactory references rather than downright realist or naturalist descriptions.[136] The first occurrence is a good example for the association of smell and memory. Across the gap of about twenty-five years, as is revealed by a hint in the frame, the narrator Vladimir Petrovich is remembering his first love, the first moment of closeness with the attractive Zinaida Zasyekin, twenty-one at the time, and five years his senior. During a game of forfeits she is playing with a group of her admirers, the narrator finds himself favored by her over all his older competitors and has the honor of sitting "beside her, both of us under the same silk scarf; . . . I remember how both our heads were suddenly plunged in a close, fragrant,

---

135. His "Russianness" is much more in evidence in *Fathers and Sons;* the focus is on matters Russian, and they are presented in a very Russian fashion. Let me quote Isaiah Berlin to convey an idea of what is meant by this. Russia, Berlin says, was "an astonishingly impressionable society with an unheard of capacity for absorbing ideas." New ideas, when

> promulgated in the west, . . . sometimes excited their audience, and occasionally led to the formation of parties or sects, but they were not regarded by the majority of those whom they reached as the final truth; and even those who thought them crucially important did not immediately begin to put them into practice with every means at their disposal. The Russians were liable to do just this; to argue to themselves that if the premises were true and the reasoning correct, true conclusions followed. (*Russian Thinkers,* 124–25)

136. The edition referred to here and in the following is Ivan Turgenev, *First Love,* trans. Isaiah Berlin (Harmondsworth: Penguin, 1988).

almost transparent darkness . . . ; and I remember the warm breath from her parted lips" (45); and he also remembers that he "could scarcely breathe" as a consequence of this new and exciting closeness. At the outset of his story, which for the main covers a few summer weeks in the country in 1833, the narrator describes his mood of heightened expectation, his fermenting blood, his fluttering fancy and his anticipation of unknown events awaiting him. He admits that the image of women had "scarcely ever [taken] definite shape in [his] mind"; but he is full of a feeling of presentiment. "I breathed it, it was in every drop of blood that flowed through my veins" (23–24).

Heat, fermentation, and smell are also the components of our second scene, even if not in an erotic but in a moral sense. It occurs after young Vladimir has come to realize that Zinaida is herself in love—but with whom? He runs through all her admirers but "could not see further than the end of [his] nose" (60). Dr. Looshin, much older, yet himself one of Zinaida's admirers, understands his agony and warns him, "Can't you see what sort of house this is? . . . The atmosphere isn't healthy for you here. Believe me, you might become infected" (60–61). The narrator does not understand him even after he repeats his warning that "the atmosphere here is bad for you. . . . Hothouses smell sweet too, but one can't live in them" (61). Interesting here is the fact that corruption—in contrast to Dostoyevsky, as we will see, and more in line with the decadent imagery of Huysmans or even Thomas Mann—has the allure of warmth and smell. Dr. Looshin is himself "contaminated" by Zinaida's charms and the unhealthy atmosphere of multiple wooing, but for him, the "old bachelor," the member of a "hard-boiled lot" (60), it does not matter anymore. Yet there is a serious note in his concern for the youth.

The third example is "the scent of herbs" in the garden (83) during that one night the narrator decides to keep watch on Zinaida. He is utterly, almost feverishly excited, and "my blood was on fire and whirling within me . . . The night was dark, the trees scarcely murmured; a soft chill fell from the sky; the scent of herbs came floating across from the kitchen garden." This is the only instance where the use of olfactory metaphor is inconsequential beyond the level of adding realist atmospheric detail to the description. While the occurrence rings true, it lacks the intimate connection to layers of signification beyond the surface, otherwise so typical and consistent for olfactory references in general. It is true, but it is gratuitous and in fact out of tune with the romantic tone of the passage, resembling other romantic passages of nature description in the text (e.g., 46, 48, 56, 75).

Much richer in its polyreferentiality—inviting contrast with Stifter's *Nachsommer*—is our last example, a scene between the narrator and Zinaida in the garden, during which she is plucking "a small red rose" (75). She is changing, has been unwell, but is now just "a little tired" (75). The narrator, and the reader with him, knows that she is in love, and the reader—better than the narrator—knows, at least suspects, what is happening to the young woman. At this moment of vague emotions, presentiment, and secret passion, the rose unfolds its full and ancient symbolic potential: first as an object, plucked by the hands of the young lover; then through its color ("Zinaida lifted the rose to her face and it seemed to me as if her cheeks caught the reflection of its bright petals"); and lastly through its smell ("Zinaida gave me the rose to smell"), invoked at the moment when her relationship to the narrator is about to be fixed as one of friendship only. Love, with its sweet tremors that were felt before, is to be put aside once and for all (75–76). Finally, the rose serves as the seal on the changed relationship between the two, a "token of [the] new dignity" bestowed upon the youth, who receives the flower "in the buttonhole of [his] jacket" (76) and is thereby confirmed as the lady's page.

The olfactory coding in *Fathers and Sons* (1862) is more robust, partly simply because there is more of it than in *First Love*, namely over twenty instances in 160-some pages.[137] *Fathers and Sons* is set on a larger scale and firmly planted within concrete historical reality. It redraws the intellectual and generational faultlines of contemporary Russian society. The existence of the latter on that 20 May 1859—and throughout the whole story, and indeed beyond—is subtly hinted at in an atmospheric metaphor early on. Nikolay Petrovich is picking up his son Arkady and his friend Bazarov from the train. He soon finds himself divided from them in the carriage on the way home by the stench of the "thick black cigar, which Arkady began to smoke promptly, diffusing about him such a strong and pungent odour of cheap tobacco, that Nikolay Petrovich, a life-long nonsmoker, was forced to turn away his head, as imperceptibly as he could for fear of wounding his son" (10). More than a semicomical incident, the scene is symbolic both for the inconsiderateness of the younger, nihilistic generation, its insensitivity toward standards of politeness in word and deed, as well as for the insecurity of the older generation in dealing with educated, modern chil-

---

137. Ivan Turgenev, *Fathers and Sons*, ed. and trans. Ralph E. Matlaw, A Norton Critical Edition (New York: Norton, 1966). All subsequent references are to this edition.

dren. While the fathers would so much like to be proud of their sons' academic achievements, they do not quite know in what these consist. In this very scene, then, the reader sees and smells the traditional values going up in smoke, and the smokescreen being raised behind which the generation of the sons, aided by sharp words and loutish behavior, sets out to change the world. Or do they? The novel tells the story of their failure and of the old order asserting itself once again, in fact symbolically securing its future beyond the middle generation of Bazarov and Arkady: the youngest character is, after all, Nikolay Petrovich's and Fenichka's baby son Mitya. Bazarov, the only true modernizer—at least in word, if not in deed—dies; and Arkady, who lacked Bazarov's authenticity from the start and was mostly aping him, regresses into an undistinguished married existence.

These generational differences, but also individual personalities, are olfactorily coded by Turgenev, subtly but consistently, and with conscious play on the allusive and elusive polyreferentiality of the medium. Pavel Petrovich is the most striking example. With his stiff, elegant correctness in dress and manners (11) he represents the older generation's Western type, while as a lodger on his brother Nikolay Petrovich's farming estate, he cannot fail but strike the reader as a kind of out-of-place dandy. His "perfumed moustaches" (11, but also 16; and "perfumed face," 116) are of immediate note and so is his lavish use of eau de cologne (25, 130, 134). In his unrestrained admiration of English manners he confirms the West-East decline of standards of social sophistication, a decline that Bazarov would like to annihilate but can do so only verbally. He calls Pavel Petrovich an "antique survival" (12) but admits a few lines further down that the English washstand in his guest room, of which he wholeheartedly approves, "stands for progress!" (13). Cleanliness and personal hygiene are associated with the West; and the fact that they are far from being widespread at the time is conveyed to the reader in their foregrounding by the author. Everything about Pavel Petrovich fits this analysis, and so does his portable bath and the fact "that he always smelt of some unusual, amazingly 'aristocratic' scent" (24).

On another occasion, "the cleanness of the room" and the "freshness of the bed-linen" make Nikolay Petrovich immediately think that "the woman of the house must be a German" (29). Although this turns out to be wrong, the woman, who soon after their initial meeting begins to work as Nikolay Petrovich's housekeeper, manages to bring "order into the household"—as well as her daughter, Fenichka (30). This young woman is also surrounded by an atmosphere of pleasant cleanliness; her room is "very clean and snug" and "smelt of the freshly painted floor and of camomile and hydromel" (27). There is no doubt: cleanliness and hygiene are Western, both in their striking upper-class foreignness and eccentricity as represented in Pavel Petrovich, as well as in their more down-to-earth, thoroughly positive, homey aspects shown in Fenichka and her mother.

Cleanliness is foregrounded and again associated with modern, western rationality for yet another person, Anna Sergeyevna Odintsov, the young widow of independent means with whom Bazarov falls in love. Turgenev draws her, as he himself points out in a letter to Sluchevsky, as a "representative of our idle, dreaming, curious and cold epicurean young ladies, our female nobility." While she would love "to stroke the wolf's fur (Bazarov's)," she would also like to "continue to recline, all clean, on velvet."[138] Indeed that cool, pleasant, touch-me-not environment Turgenev alludes to in the letter does surround her in the novel as a clean and fragrant atmosphere. The very entrance hall of her spacious house is "clean, everywhere there was a peculiar pleasant fragrance" (65); she is in the habit of taking fragrant baths (70) and loves to fall asleep "all clean and cool, in her clean and fragrant linen" (71). On the occasion of one of her meetings with Bazarov the atmosphere changes, however. "Bazarov got up. The lamp burnt dimly in the middle of the dark, fragrant, isolated room; from time to time the blind was shaken, and there flowed in the disturbing freshness of the night. . . . He was suddenly conscious that he was alone with a young and lovely woman" (77). Nothing comes of this situation. Bazarov's love for her is never reciprocated.

What about Bazarov himself? He is the controversial central character of the novel, about whom the critic Annenkov wonders in a letter to Turgenev, almost on the latter's behalf, whether to consider him "a productive force in the future or a stinking abscess of an empty culture, of which one should rid oneself quickly."[139] Of interest to us here is the ambiguity of the metaphor itself, for even if one got rid of the "stinking abscess," the "empty culture" on which it grew would still be in place, and the cure for contemporary Russian society, which the speech figure envisages, would be far from complete. After all, the novel does accomplish this very thing:

138. Turgenev to Sluchevsky, 14 (26) April 1862. Quoted in *Fathers and Sons,* 186.

139. Annenkov to Turgenev, 26 September (9 October) 1861. Quoted in *Fathers and Sons,* 177–78. The issue of how to evaluate Bazarov has been the most hotly debated aspect of the novel since its publication. For a contemporary response see Dmitry I. Pisarev, "Bazarov," *Fathers and Sons,* 195–218.

it disposes of Bazarov, yet shows the old—empty?—culture as largely intact.

This culture, lovingly drawn in Bazarov's fussy, concerned parents, has "a special sort of scent about [it]," as Arkady points out to Bazarov on the occasion of his visiting Bazarov's family and talking to him about "these little houses like yours." Bazarov, rather ungracefully, calls it "a smell of lamp-oil and clover" and goes on to comment on "the flies in those dear little houses. . . . Faugh!" (101). He detests this small-scale world, its warmth and old-fashionedness, and its smells. It makes him feel small and insignificant, and while his parents do not worry about their own "insignificance, [and] its stench doesn't sicken them," he himself feels "nothing but weariness and malice" (102). His general disaffection with the old world is not alleviated by the instances of pleasant smells that, though scarce, are strewn across the narrative to mark the countryside and country living at large. Thus the "couple of armfuls of dry and rustling but still green and fragrant grass" (101) that the two young men have thrown under themselves before starting the above discussion, evidently does nothing to improve Bazarov's mood.

It is the older generation that is aware of the good country air. Nikolay Petrovich enjoys "the sense of the fresh air in his face" (46) while walking in the garden to ponder his and Arkady's relationship. Vassily Ivanovich, Bazarov's father, invites Arkady "to come this way into the shade, to breathe the morning freshness a little before tea" (98). In contrast to this, Anna Sergeyevna asks Bazarov to "draw the blind" after he opens the window onto "the dark night . . . with its . . . faintly rustling trees, and the fresh fragrance of the pure open air" (76). The sensitivity for the finer details in both the cultural and natural surrounding is lost among the younger generation, and nothing has, as yet, taken its place. This perceptual inability produces an aesthetic deficit that has nothing to do with dysfunctional senses. On the contrary: Bazarov holds forth about his reliance on sensation and the material aspect of the world. "I maintain a negative attitude, by virtue of my sensations; I like to deny—my brain's made on that plan, and that's all! Why do I like chemistry? Why do you like apples?—also by virtue of our sensations. It's all the same thing. Men will never penetrate deeper than that" (104). Bazarov's ultimate failure, while sufficiently explicable in social and historical terms, is also a failure of aesthetic appreciation. A world in which Pushkin is replaced by Büchner (while reading the great poet still served Zinaida in *First Love* "to clear the air" [54] after Maidanov's miserable poetry) is not a world worth living in.

Finally, *Fathers and Sons* contains, just like *First Love,* a romantic rose scene that has, as it is secretly observed, some unexpected consequences. The scene takes place in the lilac arbor between Bazarov and Fenichka. She is resting there with her "heap of red and white roses still wet with dew" (118) because she feels, although it is still early, "quite weak from the heat." Their conversation has a light, bantering, yet covertly intimate tone that becomes more audible when Bazarov asks for one of her roses as payment for the small medical services he has rendered Fenichka's little son Mitya in the past. "'Which will you have—a red or white one?'" (119) Fenichka asks him, and he, of course, chooses a red one. After some more pleasantries, he invites her to smell the rose with him. "'Smell, how delicious this rose smells you gave me.'" And while "Fenichka stretched her little neck forward, and put her face close to the flower. . . . [t]he kerchief slipped from her head on to her shoulders; her soft mass of dark, shining, slightly ruffled hair was visible. 'Wait a minute; I want to smell it with you,' said Bazarov. He bent down and kissed her vigorously on her parted lips" (120). Every single symbolic quality we associate with "literary roses" is present here: their morning freshness; Bazarov's choice of a red flower; their smell and the closeness its simultaneous enjoyment forces on the two young people. Moreover, there is the erotics of the slipped kerchief, the soft shoulders, the mass of hair, everything, in short, that Stifter was afraid of and tried to purge from his roses by planting a strictly horticultural variety around his *Rosenhaus.*

The romance between Bazarov and Fenichka is not to be, for a "dry cough was heard behind the lilac bushes" (120). What Pavel Petrovich has seen and heard will lead him to challenge the young man to a duel—another more literary than realistic device at the time, and as questionable as Innstetten's duel in *Effi Briest,* even if more comical than the latter.[140] Bazarov survives, but dies a short time later from his infection after assisting in the autopsy of a typhus victim. Like old Johann Buddenbrook, he remains turned to the wall in his sickroom for most of the time (155). Anna Sergeyevna, with whom he desires a last meeting, brings a doctor with her, "a little man in spectacles, of German physiognomy" (159). Bazarov's

---

140. Jeffrey Meyers, "The Duel in Fiction," *North Dakota Quarterly* 51, (Fall 1983): 129–50 contains an overview of dueling in some major European novels. Regarding the case at hand, he writes: "By 1859, when *Fathers and Sons* (1862) takes place, duelling was no longer taken seriously by the younger intelligentsia, who are represented by Bazarov" (135). Karenin in *Anna Karenina* contemplates a duel with Vronsky but decides against it and characterizes the practice implicitly as uncivilized.

room is free from smells, but the atmosphere is one of disease and contagion. Anna does not take off her gloves and draws "her breath apprehen-
sively" in "this loathsome room" (161).

Bazarov dies the day after her visit; the "great peace of indifferent
nature" (166) takes him back.

Dostoyevsky: "The Odor of Corruption"

Isaiah Berlin is certainly right in calling Eastern Europe and Russia in the
1830s and 1840s and even beyond "intellectual dependencies of Germany,"[141] but nothing could be more wrong than trying to apply this
statement to the Russian *novel* as it emerged only a couple of decades later,
especially in Dostoyevsky: there is nothing comparable to his elemental
force, his systematic madness, his psychological intensity, or his descriptive
and evocative powers in the whole of German literature of that century.

The following short account cannot and does not attempt to do justice
to Dostoyevsky as the giant among, and most Russian of, the Russian
novelists of his century. Rather, on the more modest trail of our inquiry,
focused on all sorts of airborne matter, we will try to determine what kind
of olfactory aspects Dostoyevsky uses and to what effect. Limiting our
survey to *Crime and Punishment* from 1866 and *The Brothers Karamazov*
from 1879–80, two main areas present themselves: smells used to describe
the city of St. Petersburg in the former, and the "odors of corruption" in
the latter novel.

There is no doubt in the minds of readers of *Crime and Punishment* that
St. Petersburg, and almost everything and everybody in it, stinks. Yet in
numerical terms the frequency of olfactory instances is not much higher
here than in other nineteenth-century novels, thirty-some occurrences in
465 pages.[142] How is this impression created, then? It is the result of what

---

141. Berlin, *Russian Thinkers,* 136 and, almost verbatim, 122.

142. References for this novel are to the Norton critical edition of Feodor Dostoevsky,
Crime and Punishment, ed. George Gibian, trans. Jessie Coulson (New York: Norton,
1975). As always, these frequencies are meant to be mere ballpark figures as I am not
primarily interested in hard and fast statistics but much more in sensational, aesthetic
impressions; and second, the counting itself is difficult as decisions have to be made about
what to include, how to treat repetitions, how to deal with obviously figurative versus
concrete examples, etc. The references to Lazarus may serve as an example. The biblical
passage is alluded to four times (208, 221, 274, 277), but smell is explicitly mentioned only
on the last occasion, the actual quote from John 11. I counted it as one instance. At the

we might call Dostoyevsky's technique of the synaesthesia of the repulsive. This synaesthetic strategy has several components. The first is one of narrative perspective. There is very little distance, in descriptive and narrative passages above all, between the narrative voice and the central character of Raskolnikov. All perception is funneled through him and hardly any leeway is left for the readers to gain an independent foothold in and develop their own view of this narrative universe. Every sensation that hits Raskolnikov also hits the reader with equal and unmitigated force in the absence of an objectifying, corrective narrative voice.

Second, the perceptual consciousness at the center of the novel, Raskolnikov's, is relentlessly exposed to the oppressive world, the loathsome environment, the poverty, misery, squalor of the St. Petersburg Haymarket area, described in realistic detail. This consciousness is high-strung to the point of breaking and seems constantly on the verge of collapse under internal and external tensions. A distorted, at times paranoid perceptivity and frequent panicked reactions are the consequence of this constellation.

Third, there are two evident reasons for the permanent state of high alert in which this perceptual consciousness operates. The first is simply that it is located in a body that is always stretched to its physical limits. Raskolnikov both eats and sleeps far too little and on several occasions rejects food or rest, thus aggravating his already precarious state. The second is the constant exposure of the perceptual and psychological apparatus to strong negative emotions of shame, fear, loathing, panic, and so on. The preoccupation with such feelings is bound to impair his perceptual capacities. Finally, in a symbolic gesture, even time is abandoned in this universe. Raskolnikov, on his first encounter with the reader, is setting out to pawn his watch.

What Dostoyevsky achieves by these means in this novel, and it is the hallmark of his writing altogether, is to appeal to his readers' feelings of simple human pity, their "bourgeois," middle-of-the-road sensitivities and values, their common sense—and at the same time to utterly frustrate them by making his hero completely impervious to them. How often is one on the point of calling out to Raskolnikov to have a bite to eat, to get some rest, to just calm down a little, and everything will look different! Each

---

same time, however, the odor of the corpse is something like a subtheme in Dostoyevsky; it is also mentioned on the occasion of Marmeladov's death (201); it is a major issue in "The Odor of Corruption" chapter in *The Brothers Karamazov* where it finds further mention in connection with little Ilyushechka's death.

time, however, Raskolnikov drives on, pushes further, and becomes more and more confused and delirious.

The characters' (Raskolnikov's in particular) blatant disregard of the elementary psychophysical connection between food, rest, and comfort and a person's perception of the world is what drives the reader himself or herself almost to distraction. Thus the relief, both the reader's and indeed Raskolnikov's, is tremendous on the rare occasion when he does something as commonsensical as eating: Nastasya has just brought him "something to eat, and he ate and drank with a good appetite, indeed almost greedily. His head felt fresher, and he himself was less restless than for the past three days. He even wondered for a moment at his former fits of panic" (373). Engaging the reader in a basic ontological concern for both the physicality underlying the novel's central perceiving consciousness and the squalor of its surrounding reality is Dostoyevsky's narrative masterstroke. Regardless of how intensely intellectual, psychological, or religious this engagement also is, it is always led back to the basic creaturely level of the hero. The following instances, with our usual focus on atmospheric and olfactory aspects, may serve to illustrate the point.

There is, first, an all-encompassing olfactory-atmospheric arch spanning the city and the novel. Throughout more than ninety percent of the text, not counting the epilogue, St. Petersburg is literally under the weather.[143] "The heat in the streets was stifling. The stuffiness, the jostling crowds, the brick and mortar, scaffolding and dust everywhere, and that peculiar summer stench so familiar to everyone who cannot get away from St. Petersburg into the country, all combined to aggravate the disturbance of the young man's nerves" (2). Add to this "the intolerable reek from the public houses, so numerous in that part of the city" (2), and the mixture is quite revolting. This spell does not break until 420 pages later when finally "heavy clouds began to pile up overhead, . . . and rain swept down in a

---

143. Let us not forget that St. Petersburg was the "Western," "decadent" of the two Russian capitals. Its detailed description by Dostoyevsky, who becomes increasingly conservative, religious, Slavophile in the course of his life, is also meant as a portrait of decadence and corruption. It also serves to illustrate the theory of social determination of character (Porfiry Petrovich is a representative of this school of thought), a theory from which the later Dostoyevsky distances himself more and more. Among odors, he has his personal favorites, those of lime, brick, and mortar as characteristic of the city. On a different, but no less personal note, see D. H. Lawrence's remarks on Dostoyevsky, made in a letter to Koteliansky, calling Dostoyevsky "a rotten little stinker," among other things. The passage, with Cox's comments, is found in Gary Cox, *Crime and Punishment: A Mind to Murder* (Boston: Twayne Publishers, 1990), 19. This savory morsel I owe to Ron LeBlanc.

deluge" (422). This break in the weather changes the atmosphere altogether, and a "thick milky mist covered the city" the next morning (432).
The narrative focus during that night is on Svidrigaylov, who is about to
commit suicide. He is "beginning to shiver" (425) in his wet clothes, takes
"a cramped and stuffy room" (425) for his last night, which "smelt of mice
and some kind of leather." His sensations are generally unpleasant; "he
could not eat anything," was "beginning to be feverish," and "felt an-
noyed." The room again "felt stuffy"; he "disliked the sound of trees at
night in storm and darkness! A nasty sensation!" and he cannot sleep. It
strikes him, who will be dead in a few hours, as strange that he is not
indifferent "to all these questions of aesthetics and comfort now" (427).
In the early morning mist, after nightmares and further discomfort, "Svidrigaylov pulled the trigger" (433). With the death of this last potential
witness against Raskolnikov, things could cool down for him; the air is
clear, and it seems he could begin to breathe freely again. At this very
point, however, he decides on making or, rather, having reached the state
of psychological exhaustion, simply makes a full confession of his murder.
His entering the police station will complete a second olfactory-atmospheric movement. Before looking at it, however, let us first point out a few
pillars that support, and occasionally remind the reader of, the grand arch
of heat, smells, and stuffiness overhead.

These pillars are planted at regular intervals so that the reader is never
for a moment released from the unpleasant atmosphere. For instance,
Raskolnikov is leaving his flat to go for a walk that will ultimately take him
back to the scene of his crime. Although it is already eight, "the heat was
still as oppressive as before, but he greedily breathed the dusty, foul-smell-
ing, contaminated air of the town" (132). The following is a dream in which
he revisits the murder scene. In this dream "the air was particularly stifling"
and he noticed "a smell of lime, and dust, and stagnant water" (234). In
the next instance it is Svidrigaylov who, in talking to Raskolnikov, notices
that the city has not lost its stench in the seven years since he visited it and
adds that he "found the town fairly reeking with its familiar odours from
the first moment" (407). The careful adverbial guidance ("as before"); the
reference to the already mentioned sources of smell ("lime," "dust"); the
adjective "familiar": all point to the permanence of the phenomenon—and
to Dostoyevsky's conscious use of the device in his composition.

The second olfactory-atmospheric circle is closed when Raskolnikov
walks up the staircase at the police station to make his confession and
notices that it "was as dirty and littered as ever, the doors of the tenements

still stood open, the same kitchens emitted the same reeking fumes" (445). When was this circle opened? It happened much earlier when he set out to the police station for the first time to settle some administrative detail. Upon leaving his flat then, "the heat outside was again overpowering; not so much as a drop of rain had fallen all this time. Again the same dust and bricks and mortar, the stinking shops and public houses, the drunkards everywhere" (79). At the police station he had noticed that "the staircase was steep and narrow and smelt of dishwater. All the kitchens of all the flats on all four floors opened on to the staircase, and as all the doors stood open almost the whole day, it was terribly stuffy." Inside "the nostrils were assailed by the sickly odour of new paint which had been mixed with rancid oil" (80). The passage on page 79 reiterates the atmospheric conditions and links them to the "ground movement" we are talking about now, which takes up the better part of the novel and connects page 445 with page 80.

Those two atmospheric arches spanning the novel are connected at yet another point in a different, more pneumatic way. The central figure in this link is Svidrigaylov. When he, who has overheard Raskolnikov's confession of his murders to Sonya from a room next to hers and who thus holds some real power over him, suddenly blurts out his "Ah, Rodion Romanovich,...every man needs air, air, air!...More than anything!" (371), he extends the atmospheric theme, concrete and factual so far, into the figurative realm—with a deeply ironic twist. For he, suggesting this "airing out," is the very person who can, through his knowledge, smother and annihilate Raskolnikov altogether. But it was a "strange time" that had begun for Raskolnikov after his acquaintance with Svidrigaylov; "it was as if a mist had fallen round him" (370). The air theme, in any case, resonates with him; he quotes Svidrigaylov to Razumikhin only a short time later (375), on which occasion the latter tells him that the alleged murderer (the painter) had confessed everything. Raskolnikov seems to gain some breathing space at this news. The subsequent meeting between him and Porfiry Petrovich lends initial support to this feeling until the air theme suddenly pops up again when Porfiry tells his interlocutor that he has "needed a change of air for a long time" (388) and in an uncanny echo a little later quotes Svidrigaylov literally: "'Now you need only air, air, air!'—Raskolnikov started" (389). Something is clearly in the air and Raskolnikov is beginning to buckle under the blows of Porfiry's "double-edged weapon" of psychology (e.g., 386). Although the news of Svidrigaylov's suicide seems to save him at the last minute, Sonya's face outside the police station drives him back: he is ready to confess, to start doing penance.

Much that has been said about Dostoyevsky's technique in *Crime and Punishment* applies also to *The Brothers Karamazov*. The olfactory atmosphere, however, is of an entirely different quality. Whereas in the former novel smells were concrete, realistic elements of Dostoyevsky's heavy descriptive machinery with symbolic or metaphsyical aspects only as secondary concerns, in *The Brothers Karamazov* their role is predominantly figurative. They are real smells, no doubt, but their primary significance is symbolic. This is a general development in Dostoyevsky's writing. In the later novel, he is evidently no longer concerned with creating a full-scale sensorily concrete city environment for the reader and for his characters to operate in, like guinea pigs in a cage, but is more interested in making emotions and psychological states visible in actions, interactions, patterns of behavior, and disquisitions without direct connection to the physical environment. There is no city in the first place. Mokroe is a peasant village, and the name of the town where most of the action takes place and the narrator and his characters live is revealed only accidentally, as it were, through a gossip paper. It is Skotoprigonevsk, "Stockyardville" (542). Whether we are to associate any smells with this place can remain open, but what is clear is that the real dramas have become internalized. The tendency from concrete to figurative, in fact spiritual, uses of the medium of olfaction can be supported by examples from Dostoyevsky's *Diary of a Writer*.[144]

The two central olfactory events in *The Brothers Karamazov* are the person of Smerdyakov (and, to a lesser degree, his mother Lizaveta) and

---

144. For these hints I am indebted to Ron LeBlanc. In the strange mixture of autobiographical, literary, and journalistic materials that *Diary of a Writer* contains, written over the period of the last eight years of the author's life, Dostoyevsky shows a tendency to associate bad smell with moral corruption. A few examples will illustrate the point. From "Bobok," 1873: "that stink we scent is, so to speak, moral stink . . . Offensive odor emanating from the soul"; from "To a Teacher," 1873: "the aesthetically and mentally developed strata of society . . . are attracted by the stink, much as Limburger (unknown to the people) is relished by a refined gastronome. Here there is essentially a craving for smearing, for the odor, for relishing the odor"; from 1880: "Sin is stench, and stench is dispelled when the sun rises." F. M. Dostoievsky, *The Diary of a Writer*, trans. Boris Brasol (Santa Barbara: Peregrine Smith, 1979). In *Notes from Underground* on the other hand (1864, two years before *Crime and Punishment*), the olfactory instances are—still—largely concrete. Both texts, however, create at times an atmosphere anticipating Nietzsche's *Genealogy of Morals* (1887). The *Diary* is similar in its explicit link of odor and moral issues; *Notes*, on the other hand, is full of that feeling of resentment, so central to the creation of morals in Nietzsche's underground workshop.

the title and central occurrence of the "odor of corruption" chapter.[145] We will return to them presently.

Apart from these two instances, however, the novel is quite poor in smells. Nature receives only few olfactory epithets; there is a "stinking pool" (88), actually "our stinking little river" (118); there are a few occasions of "fresh" or "cool" air (386, 412, reviving Mitya in both cases; 584, doing the same for Ivan); in one instance (from Father Zosima's biography as written down by Alyosha) "the days were . . . full of fragrance" (267). Several examples can be found that are used to characterize groups of people, one even with a certain West-East bias (an issue that finds fuller treatment in the prosecutor's speech during Dmitri's trials).[146] Thus old Fyodor Pavlovich calls Smerdyakov a "stinking Jesuit" (118), and Smerdyakov describes the difference between a French and a Russian scoundrel as "there the scoundrel wears polished boots and here he stinks in filth" (207). It is around Smerdyakov, naturally, that a kind of olfactory aura develops. Thus, Dmitri calls him "that stinking dog" (559), Ivan a "stinking rogue" (581); and he says of himself that he is "descended from the stinking one" (206). Smerdyakov, probably Fyodor Pavlovich's illegitimate son and thus the fourth of the Karamazov brothers, is a "repressed" character, discarded by his presumed father (in this he is indeed no different from Dmitri), shunned by all of them, and regarded with a mixture of disgust and superciliousness, yet some secret fascination.[147] This social outcast, born to

---

145. There is also the intriguing scene in book 4, chap. 6, "A Laceration in a Hut," followed by one "in the open air" in the next chapter. During Alyosha's visit, Snegiryov's wife, Arina Petrovna, launches into a reminiscence about a deacon's wife who used to visit her when her husband was still in the army. The dialogue she recalls is about women's clean or unclean breath. In Russian, however, there is no mention of "breath" but only "air," *vozdukh,* which is either *chisty* or *nechisty,* "clean" or "unclean." A visiting general, whom she asks about this matter, confirms that she "ought to open a window" because the air is not fresh, *nesvezhy* (185). The fact that the Snegiryovs' quarters are "stuffy," *dushno,* has already been mentioned (180). Despite the translation, the discourse is about air, even if in an atmospheric sense, as is also hinted at in the opening line of the following chapter, where Snegiryov, having pulled Alyosha outside, remarks: "The air is fresh sir, but in my mansion it is not so in any sense of the word" (185).

146. The prosecutor Ippolit Kirillovich associates the three brothers with three main intellectual types in Russian society. Ivan is the European enlightenment figure, Alyosha the man of the people, and Dmitri the representative of Russia in her essence, in her "very scent and smell" (663). This phrase provided the title of this section.

147. Fyodor Pavlovich likes to have him around at times and absolutely trusts his honesty (114). He engages Smerdyakov as his cook. If he ever had any misgivings about this appointment, he certainly displaced them. Fyodor Pavlovich "did not like the smell of cooking" (82). It could well be the cook himself, however, that he does not want to

"stinking Lizaveta," a "mentally disturbed street person," as we would call her today, and himself given the name Smerdyakov (from *smerdit'*, to stink), gives off, figuratively speaking, an offensive smell. It is ironic, but revealing, that his expenses for "clothes, pomades, perfumes, and such things" (114) cannot mask the symbolic stink that surrounds him and that is his very essence.[148]

Dostoyevsky could hardly have chosen a more apt metaphor than odor for Smerdyakov and his role in the novel. He is elusive and allusive (through his name, to the past with its secrets); he permeates the Karamazov household like, well, an odor. His epilepsy, the "holy disease" whose fits are often preceded by short moments of aura, of altered perception, adds to his existence a spiritual dimension. Moreover, he is born of a woman who is, in the view of "our gentlemen, drunken revelers," more "an animal" than a human being (88). The narrator, however, tapping the tradition of the "holy fool," speaks of her as "an idiot, and so specially dear to God" (87). Membership in the human race is questioned for Smerdyakov, too, when Grigory, Fyodor Pavlovich's servant who has raised the boy, complains about his ingratitude and calls him first a "monster" and then asks him directly: "Are you a human being?" and answers himself in the negative: "You are not a human being. You grew from the mildew in the bathhouse" (112).[149]

The issue of humanity is also raised for Father Zosima, although not with reference to the subhuman but rather to the superhuman realm of saintliness. Although in his case the smell is concrete, that of a dead human body, its implications are spiritual. In Christian olfactory symbolism a simple binary division exists with good smells (or none at all in this case) associated with goodness, if not saintliness, bad smells with moral corruption

---

be reminded of at every meal—and so has his meals prepared in the lodge, away from the main house, although a kitchen is available there.

148. This is the only reference to artificial, good, scents in the whole novel, apart from one other instance, where Dmitri, still an officer in those days, had just "scented his handkerchief" on his way out for the evening (102). Generally Dostoyevsky's selections of smell, not only in this novel, are from the negative half of the olfactory spectrum.

149. This offers a parallel with Süskind's smell-free hero Grenouille in *Das Parfum* (see chap. 5). Grenouille, too, because he is inodorous, has his humanity questioned. Dubious paternity, mysterious birth, and either absence or prominence of (metaphorical) smells arouse suspicion about a character's human nature. Grenouille will fabricate his own *odor humanis;* Smerdyakov, inversely, cannot get rid of his "stink" regardless of the great care he takes for his cleanliness, appearance, and use of perfume.

and the devil. The *skandalon* in Father Zosima's case is the unexpected, disturbing "odor of corruption" ("tletvornyi dukh") instead of the hoped-for "odeur de sainteté" emanating from the corpse.

Much is made of this incident; it "has been minutely remembered to this day" and has become "a stumbling block to many" in their faith. The narrator admits that he "would, of course, have omitted all mention of it" if it had not formed "a crisis and turning point" for Alyosha "in his spiritual development, . . . giving a shock to his intellect, which finally strengthened it for the rest of his life and gave it a definite aim" (308). Thus are the effects of smell as Dostoyevsky uses it here, mysterious, all-pervasive, unpredictable, unforgettable. But regardless of how extraordinary the smell issuing from Father Zosima's coffin appears to the people, death *is*—among many other things—an olfactory phenomenon, and Dostoyevsky's own writing contains a number of instances. Until the end of this study we cannot spare the reader a few more corpses.[150]

In *Crime and Punishment* Dostoyevsky pointed specifically to the odor emanating from Marmeladov's dead body, which, as "the weather is very hot and there is a smell" has begun to annoy the other lodgers in the building and is "taken to the cemetery chapel" until the funeral (201). In contrast to this case and, more explicitly, to Father Zosima's, Dostoyevsky comments on little Ilyushechka's death at the end of *The Brothers Karamazov* that it was "strange to say [that] there was practically no smell from the corpse" (728). The boy, by implication, is thus proclaimed a true saint, and Dostoyevsky asserts his notion of the innocence of children, a theme also expounded by Ivan in his talk with Alyosha about the injustice of children's suffering.

The issue is further thematized in the several references to the biblical Lazarus story in John 11 (*Crime and Punishment*, 208, 221, 274, 277) where Martha is giving her doubts about Lazarus's resurrection their strongest possible form by pointing out that his body already stinks. The odor of decay, the odor of corruption, the irrefutable evidence of physical death presents a serious obstacle to a belief in transcendental existence—but in its immateriality simultaneously provides a hint at such an existence. Smell is the liminal marker, the *meta*physical sense par excellence.

Odor mortis, I am afraid, is also the focus of the next section.

---

150. Especially the deaths, increasingly "smelly," of the various Buddenbrook family members in Thomas Mann's novel (see chap. 3, but also chap. 4, "The Stench of Power").

Tolstoy: "The Smell of that Striped Leather Ball"

> Death is before me to-day
> As the odour of myr / rh,
> As when one sitteth under the sail /
> On a windy day.
>
> Death is before me to-day /
> As the odour of lotus flowers,
> As when one sitteth on the shore /
> Of drunkenness.
>
> Death is before me to-day
> As . . .[151]

The East-West theme, specifically the topic of theoretical and technological modernization in agricultural Russia by means of Western techniques and equipment, is an important aspect in *Anna Karenina*.[152] Levin is the character around whom the issue is built, and in his role of an active landowner and farmer he also provides a counterfigure to the absentee landlords so common among the Russian nobility of the time. However, the novel does not, unlike *Fathers and Sons*, exhibit any olfactory coding of the theme; it is, in fact, an almost odor-free book. A few illustrative examples shall therefore suffice before we turn to *The Death of Ivan Ilych* (1886) and thereby return to our theme of *odor mortis*.

A first premonitory whiff issues from the shabby hotel room where Levin's brother Nicholas Dmitrich lies dying, another of the numerous "consumptive cases" (*Anna Karenina*, 446) whose end we witness in the nineteenth-century novel. The hotel is one of those places that have been arranged "after new and improved models, with the best intentions of cleanliness, comfort and even elegance" in mind but that has soon deteriorated so far that "these very pretensions [make it] worse than the old-fashioned inns which were simply dirty" (444–45). "In the dirty little room, its dado filthy with spittle . . . , and its air impregnated by the stifling smell of impurities," lies Nicholas, already far gone. He himself realizes that "it is dirty here, and it smells, I should think." Levin is helpless,

---

151. Adolf Erman, *The Ancient Egyptians: A Sourcebook of Their Writings,* trans. Aylward M. Blackman (New York: Harper and Row, 1966), lxvii.

152. Leo Tolstoy, *Anna Karenina,* trans. Louise and Aylmer Maude, ed. George Gibian (New York: Norton, 1970). All subsequent references are to this edition.

overwhelmed by "painful sensations," and says that "he would fetch his wife" (447). It is Kitty, whom he only reluctantly permitted to make the trip with him in the first place, who begins to clean up and take care of Nicholas. With her innate sense for the practical and her natural disregard for the proper, Kitty has no qualms about collaborating in cleaning up with Mary Nikolayevna, Nicholas's mistress, who is staying with him. When Levin returns from an errand to the doctor where Kitty has sent him to have him out of her way, "he found the invalid arranged in bed and everything around him quite altered. Instead of the foul smell there was an odour of vinegar and of scent, which Kitty—pouting her lips and puffing her rosy cheeks—was blowing through a little glass tube" (449).

Odors are—or once were, before they came under attack from public health, hygiene, and sanitation forces at work in the name of enlightenment progress—a natural phenomenon present at both extremes of human life, birth and death. They mark, as will be discussed in more detail later, both phenomenologically and symbolically the creation of human bonds (between mother and child, for instance) as well as their final destruction, their biological dissolution. We have already witnessed several instances of the latter kind; but *Anna Karenina* also contains one of the former. Serezha, Anna's and Karenin's son, about nine years old at the time, has been told that his mother is dead after she moved away with Vronsky. Serezha, however, "did not believe in death in general, and especially not in *her* death," and on every walk he takes he hopes to see his mother, who would approach him "and lift her veil. Then he would see her whole face, she would smile, embrace him, and he would smell her peculiar scent, feel the tenderness of her touch, and cry with joy as he had done one evening when he lay at her feet and she tickled him, while he shook with laughter and bit her white hand with the rings on the fingers" (476).[153] A broad sensory and emotional range is exposed in Serezha's longing (or, inversely, is drawn upon by the narrator to express this longing), with his mother's smell an important element of his desire for closeness, shelter, tenderness. Karenin and the boy's private tutor, however, have no feelings for this nor any understanding for his slow learning. The issue is discussed between the narrator and the reader and the former points out to the latter that "there were more urgent demands on his soul" than learning the names of the Christian patriarchs, for instance. Serehza "knew his soul, it was dear to

---

153. The olfactory reference in Russian is *"slyshat' zapakh,"* literally, "to hear a smell." It is a common expression, still used in colloquial speech. I do not know of any similar mixed sensory reference in either German, English, or French.

him, and he guarded it as the eyelid guards the eye, and never let anyone enter his heart without the key of love" (478). Karenin does not have that key, elusive as it may be, like a smell from Anna's warm and fragrant body.

The odors described in *The Death of Ivan Ilych* are from the opposite end of the spectrum of life, foreshadowing its end, premonition and warning simultaneously.[154]

Sequentially, Tolstoy organizes the story in two temporally reversed parts. We learn right at the beginning that Ivan Ilych, a government legal official who has spent many years in the provinces, but more recently has been living in St. Petersburg, has died. We learn about his wife's and his colleagues' reactions and follow one of them, Peter Ivanovich, on a condolency visit to Ivan Ilych's house. The second, longer part of the narrative is dedicated to a short biographical sketch of Ivan's career, marriage, and move from the provinces back to St. Petersburg, but above all to a detailed description of his sickness, dying, and death; to his slow, reluctant acceptance of the reality of his dying; and to the torments, both physical and psychological, brought upon him.

There is little true mourning or compassion among Ivan's colleagues when they learn about his death; their thoughts immediately turn to hopes of promotion and they assume that irresistible stance of the survivors, summed up as "the complacent feeling that 'it is he who is dead and not I'" (96).[155] Peter Ivanovich's condolency visit to Praskovya Fëdorovna, Ivan's widow, is marked by olfactory episodes. A "faint odor of a decomposing body" (98) is noticeable as soon as he enters the room where the dead man is kept; at the end we notice his appreciation of the fresh air "after the smell of incense, the dead body, and carbolic acid" (104). Life goes on—Peter Ivanovich arrives just in time at Fëdor Vasilievich's house for the second round of a game of whist (104)—but the odor lingers. Traces of it accompany Ivan throughout his illness in the second part of the story.

One of the issues initially at stake is to determine the nature of his disease, to give a name to his condition. The doctor is sufficiently vague, "said that so-and-so indicated that there was so-and-so inside the patient,

---

154. Leo Tolstoy, *The Death of Ivan Ilych and Other Stories* (New York: New American Library, 1960). All references are to this edition. Aylmer Maude is the translator of *The Death of Ivan Ilych*.

155. Elias Canetti in *Masse und Macht*, 2 vols. (1960; Munich: Hanser, 1976) has more to say about this. (English: *Crowds and Power*, trans. Carol Stewert [New York: Viking, 1962].) See chap. 5.

but if the investigation of so-and-so did not confirm this, then he must assume that and that. If he assumed that and that, then . . . and so on" (121). Throughout, the ultimate cause of the disease, human mortality, the fact that we all have to die, is never stated by the various medical authorities he comes to consult. It is the one great discovery he has to make alone and accept for himself; and it is all the harder as the terrifying possibility dawns on him of a life lived wrongly, of an existence wasted in conventionality and without any inner conviction. In the process, he is granted none of the alleviations (and illusions) that lie in "taming by naming," the sense of relief at having a label for the phenomenon and thus a certain control over it. Ivan's feeling of separation from everybody, his rejection of the human condition for himself, is expressed most poignantly in instances of olfactory and gustatory memory. At the time in question, Ivan recognizes "that he was dying, and he was in continual despair" (131). He remembers a syllogism from his schooldays: "'Caius is a man, men are mortal, therefore Caius is mortal'" (131). This

> had always seemed to him correct as applied to Caius, but certainly not as applied to himself. . . . he was not Caius, not an abstract man, but a creature quite, quite separate from all others. He had been little Vanya . . . with all the joys, griefs, and delights of childhood, boyhood, and youth. What did Caius know of the smell of that striped leather ball Vanya had been so fond of? Had Caius kissed his mother's hand like that, and did the silk of her dress rustle so for Caius? . . . "Caius really was mortal, and it was right for him to die; but for me, little Vanya, Ivan Ilych, with all my thoughts and emotions, it's altogether a different matter." (132)

Nothing can be more appropriate than the choice of an olfactory example to illustrate the point. Taste, as Proust shows, has similar characteristics. Both chemical senses are strongly and idiosyncratically linked to memory; "the smell of that striped leather ball" is something so inalienably individual and personal for Ivan that he is almost determined to claim an exemption for himself on the strength of it from the one certainty in human life, death. There is, in fact, an analogous gustatory incident that occurs to Ivan during his weeks of sickness. Pictures of his life are floating through his head.

> They always began with what was nearest in time and then went back to what was most remote—to his childhood—and rested there. If he

thought of the stewed prunes that had been offered him that day, his mind went back to the raw shrivelled French plums of his childhood, their peculiar flavour and the flow of saliva when he sucked their stones, and along with the memory of that taste came a whole series of memories of those days. (150)

But smell and taste phenomena also accompany his physical deterioration as irrefutable signs of decay, of that loosening of bonds which, as its last stage, produces an odor of corruption. Thus his special foods become "increasingly distasteful and disgusting to him" (135). It even seems to him that everything, especially his medicine, has a "familiar, sickly, hopeless taste." Even his tea acquires it, and with this realization "the pain also returned" (140). Ivan is embarrassed about the "special arrangements" necessary for his excretions, which are a torment to him because of "the uncleanliness, the unseemliness, and the smell, and from knowing that another person had to take part in it" (135). This other person is his servant Gerasim with "the even white teeth of a healthy peasant" (105) as Peter Ivanovich had noticed. He discharges his sick-nurse duties "with a firm light tread, his heavy boots emitting a pleasant smell of tar and fresh winter air" (135).

It is at the most basic level of breathing, drinking, and eating and the sensations of smell and taste associated with these essential vital functions that Ivan's deterioration is brought home to the reader (and, partially, contrasted with the aura of the healthy peasant). These sensory modes, generally thought incapable of abstract conceptualization and thus of artistic expression because too close to home so to speak, serve to integrate in their *literary* form the disparity between the concrete and the abstract, the individual and the general. Sensory and perceptual peculiarities (the strong memory component, the perceived bad tastes and smells) are results and symptoms of physiological processes. They signal with unmitigated immediacy both to the character in question and to the reader the seriousness of the former's condition, his existential individuality, and his impending end.[156]

---

156. In addition, there is also Ivan's screaming, which "was so terrible that one could not hear it through two closed doors without horror" (154). This he has in common with Kammerherr Detlev Brigge in Rilke's *Malte Laurids Brigge*. Brigge's death chamber, moreover, is full of smells and thus attractive for the Kammerherr's dogs. See chap. 3.

"Apple Fragrance": "A Smell of Honey and Autumn Freshness"

Despite being the recipient of the Nobel Prize for literature in 1933, Ivan A. Bunin (1870–1953), who lived in the West after 1918, does not have quite the stature of his great nineteenth-century narrative predecessors. His short reminiscence "Apple Fragrance" from 1900 is typical of his preference for shorter forms and an impressionistic style, not unlike Chekhov's at times.[157] "Apple Fragrance," although dealing with landlords and peasants, ubiquitous figures in all the Russian texts discussed here, has none of the social urgency or the clamor of contemporary political, philosophical, and psychological actuality. Instead, it takes us into the fin-de-siècle with its nostalgic, languorous reminiscences of the past and its narrative structure of an act of memory. It is saturated with the autumnal spirit that Mirsky must have had in mind when he called Chekhov "the autumnal genius" of Russian prose.[158] Indeed, the season in "Apple Fragrance" is the fall. " . . . I remember a fine, early autumn" (7), the opening sentence, including the ellipsis, sets the tone, and the "I remember" resonates through the text as its structuring device, calling up image after image, scene after scene of pleasant boyhood recollections by an unidentified male narrator from the landed gentry. It is a purely lyrical, atmospheric piece of prose, vaguely set during one autumn in a village called Veselki, but recalling many similar autumns and the passing of the years between them. Temporal progress is telescoped, its autumnal deposits superimposed on each other in this composite picture of which smells form such an important part.[159] "The fragrance of Antonovska apples is disappearing from the country houses. Those days were such a short while ago and yet it seems to me that a whole century has passed since then" (32). The flow of time is arrested in memory, and fall after fall, with their fires, the hunting trips, the eating and drinking, and the old books, is captured and condensed to the length of the story and recalled above all by its smells. Dominant among these is "the smell of Antonovska apples—a smell of honey and autumn freshness" (8). All the remembered scenes are set in the country-

---

157. Ivan Bunin, "Apple Fragrance" ("Antonovski Jabloki"), *Shadowed Paths,* trans. Olga Schartse, ed. Philippa Mentges (Moscow: Foreign Languages Publishing House, n.d.), 7–37. The title of this text is more commonly translated as "Antonov Apples." I chose this Soviet translation for its lyrical quality.

158. Mirsky, *A History of Russian Literature,* 354.

159. There are more than twenty olfactory-atmospheric references in this text of fourteen pages in its Russian, thirty pages in its loosely printed English version.

side; the smells recalled are those of nature; they are all pleasant, intrinsically so, or at least remembered as such by the narrator as he purifies and glorifies in the glow of his recollection the activities and objects from which they detach themselves. Even when the group of hunters, as it sometimes happened, returned with "[their] faces flushed, covered with dirt and [their] clothes drenched through and through with the stench of horse sweat and the hide of the run-down beast" (28), there is nothing unpleasant about it. For the house the men return to is bright and warm; there are lots of food and drink after which "you feel so deliciously tired, so sweetly drowsy" (28). The next morning would find one in bed for a long time and later on in the library where there was "a nice smell about those volumes, . . . a smell of old perfume and a pleasant tang of mustiness" (30).

It is common for the long-forgotten olfactory or gustatory experience, upon re-encounter, to trigger extensive memory-recall. What Bunin does here, however, is the reverse: an unknown cause has started the narrator's reminiscence, and as part of it he recalls a rich store of smells. A whole era, a whole way of life becomes thus infused with and described as a collage of odors. This use of olfaction lies somewhere between the strictly realist on the one hand, with scents clinging to and emanating from objects or persons in the actual fictional reality of the text (such as in Dostoyevsky's St. Petersburg), and on the other a use such as Huysmans (and other "decadents") will make of scents for the very creation of a fictional reality of the second order.[160] Bunin belongs to the older school of literary olfactorists by relying (like Dostoyevsky and the realists) on natural fragrances, whereas Huysmans (but already Baudelaire before him and later Huxley) use artificial scents—in fact emphasizing and relying on their very artificiality—for the creation of their aesthetic, political, and other effects.

With the richness of his olfactory vocabulary and its application in a text of remembered, impressionistic images and events, the Bunin of "Apple Fragrance" stands on the threshold to the modernist, more aggressive use of olfaction in narrative prose that we will discuss further. As such he can serve us here as a figure of transition into the twentieth century (as could his better-known contemporary Chekhov, whose short stories often have a similar lyrical and impressionist quality).[161]

160. The fictional character Des Esseintes in *Against the Grain* uses perfumes and a perfumer's tools to create a visionary secondary reality of summery fields and factory smokestacks for himself (see chap. 3). The reference is to Huysmans's chap. 10.

161. A detailed discussion of Chekhov would exceed the frame of this chapter, whose aim is an exemplary sampling rather than a systematic survey of olfaction. There is no

Before we step into the twentieth century ourselves let us briefly check the initial hypothesis for this discussion, the postulated "existence of an abundance of smells in Russian nineteenth-century realist prose." It clearly needs specification. There are indeed numerous olfactory instances in *Fathers and Sons,* fewer in *Crime and Punishment,* and really only one major olfactory complex in *The Brothers Karamazov.* Tolstoy, overall, is not very rich; and the "impressionists" seem comparable to their Western counterparts. This simple quantitative account, however, cannot do justice to the reader's subjective impressions (especially if he or she has been brought up on contemporary German literary fare) nor to our varied findings; only a qualitative-topical formulation adequately sums up the results. What is remarkable for each single author is the high awareness of the olfactory medium as such, resulting in its clearly focused, structured application to great descriptive effect. This is achieved, for instance, by synaesthetically compounding olfactory effects with other descriptive elements to create a vivid impression of the misery and squalor of the city; by the clear generational olfactory coding Turgenev uses; by applying olfactory elements in well-circumscribed thematic instances, such as the partial representation of death; by tapping the memory characteristics of the medium; or by representing through smells the symbolic and spiritual dimension in a religious or moral context.

All these aspects testify to the conscious and focused utilization of the olfactory medium in Russian nineteenth-century narrative prose. The overall impression for the reader, compared with that gained from our survey

---

shortage, however, of olfactory phenomena in Chekhov. One particularly vivid scene from *The Steppe* may suffice here as an example. The story is the leisurely, impressionistic description of a small boy's journey from his village to a distant town where he is to go to school. The trip on top of a peasant cart full of wool vividly traces the slow, uneventful, profound lostness of existence in the steppe. The scene occurs during a stop at an inn, when the boy's uncle starts counting a large sum of money he is carrying with him. The way the money, the rarest of commodities in the vast emptiness of the steppe, is shown lying on the table as "filthy lucre," with the soil, the sweat, the smells of the land where it grew in an almost organic process still clinging to it, is unforgettable. "Out of [Kuzmitchov's] bag fluttered whole packets of paper money.... Never in his life had Egorooshka seen such a heap of money as now lay on the table.... He looked at it now, however, unmoved, and was only aware of a loathsome smell of rotten apples and kerosene which emanated from the pile." While the boy tries to fight off his sleepiness after a tiring day, his vision blurs, "the flame of the lamp, the glasses, the fingers all seemed doubled; the samovar rocked, and the smell of the rotten apples became even more sour and loathsome" (Anton Chekhov, *The Stories of Chekhov,* ed. Robert N. Linscott [New York: Modern Library, 1923], 356–57). "Filthy lucre" is the term from Brown, *Life against Death.*

of contemporary German novels, is infallibly one of a more frequent and more impressive deployment of olfaction in the Russian texts. This finding may also be the reflection of a more physical, passionate, phenomenological (literary) approach to the world, and thus of a literary project that is not aimed at instilling a sense of law and order in its readers or at mapping good, bourgeois values and behaviors onto them by offering them models of identification such as Anton Wohlfart or Heinrich Drendorf. It seems, rather, that the Russian literary project of the second half of the nineteenth century is interested in questioning such (German) models by playing them through in the novel and taking their major philosophical underpinnings to their literary extremes, as so many of Dostoyevsky's characters do. This, infallibly, reveals their aporias.

CHAPTER 3

The Turn of the Century: New Nervousness and the Olfactory Explosion

Wer den Leser kennt, der tut Nichts mehr für den Leser. Noch ein Jahrhundert
Leser—und der Geist selber wird stinken.
—(Nietzsche, *Zarathustra I*, Vom Lesen und Schreiben)

As for the olfactory reference, Nietzsche is partly right, although it is not
stench but pleasant scents that begin to waft through the age; but he is
wrong as to the projected time frame. In the literary manifestations of the
Geist Nietzsche alludes to, the olfactory element becomes prominent already a few years after his pronouncement. In fact, smells and odors, scents
and stenches have begun to emanate from literature even before the moment of his remarks in the 1880s. There are authors such as Hugo (1802–85),
Baudelaire (1821–67), Zola (1841–1902), Huysmans (1848–1907), Wilde
(1854–1900), and, a little later, Proust (1871–1922) and Joyce (1882–1941),
in whose oeuvres the olfactory element cannot be overlooked.[1] And from
then on smells are to stay with us. The *spirit* of literary imagination and its
phenomenological reference system have indeed begun to reek. Literary
texts will now not only open our eyes and unplug our ears, they will also
penetrate our nostrils. The above list of authors for whom the olfactory is
an important descriptive element can be extended *ad libidinem*—with German authors now being a part of it: Schnitzler (1862–1931), Hofmannsthal
(1874–1929), and Rilke (1875–1926), to name but three great ones. They all

---

1. It is true, that "overlooked" is not the right metaphor for the sensory realm under
investigation here. It is, however, one of the numerous examples of the visual basis
underlying the sensory-metaphoric structure of language.

use olfaction as a signifying component in their textual strategies to an extent unimaginable for their bourgeois realist and Victorian predecessors.

The above names and the chronology underlying them reveal that French literature above all "raises a stink" before German literature does. In cultural discourse in general and literary criticism in particular, the olfactory, discussed from a variety of perspectives, first becomes a topic in France.[2] Thus the stereotypical view of the French by the Germans, or more generally, of Latin culture by the Germanic as more *sinnenfreudig,* more extrovert, more spontaneous, and better versed in *savoir vivre* with its strong hedonistic undertones, finds corroboration at this literary conjunction.[3] The interest in the senses, the sensory, and the sensual, however, is by no means limited to its hedonistic aspects. It already surfaced, as we pointed out in the preceding chapters, in such realms as medicine, sanitation, and both public and personal hygiene. But here too, it is the French who prove to be ahead of the Germans.[4]

The time lag between the emergence of smells in French literature and German literature must also be viewed in terms of different literary historical traditions. French realism and naturalism are not as distinct from one another as German bourgeois realism and naturalism are. French realist writing by such authors as Balzac, Flaubert, Zola, and Hugo, from its more romantic to its more naturalist brand, deals with a broader spectrum of reality than its German counterpart. Above all, French realism does not exclude the two topics that will become the focus of interest for German naturalism where it most directly opposes and challenges realism, first, the working class, the poor, the emerging city masses, and second, sexuality. The exclusion or at least explicit marginalization, as in Freytag, of these two topics in German bourgeois realism eliminates, of course, a lot of natural, realistic possibilities for smells and stenches. To state it positively: the more central position that the lower classes and sexuality and sensuality have in French realism makes phenomenologically plausible the existence of so many more olfactory instances in the French than in the German

---

2. There exists an early conference paper from 1899, *Les odeurs dans les romans de Zola,* explicitly linking literature and the olfactory. Léopold Bernard, *Les odeurs dans les romans de Zola.* Conférence faite au cercle artistique (Montpellier: Coulet, 1899). It is the first, if not the only, study known to me explicitly connecting smells and literature.

3. On eighteenth-century mutual (stereotypical) perception see, for instance, Mme de Stael's account, *De l'Allemagne* (1813).

4. Cf. Virchow's references to France and Great Britain as more advanced in terms of social hygiene and statistical data on epidemics, birth- and mortality rates, and so on. For a more recent account see also Corbin, *Le miasme.*

context. This model works as long as we accept the premises of realism and mimetic representation. The turn of the century challenges them both.

Smell, then, present throughout the second half of the nineteenth century in French literature, emerging only around the turn of the century and more generally only after 1900 in German literature, enters literary description along two main lines. First, along the line of class and, by extension, of the general social, hygienic, medical, and sanitary conditions of a significant part of the population; and second, along the line of gender, sexuality, sensuality, the erotic. For both these openings we have been able to show first traces in the novels discussed in the preceding chapters. To these two inlets at the lower end of the social scale (sexuality, although not in practice, is nevertheless in theory—and certainly from a susceptible bourgeois Victorian perspective—considered as low and vulgar, and thus undergoes severe repression) must now be added a third at the very top of the social scale. We hinted at it in the discussion of Fontane's novel. The aristocracy and the wealthy bourgeoisie, the rich leisure class overtaxed by nervous strain, open themselves up to, in fact actively seek, pleasure, hedonism, and entertainment on a level and with an expense and lavishness hitherto unknown. Olfactory pleasures are increasingly part of this.

This chapter, focusing on great authors and well-known texts as did the preceding ones, will turn to German literature only in its second half after a review of some French texts. The pièce de résistance is J. K. Huysmans's novel *Against the Grain*,[5] marking the culmination of aestheticism and decadence. Its protagonist, Duke Des Esseintes, is going to be our reference in all matters sensual. He is the owner of an extensive library and, among other things, is an avid reader who makes no bones about his literary likes and dislikes. It will deepen our understanding of fin-de-siècle to look over his shoulder for a while and only then, having studied some of his books with him, proceed beyond the realm to which he is introducing us. For German literature Rilke's *Aufzeichnungen des Malte Laurids Brigge* represents most clearly the break with nineteenth-century bourgeois realism and the push toward twentieth-century modernist models of perception and writing as they are implied for instance in the works of Freud in psychology or Bergson in philosophy.

Our label for that time period as the age of "new nervousness and olfactory explosion" is only one brushstroke on a much larger canvas, but

---

5. J. K. Huysmans, *Against the Grain (A Rebours)*, introd. Havelock Ellis (New York: Dover Publications, 1969). All references are to this edition.

it is meant to outline a development that indeed characterizes the *fin d'un siècle* but marks, by the sheer inevitability of chronology, also the beginning of the next. The shift implied is the emergence of the modernist paradigm out of the bourgeois tradition.[6] From our phenomenological angle it is sufficient to define modernism as just that: the surfacing of the olfactory as an essential element in writing. Even this simple concept will allow us to point out important developments within the time period and national literatures covered in this chapter and make visible the line that leads from Huysmans and prior authors to Rilke.

One such development is the unfolding of the new story of the individual in psychoanalysis. There also begins to emerge a new concept of time and memory in philosophy through Bergson. And the years after 1900 witness the beginning of a new understanding of language originating in the famous lecture notes of de Saussure's *Cours de linguistique générale*, first put together and published in 1916. These events are not unrelated; in fact it is literature above all that draws their findings together, in the works of Proust and Joyce for example.[7] We witness in those years the spinning of

---

6. For a discussion of some of the questions in that context, see Monique Chefdor et al., eds., *Modernism: Challenges and Perspectives* (Urbana: University of Illinois Press, 1986). This collection of essays deals with the historical roots of the terms modernism and postmodernism. Cf. Chefdor, "Modernism: Babel Revisited?," Ihab Hassan, "The Culture of Postmodernism," and Clement Greenberg, "Beginnings of Modernism." Greenberg stresses the French roots of modernism, a view with which our findings so far concur, addresses the issue of various strands of modernism (cf. Berman, "Modernism, Fascism, and the Institution of Literature"), as well as manifestations of modernism in various arts and, as an outlook, criteria of distinction between modernism and postmodernism (cf. again Hassan's contribution). Since its successor and terminological derivative, postmodernism, has taken center stage, modernism itself has been frequently "revisited" and revised in recent research. And it is precisely questions as to their relationship (is it one of chronological succession, of conceptual opposition, or of representing two sides of the same coin?) that have directed renewed attention at the older of the two. Cf. Frederick R. Karl, *Modern and Modernism: The Sovereignty of the Artist 1885–1925* (New York: Atheneum, 1985), esp. chap. 9, "Modern and Postmodern, Modernism and Postmodernism," 401ff., and Huyssen, *After the Great Divide*. In the introduction Huyssen explains the "Great Divide" as the discourse that aims at maintaining a categorical distinction between high art and low mass culture. Adorno appears as the theorist of the "Great Divide policy." For Huyssen, postmodernism is the most recent challenge to that established distinction (earlier ones are the historical avant-gardes). This is the view we will by and large share. Cf. also recent work by Christa and Peter Bürger.

7. One cannot fail to notice that these three events and their offshoots constitute that part of the modernist heritage that everybody more or less agrees on and that spans the modernist core period from about 1900 to 1940. (For a more detailed account of much earlier modernist manifestations, going as far back as the 1850s and Baudelaire, see Green-

important threads that will be woven into the larger pattern of the next three or four decades.

While bearing these developments in mind, our analysis is not operating in a universe of purely intralinguistic cross-references, a forbidding world of differences among and hence meaning derived exclusively from textual signifiers. There exists an object world to which language, however precariously, refers. The linguistic grounding of smells itself regularly tears holes into the language network, hinting at the primacy of perception and clearing the view for a reality beyond. The need for circumlocution ("the smell of"), the fascination with a sensory object that acts as a filler in the interstices between subjects and objects and provides a medium, a *Fluidum,* around them constitutes to a large extent, I believe, the attraction smell has for a modernist approach to the world.

In the time from about 1880 to the 1910s, significant shifts take place in olfactory perception. First of all, smells *are* becoming a topic.[8] Second, however, there occurs a change in their perceptual structure. They are no longer mere object smells, but they enter into an interactive perceptual relation with that vibratory organism the modern human has become, breaking down borders of subject and object, transgressing present and past, linking immediacy and memory.[9] The key terms are *extase* (Baudelaire), and *dérèglement des sens* (Rimbaud). In the more staid Thomas Mann, for instance in *Tod in Venedig* from 1912, it will be the protagonist's

---

berg, "Beginnings of Modernism." As an isolated even earlier instance *Tristram Shandy* is frequently mentioned, more and more also in connection with postmodernism.) The three realms of psychoanalysis, time, and language are again at the center in the postmodernist debate, where they are discussed in their mutual effect on each other. In Lacan, Derrida, Heidegger and others, in psychoanalysis and poststructuralism, the various approaches are acting on each other. We may take this as a confirmation of our assumption that the phenomena commonly understood as postmodernism have indeed been an undercurrent of modernism all along, as Huyssen argues. (For a handy list of general "postmodern characteristics," see Hassan, "Culture of Postmodernism.")

8. There is an abundance of works dealing with smells in terms of psychology, sexuality, pathology, and human relations in general by authors such as Haeckel, Fliess, Ivan Bloch, Havelock Ellis, Krafft-Ebing, and Zwaardemaker. For a concise and highly informative essay on nineteenth- and early twentieth-century investigations of olfaction, see Stephen Kern, "Olfactory Ontology and Scented Harmonies: On the History of Smell," *Journal of Popular Culture* 7 (1974): 817–24.

9. Roger Shattuck, *The Innocent Eye: On Modern Literature and the Arts* (New York: Farrar, Straus, Giroux, 1984). In "Vibratory Organism: Baudelaire's First Prose Poem," 135ff., Shattuck goes as far as to argue that "the passage by Baudelaire contributed to a line of thinking and looking in Western art that would eventually lead to non-figurative or abstract painting" (143).

languorous slide down into the arms of Dionysos and death, desired and feared at the same time.

Decadence, fin-de-siècle, and aestheticism, the categories often associated with Huysmans, must be revalued for our purpose. Huysmans stands as much at the beginning of a new tradition of olfactory perception as he marks the end of an older one. Des Esseintes is an olfactory entrepreneur; he (still) uses scents as objects, as deliberate stimuli in his psychoartistic experiments. The olfactory landscape he creates is the laboratory practice piece before Malte Laurids Brigge applies his own perceptual sensitivities to the real world, where smells are immanent and transcendent at the same time, forming part of his natural universe.

Smell in literature has come a long way, mutated from "bad" to "good," promoted from masking to highlighting. Smells have entered both the science and humanities discourse and, in our very present, are emerging with unforeseeable potential in the economic and political sphere.[10] They have followed the dialectical pattern of enlightenment, where any given historical knowledge becomes an obstacle to and has to be cleared away by future knowledge. This is how Kant devised a role for olfaction, although he seems to have had some misgivings about its dialectical nature, which vacillates between epistemological and hedonistic functions. His ultimate dismissal of olfaction once it has served its enlightenment purpose now appears as somewhat premature. But by pitting epistemology on the one hand against hedonism on the other as dialectically opposed poles in the first place, Kant makes an important statement about where enlightenment puts its emphasis in the construction of meaning. It shows that the cognitive aspect wins out over the sensory or hedonistic, the intellectual gains over the physical, and the cognitive potential of pure sensate experience is notoriously underrated.[11] The distrust of the senses, let alone emotions, is endemic in our society.[12] Kant sees three senses as "mehr objektiv

---

10. "Search is on for Emotion-Eliciting Scents"; "So-called environmental fragrancing systems may be used to keep truckers alert on the road or to reduce anxiety in New York City's subways"; "Inhaling the right scent also makes workers more productive"; "The dark side is mind control." All quotes are from Alix M. Freedman, "Search is on for Emotion-Eliciting Scents," *The Wall Street Journal* 13 October 1988.

11. "Es gibt in userer Gesellschaft keinerlei Vertrauen in die Wahrnehmung." ("There is no trust in perception in our society.") Hoffmann-Axthelm, *Sinnesarbeit*, 13.

12. Everyday expressions such as "I couldn't believe my eyes" and "you can't trust your senses" testify to this inherent distrust, which is fed also by all kinds of examples of (optical) illusions as found in any textbook on perceptual psychology. There lies a certain intellectual satisfaction in proving one's senses wrong.

als subjektiv, d. i. sie tragen als empirische Anschauung mehr zur Erkenntnis des äußeren Gegenstandes bei, als sie das Bewußtsein des
affizierten Organs rege machen," and two as "mehr subjektiv als objektiv;
d. i. die Vorstellung durch dieselbe ist mehr die des Genusses, als der
Erkenntnis des äußeren Gegenstandes."[13] The olfactory is, of course, together with taste, located in the second group, its subjective and hedonistic
element stressed. Only begrudgingly, as it were, does Kant allow for a
certain amount of olfactory insight:

> Welcher Organsinn ist der undankbarste und scheint auch der entbehr-
> lichste zu sein? Der des Geruchs. Es belohnt nicht, ihn zu kultivieren
> oder wohl gar zu verfeinern, um zu genießen; denn es gibt mehr Gegen-
> stände des Ekels (vornehmlich in volkreichern Örtern), als der An-
> nehmlichkeit, die er verschaffen kann, und der Genuß durch diesen Sinn
> kann immer auch nur flüchtig und vorübergehend sein, wenn er
> vergnügen soll.—Aber als negative Bedingung des Wohlseins, um nicht
> schädliche Luft (den Ofendunst, den Gestank der Moräste und Äser)
> einzuatmen, oder auch faulende Sachen zur Nahrung zu brauchen, ist
> dieser Sinn nicht unwichtig.[14]

This role the sense of smell has played for centuries. It has contributed
in the seventeenth, eighteenth, and nineteenth centuries to the elimination
of the endemic olfactory ills of the big cities from Paris to London and
Berlin; and it has quietly served its enlightenment purpose. Now, however,
around the turn of the century, the tide is turning against Kant with an
increasing number of nervous contemporaries working hard to push olfaction into the aesthetic realm of *Genuss, Kultur,* and *Verfeinerung*—pleasure,
culture, and refinement, the very spheres Kant thought closed to it.

---

13. Kant, *Anthropologie,* 47–48. Three of the five senses are "more objective than
subjective" for Kant, "i.e., due to their empirical thrust they contribute to the perception
of the external object rather than emphasizing an awareness of the affected organ of
perception." The other two, however, are "more subjective than objective; i.e., the
impression they provide is more hedonistic than perceptive of the external object."

14. Kant, *Anthropologie,* 53–54. "Which sense is the least rewarding and the most easily
dispensable? The sense of smell. It is not worth cultivating or refining in order to enjoy
it, for there are more objects of disgust (especially in densely populated places) than of
pleasure; and the pleasure provided by this sense can always only be fleeting and transitory if it is to be enjoyed.—As a negative condition of well-being, however, in order not
to inhale noxious air (the smoke from heatings, the stench of cloacas and cadavers), or
not to eat rotting food, this sense is not unimportant."

The attempted enlightenment suppression, more accurately called by its psychoanalytical term, repression, forces us to undertake a brief detour through psychoanalysis. For Freud smell is, literally, only a footnote to his work. His view, like Kant's, is an enlightenment view that places the sense of smell in a teleological process that leads, in fact has already led, to its demise. The decisive step in this course of events, according to Freud's admittedly speculative remarks, occurs very early in prehistory when humans began to walk upright. The olfactory, before this event the guiding sense in man's sexual behavior, loses this function of regulating male-female attraction, which is taken over more and more by vision. The sense of smell, therefore, disconnected from its sexual function at such an early developmental stage, never undergoes the demands of civilization, namely sexual sublimation, the *conditio sine qua non* in Freud's concept of culture. He indeed discusses smell, this sensory relict from an ancient past, only as a passing phenomenon in the anal phase of childhood in accordance with the basic psychoanalytic tenet that individual human development mirrors the process of civilization at large. This, however, is not the whole story. A sensory modality as sophisticated as the olfactory and developed in an evolutionary framework does not simply atrophy once its central function of regulating sexuality is allegedly diminished. The loss of importance that Freud diagnoses is certainly not one of actual physiological capacities but rather one of social functionality. The sense of smell may be idling for millenia, but its presence is nevertheless felt, a fact Freud himself hints at when, in connection with childhood development, excrement, and hygiene, he points out that

> die Erziehung dringt hier besonders energisch auf die Beschleunigung des bevorstehenden Entwicklungsganges, der die Exkremente wertlos, ekelhaft, abscheulich und verwerflich machen soll. Eine solche Umwertung wäre kaum möglich, wenn diese dem Körper entzogenen Stoffe nicht durch ihre starken Gerüche dazu verurteilt wären, an dem Schicksal teilzunehmen, das nach der Aufrichtung des Menschen vom Boden den Geruchsreizen vorbehalten ist.[15]

---

15. Freud, *Das Unbehagen in der Kultur,* 458–59. "Education here places particular emphasis on accelerating the process that is to make excrement worthless, disgusting, revolting, and objectionable. Such a revaluation would hardly be possible if these bodily matters were not condemned by their strong odors to share the fate of all olfactory stimuli after man's rise from the ground."

It becomes obvious that in civilizational repression, in the attempts at eradicating smells, a collective unconscious fear of two things manifests itself and acts as the main reason for the low cultural status of that sensory mode: the felt threatening presence of that idle sensory modality, not harnessed to cultural usefulness by sublimation; and the shameful collective unconscious memory of (the female) genitalia and (the male) nose being on the same level.[16] The first is fear, the second is shame, and both feelings are present in Freud's account. In fact, they are still dominant in present cultural discourse where "b. o." is either a massive insult or the reason for terrible embarrassment or both. Thus deodorants have become the guardians of everybody's subjective and objective olfactory peace.

Adorno and Horkheimer in *Dialektik der Aufklärung* come closer than Freud—on whom they nevertheless build—to the essential functioning of smell and the combination of fear, shame, and desire that modern civilization associates with this sense.[17] "Von allen Sinnen zeugt der Akt des Riechens, das angezogen wird, ohne zu vergegenständlichen, am sinnlichsten von dem Drang, ans andere sich zu verlieren und gleich zu werden. . . . Im Sehen bleibt man, wer man ist, im Riechen geht man auf." This is a powerful comment on, for instance, Stifter's *Nachsommer,* in line with our findings. Horkheimer and Adorno continue:

Dem Zivilisierten ist Hingabe an solche Lust nur gestattet, wenn das Verbot durch Rationalisierung im Dienst wirklich oder scheinbar praktischer Zwecke suspendiert wird. Man darf dem verpönten Trieb frönen, wenn außer Zweifel steht, daß es seiner Ausrottung gilt. (165)

This is a concise summary of Kant's position. It seems that a combination of psychological and sociohistorical aspects, more precisely of the theses

---

16. Cf. Calvino's wonderful piece on early man, sniffing for his preferred female in the herd (chapter 5, below).

17. Max Horkheimer and Theodor W. Adorno, *Dialektik der Aufklärung. Philosophische Fragmente* (1947; Frankfurt am Main: Fischer, 1984). (English: *Dialectic of Enlightenment,* trans. John Cumming [New York: Herder and Herder, 1972].) "Of all the senses smelling, which is stimulated without objectifying, testifies most clearly to the urge to abandon and assimilate oneself to the other. . . . In the act of seeing one remains oneself, in smelling one dissolves." The continuation reads: "Civilized man is permitted such pleasure only when it can be justified in the name of real or seemingly practical purposes. The tabooed drive can only be indulged when it is unmistakable that such indulgence aims at its eradication" (*Dialektik,* 165). Cf. also 208, the reference to "Freud's genialer Ahnung" about the disgust originating in man's upright gait. Further references to the (a)social role of smell are to be found on 59 and 65–66.

offered by psychoanalysis and the thought patterns of enlightenment, can provide the most complete explanatory model for the cultural role of olfaction. The discrepancy between Freud's account of the anthropological and sexual function of the sense of smell and its diminished importance on the one hand, and the literature from his very day and age that tells a different story on the other, can be elucidated by juxtaposing his account with Horkheimer and Adorno's basic tenets.

Ernest Schachtel provides another extremely lucid complement to Freud with a direct bearing on our inquiry.[18] Starting from the problem of childhood amnesia, the fact that we can hardly remember anything prior to about our fourth year, he points out that while those first years of childhood are extremely rich in experiences, they are poor in terms of language, which, after all, we are only learning during that time. And in the process of language acquisition, we are imperceptibly pushed into the straitjacket of words, terms, expressions, concepts, the limited, in fact inadequate, set of verbal means available for the stunning wealth of a child's day-to-day discoveries. Schachtel's critique of Freud is based on the latter's exclusive focus on sexuality as the one and only formative force in those years. It does not seem "sufficiently clear why a repression of sexual experience should lead to a repression of all experience in early childhood" (285). The additional, more comprehensive reason lies in adult language and the memory that corresponds to it. "Adult memory reflects life as a road with occasional signposts and milestones rather than as the landscape through which this road led" (287). Experience "turns into a barren cliché" (289). The forces of convention and conformity inherent in, and socially exercised through, language lead to mnemonic blanks.

> Memory, in other words, is even more governed by conventional patterns than are perception and experience. . . . The object of memory has less chance than the objects of experience and perception have to penetrate and do away with part of that glass, colored and ground by the social mores and viewpoints, through which man sees everything or fails to see it. Memory is a distance sense, as it were, and—to an even greater degree than the two other distance senses, vision and hearing—less

18. Ernest G. Schachtel, *Metamorphosis: On the Development of Affects, Perception, Attention, and Memory* (New York: Basic Books, 1959). This study links psychology, language, and social forces as they bear on the individual, and establishes an explicit link with literature. All references are to chap. 12, "On Memory and Childhood Amnesia," 279ff.

immediately related to its objects than the proximity senses of smell, taste, and touch. (291–92)

Schachtel makes repeated reference to Proust and his preoccupation with precisely those lost landscapes of remembrance beyond voluntary recall. "Voluntary memory recalls largely schemata of experience rather than experience. These schemata are mostly built along the lines of words and concepts of the culture" (294). This "beyond" is what the (linguistic) artwork should aim at, according to Schachtel, thus helping to pry open the locked treasures of original experience, preparing new (actually old) ground for the human senses. He makes clear that "the quality of early childhood experience does not fit into the developing schemata of experience, thought and memory since these are fashioned by adult culture and all its biases, emphases, and taboos" (298). This fact affects sensory perception, especially the olfactory, because

> phylogenetically as well as ontogenetically the distance senses, sight and hearing, attain their full development later than the proximity senses. . . . The latter senses, especially smell and taste, are neglected and to a considerable extent even tabooed by Western civilization. They are the animalistic senses *par excellence*. (298)

Schachtel goes on to point out the central characteristics of the sense of smell, such as its anarchic component, its connection to earlier human developmental stages, its sharp contrast to vision and distance, and the social power constellations involved. "The emphasis on distance and the taboo on smell in modern society is more outspoken in the ruling than in the laboring class, distance being also a means of domination and of imposing authority" (300). He is even more explicit on that point in the following passage on Western society in general as one where "it becomes necessary for the society that remembrance of a time in which the potentialities of a fuller, freer, and more spontaneous life were strongly present and alive be extinguished" (320). Smell, for Schachtel, is a sensory mode that allows for "trans- or nonschematic," that is, fundamentally liberating experience. This is its most outstanding modernist feature, which sets it in contrast to bourgeois reality.[19] Such experience is a requirement for true art. "The

---

19. There is a twist of enlightenment irony in the fact that Freud in "liberating" childhood in fact creates a new layer of explanatory concepts that, while enlightening

artist, the writer, the poet, if they have any real claim to their vocation, must be capable of 'nonschematic' experience. They must be perceptive; that is, they must experience, see, hear, feel things in a way which somewhere transcends the cultural, conventional experience schemata" (317). This is precisely the claim made for the sense of smell in this study.

Before turning to Des Esseintes let us briefly trace some developments in French literary history that run parallel to German bourgeois realism but with different parameters. This digression will enable us to see the German situation in a larger context.

From Baudelaire to Rimbaud: "Des Senteurs Confondues"

Baudelaire's *Les Fleurs du Mal*,[20] published in 1857, takes us back to the very years where our inquiry starts, but puts us on a different track indeed from bourgeois realism. Baudelaire can be said to represent the very world, the very emotions, sensations, the very life that is cut out from the works of authors such as Freytag and Stifter. And indeed, Baudelaire's worldview, which is explicitly more than a view, an ocular phenomenon, relies on all the senses to an incomparably greater extent than contemporary (German) realist narrative does. A simple quantitative check confirms this claim easily.[21] Among the vocabulary pertaining to beauty and the body that is used in the 160 poems that constitute the collection, *oeil* (eye) is the most frequently used noun with 143 occurrences, followed by *coeur*, the heart (142); *beauté* (beauty) with 45 instances is ranked ninth, *corps*, (the body) is eleventh with 42 occurrences; *femme* (woman) appears in 34 instances, *homme* (man) with its more general meaning is hardly ever used for an individual subject and appears about 40 times. There are 3 occurrences of *nez* (the nose, of which only one has to do with smell, the others being fixed expressions, e. g., "le nez en l'air"), and *narine* (nostril) is mentioned once. These bare figures alone give us a first outline of the sensory geography, the landscape of the body mapped here.[22] Moving from the corporeal base

what they set out to enlighten, throw into even greater darkness alternative or competing views.

20. Charles Baudelaire, *Les Fleurs du Mal,* ed. Edouard Maynial (Paris: Société des belles lettres, 1952).

21. Robert T. Cargo, ed., *A Concordance to Baudelaire's "Les Fleurs du Mal"* (Chapel Hill: University of North Carolina Press, 1965).

22. As Baudelaire's main work is poetry, of course, it falls, strictly speaking, outside our sphere of investigation, and indeed, with the few remarks made here, I do not in any

to the objects of perception, including the verbs denoting perceptual activity, we find *parfum* mentioned 33 times, *odeur* 14 times (compared with *regard,* look, which occurs 19 times), *senteur* (smell, three times), *puanteur* (stench, once; the same frequency as the verb *puer*). The verb *sentir* occurs 21 times, but is used more frequently in its general meaning of "to feel" rather than "to smell." Moreover, there exists, not only for Baudelaire, an additional recessive or borderline vocabulary of atmosphere. From Baudelaire's poetry, definitely, "une senteur montait, sauvage et fauve."[23]

Baudelaire's is a sensuousness that does not shun olfactory phenomena.[24] The case for the sense of smell appears especially striking in Jean-Paul Fenaux's study on "Spleen et Idéal," the first and largest of the six parts of *Les Fleurs du Mal.*[25] Within those eighty-some poems *beauté* occurs 76 times, *parfum* 32 times, *odeur* 10 times.[26] Fenaux is able to outline a "corps du désir et des sens" (73), and notes specifically that

> organes des sens, verbes, object sensibles occupent en effet plus de trois cents termes, mais on observe un grand déséquilibre entre le goût et le toucher d'une part, et d'autre part la vue, l'ouïe et l'odorat. . . . La part

way presume to interpret or explain Baudelaire's masterpiece. I merely take him as a landmark at the gate of a new literary treatment of the body, the sensory-sensual, and aesthetics, and I am placing him (and later French poets from the Parnassian, symbolist, and decadent movements) in sharp contrast to his German contemporaries Freytag and Stifter in this respect.

23. "Le Parfum"; part 2 of "Un Phantome." From Baudelaire's poetry "rises a wild and savage odor."

24. Cf. also Lawrence E. Marks, *The Unity of the Senses: Interrelation Among the Modalities* (New York: Academic Press, 1978). In his last chapter, on synaesthesia, Baudelaire figures prominently.

25. Jean-Paul Fenaux, "Spleen et Idéal: Lexique et Thématique," *Analyse et Réflexions sur Baudelaire "Spleen et Idéal"* (Paris: Edition Marketing, 1984). This beautifully illustrated volume of short essays deals with a wide range of aspects of "Spleen et Idéal," but centers around the two terms *misère et beauté.*

26. Those figures include derivatives, such as *beau, belle,* etc. in addition to *beauté,* as well as verb forms; hence the higher numbers than in Cargo's *Concordance,* where each word is counted individually. Fenaux describes "a body of desire and the senses" ("Spleen et Idéal," 73). The following quote reads: "Sense organs, verbs, and sensory objects occupy in fact over three hundred terms; but what is noticeable is a considerable imbalance between taste and touch on the one hand and vision, hearing, and smell on the other. . . . The share of smell is no doubt exceptional. The number of occurrences of *perfume, odor,* and *smell* (46 altogether) is enough to give us an idea, but one cannot neglect an additional twenty-some instances of heady emanations where the poet gets into a quasi-toxicomaniacal extasy. These include *benzoin, incense* (9) also called *oliban; tar,* Havanna cigars, *musk* (4), and *myrrh.* Other *exhalations* seem less pleasant: *to stink, pestilence, stench.*"

réservée à l'odorat est incontestablement exceptionelle: les occurences de *parfum, odeur* et *senteur* (en tout 46) suffisent à la situer, mais on ne doit pas négliger, en outre, l'existence d'une vingtaine d'émanations entêtantes, où le poète trouve une extase quasi-toxicomaniaque. Ce sont le *benjoin*, l'*encens* (9) appelé aussi *oliban*, le *goudron*, le havane, le *musc* (4) et la *myrrhe*. D'autres *exhalaisons* apparaissent moins agréables: *empester, pestilence, puanteur*. (74)

Let us also bear in mind the following numbers: the eye is mentioned 61 times; *âme* (soul) has 34 occurrences, *corps* (body) 24; *pied* (foot) is used 17 times, as often as the terms used to refer to hair. *Volupté* (pleasure, voluptuousness) is mentioned 14 times, and *voix* (voice) 12 times, *main* (hand) 11 times, as frequently as *caresse* and *sein* (breast, bosom).[27] Fenaux's commentary, supported by these figures, makes one thing clear: the Baudelairian body is not aimed at scientific or cognitive experience, but is a sensual subject-object giving, as well as given to, both pleasure and pain. It is a body of desire and imagination, of eroticism. Despite the fact that the nose as a body part is virtually missing, the olfactory forms an important component of the sensual and hedonistic aura that is surrounding this body. Yet even in France Baudelaire's body is pushing against an invisible borderline of common bourgeois decency. Immediately after its publication, the first edition of *Les Fleurs du Mal* was confiscated and Baudelaire forced to remove 6 poems of the original 100 because they were considered immoral or blasphemous.

The following remarks about the writings of Stéphane Mallarmé (1842–98), Paul Verlaine (1844–96), Arthur Rimbaud (1854–91), and Guillaume Apollinaire (1880–1918) cannot be more than cursory observations indeed, providing some examples of the use of sensory perception by these poets. All I hope to show is the emergence of a new understanding of sensory perception that steers away from an object-oriented hermeneutic activity toward a subject-centered sensory-sensual event. This shift of representational paradigms can be read as one of the fundamental markers of (literary) modernity. It must be seen against the background of the older, much broader and still vital realist tradition of writing that continues unabated to this day. Romantic realism, a term occasionally applied to Balzac, for instance; bourgeois realism, the standard German term; and naturalism are all variations of that underlying broad and continuous stream. That the

---

27. All figures for "Spleen et Idéal" according to Fenaux, "Spleen et Idéal," 70.

new nervousness, the new sensitivity appears and develops first in poetry and only then spreads to prose is not surprising; in fact, it fits in with the most standard accounts of the three fundamental literary genres of prose, poetry, and drama and the characteristics traditionally associated with them. An almost exemplary transition stage is represented by Mallarmé's "Poèmes en prose," of which "La pipe" provides an outstanding example of the use of the sense of smell and its memory-triggering function; a different transition is found in Apollinaire's symbolist concrete poetry.[28]

The new conceptualization of the sensory-sensual event brings with it *désir* and *extase,* phrased in openly physical terms, a dimension that is clearly absent from bourgeois realism. (Even Keller's most daring scene in this respect, the nightly bath of Judith in the lake, is truncated.) It expresses the melting of two subjects into each other or, more generally, the imminent dissolution of the subject in the chaos of the world surrounding it, a world that is no longer constructed in the manner of a rational realist text.[29]

Suffice it here to list a few examples from each poet of the sensory mode under discussion. There is Mallarmé's "Renouveau" (34), where "Le printemps maladif a chassé tristement / L'hiver, saison de l'art serein" and the "I" says of himself: "Puis je tombe énervé de parfums d'arbres, las." Nerves, the scent of blossoming trees, a lassitude, later in the poem an "ennuie": this is Mallarmé's spring. Certain themes, leitmotivs of the second half of the nineteenth century, surface in nearly all the writers of the time, trends that cut across the borders of the movements to which the artists belong or in which they have been classified by posterity. The common vocabulary and common pool of themes includes nerves, nervousness, sensations, desire, and ecstasy, a keen sense of art and the artistic and aesthetic, as well as the artificial. These thematic commonalities have a parallel in the fact that most artists from symbolism, decadence, aestheticism, as well as the Parnassians and the impressionists both in poetry and

---

28. Stéphane Mallarmé, *Oeuvres complètes,* ed. Henri Mondor and G. Jean-Aubry, Bibliothèque de la Pléiade (Paris: Gallimard, 1945), 275f. Guillaume Apollinaire, *Calligrammes: Poèmes de la paix et de la guerre (1913–1916)* (Paris: Gallimard, 1925). Particularly interesting for our purposes is "La mandoline, l'oeillet et le bambou," 70. "L'oeillet," printed in the shape of a flower, is about the sense of smell: "que cet oeillet te dise la loi des odeurs qu'on n'a pas encore promulguée et qui viendra un jour régner sur nos cerveaux bien + précise & + subtile que les sons qui nous dirigent. Je préfère ton nez à tous tes organes ô mon amie. Il est le trône de la future SAGESSE."

29. For occurrences of the two terms, *désir* and *extase,* see Cargo, *Concordance* to Baudelaire; for Mallarmé, cf. "Prose (pour Des Esseintes)," *Oeuvres,* 55. For a similar moment of dissolution of the subject, see also Rilke, the "Verkleidungsszene" in *Malte.* The theme also permeates Mann's *Tod in Venedig.*

in painting know each other or at least read each other and comment on each other's work.[30] Thus Mallarmé's "Prose de Jeunesse II" is a reflection on Baudelaire's *Les Fleurs du Mal*[31] ("je me plonge avec délice dans les chères pages des Fleurs du Mal") and contains the following remarkable passage, an evocation of a landscape as seen under the influence of opium: "C'est le couchant. O prodige, une singulière rougeur, autour de laquelle se répand une odeur énivrante de chevelures secouées, tombe en cascade du ciel obscurci! Est-ce une avalanche de roses mauvaises ayant le péché pour parfum?" (*Oeuvres*, 263). His later "Poème en prose," "La pipe," structures smell as Proust does in the *Recherche*, including taste as a trigger of memory. The "I"-narrator states that after a long period of smoking cigarettes he is returning to "ma grave pipe" and goes on to describe the effect of the first few puffs:

Mais je ne m'attendais pas à la surprise que préparait cette délaissée, à peine eus-je tiré la première bouffée, j'oubliai mes grands livres à faire, émerveillé, attendri, je respirai l'hiver dernier qui revenait. Je n'avais pas touché à la fidèle amie depuis ma rentrée en France, et tout Londres, Londres tel que je le vécus en entier à moi seul, il y a un an, est apparu; d'abord les chers brouillards qui emmitouflent nos cervelles et ont, là-bas, une odeur à eux, quand ils pénètrent sous la croisée. (275)

---

30. For a short account of some of the interconnections among movements in France in the 1880s, see Philip Stephan, *Paul Verlaine and the Decadence 1882–90* (Manchester: Manchester University Press, 1974), esp. ch. 1, 1–16. For further links, especially with visual art and fashion, crafts, etc., see Gerhard Goebel, "Mode und 'Neue Kunst': Zum Beispiel Poiret," in *Naturalismus/Ästhetizismus*, ed. Christa Bürger, Peter Bürger, and Jochen Schulte-Sasse (Franfurt am Main: Suhrkamp, 1979), 175–89.

31. Following is the translation of the Mallarmé quotes in this paragraph. Mallarmé "is launching himself with delight into the beloved pages of *Les Fleurs du Mal*." From "Prose de Jeunesse II":

The sun is setting. Oh, what a miracle, a spectacular red, around which a dizzying odor of loosened hair is spreading, cascading from the darkening sky! Is it an avalanche of evil roses steeped in the odor of sin?

From "La pipe":

But I wasn't ready for the surprise the abandoned pipe had in store for me. Hardly had I smoked the first puff that I forgot the grand books I was going to write. Amazed and touched, I was breathing the smells of the past winter which came back to me. I had not touched my faithful friend since my return to France, and London, the London I had experienced all by myself in the past year, came back to me. First the beloved fogs that wrap themselves around one's brain and have a smell all of their own when they penetrate through the window.

The difference to Proust lies, of course, in the fact that Mallarmé's narrator forgets his "grands livres" whereas Proust's really only gets started on them . . .

Verlaine's case is different, but he leaves no doubts about two points made so far: his involvement with other literary figures of the time, for instance in his scandalous relationship with Rimbaud that certainly fully served, if nothing else, the purpose of *épater le bourgeois;* and his liberal use of the sensory-sensual element in his writing, both poetry and prose. His collections *Femmes* (originally published in 1890) and *Hombres* (posthumously in 1903 or 1904) leave nothing to be desired in sexual explicitness. As for smells, they are associated with the topic of both straight and gay sexual activities in various forms.[32] The poem most directly linked with our investigation is "Goûts royaux,"[33] but there are plenty of others. Here,

---

32. Paul Verlaine, *Femmes/Hombres,* trans. William Packard and John D. Mitchell, introd. Hugh Harter, illustr. Michael Ayrton (Chicago: Chicago Review Press, 1977). The publication dates are taken from the introduction, 21. The book is bilingual French-English and represents the first English translation. The poetry was suppressed for years and indeed as late as the 1930s was not included in Verlaine's collected works. Cf. Paul Verlaine, *Oeuvres poétiques complètes,* ed. Y. G. Le Dantec, Bibliothèque de la Pléiade (Paris: Editions de la nouvelle revue française, 1938).

33. "Goûts Royaux."

Louis Quinze aimait peu les parfums. Je l'imite
Et je leur acquiesce en la juste limite.
Ni flacons, s'il vous plait, ni sachets en amour!
Mais, o qu'un air naïf et piquant flotte autour
D'un corps, pourvu que l'art de m'exciter s'y trouve;
Et mon désir chérit, et ma science approuve
Dans la chair convoitée, à chaque nudité,
L'odeur de la vaillance et de la puberté
Ou le relent très bon des belles femmes mures.
Même j'adore - tais, morale, tes murmures -
Comment dirais-le? ces fumets, qu'on tient secrets,
Du sexe et des entours, dès avant comme après
La divine accolade et pendant la caresse,
Quelle qu'elle puisse être, ou doive, ou le paraisse.
Puis, quand sur l'oreiller mon odorat lassé,
Comme les autres sens, du plaisir ressassé,
Somnole et que mes yeux meurent vers un visage
S'éteignant presque aussi, souvenir et présage
De l'entrelacement des jambes et des bras,
Des pieds roux se baisant dans la moiture des draps,
De cette langueur mieux voluptueuse monte
Un goût d'humanité qui ne va pas sans honte,
Mais si bon, mais si bon qu'on croirait en manger!

the sense of smell (re)claims its very animal function in sexual attraction and stimulation. This role, however, is different from the one Freud will describe as lost a few decades later. Freud comments on the olfactory's diminished biological importance in regulating sexual behavior whereas Verlaine presents the triumphant (re)appearance of the olfactory as a part of sexual pleasure, quite unregulated in the physiological as well as in the sociolegal sense.[34]

The mention of Verlaine inevitably leads to Rimbaud, his lover and kindred spirit, his seducer and victim simultaneously. For Rimbaud too, the senses are the primary means of orientation in a world that for him only begins where for most any bourgeois *bonhomme* it ends. It is a world that does not make sense, but into and in fact through which the senses have to penetrate toward a vision beyond. "Je dis qu'il faut être *voyant,* se faire *voyant.* Le poète se fait *voyant* par un long, immense et raisonné *dérèglement* de *tous les sens.*"[35] The unleashing of the senses that Rimbaud propagates for the seer and which clearly includes the sense of smell in ways new and daring and untried so far has become reality in French literature of the 1880s and 1890s. It is found in poetry and shorter prose, as well as in theoretical statements, but it is also acted out in the daily lives of some of the figures mentioned, the *poètes maudits.* Parallel to this development, which originates in poetry and is essentially poetic in nature, runs a similar, if less revolutionary increase in matters sensory and sensual in the novel. In fact, "the naturalist novel, as it was handled by Zola and by the brothers Jules and Edouard de Goncourt, is of considerable relevance to the history of decadent poetry."[36] While the various movements—espe-

---

Dès lors, voudrais-je encore du poison étranger,
D'une fragrance prise à la plante, à la bête,
Qui vous tourne le coeur et vous brûle la tête,
Puisque j'ai, pour magnifier la volupté,
Proprement la quintessence de la beauté!

34. Noteworthy is the comment made by the Hansons in their defense of the collections against the stigma of pornography. "There is much of the schoolboy in these poems, a good deal of the poet too; one of the best ["Goûts royaux"] describes the various feminine odors and is, if the subject be admitted, beautifully written, full blooded, taut, expressive, and with a wealth of exact and original imagery." Lawrence and Elizabeth Hanson, *Verlaine: Fool of God* (New York: Random House, 1957), 234.

35. Arthur Rimbaud, *Complete Works, Selected Letters,* trans. Wallace Fowlie (Chicago: University of Chicago Press, 1966), 306–7. "I say that one has to be a *seer,* to become a *seer.* The poet makes himself into a *seer* by means of a long, massive and reasoned *deregulation* of *all the senses.*"

36. Stephan, *Verlaine and the Decadence,* 8.

cially naturalism, decadence, and impressionism—pursued slightly different approaches and goals, they all aim at the present, "and all three believed in portraying the subject as it is perceived by our senses, rather than in analysing it rationally" (Stephan, 10). In the framework of the numerous relations that existed among novelists and poets, painters and art critics, as well as within these groups; in all the cross-influences on a critical and theoretical level; in all the links of personal acquaintances, friendships, or enmities; in this whole, complex, creative breeding ground of modernity rather than in any of its isolated components must be sought the relevant developments for the emergence of the olfactory sense as a literary narrative tool.

After this excursion into the poetry of the 1880s and 1890s we are now better positioned to appreciate Baudelaire's sensory avant-garde position in the 1850s. A tentative comparison with the contemporary novel will confirm this view. It is easy to see that Baudelaire in *Les Fleurs du Mal* in 1857 is more modern in this respect than Victor Hugo in *Les Misérables* five years later.[37] And yet, Hugo, in turn, is sensorially infinitely richer and more explicit than his German contemporaries. His novel, in the vein of romantic realism of the Dickensian kind with an authoritarian, omniscient narrator leading the reader through an often literally labyrinthine plot, is much closer to the German and Russian novels of the time than are Baudelaire's poems—and yet, it is also a world away. The extraordinary "Book Two: The Intestine of the Leviathan" from the last part of that long novel is both the epitome of the bourgeois worldview and its complete subversion. The Western city, "Paris, die Hauptstadt des XIX. Jahrhunderts,"[38] reveals in Hugo's description its nether parts, its repressed lower body. "Paris has another city under herself" (1259). The narrative detour through this other city, the sewer system of the Western metropolis, sheds light on the flipside of bourgeois life, breaks down the social distinctions that are artificially created in the world above by adhering to a strict social *comme il faut*. It tells a story that is not told above, one of shit and stench, one of

---

37. Victor Hugo, *Les Misérables,* trans. Lee Fahnstock and Norman MacAfee, based on the C. E. Wilbur translation (New York: New American Library, 1987). The book runs to over 1400 pages.

38. Walter Benjamin, "Paris, die Hauptstadt des XIX. Jahrhunderts," vol. 1 of *Schriften,* ed. Th. W. Adorno and Gretel Adorno with Friedrich Podszus (Frankfurt am Main: Suhrkamp, 1955), 406ff.

"impurity and danger,"[39] where suddenly "in the humid haze, the rat appears" (1260), the animal of fear and loathing.[40] Yet at the same time, this underworld is presented by Hugo, tongue in cheek, as representing the epitome of bourgeois positivist, utilitarian, and entrepreneurial thinking: the subterranean mass of shit constitutes an incredible fortune.[41] Hugo, fully aware of the "filthy lucre" of money, presents the following simple equation: "If our gold is manure, on the other hand, our manure is gold" (1257), and fleshes it out poetically:

> This garbage heaped up beside the stone blocks, the tumbrils of mire jolting through the streets at night, the awful scavengers' carts, the fetid streams of subterranean slime that the pavement hides from you, do you know what all this is? It is the flowering meadow, it is the green grass, it is marjoram and thyme and sage, it is game, it is cattle, it is the satisfied lowing of huge oxen in the evening, it is perfumed hay, it is golden wheat, it is bread on your table, it is warm blood in your veins, it is health, it is joy, it is life. (1257)

But if excrement is money, it is also truth. The false appearances, desperately maintained in the upper world are unmasked, the high is jumbled together with the low, the respectable with what it despises. There is "more than brotherhood" in the sewer, there "is closest intimacy. All that used to be painted is besmirched. The last veil is rent. A sewer is a cynic. It *tells* all" (1262, emphasis added). Sewage and truth, sewage and narrative, the upper and the nether world: above, a mixture of discourses aiming at demarcation and supremacy—below, the truth of shit. "Above[,] the unintelligible, below, the inextricable; . . . Labyrinth underlay Babel" (1263). And smell? Smell links the two worlds, invisibly, yet powerfully, as Corbin argues. Like the rat, it passes from one into the other as the bourgeois

---

39. Cf. Mary Douglas, *Purity and Danger: An Analysis of Concepts of Pollution and Taboo* (London: Routledge and Kegan Paul, 1966). Her argument is in terms of ethnic and religious symbolism. Although such an angle is somewhat marginal to our project, it highlights the importance of cleanliness, purity, and social values in a different societal sphere.

40. On the sewer and its symbolic meaning, cf. Stallybrass and White, *Politics and Poetics of Transgression*, chap. 3, "The City: the Sewer, the Gaze and the Contaminating Touch," 125–48. Hugo is one of their primary references.

41. Cf. on this issue Corbin, *Le miasme*, 136ff. See also Charles Bernheimer, "Of Whores and Sewers: Parent-Duchâtelet, Engineer of Abjection," *Raritan* 6, no. 3 (1987): 72–90. Parent-Duchâtelet is one of the foremost hygienists of the nineteenth century, an avid smeller and walker of the Paris sewer system.

nightmare come true. It is the symbol of truth that emanates from the underworld; it hints at the true story that is being told underground, the ugly truth of a dissembling society.

A key point to keep in mind about "The Intestine of the Leviathan" is the dialectical nature of the process of enlightenment taking place here. To talk about the repressed—a tremendous progress over the silence in those matters in contemporary German literature—also means to search for new ways of repressing it further, of eradicating the offensive, and thus of inverting the moment of insight that Hugo provides in this trip through the sewers. The repressed that momentarily returns leads, in turn, to even greater repression. Hugo provides us a memorable example of this, too, in the cloaca that "flowed back into the city's throat, and Paris had the aftertaste of its slime" (1264). Notice the metaphor in terms of the other sense of proximity, the other subjective sense, in Kant's terminology, that is more often linked with *Ekel* than with pleasure, the sense of taste. For all literature and, for that matter, for all discourse, Barthes's dictum is true: "écrite [and, we might add by way of generalization, *verbalisée*], la merde ne sent pas."[42] Writing is the door through which smell, disgust, and the bourgeois fascination with those things enter the very bourgeois world that is on the surface level so much bent on banishing them. They enter on paper, as discourse.[43]

One last point needs to be made about Hugo in comparison both with the German bourgeois realists and with Baudelaire and French poetry. As open, visceral, nasal as he is compared with his German contemporaries, he is still clearly more traditional in his use of the olfactory than Baudelaire. By this is meant that, whenever (narrative) literature up to around 1900 uses the olfactory as a descriptive modality, it generally employs it in an objective role. Smells appear as a phenomenon of the real world where they have their origin and where they are perceived by a subject and deciphered as to their meaning. Smell is an objective cognitive phenomenon, and even when subjective effects are mentioned (such as in the few hints in Stifter or in Keller), they are the exceptions rather than the rule. For generally even such effects are fairly rigidly and predictably paired with

---

42. Roland Barthes, *Sade, Fourier, Loyola,* Collection Tel Quel (Paris: Edition du Seuil, 1971), 140.

43. Cf. Stallybrass and White, *Politics and Poetics of Transgression,* 125. They talk about "disgust and fascination," which are "recreated for the bourgeois study and drawing-room." We have been tracing their olfactory path from actual reality into scientific discourse first, and now into the literary and aesthetic realm.

their originating object. Hugo takes what we may call the realist and naturalist use of smells in literature to its extreme, far beyond his German
contemporaries, with the exception of the slightly younger Raabe, who
describes smells in a nexus similar to Hugo. Both writers are beginning to
tap the revelatory potential of olfaction to a much larger extent than the
bare traces found in German realism. Yet Hugo still remains in the objective mode of using smells.[44]

Zola's work is permeated by smells that are an essential aspect of the
reality he depicts and that he is known to have carefully investigated before
writing. His writing, as *littérature engagée,* operates on the assumption of,
in Bürger's terminology, a close connection between art (in this case literature) as a public institution and private life. For Huysmans and aestheticism the opposite holds true: the individual withdrew into his or her
private sphere, which appears as disconnected from the public realm, including art as an institution.[45] In Zola's assumption, then, the olfactory is

44. A similar statement could be made about Zola, the grand master of naturalist
prose and the only author so far on whom a study has been written explicitly investigating
the role of smells in his work, Léopold Bernard's *Les odeurs* (see footnote 2 of this
chapter). The aim of Bernard's talk is to present to his audience "le musicien, . . . le
symphoniste des odeurs" (7). "Avant [Zola] la langue des odeurs était pauvre: il l'a
prodigieusement enrichie; il a poussé . . . la notation . . . de cette manière originale de
sentir, longtemps regardée comme inférieure et purement animale par les romanciers
idéalistes" (7). Bernard refers to Baudelaire, "un autre gourmet d'odeurs" (8), and Gautier, and then goes on to list examples from all of Zola's works. The description, as above,
tends to be in musical terms ("une musique des odeurs," 9). He attributes Zola's use of
smells to both personal idiosyncrasy and the theoretical doctrine of naturalism. Bernard
points out, with an undertone of criticism, the raw social-Darwinist underpinnings of a
crude naturalism of survival that Zola uses, e.g., in the *Rougon-Macquarts.* "Puisque . . . Zola a voulu peindre la brute qui sommeille toujours au fond de la nature
humaine, il est tout naturel qu'il ait mis sur le pied d'égalité, avec les sens intellectuels et
esthétiques, les sens qui sont plus particulièrement préposés à la vie végétative et animale.
Je veux dire: l'*odorat* et le *goût*" (21). This repeats the Kantian (and general enlightenment)
distinction of higher/lower senses, and Bernard continues in terms distinctly reminiscent
of Descartes and Locke as well as Baumgarten: "Tandis que la vue, l'ouïe et le toucher
fournissent à la pensée la matière des *idées claires et distinctes* dont elle fera la science et
l'art, le nez et la bouche ne servent guère qu'à nous *avertir* de ce qui agrée ou répugne à
l'estomac, à nos poumons, d'une manière générale" (21, emphasis added). In this traditional framework Bernard recognizes, however, a sexual dimension of smells, as there are
such "qui réveillent ou assoupissent l'appétit sexuel" (22). He concludes by raising the
question whether Zola did not go too far "en mettant ainsi ses personnages dans une si
étroite dépendance des impressions de leur odorat" (28).

45. On Zola and Huysmans esp. see Hans Sanders, "Naturalismus und Ästhetizismus:
Zum Problem der literarischen Evolution," in Bürger, Bürger, and Schulte-Sasse, *Natu-
ralismus/Ästhetizismus,* 56–102. *A Rebours* does contain a good deal of explicit sociological critique, channeled through Des Esseintes, and the gesture of withdrawal from society

placed between the two poles of a public-objective phenomenon and the private-subjective perception of it. This constellation is essentially the same as in realist novels, except that the sheer quantity of instances lifts that perceptive mode from an occasional, attributive, descriptive comment onto the level of a continuous, atmospheric characterization. In bourgeois realism individual instances of smell seem to mark momentary breakdowns, involuntary revelations, Freudian slips of the nose, so to speak, in a narrative structure that attempts to isolate olfactory reality and prevent it from breaking through the impenetrable, nonolfactory overall description. Zola is bent on tearing this *veil*.[46] In his naturalism, however, a large number of olfactory characteristics open up this described reality and offer an additional communicative channel of represented and representative perception. His own tenets confirm this view. What he strives for is the "déchéance de l'imagination,"[47] the "disempowerment" of the very imagination that in romanticism and German bourgeois realism serves to weave an all-enveloping narrative veil over reality. The naturalist novel is "le roman d'observation et d'analyse," and the writer tries to "cacher l'imagination sous le réel" rather than the other way around (1285). The "sens du réel" (1286) is the *conditio sine qua non* of the naturalist novel, but it has to be combined with "l'expression personelle" (1290). As a living representative of such writing Zola names Alphonse Daudet, whose every page "prend une couleur, une odeur, un son" (1291), whereas with some other famous writers "on sent la rhétorique, l'apprêt de la phrase, une odeur d'encre se dégage des pages" (1293).[48]

Zola describes the "sens du réel" in terms of painting (1286–87) and explains its essence in terms of the aural. One does not need "des oreilles délicates" to understand the real, it is enough to have "des oreilles justes, pas davantage" (1288). It is when he talks about "l'expression personelle" that he refers to smells. Bernard observes that for Zola "le parfum est l'âme

---

is itself an act of criticism, if not rejection. The thrust, however, is different: Zola's occurs in the ethicopolitical, Huysmans's in the libidinal-aesthetic realm.

46. On the veil and the links between Hugo and Freud, see: Stallybrass and White, *Politics and Poetics of Transgression,* 140–41.

47. Emile Zola, "Le roman expérimental," *Oeuvres complètes,* ed. Henri Mitterand (Paris: Cercle du livre précieux, 1966), 10:1143ff.

48. For Zola, Daudet's pages "have a color, a perfume, a sound" whereas in other writers' texts "one hears the rhetoric, the stiffness of the sentence, an odor of ink flows from the pages." The quotes in the following paragraph read: There is no need for "subtle ears"; all that is required is "just ears, not more." Bernard thinks that for Zola "perfume is the subtle soul of objects, the only soul a materialist would admit to."

subtile des choses, la seule qu'un matérialiste puisse admettre" (Bernard, 22).

In German literature, naturalism is above all represented by Gerhart Hauptmann and the dramatic genre.[49] While his topics, the social milieu, and the *engagé* stance are similar to Zola's, Hauptmann makes little use of smells as a characterizing tool. This has to do with the medium. Hauptmann finds himself caught between two demands. On the one hand, as a naturalist, he should use smells. As a dramatist, on the other, he is limited in this by the genre. As German naturalism reacts to bourgeois realism precisely in talking about the topics the latter shunned and which we suspect of being "smelly," the poor, the masses, and sexuality, we have reason to expect that our observations made for French naturalism will be confirmed for German naturalism. Hauptmann, indeed, does present poverty, misery, filth, for instance in *Die Weber*,[50] yet there are only two instances of smell in the play, both of the old-fashioned kind of a person commenting on object smells. Both however, have to do with one of the central topics of the play, hunger and eating. Ansorge as well as the old Baumert in act 2 are described as "schnüffelnd" when they notice the meat frying in the pan, which is their own dog they had killed earlier. In act 3, Hornig, the rag collector and pedlar, recollects that some people had so little to eat that they ate "stinkende Schlichte."[51]

In *Der Biberpelz*[52] there is one similar use of smell. The Moteses, upon entering Frau Wolff's kitchen, notice the smell of frying meat in act 1: "Das riecht ja hier so nach Hasenbraten." In this instance smell does have a dramatic function in that it almost betrays the Wolffs' poaching. Frau Wolff had just removed everything visible that could possibly reveal the "Rehbock-Episode" (stage directions), but smell she cannot remove so easily and quickly. The indexical sign almost gives away its source and thereby increases the dramatic tension. Smell can only be a limited device in plays because of the stage's intermediate status between reality and the written or spoken text. Barthes's statement that "écrite, la merde ne sent

---

49. For a general introduction and characteristic of German naturalism and its salient features, see Günther Mahal, *Naturalismus* (Munich: Wilhelm Fink, 1975).

50. Gerhart Hauptmann, *Die Weber*, vol. 2 of *Das gesammelte Werk: Ausgabe letzter Hand. Zum 80. Geburtstag des Dichters am 15. November 1942* (Berlin: Suhrkamp, 1943).

51. Cf. Keller, *Der grüne Heinrich*, 254. Here, too, *Schlichte* is described as stinking. *Schlichte* is a gluelike liquid used to treat threads for weaving in order to smooth their surface.

52. Gerhart Hauptmann, *Der Biberpelz*, vol. 2 of *Das gesammelte Werk*.

pas" has its application here too. While it accounts for unlimited reference to smells on the written page and in the spoken dialogue, it makes clear that in the semireality of the stage the use of smell is more problematic. It may have a dramatic function, but in most situations is not a gratifying dramatic event. Theater relies on the eye and the ear; for smells, there is no channel in the spatial setup of actors and audience in the bourgeois theater.[53]

What we should take of the discussion so far into the following analysis of *Against the Grain,* is the beginning fundamental revaluation of the object-subject relation in olfactory perception that characterizes modern literature. In the new assessment of olfactory significance smells are no longer perceived as a reality "out there" that leaves a sensory imprint on a subject. Rather, their meaning is constituted in and by the perceiving subject itself. Smells do leave *impressions* on a subject, but also, and perhaps even more so, they are now *expressions* of a subject. In this new role they lose their objective element, their unambiguous indexical quality, and must instead be understood through a literary subject. This shift occurs first in poetry, the genre described as subjective par excellence. After that, the phenomenon manifests itself in decadent prose. "*A Rebours,* as we shall see, describe[s] the principles of decadence for the general public."[54]

Against the Grain: All Nerves

Calling a style decadent means, as Havelock Ellis points out in the introduction to the novel, having in mind a classicism, measured against which the style under discussion falls short. This plausible literary-historical assumption, however, runs counter to Des Esseintes's experience as a man of the 1880s and a reader of precisely such classical (Latin) texts. For him it is those texts that have, indeed, not fallen *down,* but fallen *behind* in terms of the experience that he, Des Esseintes, the modern reader, the representative of the "new nervousness," has. His life experience does not "make sense" in terms of classical textuality. Virgil appears as a "pedant" (26); for Horace's "elephantine graces" Des Esseintes feels "disgust" (27); and for Cicero, "his enthusiasm was not a whit greater" (27). Caesar is hardly to

---

53. Cf., however, the character Solyony in Chekhov's play *The Three Sisters* from 1901. He sprinkles himself repeatedly with perfume to mask his odor of a corpse. He is a thoroughly negative and destructive type.

54. Stephan, *Verlaine and the Decadence,* 9.

his taste, and Livy is called "sentimental and pompous," Seneca "turgid and jejune." Suetonius seems "lymphatic and horrifying" (28). Classical textuality is too rigid in form and content, but above all in terms of representing sensuous experience. Classical authors use "mechanically bisected" verses, and are "full of useless verbiage." They are "a torment to his sensibility" (27) and have "wearisome habits of tautology" (28). All this, for Des Esseintes, is the essence of Latin classicism, rigid formal and structural grids out of which the sensory—and thereby the sense—has evaporated, provided they were ever there. Among the authors "he really loved" (28) on the other hand, is Petronius, who discloses "the trivial, everyday existence of the commonality, its incidents, its bestialities, its sensualities" (29). He depicts the real stuff, "old wantons of the male sex," "women frantic with hysteria," a "slice from the raw of Roman life" (29). And Des Esseintes also likes Apuleius. This "African rhetorician was his delight," his language, this "copious flood, fed by many tributary streams from all the Provinces of the Empire . . . form[s] one strange, exotic dialect, hardly dreamed of before" (30). For Des Esseintes, however, it is not only a matter of reified (classical) form on the one hand and a sensuous content on the other that distinguishes between the rejected classicism and the more fitting decadence. A third element, the tenets of a new poetics, is revealed in his comments on Tertullian, whom he once liked with his "style rigorously compressed," with his "continual antitheses, crammed with puns and plays upon words" (31). Now Des Esseintes realizes how far he has moved away from Tertullian's ideas, which have become "the precise opposite of his own" (31). The reason is that Tertullian, in "De Cultu Feminarum," charges women "not to bedeck their persons with jewels and precious stuffs and forbids them to make use of cosmetics because they are thereby trying *to correct and improve on Nature*" (31, emphasis added).[55] This is the turning point where the aesthetic paradigm of classicism (imitating nature as the highest ideal of beauty) veers toward decadence, the emerging aesthetic sensuality or sensual aesthetics. Des Esseintes wants "the precise opposite" of Tertullian: "Nature has had her day. . . . [H]er productions must be superseded by art" (22).

The essence of decadence for Des Esseintes and his time, then, is the awareness of, in fact emphasis on, the undeniable cultural and historical

---

55. This very aesthetic aim is what Utitz (cf. chap. 2) associates with the "empiricists." In terms of his argument about Heinse, this is the "romantic" form of classicism. The other group that he establishes, with Greek antiquity as its model, Utitz calls the "classicists."

element that has entered an aesthetic discourse still hopeful of establishing nature supreme. Time for the latter is up. And not only is it up in terms of the object world, the side of the product in such an aesthetics, but it is over above all from the perspective of the consumer, the hedonist, the connoisseur whose very sensory as well as sense-making capacities have developed away from the natural, requiring clearly the cultural and artificial as the object of their interest. Thus Rousseau's "back to nature," seen from the vantage point of a century later and interpreted as an aesthetic maxim, stands for a lost cause. It is seen by Des Esseintes and his jaded bunch as what it really is: hopelessly romantic.

In the turn-of-the-century aesthetic climate a new attitude toward the olfactory unfolds. The joint development of general public cleanliness and sanitation, of sewage and waste disposal, of public and private hygiene on the one hand and individual as well as general olfactory sensitivity (in a cultural and psychological rather than in an evolutionary and physiological sense) on the other have reached a level that shifts the battle between good and bad smells in favor of the good. This battle, induced by, and forming part of, the process of civilization has in historical times been characterized by relentless pressure on everything bad. It was, in fact, often only in this very process that the "opponent was constituted and badness defined with increasing sophistication as the level of civilization rose. Around the turn of the century, with the enemy lines clearly thinning out and the good or at least neutral forces gaining ground, the question arises for the upper and upper middle classes, of how to divide, govern, and rule the newly won territory. The ground wrestled from the negative forces in both the public and the private space down to the individual body, is waiting to be mapped out and infused with new standards. A new realm has been gained for aesthetics. The territory once occupied by stenches and miasmas, now neutralized, is taken over by perfumes and pleasant fragrances. It turns out that while there probably are inherently and universally bad smells (their badness having its root in the anthropological and evolutionary past of the human species), the majority of the good/bad distinctions have arisen in the civilizing process and are socially coded. A first stage of explicit aesthetic exfoliation is reached around the time period discussed in this chapter. It has been a long way from the use of aromatics in cultic and religious practice or the odors produced as by-products in the processes of washing and anointing the dead, preserving, or mummifying[56] to the use of fra-

---

56. Cf. Cynthia Shelmerdine, *The Perfume Industry of Mycenaean Pylos* (Göteborg: Astroms, 1985).

grances as a tool in the fight against the stench of the unwashed living human body;[57] and from the use of aromatics as (self-)conscious masking devices of odors that have come to be perceived as bad to the deliberate release of good, precious scents into the purified space of the body and the body politic with pleasurable and aesthetic, semiotic intentions.

In this process of olfactory aestheticization, the focus as well as the locus of the debate is shifting from speculative medicine, the humoral model and the phlogiston theory, via the miasma concept, to the discovery of the bacterium. It enters the modern scientific discourse on the one hand and aesthetics on the other. The cleared, neutralized, disinfected olfactory medium, air, can now be recharged with scents, smells, perfumes. This is indeed happening around the turn of the century on a remarkable scale, and in the process the olfactory penetrates beyond the scientific into the literary realm. It openly spills from the cognitive and, partially, the ethico-political domain into the libidinal-aesthetic. This shift reveals that the existing vocabulary for smells in their newly entered aesthetic surrounding is defective, awkward, and incomplete because it antedates—to the extent that it exists at all—the aesthetic stage of that sensory modality. It has one part of its roots—and there are, indeed just roots, rudiments, without rhetorical blossoms—in a preanalytical stage of tracing origins or causes and effects (the smell of . . .; it smells like . . .). The other part is embedded in ethicopolitical soil: good, bad; pleasant, unpleasant; the categories of attraction and repulsion, of desirability and avoidance. It is only around 1900, with the emergence of smell in the libidinal-aesthetic realm, that the potential for an olfactory aesthetic, as well as the characteristics of its terminology, come into focus. But despite significant innovations, the olfactory remains caught in the backwardness of its phenomenological, ethicopolitical, and linguistic history. Its most recent surge in our own time is due precisely to these characteristics, and the potential for a new, postmodern mythology is thereby created.

Before returning to Des Esseintes, let us take a short detour through hermeneutics and philosophy. *Against the Grain* is a prose text in which beats the sensory heart of the poetry of its time. This heart, however, is no longer the same as in bourgeois realism, an organ both sensitive and sentimental, normative but without aesthetic standards other than *Gemütlichkeit*. The decadent heart is a skein of nerves, high-strung, hypo-

---

57. Cf. Madame de Maintenon's comment on, of all people, the Sun King: he stinks "comme une charogne." Quoted in Stefan Winkle, *Johann Friedrich Struensee: Arzt, Aufklärer und Staatsmann*, 452.

chondriacal, and egocentric. It is alert and attentive, critical but self-indulgent, and its neurons extend into each and every sensory surface of the body. It is with these physical aspects that we are concerned here, the outstanding role of the senses in general, the olfactory in particular.[58]

For this inquiry *Against the Grain* is a veritable treasure trove. In just over 200 pages it contains more than thirty references to smell. The whole of chapter 10 is devoted to olfactory experiments that, as it turns out, leave Des Esseintes devastated, shattering his nerves, "prostrating him to such a degree that he fell swooning and half dying across the window sill" (116). It is from the long-term effects of this olfactory shock—the causal link is explicitly mentioned again later on (195)—that Des Esseintes suffers through the rest of the book.

Chapter 1 is preceded by a "Notice" that provides a short summary of the hero's career so far. The old noble family of the Des Esseintes has decayed to its last offspring, Duc Jean. From the sturdy warrior figures, who in all their physical vigor looked as if "imprisoned in the old-fashioned picture frames that seemed all too narrow to contain their broad shoulders," the family has degenerated into "an exhausted race" with an "excess of lymph in the blood" (1). The last in this long declining line of generations is "Duc Jean Des Esseintes, a frail young man of thirty, anaemic and nervous, with hollow cheeks, eyes of a cold, steely blue, a small but still straight nose, and long, slender hands" (2). He is brought up at a Jesuit boarding school and hates his older family members and their friends, "these mummies," these "empty-headed folks" (5), those "solemn humbugs and silly idiots" (6). "His nerves [are] on edge"; he has only "one passion and one only, woman" (6), but he overindulges. "Ennui weigh[s] him down," "his senses [fall] into a lethargy, impotence [is] not far off" (7). In this desolate situation he sells the family chateau, thus providing himself with a handsome income. He buys a cottage in Fontenay, outside Paris, and one day "he got rid of his furniture, dismissed his servants and disappeared without leaving any address with the concierge" (8) in order to start a new and solitary life in the countryside.

The novel thus begins with an ending, but every ending, as we know,

---

58. A further inquiry would have to discuss *Against the Grain* as the spiritual account of a seeker at the beginning of a new age who moves through Schopenhauer's pessimism ("the German quack," xxxvii) back into the fold of Catholic mysticism and in the process denounces certain aspects of sensory-sensual experience as excess. The latter position is outlined in Huysmans's "Preface: Written Twenty Years After the Novel" (dated 1903) that has been added to the Dover edition here referred to.

is the start of something new. Just what is it that is beginning here? First, the parallels and differences to Stifter cannot be overlooked. As in *Der Nachsommer*, the material background of the hero is secured. Then an isolated locale is chosen where the larger part of the plot is going to take place. Strict social regulations are installed, admitting only a select few. Servants, of whom there are plenty in Stifter, exist here, too, but are virtually invisible. Des Esseintes explicitly retains two and isolates himself from them as much as possible (17). The central difference between the novels lies in the perspective. *Der Nachsommer* is an *Erziehungsroman*, therefore future-oriented, even if that future lies in past forms of social interaction and structures. *Against the Grain* is beyond that. It does not envisage a community in which the hero is to be integrated. Its solipsistic subject is largely disconnected from social reality. Perception located in the economic structure of *Soll und Haben* and in a phenomenological, aesthetic framework in *Der Nachsommer*, is now turning into a phenomenon of the philosophical and aesthetic superstructure. Whereas Freytag and Stifter, as well as Keller, educate their heroes with a view to their integration as useful members in bourgeois society, Huysmans's Des Esseintes has left the realm of social utility behind and put a distance between himself and the economic base that serves as a "cordon sanitaire"[59] and creates space to pamper his ego.

There are basically two strands of activity that Des Esseintes turns to, reminiscing over and assessing his past, and shaping his present surroundings according to his esoteric tastes, a combination of rococo opulence and monkish starkness. The first activity involves time and memory, the second aesthetics. One of Des Esseintes's foremost concerns is with isolation, segregation, rarification, purity. The inner sanctum of his house is linked to the other rooms by "a padded passage . . . in such a way as to absorb every unpleasant smell and disturbing noise" (20). He maintains that fictitious pleasures are "every whit as good as the true" (21), and that it is possible to "substitute the vision of the reality for the reality itself" (22). In chapter 10 we will find him substituting the *smell* of reality for reality itself. "Artifice was in Des Esseintes' philosophy the distinctive mark of human ge-

---

59. It is a telling coincidence that the term "cordon sanitaire" was first used by Marcel Proust's father Adrien (1834–1903), a medical doctor and eminent hygienist of his time. Cf. Adrien Proust, *Traité de l'hygiène*, 2d ed. (Paris: A. Masson, 1881). His son will, like Des Esseintes, withdraw into his shuttered and vapor-filled study in order to reflect on the ways of the world.

nius . . . Nature has had her day . . . [h]er productions must be superseded by art" (22).

In retrospect Stifter's world seems naive compared with Huysmans's. The former's tripartite hierarchical structuring of the object world consisting of nature, human products of use and consumption, and artworks providing guidelines for an education culminating in aesthetics is inverted and subverted by Huysmans. Des Esseintes has already gone through his education and reached the final plateau of art. The human production on the intermediate level of economic necessity interests him only insofar as he takes it for granted and its commodity status as given; and the bottom rung, nature, is explicitly dismissed. Stifter painstakingly sets up hierarchies of objects and usages, of procedures and purposes and garnishes every step with verbose supporting arguments. In this process which is purely object-oriented, indeed reifying, he skips the senses and the sensual, the subjective and the personal altogether. Huysmans's Des Esseintes, an object fetishist like Stifter's Heinrich, is of a different caliber. The natural order does not interest him, an order of economic purpose he ignores, and the only order he accepts is that of his own tastes. His object world is completely determined by the subject, by its memories and senses. Des Esseintes's country retreat is a laboratory where experiments in these two fields can be carried out. His withdrawal allows him, who has been out in the world, who has seen it all, to catch up intellectually and emotionally, to reflect on and work through, the experiences that he has had. The means for this are reminiscences, the trigger mechanisms are intellectual (religious, literary, etc.) and sensory (self-)stimulation. Chapter 10 can serve as a model for the second approach; its sensory mode is the olfactory.

In the context of the new mode of perception rising with Baudelaire, perception is understood to mean more than just the sensory. It is the "gesamte Daseinsweise" as well as "Sinneswahrnehmung."[60] "Die Art und Weise, in der die menschliche Sinneswahrnehmung sich organisiert—das Medium, in dem sie erfolgt—, ist nicht nur natürlich, sondern auch ge-

---

60. Benjamin, "Das Kunstwerk im Zeitalter seiner technischen Reproduzierbarkeit," vol. 1 of *Schriften*, 372. "Kunstwerk," "Paris, die Hauptstadt des XIX. Jahrhunderts," "Über einige Motive bei Baudelaire," and the fragments "Zentralpark" (all in vol. 1 of *Schriften*) contain some important terms and concepts that we will be drawing on for parts of the following analysis. An extremely rich collection of facts, data, concepts, and perceptions as well as an account of their rapid change is contained in Stephen Kern, *The Culture of Time and Space 1880–1918* (Cambridge: Harvard University Press, 1983).

schichtlich bedingt" (Benjamin, 372).[61] What we tentatively described as a shift from perception as a hermeneutic act to perception as a sensual event, Benjamin phrases in terms of his two concepts of *Aura* and *Chok*. These must be evaluated against the background of newly emerging mass phenomena—both economic processes, such as the mass production of identical units, and social developments, with masses of people in cities. The mass as a part of the modern individual's self-conceptualization—but also as that in distinction to which the individual conceptualizes himself or herself—is largely absent from *Against the Grain*. Des Esseintes defines himself through the object world and the sensory-sensual experience it affords him, and through art. But the background noise of the mass, so characteristic for modernism, always present in Baudelaire for instance and an important factor in Rilke, can already be felt.

In order to deal fruitfully with Huysmans's chapter 10, we need, in addition to Benjamin's concepts of aura and shock, a new understanding of time as it appears in memory.[62] Such a concept exists, and it has the additional advantages of being contemporary with the literature discussed here and of being connected to memory in its very conception. This is the notion of *durée* and the related concepts of *mémoire volontaire* and *mémoire involontaire* as developed by Bergson.[63] The dawn of modernity brings with it increased speed, higher density, and permanent sensory overload of the individual in the city. This reaches the point where the individual can no longer deal with this sensory overstimulation at the moment of its occurrence. The brain continues registering events (*Ereignisse*), but there is no time for working through them and converting them into experience (*Erfahrung*). The result is a stance of detachment, the typical social attitude of the aesthete. Individual consciousness itself, as Benjamin points out, develops a protective mechanism and immediately relegates large parts of the constant influx of impressions to the subconscious. Analogous to the

---

61. Perception is a "whole way of being" not just "sensory perception." "The manner in which human sensory perception is organized—the medium in which it occurs—is not only naturally but also historically determined."

62. The concept of aura is potentially a valuable tool for the exploration of the use of perfumes. The modern subject is answering the threat of being made into just another object in the all-pervasive commodities-exchange by attempting to recreate a personal aura, a mystique—and perfume advertising with its stress on exclusivity, irresistibility, and eroticism highlights precisely this.

63. Henri Bergson, *Oeuvres*, 3d ed., annotated André Robinet (Paris: Presses Universitaires de France, 1970). Esp. "Essai sur les données immédiates de la conscience" (1889) and "Matière et Mémoire" (1896).

dream acting as the guardian of sleep, the ever-alert, permanently stimulated and distracted consciousness becomes the guardian of mental sanity.[64] The effect of this is a characteristic of modern life to this day: dramatically increased but thinned out, shallow perception; increased data processing— but without personal, emotional gain. Innumerable objects flicker into and out of an individual's field of vision, an endless soundtrack accompanies his or her life, which, even as it can be recalled in consciousness, is watered down to a *curriculum vitae*.[65] One's *real* life with its experiences, its emotional richness, has emigrated inward, is located in the *mémoire involontaire* with its very precarious access. For Proust, indeed, the access hinges on pure chance. It depends on the savoring of a madeleine whether we ever come to know the rich, sensual Combray of our childhood or whether we will forever have to make do with the bland version that the *mémoire volontaire* is willing to yield on demand. As keys for accessing the locked treasures of our past, the senses of taste and smell seem particularly well suited.[66]

Against the Grain is a model of working through a whole past *à distance* that has been given up in search of a meaning that was impossible to find in times of permanent and excessive sensory stimulation. As a process, however, this working through differs significantly from Malte Laurids Brigge's. Des Esseintes still trusts his language; it does not seem to interfere with, in fact codetermine, his perceptual experience. For Malte, on the contrary, the world only comes together insofar as it can be turned into language. He is a writer, after all. Des Esseintes is, still, a reader. Huysmans takes care of Des Esseintes's material security and thus buys him time; he puts all the tools at his disposal for experimenting with his previous life, such as a knowledge of art, religion, philosophy, literature, perfumery, and so forth. Ultimately, however, Des Esseintes is concerned with sense making beyond himself. He is in search of a belief, a God. We will not be able

---

64. Cf. Benjamin, "Kunstwerk," 394. "Die Rezeption in der Zerstreuung, die sich mit wachsendem Nachdruck auf allen Gebieten der Kunst bemerkbar macht und *das Symptom von tiefgreifenden Veränderungen der Apperzeption ist,* hat am Film ihr eigentliches Übungsinstrument" (emphasis added).

65. Cf. Schachtel, *Metamorphosis,* on this point, esp. the link of perception, experience, and language.

66. Our combination of concepts hinges, like psychoanalysis, on the unconscious. It differs from psychoanalysis in the routes of access to the unconscious—sensory impressions instead of dreams or linguistic utterances. And it is different in its perspective—we rely on narrative that may or may not constitute a process of "working through" as opposed to "working through" in psychoanalysis that may or may not be in the form of narrative.

to follow him along this entire path, but we can witness the role that the senses play en route to that theological goal in his quasi-medieval framework of moral concepts. Sensory perception overarched by a (im)moral superstructure of lust and disgust plays a different role here from the one it played in the enlightenment tradition. There it stands in the service of reason, a tool in the quest for knowledge, which serves as its own motor force. Here such "pure knowledge" is no longer enough. For Huysmans the rationalist, hermeneutic optimism based on mechanically expanded sensory perception (microscopes and telescopes, photography and telegraphy) appears deflated. Human existence is "brought back to its senses," and it is taste and smell, which "never strayed far from the body," that reveal most drastically the meaninglessness resulting from sensory overindulgence.[67]

Against the Grain is a novel of extremes and borderlines. It marks a move from the center (Paris) toward the fringe (Fontenay). It describes a transition from worldly society through intellectual privacy to, ultimately, a spiritual community. In literary-historical terms it was widely influential in modernist artistic circles but largely rejected by bourgeois, Victorian criticism and readership. In its narrative techniques, it shows a strong authorial voice, counterbalanced by indirect interior monologue. And it relies heavily on the senses as a liminal area between the individual and the world. The structure of this area is described in chapter 4 for the sense of taste. Des Esseintes has just received the gold-plated turtle, inlaid with precious stones, and he feels "perfectly happy" (43); he drinks a cup of tea, "liquid perfume" (43), but the mere gust of cold wind coming in through the window as he opens it gives him "a shock" from which "a dose of spirits" should "restore his bodily temperature" (44). The taste organ, the elaborate contrivance of "a row of little barrels," allows him to play "symphonies on his internal economy, producing on his palate a series of sensations analogous to those wherewith music gratifies the ear" (44). Players in this orchestra of spirits are, to give just a few examples, "kirsch, blowing a wild trumpet blast; gin and whisky, deafening the palate with their harsh outbursts of cornets and trombones; liqueur brandy, blaring with the overwhelming crash of the tubas" (44). The characterization and classification of taste sensations in terms of another sensory mode (hearing in this case)

---

67. Cf. Huysmans's adoption of Trappism, the ascetic reform movement within the Cistercian order, strict and frugal in its life-style; and Des Esseintes who sets up his bedroom as a monk's cell.

and of an established art form (music) is something not unusual for smell either. In fact such a transposition of the semantic fields of smell and taste sensations almost suggests itself, given the lack of a terminology of their own. The problem has a documented history, above all in science.[68] Attempts to solve it have followed the traditional precarious route between the Scylla of the signifier and the Charybdis of the signified. Taming by naming has been the grand gesture of rational exorcism since man started conceptualizing—even if for one subject matter in terms of another, as is the case for the taste organ; and even if as a figure of speech, as metaphor. *Metaphor* is used here as a designation in "un-actual" terms. For smells, technically speaking, the designatory relation is metonymy, the relation of contiguity rather than similarity or dissimilarity. Taming by naming, however, is unsuccessful in both the case of taste and smell. The resistance of the chemical senses to a classification in their own terms makes them unpredictable, and Des Esseintes, attempting to sound "one single note on the keyboard of his instrument" (46), the note of Irish whisky, arouses "by a fatal similarity of taste and smell" some half-obliterated recollections of years ago: "The acrid, carbolic flavour forcibly recalled the very same sensation that had filled his mouth and burned his tongue while the dentists were at work on his gums" (46). He has to relive the "abominable" experience of a tooth extraction. When it is over, "he shivered, horrified at these dismal reminiscences. He sprang up to break the horrid nightmare ... and ... began to feel anxious about the turtle" (48). But the turtle is dead. Death has defied aesthetics. Aestheticization-as-objectification of a living being does not prevent its death. Similarly, the aestheticization of one sensory modality in terms of another cannot prevent the former's true nature from surfacing, and the linguistic support structure of one sense

---

68. Cf. Edward Sagarin, *The Science and Art of Perfumery* (New York: Mc Graw-Hill, 1945). Chapter 12 bears the title: "A Science in Search of a Language," 137ff. Sagarin mentions the famous French perfumer Septimus Piesse's "odophone," a concept for the transposition of scents into the system of musical notation (145–48). Cf. S. Piesse, *Histoire des parfums et hygiène de la toilette* (Paris, 1905). "Un parfumeur experimenté a quelquefois deux cents odeurs dans son laboratoire et sait distinguer chacune d'elles par son nom. Quel musicien pourrait, sur un clavier comprenant deux cents notes, reconnaître et nommer la touche frappée sans voir l'instrument?" (4). Sagarin's little book, although somewhat dated now, is still fascinating and touches on the fundamental quandaries of the olfactory sense in terms of art, language, science, and business and its eternal in-between state. Cf. also Carterette and Friedman, *Tasting and Smelling*, and Engen, *Perception of Odors*, for a more scientific and historical outline. The name of H. Zwaardemaker appears in all three accounts in connection with classificatory attempts in olfaction. For some of Zwaardemaker's publications on the topic, see Sagarin, 251.

cannot prevent another, to which it is applied, from cutting through its verbal surface to the quick of the subject. The sharp note of remembered pain cannot fail to pierce through the borrowed harmony of another sense.

At the beginning of chapter 10 Des Esseintes enjoys a respite from his nervous ailments, a "delightful clearness of the brain" (105). It is of short duration, however, for "in a moment, one afternoon, hallucinations of the sense of smell appeared" (105). He decides to exorcise this devil by calling in Beelzebub and "resolved to plunge himself in a bath of real perfumes, hoping [to] moderate the force of the overpowering frangipane" (105). "Needless to say, he possessed a collection of all the products used by perfume-makers" (109). Two things are striking in Des Esseintes's reflections on perfumery: the ambivalent status of smells between an art and a craft, and his conceptualization of the history of perfumery in terms of the history of language:

> Years ago he had trained himself as an expert in *the science of perfumery* [emphasis added]; he held that the sense of smell was qualified to experience pleasures equal to those pertaining to the ear and the eye, each of the five senses being capable, by dint of a natural aptitude supplemented by an erudite education, of receiving novel impressions, magnifying these tenfold, coordinating them, combining them into the whole that constitutes *a work of art* [emphasis added]. It was not, in fact, he argued, more abnormal than [*sic*] an art should exist of disengaging odoriferous fluids than that other arts should whose function is to set up sonorous waves to strike the ear or variously coloured rays to impinge on the retina of the eyes; only, just as no one, without a special faculty of intuition developed by study, can distinguish a picture by a great master from a worthless daub, a *motif* [italics in original] of Beethoven from a tune by Clapisson, so no one, without a preliminary initiation, can avoid confounding at the first sniff a *bouquet* [italics in original] created by a great artist with a pot-pourri compounded by a manufacturer for sale in grocers' shops and fancy bazaars. (106)

Given the two ingredients, a natural aptitude and some erudite education, Des Esseintes sees no reason why the *science* of perfumes should not be able to produce a *work of art*. The possible conflict between science and art can be solved in Benjamin's terms where the characteristic of the true work of art (the original) versus its copies lies in the fact that the former retains the trace of its historical origin, its "geschichtliche Zeugenschaft" ("Kunstwerk," 371). This, precisely, perfumes cannot do. Their essence lies in their volatility. They are, in fact they have to be, products of technical reproducibility, as their purpose is to disperse and dissolve. They are therefore not works of art but products of a craft. The situation is similar, both in factual and in linguistic terms, for the culinary: the gourmet meal reveals itself as such only in its consumption.

Benjamin's claim can be developed a step further and linked to Freud. For humankind there is only one type of smell with an indelible historical, in fact, anthropological origin: the smell of the human (sexual) body. This smell, however, it will be objected, is far removed from art. Indeed it is. It is the dialectical opposite of art qua perfumery. Yet it is as perfumery only that smells could possibly lay claim to the status of an art, namely in perfumery's age-old attempt at subduing sexual smells; as man's eternal endeavor to cover up his or her primal origin. In this one respect perfume points to a historical, in fact primordial, origin and appears as the ersatz body smell. It reveals its Benjaminian (pre)historical locus that, as the actual bottled commercial product, it is designed to deny. The steamy discourse on eroticism, seduction, and irresistibility that accompanies perfumes in modern marketing helps deflect attention from this ancient connection and does a first-rate job at covering up by pointing out the very thing that perfumes are designed to cover up: their origin in sexual odors.

Des Esseintes hints at the slippery nature of the art of perfumery by phrasing its processes and effects in terms of language and literature, which in more recent theoretical approaches have increasingly been understood as revealing and covering up meaning. Revealing, in fact, occurs through covering up and displacing.[69] Thus Des Esseintes had learned step by step "the arcana of this art, the most neglected of all" so that he was enabled to "decipher its language,—a diction as varied, as subtle as that of literature itself, a style of *unprecedented conciseness under its apparent vagueness and uncertainty*" (107, emphasis added). First he had had "to master the grammar, to understand the syntax of odours" (107). Only then is he able to see the larger outlines. "Its history followed step by step that of the French language" from Louis XIII, "perfumed and full-flavoured" (107) to "the pomp and stateliness of the *Grand Siècle*" (107) and "the wordy style of Bossuet"; from "the well-worn sophisticated graces of French society un-

---

69. Cf. the striking sonnet "Correspondances" by Baudelaire in *Les Fleurs du Mal*, where specific links are drawn between nature, language as symbols, and the senses, above all the olfactory, and where "les parfums, les couleurs et les sons se répondent" and, in the last line, perfumes "chantent les transports de l' esprit et des sens."

der Louis XV" through "the indifference and incuriousness of the First Empire, which used Eau de Cologne and preparations of rosemary to excess" (108). Perfumery "ran for inspiration, in the train of Victor Hugo and Gautier, to the lands of the sun; it created Oriental essences, *selams* overpowering with their spicy odours" (108). He repudiates "the voluntary decrepitude to which the art had been reduced by the Malesherbes, the Andrieux, the Baour-Lormians, the vulgar distillers of its poetry" (108). Des Esseintes, not having dealt with perfumery recently, is a little rusty at first, and "the phrases, the processes had escaped his memory" (109). But he soon becomes bolder and decides "to strike a thundering note, the overmastering crash of which should bury the whisper of that insinuating frangipane which still stealthily impregnated the room" (110). "Of old," Des Esseintes

> had loved to soothe his spirit with harmonies in perfumery; he would use effects analogous to those of the poets, would adopt, in a measure, the admirable metrical scheme characterizing certain pieces of Baudelaire's, for instance "*l'Irréparable*" and "*le Balcon*," where the last of the five lines composing the strophe is the echo of the first, returning like a refrain to drown the soul in infinite depths of melancholy and languor. (110)

He builds up to the climactic creative act in terms of poetry once more, and of music:

> He wandered, lost in the dreams these aromatic stanzas called up in his brain, till suddenly recalled to his starting point, to the original *motif* of his meditations, by the recurrence of the initial theme, re-appearing at studied intervals in the fragrant orchestration of the poem. (110)

Then he rises to the synaesthetic climax crowned by the olfactory. He roams in "a landscape full of surprises," beginning with "a simple phrase,— ample, sonorous, at once opening a view over an immense stretch of country" (110). "With the help of his vaporizers," he injects "extract of meadow flower" into the whole room, creates "artificial lilacs" and "lindens sway[ing] in the breeze." Into this scene, which he sees "under his closed eyes," he introduces woman by means of "half feline essences, smacking of the petticoat." Later, "he let[s] these fragrant waves escape by a ventilator." Woman, "the feminine aroma[,] disappeared, the country was left without inhabitants." Instead, industry emerges. There "rose a row of factories whose tall chimneys flamed at their tops like so many bowls of punch." Des Esseintes revivifies lindens and meadow grass and adds "new mown hay" (111), and instantly there "rose mounds of hay, bringing with them a new season, scattering their delicate odours reminiscent of high summer.... [W]hen he had sufficiently savoured the sight," he moves to the last, synaesthetic flourish. He "hurriedly scattered about exotic perfumes, exhausted his vaporizers, concentrated his strongest essences, gave the rein to all his balms...." An "atmosphere, maddening and sublime" arises; he forces "to grow together, in despite of seasons and climates, trees of diverse essences, flowers of colours and fragrances the most opposite." Then, "suddenly a sharp agony assailed him.... He opened his eyes, to find himself once more in the middle of his study." He lets in some air through the window, "but his eyes were still heavy" (112). After "carefully recorking the bottles of scents and essences" he turns to the toiletry and makeup utensils, of which he owns plenty, left over from former lovers. It is here that a truly Proustian moment of recollection occurs.

> He handled all this elaborate apparatus, bought in former days to please a mistress who found an ineffable pleasure in certain aromatics and certain balms, ... who loved to have her nipples macerated in scents, but who only really experienced a genuine and overmastering ecstasy ... when ... she could ... breathe the smell of chimney soot, of wet plaster from a house building in rainy weather, or of dust churned up by the heavy thunder drops of a summer storm. He pondered these recollections, recalling particularly an afternoon spent ... in this woman's company ... the memory of which stirred in his breast a whole forgotten world of long-ago thoughts and old-time scents. (113)

His recollection is so vivid that Pantin, the small town and scene of the remembered events, "lay there in front of his eyes," and he recites his own words, written down after that moment in the past. At Pantin are located some perfumeries, and Des Esseintes enjoys the fact that "it is to industry, to commerce ... that Pantin owes this artificial spring.... [T]he spring-like fragrance floating in through the cracks of the window-frame, is exhaled by the neighbouring factories where Pinaud and Saint-James make their perfumes" (114–15). But once again, "by a sudden failure of all his bodily powers" (115), Des Esseintes is interrupted in his wanderings. "He threw the window wide open; ... but the next moment the wind seemed to bring with it a vague breath of bergamot." He shudders, he feels possessed, and when indeed the smell of frangipane fills again "all the air from the valley of Fontenay away to the Fort, assailing his exhausted sense of smell, . . . he fell swooning and half dying across the window sill" (116). That is where we found him at the beginning of this discussion.

I have quoted extensively from this chapter because it contains a sufficient number of angles on the phenomenon of olfaction for a full panorama of the contemporary olfactory landscape. This landscape, first of all, has largely been rid of bad smells. The dominant theme is no longer, as in previous discourse, eliminating repugnant odors but rather the qualities and effects of manufactured good scents. Whenever at this point stenches and bad odors appear in literary description, such as in Zola, they are introduced deliberately and for specific effect, no longer as the lamentable but seemingly unavoidable condition of human life. The cultural progress of hygiene shows its effect on the literary discourse of smells. In this process, the olfactory landscape is taking on more and more the contours of the human (female) body, and special emphasis is placed on sexuality and memory.[70]

The fundamental shift from avoidance to creation liberates the nose. The handkerchief pressed to it, drenched with fragrant essences in an effort to protect the subject from miasmatic vapors, can be removed. New pleasures open up. A sense is set free to pursue artistic goals, insofar as perfumery and art go together. This issue, broached above in connection with Benjamin and Freud, needs elaboration. Olfactory perception, in Freud's hypothesis, is the sensory modality directly linked with sexuality. It loses this function in the very early stages of the civilizing process and remains therefore unaffected by it and primitive in its structure. It retains its insistent reference to man's rise from the ground and the evolving shift of the sensory base of sexual attraction from the olfactory to the visual mode of perception. This is the official story. What is emerging with growing clarity, however, is the insight that the olfactory has in no way lost or even only weakened its hold on the attraction between the sexes.[71] On the contrary, this ancient story of olfactory attraction is more and more openly expressed in beginning modernism. It seems that Freud underestimated the tenacity of the sexual-olfactory link. Indeed, olfactory phenomena can-

70. For a link of these two, see also Rilke, *Malte Laurids Brigge,* 724.

71. As we are discussing only texts by male writers—due to no intentional bias by the author of this study, but certainly for reasons having to do with the historical male hegemony in literary canons—this claim, strictly speaking, must be modified to "sexual attraction of the male by the female" at this point of our investigation.

not be explained by the concept of sublimation that underlies his notion of artistic and cultural production in general. Creation and use of artificial scents—unlike artworks in established media that are the result of processes of displacement—take place in the same medium as their noncivilized driving mechanisms and are therefore unaffected by displacement. This can be taken literally: whereas in painting, for instance, desire for the body is abstracted, transferred to a canvas, and framed, perfumes are worn on the body, the object of desire itself. Smells, the wonderful archaic odors once regulating sexual behavior, and still stimulating it, remain smells. The only effect on them by the civilizing process has been a "revaluation of all values," in calling good the artificial and bad the natural. Deep down, of course, we all know better. The direct link of all scent on the human body to sexuality has never really been broken. Perfumery, then, appears as an art indeed—in the more general sense of the term, bordering on *artifice*. It has claimed for centuries to conceal what it was revealing, to reveal what it was pretending to conceal. Perfume is the last piece of clothing to come off (in fact, it does not come off) in the historical process of undressing the human (female) body in (European) literature. Perfume is the smell of pudenda by a different, respectable name.

One effect, however, does seem to have been wrought on olfactory perception in its history. In its emergence in literature as a sense of attraction rather than repulsion as previously outlined for the nineteenth century, it is frequently expressed in a specific rhetorical frame, the trope of remembering and invocation. In Huysmans's novel, there are numerous examples for this added element of indirectness. In the following, for instance, Des Esseintes is describing a painting of Salomé by Gustave Moreau, one of his favorite painters (chapter 5). While "the clouds of scented vapour" (51) rising from burning cressets surrounding the figure of Herod may actually be visible in the picture, the Tetrarch's perception of Salomé after the deed is pure olfactory projection by the viewer, Des Esseintes, who describes the Tetrarch as "still pant[ing], maddened by the sight of the woman's nakedness, reeking with heady perfumes, dripping with balms and essences, alluring with scents of incense and myrrh" (55). This description is mediated through the narrator of the novel who describes a figure in a picture, through whose perception of another figure in the picture we, the readers, are made aware of the latter's scents, which are invisible, of course. And yet, the literary representation of the scene in its compounded sensuality hits home with surprising force of titillation, both for the narrator, who is "overwhelmed, overmastered, dizzied before this figure of the dancing girl" who is so "ensnaring to the senses" (55), and for the reader. The fact that smell cannot be recalled as smell but most often as an image is exploited in this synaesthetic epiphany. Smell is the added ensnaring web of eroticism that enhances the charged sensuous atmosphere and wafts out of the painting, out of the book to envelope both narrator and reader.

More straightforward examples of the triggering of memory by smells—straightforward in their mechanics, but never in their effect—are the following. In the flower chapter (chapter 8), it is the very last orchid brought in by Des Esseintes that he comes to regret "having admitted among the scentless" plants already present in the room. It is the Cattleya, "the orchid that brought up the most unpleasant associations." It does so by its smell, not by its unobtrusive visual appearance of "an almost invisible mauve." Des Esseintes "drew near, put his nose to it and started back; it exhaled an odour of varnished deal, just the smell of a new box of toys, recalling irresistibly all the horrors of the New Year and New Year's presents" (88).

In chapter 9, after the flowers have withered, Des Esseintes's nervous condition is once more shaky at best. He has nightmares; "he was afraid to go to sleep. . . . He was consumed by infinite ennui. The pleasure he had felt in the possession of his amazing flowers was exhausted" (94–95). He goes through his artists' portfolio; he reads Dickens—nothing brings alleviation until he opens "a little box of silver-gilt . . . full of bonbons." They remind him that "formerly . . . when his impotency was an established fact . . . he would place one of these sweetmeats on his tongue; . . . then, in a moment, would recur with an infinite tenderness recollections, almost effaced, altogether soft and languishing, of the lascivious doings of other days" (97). This remembrance of remembering is triggered in the medium of taste, but as he sets it in motion, the woman who first comes to his mind does so because "if she had made a deeper impression on his mind than a host of other women . . . this came of the smell she exhaled as of a sound and wholesome animal" (100). This set of sensory Chinese boxes, of a smell memory within a taste memory within the larger framework of erotic reminiscing, cannot be surprising when one reads that the bonbons "consisted of a drop of sarcanthus scent, a drop of *essence of woman,* crystallized in a piece of sugar" and that they evoke "reminiscences of water opalescent with rare vinegars" and of "deep, searching kisses, all fragrant with odours" (97, emphasis added).

These examples suffice to highlight once more the general argument put forward here. Smells in the literature of beginning modernism appear predominantly as the gate to memory or within memory itself. In both cases, memory is the Bergsonian and later Proustian *mémoire involontaire*. The *general* unpredictability of what a smell will recall is contrasted to the solid bond of a smell with a *specific* instance of memory in each *individual* case. The low general determinacy and the extremely high individual determinacy of phenomena triggered by olfaction is precisely what bourgeois realists feared and what decadence with its nonsocial, certainly antibourgeois stance relishes. Odors, man-made scents, as we determined, do not constitute an art, neither in Benjamin's sense nor in that of Adorno's autonomous work of art nor, for that matter, in Kant's terms of disinterested beauty.[72] Smell is always tied up with an Other, seemingly *any* Other, ultimately, however, always with sexuality and the erotic—or, which remains to be shown, with death. This gives smell a degree of freedom far beyond that of those sense modalities that *have* developed art forms. Above all, it exempts it from being caught in a movement that, around the turn of the century, attempts the last integration of technology and utility with the aesthetic: *Jugendstil*, art nouveau, art deco.[73] Beyond smell's technical aspects (qua perfumery) and its status as a craft, it cannot be co-opted into the aestheticization of technological progress that takes the form of a style.

In the past, bourgeois realism had been the style of mediation between social and technical progress on the one hand and aesthetics on the other. It characterized the epoch of mapping onto the individual the necessary role changes demanded by rapidly shifting social structures. Naturalism had taken a critical stand vis-à-vis these processes, but had done so precisely by applying advanced, scientific, and technical methods in an attempt, so to speak, to beat the system on its own terms. Aestheticism as the umbrella term for the various antinaturalist movements, from symbolism and impressionism to decadence, voices its critique in a different way, namely by

---

72. Cf. on this point also Winterbourne, "Is Oral and Olfactory Art Possible?" His answer is negative, because the artistic dimension does not lie in either of these sensory modes themselves, but is only triggered by them. "It is simply a confusion to say that such examples [Proust's madeleine] show how munching buns and drinking tea can *as such* be aesthetic experiences" (96–97). Cf. also Osborne, "Odours and Appreciation." Insofar as the "aesthetic act" is understood as "attention directed upon the sensory content of an experience without ulterior motive other than bringing that content more fully into awareness," the olfactory is capable of aesthetics. Aesthetic judgment, then, "is concerned with the adequacy of any such sensory content to sustain attention at an enhanced level of awareness" (47).

73. For a more detailed discussion, see Gerhard Goebel, "Mode and 'Neue Kunst': Zum Beispiel Poiret," in Bürger, Bürger, and Schulte-Sasse, *Naturalismus/Ästhetizismus*, 175–89.

stressing the individual, the extra-ordinary. To that end it proclaims a realm of artificial beauty and artificiality in general. Its position includes both antimodern and modernist elements. And now, in the aftermath of decadence, *Jugendstil* attempts to weld together aesthetics and technology, use value and cult value, mass production and individual appointment. In the English context, the line of development can roughly be sketched by starting with John Ruskin, for whom the good and the beautiful are still inextricably linked and the realms of ethics and aesthetics have common roots. It continues and can still be detected in Walter Pater's collection of essays on the Renaissance, where beauty is disconnected from morality and located in the fleeting, impressionist moment. He provides the old *carpe diem* motif with the philosophical and emotional underpinnings of the times. William Morris finally tries to integrate and realize in crafts and designs some of the aesthetic ideas dominant in the Victorian age, and to give some body to the ethereal shapes of the Pre-Raphaelites. Among writers, it is above all Swinburne (1837–1909) who, influenced by Baudelaire, represents the new sensualism of the second half of the nineteenth century. As regards the olfactory, he confesses in a letter to D. G. Rossetti in 1869 that he likes it and is "especially and extravagantly fond of that sense and susceptible to it."[74]

Future styles, the avant-garde of expressionism, dadaism, and surrealism, will do precisely the opposite of *Jugendstil* and point out, each in its own fashion, the irreconcilable antagonism between, on the one hand, technological progress and social change praised in its name, and, on the other, aesthetic principles that seem to be pushed aside only to be hailed eventually as the "form that follows function." The process will have come full circle when Marcel Duchamps in 1917 declares his infamous *urinoir* (La fontaine), the mass-produced item of everyday use, associated with a host of unnameable emotions, to be a work of art, to be the aesthetic expression of the age.

The olfactory—not being an art, but being a sensory modality capable of aesthetics after shedding its negative enlightenment image and breaking through the ice of the bourgeois, Victorian conspiracy of olfactory silence—emerges in literature as the instrument of exquisite individuality,

---

74. Quoted in Ann Walder, "Swinburne's Flowers of Evil: Baudelaire's Influence on Poems and Ballads, First Series" (Ph.D. diss., Uppsala University, 1976), 30. Although Swinburne does use many sensory-sensual images, overall his style is somewhat mannered, his diction deliberately archaic, and he is far from creating Baudelaire's immediacy. Too many of his *bitter* and *sweet,* too many of the *flowers* and *lips* are clichés rather than the sharp, sudden revelations they are in Baudelaire.

playing on the memory of both the individual and the species. It cannot be contained inside any one field, but infallibly knocks on the door of two: memory and sexuality. It aims at the latter through the former, and inevitably the process takes place in language. "Nous tendons instinctivement à solidifier nos impressions, pour les exprimer par le langage. De là vient que nous confondons le sentiment même, qui est dans un perpétuel devenir, avec son objet extérieur permanent, et surtout avec le mot qui exprime cet objet."[75] By putting experience, especially sense impressions, sensations, and emotions into words, we replace their complicated, multilayered, and many-faceted composite nature by a temporal succession of these individual aspects. This Bergson calls "reconstituer de la durée avec de l'espace" (84). In other words, we dissect a compounded *Miteinander* into an elemental *Nacheinander*. In a written text, in the pages of a book, time is thus replaced by space, which, however, in the process of reading is converted back into time. Time and space, this is Bergson's underlying argument, are of the same nature. The olfactory with its inability to recall smells will always recall objects, places, people, in other words, spatial concepts impregnated with time, remembered time. Due to the close connection of this sense impression with external objects (and the words designating them), the olfactory, lacking a terminology of its own, will therefore, by metonymy, reach out in each and every sphere of reality. It is predestined to become the sensory mode for mediating space and time in memory, to recreate space and time *as* memory. The stabilizing effect of language on perception, as Schachtel would call it, its conventional and schematizing pressures, are further elaborated by Bergson in the realm of taste and smell.

Telle saveur, tel parfum m'ont plu quand j'étais enfant, et me répugnent aujourd'hui. Pourtant je donne encore le même nom à la sensation éprouvée, et je parle comme si, le parfum et la saveur étant demeurés identiques, mes goûts seuls avait changé. . . . Mais en réalité il n'y a ni sensations identiques, ni goûts multiples; car sensations et goûts m'apparaissent comme des *choses* [italics in original] dès que je les isole et que je les *nomme* [emphasis added]. (87)[76]

---

75. Bergson, "Essai sur les données immédiates de la conscience," 86.

We instinctively tend to solidify our impressions in order to express them in language. This is the reason why we confuse the feeling, which is in an eternal state of becoming, with its fixed external object and with the very word that names this object.

76. Following is the translation of the three Bergson quotes in this paragraph. "This taste or that smell pleased me when I was a child, and now repulse me. And yet I still

Isolating, simplifying: taming by naming is what Bergson sees occurring in the transformation of sensory perception into language. The olfactory, however, remains flexible and unpredictable because it is hardly grounded in language at all. Despite, or perhaps because of this, "sensations et goûts m'apparaissent comme des *choses*" (87), and smells can be associated with all kinds of *choses*. "Ce qu'il faut dire, c'est que toute sensation se modifie en se répétant et que si elle ne me paraît pas changer du jour au lendemain, c'est parce que je l'aperçois maintenant à travers l'objet qui en est cause, à travers le mot qui la traduit" (87). This bond between an object represented as a word and its memory indeed becomes fixed, but for smells this fixation is a strictly individual one, and no general social links can be established such that words and phrases referring to smells would trigger an identical or at least comparable image among a group of people. Bergson's statement then that "cette influence du langage sur la sensation est plus profonde qu'on ne le pense généralement" (87) is, as regards the olfactory, true only when applied to individuals but not to groups, except that a certain common understanding exists of what is a *good* and what is a *bad* smell. Good or bad, however, are not inherent qualities. They are convenient tags to place olfactory sensations on a social scale of values.

The common understanding of good and bad is promoted for a variety of socioeconomic reasons. The attempt to deal with the most intimate and personal, however, the body and its odors, is strangely curtailed in its linguistic expression. "B. o.," the squeamish signifier, puts a semitaboo on the signified; "b. o." imposes a hushed silence on body odor but is infallibly vociferous about the products advertised to cover it up. Below that signifier, however, flowers the age-old bond of bodily smells and sexuality, and the words, indeed "à peine formés," are incapable of turning around "contre la sensation qui leur donna naissance" (87). Every artificial scent on the body is the admittance of the existence of its dialectical opposite.

---

give the same name to these sensations and talk as if the smell and the taste had remained the same and only my predilections had changed. . . . But in reality there are no identical sensations and repeated tastes; for sensations and tastes take on the form of *things* once I isolate and name them."

"What needs to be said is that all sensations are modified through repetition, and the fact that they do not seem to change from one day to the next lies in the fact that I perceive them now through the object that is their cause, and through the word that describes them." Bergson continues: "This influence of language on sensations is greater than we generally assume."

"B. o." is the indispensable Other of the perfume and fragrance industry, despised and feared at the same time; to be eradicated, yet its *raison d'être*.

The Picture of Dorian Gray: Scents of Flowers

Despite certain similarities—both heroes are provided by their creators with enough material support to allow them to live their aesthetic whims— Dorian Gray[77] is not simply the English Des Esseintes.[78] In a certain sense, Des Esseintes begins where Dorian Gray leaves off. Des Esseintes is about thirty, worn out, not especially good looking; he has been in society and is on his way out of it; he wants to live exclusively for his own purposes. Dorian Gray is younger, fresher. This, in fact, is his foremost characteristic. That he will remain young is central to the plot, the novel's stroke of genius. Dorian is entering society; he enjoys it and mingles with it as much as possible. Des Esseintes is the aesthetic intellectual, whereas Dorian Gray is more the "dumb blond" ("his frank blue eyes, his crisp gold hair," 19) who only wakes up to his aesthetic vocation after his first meeting with Lord Henry Wotton who declares on that occasion, a "new hedonism,— that is what our century wants," and goes on to suggest that, thanks to Dorian's beauty, "the world belongs to [him] for a season" (25). Lord Henry is the theoretician of an aestheticism much more malicious than Des Esseintes's. He is the tempter, the advocate of a purely selfish life-style that will bring about beauty out of its very disregard for moral values. "The terror of society, which is the basis of morals, the terror of God, which is the secret of religion,—these are the two things that govern us" (21). If we were to "give form to every feeling, expression to every thought, reality to every dream," only then would the world "return ... to something finer, richer than the Hellenic ideal." But we do not do this; "the bravest man among us is afraid of himself," when in fact "the only way to

---

77. Oscar Wilde, *The Picture of Dorian Gray (Urfassung* 1890), ed. Wilfried Edener, Erlanger Beiträge zur Sprach- und Kunstwissenschaft, vol. 18 (Nuremberg: Verlag Hans Carl, 1964). This is a critical edition of the first publication of the novel in *Lippincott's Monthly Magazine,* 1890, divided into thirteen chapters. The 1891 and following book editions were expanded to twenty chapters. All references are to this edition.

78. For an extensive study of the relations that exist between the two novels, especially about the mysterious "yellow book" from Lord Henry by which Dorian becomes so fascinated in chapter 8 and that has often been suggested to have been Huysmans's *A Rebours,* see Wolfgang Maier, *Oscar Wilde: The Picture of Dorian Gray. Eine kritische Analyse der anglistischen Forschung von 1962–1982* (Frankfurt am Main: Peter Lang, 1984), esp. chap. 2: "A Rebours und Dorian Gray," 102ff.

get rid of a temptation is to yield to it" (21). Not only do the realms of ethics and aesthetics sharply diverge here, they become mutually exclusive. The mapping of social norms onto the individual by aestheticizing them is inverted and in its inversion taken to its limits: aestheticization (of the body, the least durable of beautiful objects) perverts ethics. Dorian ends up becoming a murderer.[79] Dorian, who is exempt from aging and can thus count on his beauty as a solid asset, is also removed from the nexus of time and ethics. What Bergson links in the philosophical concept of *durée,* space and time, is posited as separate in the fiction of *Dorian Gray.* Aging, the passing of time, leaves no marks on its spatial incorporation, Dorian's body. Dorian has no incentive to be moral (i.e., to "act beautifully") because he *is* beautiful. Indeed, whenever rumors rise about his life, "that he had been seen brawling with foreign sailors in a low den in the distant parts of Whitechapel, and that he consorted with thieves and coiners," and when "men would whisper to each other in corners, or pass him with a sneer" (118), it is always his "frank and debonair manner, his *charming* boyish smile, and the infinite *grace* of that *wonderful* youth that seemed never to leave him" that provides "a sufficient answer to the calumnies" (119, emphasis added). Thus the fictional separation of time and space (the body) splits aesthetics and ethics.

We will not follow Dorian through the good times he is set up to have, but instead stick our noses briefly into his surroundings. They are elegantly appointed and pleasantly scented. Aromas and olfactory characterization are an unobtrusive element in the descriptive structure of the novel. They play a distinct, if somewhat lesser role than in *Against the Grain.*[80]

---

79. For a multifaceted, illustrated overview of aspects of life, including its seamier side, in the Victorian city, see Wolf von Eckardt, Sander Gilman, and J. Edward Chamberlin, *Oscar Wilde's London: A Scrapbook of Vices and Virtues, 1880–1900* (New York: Doubleday, 1987).

80. The olfactory plays an important role, however, in the criticism in which Wilde finds himself embroiled immediately after publication. In a review in the *St. James Gazette* from 1890, the writer states, "Not being curious in ordure, and not wishing to offend the nostrils of decent persons, we do not propose to analyse 'The Picture of Dorian Gray'" (25); and later in the same review it is pointed out that Wilde seems to "derive pleasure from treating a subject merely because it is disgusting." This attitude has, according to the writer, "a root which draws its life from malodorous putrefaction" (33). In the first of his several replies Wilde states that he does not see "how any work of art can be criticised from a moral standpoint. The sphere of art and the sphere of ethics are absolutely distinct and separate" (35). All quotes from Stuart Mason, *Oscar Wilde: Art and Morality. A Record of the Discussion which Followed the Publication of Dorian Gray* (New York: Haskell House, 1971).

Smells are present from the very beginning. "The studio was filled with the rich odor of roses, and when the light summer wind stirred amidst the trees of the garden there came through the open door the heavy scent of lilac, or the more delicate perfume of the pink-flowering thorn" (3). These are the opening lines of the novel, and by means of the olfactory an ambiance is created of aesthetic purity and natural sensuality.[81] Floral scents are mentioned at other times (23, 67) and so are perfumes, incense, or other aromatic and exotic substances.[82] Chapter 9 with its paragraph on perfumes is reminiscent of chapter 10 of *Against the Grain*. The passage itself does not tell us much new; what is more revealing is its position in the context of sensory and aesthetic reflection. The chapter contains no dialogue and is partly written in the same indirect interior monologue as are large parts of *Against the Grain*. It reveals a more pensive, reflecting Dorian than the one we find in the rest of the book. He is pondering a philosophy that would have "the spiritualizing of the senses" as its highest goal.

The worship of the senses has often, and with much justice, been decried, men feeling a natural instinct of terror about passions and sensations that seem stronger than ourselves, and that we are conscious of sharing with the less highly organized forms of existence. But it appeared to Dorian Gray that the true nature of the senses had never been understood, and that they had remained savage and animal merely because the world had sought to starve them into submission or to kill them by pain, instead of aiming at making them elements of a new spirituality, of which a fine instinct for beauty was to be the dominant characteristic. As he looked back upon man moving through History, he was haunted by a feeling of loss. (107)

The passage fits well the history of the sense of smell traced here. There are the elements olfaction has in common with "less highly organized forms

---

81. Stifter's world, as we recall, contains all the material preconditions for a similar sensual experience that, however—expression of a different sensibility—is never allowed to surface. This reflects more than an author's idiosyncrasy, as we begin to understand now, although it is this too. It is the expression of a worldview that for Stifter can be summed up in his "untergehenden Völkern verschwindet zuerst das Maß," but that for Wilde and his age amounts to something more akin to Rimbaud's "dérèglement de tous les sens."

82. Dorian puts "some perfume on his handkerchief," 47; "patchouli" is worn by Lady Henry, 37; "incense" is mentioned on 103; Dorian has a "delicately scented chamber," 106.

of life" (the Freudian trace); there is its "true nature" that has "never been understood," as well as the attempts "to starve [it] into submission" (the bourgeois repression). Dorian's sense of loss, however, is only half the truth about the civilizing process; the other is the cleaning of the air to make room for scents and allow for increasing refinement of perception, which serves as a basis for the contemporary enjoyment of that sensory modality in all its nuances. The new hedonism proclaimed by Lord Henry "was to re-create life.... Its aim, indeed, was to be experience itself, and not the fruits of experience, sweet or bitter as they might be" (108). This advocating of *Erlebnis* over *Erfahrung* is an open invitation to *carpe diem* and not think about it. "Of the asceticism that deadens the senses, as of the vulgar profligacy that dulls them, [Lord Henry's hedonism] was to know nothing" (108). Instead, it was to teach man about the fleetingness of the moment. Dorian, exempt from the ravages of time, has no incentive to "make sense," either in the modernist understanding with its increased emphasis on the senses and the sensual as taking place in some kind of *durée* or in the contrasting premodern concept of transcendental ascetic practices. Such practices push the promise of sense—both as meaning and as the sensual—into the hereafter, while maintaining in this world, as Dorian points out, a hostility toward the senses, a desire to "starve them into submission or to kill them by pain" (107). From his position "out of time" Dorian can briefly flirt with the Catholic Church, even with Darwinism, but he can also admit that ultimately "no theory of life seemed to him to be of any importance compared with life itself" (110).

The place allocated to the olfactory is close to the mysteries, both of the senses and the soul. Scents are the first among the several objects of Dorian's studies undertaken under the spell of the French book, of which the narrator at the end of chapter 9 tells us that "Dorian Gray had been poisoned by a book. There were moments when he looked at evil simply as a mode through which he could realize his conception of the beautiful" (123). So he begins to study perfumes. He is especially interested in the psychological effects attributed to certain fragrances. These effects are simply mentioned without further analysis, and in its depth this passage in *Dorian Gray* does not match the direct intense olfactory experiments that Des Esseintes undergoes. Yet Dorian saw "that there was no mood of the mind that had not its counterpart in the sensuous life, and set himself to discover their true relations, wondering what there was in frankincense that made one mystical" (110–11). Also linked are ambergris and passion;

violets and "the memory of dead romances"; musk and a troubled brain; champak and imagination. Ultimately Dorian seeks "to elaborate a real psychology of perfumes" (111)—a feat that has not been accomplished to this day.

In *Dorian Gray* the olfactory is part of a sensory realm that is less directly sexual and erotic than in the French poets and in Huysmans. Yet it plays a general role that we may now call well established in the upper-class life-style presented here, contributing to the "delightful," "exquisite," "delicate," and "quite marvellous" atmosphere reminiscent of the soft-focus-lense interiors and precious objects we find in the high-gloss life-style journals of our own day. And although memory, *the* locus of the olfactory, plays a minor role in this novel, largely due to the structural elimination of time and the eternal present surrounding the hero to the last moment, it is twice placed in that context by Lord Henry: "Life is a question of nerves and fibres. . . . You may fancy yourself safe. . . . But a chance tone of color in a room or a morning sky, a particular perfume that you had once loved and that brings strange memories with it . . . I tell you, Dorian, that it is on things like these that our lives depend." And he goes on to give an example from his own experience: "There are moments when the odor of heliotrope passes suddenly across me, and I have to live the strangest year of my life over again" (157). The Proustian moment of olfactory revelation is already known to Lord Henry.

Two further examples deserve brief mention here, which we may now call traditional, as they are object smells. They characterize the bad side of the moral spectrum through bad smells. One instance occurs in chapter 10, when Dorian shows the changed portrait to Basil Hallward, its painter. It is an ugly moment, indeed; Hallward will be murdered by his companion within a few minutes. "The lamp cast fantastic shadows on the wall and staircase" as the two men climb up to the attic; "the windows rattle" and "a cold current of air passed them" (130). There is dust and even a mouse, and "there was a damp odor of mildew" in the air (131). Later, after Campbell has removed the traces of Hallward's dead body, Dorian goes up into the attic to convince himself that "the thing" had indeed disappeared, and he notices that "[t]here was a horrible smell of chemicals in the room" (150).

These are realist or naturalist instances of the use of smell as a trace, here the trace of a crime and of death. We will find more, much more, of those.

German Literature: Going Beyond "grauer Kartoffeldunst"

The German literary fare of the second half of the nineteenth century is, as we established in the previous chapter, fairly bland in sensory terms. It is devoid of the flavors and fragrances, the aromas and scents of English, and above all French, contemporary writing. The German world of that time lacks more than anything a city, a center, a metropolis where all the ingredients are present in a critical mass to start the unforeseeable reactions—unforeseeable indeed, as they concern the nose—that have started to bubble and boil in varying degrees of pleasantness across the whole social spectrum of French and English literature. France has her Paris, the capital of the nineteenth century, with a million inhabitants in 1850, more than 2.7 million in 1901. England has her London, the world's largest city, with 4.7 million inhabitants in 1879 when Wilde arrives there and over 6 million when he leaves.[83] In contrast, the German cultural area is not at all centralized. None of its major cities has the right mix, builds up enough momentum, contains the ferment necessary to distill the essences of modernism quite as early as Paris and London do; none of them possesses the know-how for the *enfleurage* of the *Zeitgeist*. Berlin, in 1861, has only just over half a million inhabitants; it starts growing more rapidly after 1871 when it is made the capital of the Empire, and by 1880 has about 1.3 million inhabitants. The rapid growth of the *Gründerjahre* leads to shoddy, unsanitary mass-housing projects, and only around 1900 and later do the hygienic and sanitary conditions significantly improve.[84] But Berlin is only a regional center of German culture at that time. There is Prague, with about a quarter of a million inhabitants in 1910 and a Czech-speaking majority in the city parliament only after 1866; before that, German was dominant. Then there is Leipzig, the old commercial and above all printing and publishing center in the southeastern part of the German-speaking world, a city of about 450,000 people in 1900 and ranking before Frankfurt in terms of the publishing business. And there is Munich, with about 350,000 inhabitants in 1892. By 1910 it grows to over 600,000. And of course, there is Vienna, capital of an empire long before Berlin receives that same status, a city of 1.4 million inhabitants in 1890, of just over 2 million in 1910.[85]

---

83. Cf. von Eckardt, Gilman, and Chamberlain, *Wilde's London;* x.

84. Cf. on this topic Virchow, *Collected Essays,* esp. vol. 2, section 6: "Municipal Sanitation," dealing specifically with contemporary Berlin.

85. For historical information and further references about German society in the eighteenth and nineteenth centuries see Sheehan, *German History 1770–1866.* On Vienna

Since the turn of the century and even more dramatically since the end of World War II, radical shifts have taken place in the German-speaking world. Prague, after sending forth Kafka (1883–1924) and Rilke (1875–1926), two of the most eminent writers of German modernism, virtually drops out of the consciousness of the completely reshuffled postwar Western Europe. A similar fate touches Leipzig, while Frankfurt rises, once again, to the dominant position in the German publishing industry that it held already in the eighteenth century. Vienna, since WW I the too-large capital of too small a country, as well as Berlin, the split and insular curiosity from another age, both have to define new roles for themselves. Paris and London, however, have remained the undisputed centers of their nations.[86]

Literary geography, however, is only one piece of the explanatory model attempted here on the way to completing our olfactory agenda for the period of the late nineteenth and early twentieth centuries. We must first of all bear in mind the writers themselves. There is clearly a changing of the guard taking place. The great old figures are dying out. Stifter has been dead since 1868. Storm dies in 1888, and Keller in 1890. Freytag's death occurs in 1895, three years before Fontane's in 1898. With four authors from our previous chapter dead at the turn of the century (Raabe dies in 1910), the question must be asked, who are the authors during the period under investigation here? From today's perspective the question is not merely rhetorical, for many of the names well known during that epoch have not lasted. Fritz Martini, not generally known for any radicalism, has made the following remark about German writing in the second half of the nineteenth century in a European comparison:

> Die große Erzählkunst des 19. Jahrhunderts in deutscher Sprache (Stifter, Keller, Gotthelf, Raabe, Fontane, Ebner-Eschenbach) ist in Stoff, Sprache und Stimmung landschaftlich gefärbt und auf einen begrenzten, vertrauten Lebenskreis gerichtet. Während in Frankreich (Stendhal, Balzac, Flaubert, Hugo, Maupassant) oder in England (Scott, Dickens, Thackeray) sich eine große Erzählkunst in einheitlicher Tradition für die gesamte Nation gültig entwickelte, gelang es dem

---

and Berlin see 55; on the demographics of urbanization, 451ff., esp. 485–86. Sheehan's book is a valuable source of historical information on German society and culture, and provides even a short chapter on "Literary Realism," 820ff.

86. The opening of the Berlin Wall in November 1989 has not ended this process of redefinition; it has just added another twist.

deutschen Roman nicht recht, über das Provinziell-Eigenbrötlerische in eine gesamtdeutsche oder gar europäische Weite vorzudringen.[87]

Let us, then, mention just two writers here, Paul Heyse (1830–1914) and Wilhelm Raabe (1831–1910), whose short novel, *Pfisters Mühle,* we discussed in the preceding chapter. Raabe begins in the late 1850s to put together quietly and laboriously an impressive oeuvre in the realist tradition. Without the nationalist fanfare of a Freytag or the upper-crust polish of a Fontane, he focuses more on individual portraits, rural or small-town settings. In *Der Schüdderump* (1869–70) for instance, a story set in the northern German town of Krodebeck, the far-away city of Berlin only appears on the horizon of the daily lives of the people as a rumor, a locus of the unknown. The few Krodebeck citizens who do get as far as Berlin "verloren in dem ungewohnten Gewirr und Getümmel . . . ihre schlaue ländliche Unbefangenheit."[88] In terms of olfactory characterization, Raabe is generally unexciting.

Paul Heyse, together with the poet Emanuel Geibel, is the leading figure in the *Münchner Dichterkreis.* Heyse is an astonishingly prolific writer of verse dramas and novellas. Together with Hermann Kurz he edits the voluminous *Deutscher Novellenschatz* in the 1870s. Despite the fact that he is the first German author to receive a Nobel Prize for literature in 1910, he is largely forgotten today.[89] Heyse marks the tail end of that eminently German tradition of novella writing that starts with Goethe's "Unterhaltungen Deutscher Ausgewanderten" in 1795, lasts through the nineteenth century, and finds its great bourgeois representatives in Storm, Keller, Meyer, and Heyse, not to forget Kleist as a more romantic, critical contributor in its earlier, and Thomas Mann as a formal innovator in its later, phase. It is the novella, the story of law and disorder and return to

---

87. Martini, *Deutsche Literaturgeschichte,* 380. "The great nineteenth-century narrative art in German (Stifter, Keller, Gotthelf, Raabe, Fontane, Ebner-Eschenbach) has a local color to its material, diction, and mood and centers around a limited, known everyday world. Whereas in France (Stendhal, Balzac, Flaubert, Hugo, Maupassant) and in England (Scott, Dickens, Thackeray) great narrative art developed a unified national tradition, the German novel did not succeed in pushing beyond the provincial and eccentric into the whole of the German-speaking lands or even into the European space."

88. Wilhelm Raabe, *Der Schüdderump,* vol. 8 of *Sämtliche Werke,* 43. Further examples on 37–38, 44.

89. On Heyse and the thought processes underlying the edition of the *Deutscher Novellenschatz,* see Monika Walkhoff, *Der Briefwechsel zwischen Paul Heyse und Hermann Kurz in den Jahren 1869–1873 aus Anlaß der Herausgabe des Deutschen Novellenschatzes* (Munich: Foto-Druck Frank, 1967).

law that tells most explicitly the German bourgeois master plot of the century. This narrative has no room (yet) for solipsistic individualism. It still struggles with the individual vis-à-vis society, with individual passions versus general norms. The novella is the shortcut version of the *Erziehungsroman,* that other German genre of the earlier nineteenth century. It is the literary practice drill of weighing the claims of the individual against those of the community. This is an older set of problems than those discussed in Huysmans and Wilde, where community demands are shown as having receded from the individual sphere, replaced by the more subtle pressures of specific social cohorts. The central question is no longer how to fulfill society's demands but rather how to fill out the space gained for individual (self-)determination and self-realization and how to fight ennui and nerves that threaten to take a hold of the individual in the vacuum of social values. The novella is by and large an odorless genre.

This summary treatment admittedly gives short shrift to a whole epoch in German literary history and can only be justified by the fact that we have already drawn a tentative line of development from the middle of the nineteenth century through to its end in the previous chapter and that we will, in continuing this line in the following pages, cover the last decade of the old century and the first of the new once more and in greater depth.

Among the new generation, displaying a dramatically increased olfactory sensitivity, we will focus in detail on Rilke only. But it is helpful to gain a quick general overview. It includes, in chronological order, Arthur Schnitzler (1862–1931), Stefan George (1868–1933), Hugo von Hofmannsthal (1874–1929) and Thomas Mann, who was born in 1875, the same year as Rainer Maria Rilke, but who survived the latter by almost thirty years. This group of writers has, if nothing else, their cosmopolitanism in common, a traveling, urban life-style. There exists a network of discourse among them, both factually and ideally. For example, we may compare the correspondence between Rilke and Hofmannsthal, George and Hofmannsthal, George and Rilke, in addition to the personal acquaintance of Hofmannsthal and Schnitzler, with the correspondence network between Storm, Keller, Fontane, and Heyse in the older generation. Via George and Rilke in particular, another link can be drawn, important in terms of the sensual and erotic, to Mallarmé and Baudelaire, both of whom George translated into German, while Rilke, translator of Valéry, spent time in Paris as Rodin's biographer and amanuensis. Schnitzler is probably the most "local" in this group, and Thomas Mann the most marginal and certainly impossible to grasp in fin-de-siècle terms alone. But for the few years discussed here, he has at least two things in common with the others: the sensory sensitivity and, explicitly, the theme of decadence, the "Verfall einer Familie" for instance, as the subtitle of *Buddenbrooks* has it.[90] Moreover, Thomas Mann is of particular interest to us here in that he represents most clearly the bourgeois realist heritage in narrative prose, as well as the changes that it is undergoing at his hands and the astonishing metamorphoses it is capable of. Mann himself likes to think of *Buddenbrooks* as naturalist (cf. de Mendelssohn, 804), but if we are to accept this view, we will at least have to qualify his as a naturalism very different from Zola's or Hauptmann's, an upper-class naturalism that has more in common with Fontane, draws on the leitmotiv technique of Wagner, and outlines the developing nervousness and decay of a single family over three generations. I prefer to place it within the realist tradition, bourgeois in its fundamental assumptions, yet beginning to show the authorial narrative stance of ironic distancing (unknown in Stifter or Freytag, benevolently visible in Keller and to a greater extent in Fontane, but completely absent in the engagé stance of naturalism) that is to become one of Thomas Mann's trademarks and a characteristic of German realist narrative in the twentieth century. Mann's realism is open to sensory characterizations, including the olfactory, which is not in any way obtrusive but overall marks a development far beyond bourgeois realism of the old kind.

In support of this statement, let us briefly turn to *Buddenbrooks*. It will become clear that in the progressive decay of the family, there appears an increasing olfactory component surrounding the deaths of its individual members, most dramatically so in the Konsulin's death of pneumonia toward the end of the novel. The obsession with air and breathing that we already encountered in Fontane and which in the Konsulin's case amounts to sheer asphyxiation will be made into one of the central motives in the later *Zauberberg*. *Buddenbrooks* (1901) can serve as a veritable literary paradigm for the development of sensory and perceptual sensitivity up to the time period under investigation here. The novel spans about four decades, from 1835 to 1877. Woven into it is much of Thomas Mann's own social and aesthetic perception for the years around 1900. The picture of the epoch is completed with *Tod in Venedig* (1912) and *Der Zauberberg* (1924). The

---

90. Thomas Mann, *Buddenbrooks,* Gesammelte Werke in Einzelbänden. Frankfurter Ausgabe, ed. Peter de Mendelssohn (Franfurt am Main: Fischer, 1981). See esp. de Mendelssohn's "Nachbemerkungen," an informative essay on the genesis of the novel as well as its publishing history and its blossoming into the sales success that it ultimately turned out to be, 775ff. All subsequent references are to this edition.

representatives of the upper-class bourgeoisie are shown in transition from their solid and real world—realistic as well as realist—through decadence toward a contemplative and aestheticist attitude of nonbelonging. The loss of their fortunes is compensated with psychological and artistic insight, the nervous tension results in heightened (olfactory) perception.

Not only death, the exit from life, but birth too, the entry into it, is marked by odors in *Buddenbrooks*. In the bedroom where Clara is born there is a "Stimmung von Erholung und Frieden nach überstandenen Ängsten und Schmerzen . . . in der Luft, die vom Ofen noch leise erwärmt, mit einer Mischung von Eau de Cologne und Medikamenten durchsetzt war."[91] Old Johann Buddenbrook "atmete während einer Minute den warmen, gutmütigen und rührenden Duft ein, der von [dem Baby] ausging" (58–59). Only a short time after the birth of the girl, the old Konsulin dies with a "kurzen und kampflosen Seufzer" (71), and again only shortly thereafter, old Johann Buddenbrook, her husband, follows her, mumbling his last "Kurios!" and simply turning against the wall (73). This first generation dies easy, but death gets harder and more painful (and the narrative dwells more on death scenes and their immediate aftermath) as the family history unwinds. Old Konsul Kröger, upset by the revolutionary events in his city, dies in his coach on the way home from a political meeting. "Der Kopf fiel so schwer auf die Brust, daß der hängende Unterkiefer mit klappendem Geräusch gegen den oberen schlug." This horrible sound is the last sign of life before "die Augen verdrehten sich und brachen" (200). After Johann Buddenbrook, Jr.'s death, while the family gathers to settle some open matters, "die Trauerstimmung lag noch schwer und ernst in der Luft" (254).

Onkel Gotthold's death is only mentioned (279), not described, but thereafter, the religious element becomes more and more prominent in the family. A horrible death, and somewhat hushed up for this reason, is James Möllendorpf's, the old senator's: he died "auf groteske und schauerliche Weise" (414). The old diabetic man, longing for sweets, stuffs himself with cake and dies of a sudden collapse, "den Mund noch halb voll zerkauten Kuchens" (414). His death vacates the senatorial seat for Thomas with his "parfümierten, lang ausgezogenen Schnurrbart" (475).

The more the family declines, the more sensitive their olfactory percep-

---

91. There is a "mood in the air of peace and relaxation after anxieties and pain are overcome. . . . The air, still gently warmed by the stove, is saturated with a mixture of eau de cologne and medications." Johann Buddenbrook "inhales for a minute the warm, benevolent, and touching scent that emanated from the baby."

tion becomes. This is made especially poignant in the Christmas celebration and the vigils following Konsulin Buddenbrook's death, which are presented through Hanno, the last male Buddenbrook, the oversensitive, *lebensuntüchtig* child. The whole room smells, is "erfüllt von dem Dufte angesengter Tannenzweige" (546), and "Hanno genoß die weihnächtlichen Düfte und Laute mit Hingebung" (551).[92] After the long, hard death struggle of his grandma, he finds himself in the room, "den Sinn umnebelt von den Düften, welche den Mengen von Blumengebinden und Kränzen entströmten, und mit denen sich, ganz leise und nur bei diesem oder jenem Atemzug bemerkbar, ein anderer, fremder und doch auf seltsame Art vertrauter Duft vermengte" (599). The strange, hardly perceptible odor persists.

Er atmete langsam und zögernd, denn bei jedem Atemzug erwartete er den Duft, jenen fremden und doch so seltsam vertrauten Duft, den die Wolken von Blumengerüchen nicht immer zu übertäuben vermochten. Und wenn er kam, wenn er ihn verspürte, so zogen sich seine Brauen fester zusammen, und seine Lippen gerieten einen Augenblick in zitternde Bewegung. (600)

Hanno smells death in the air, a subtle foreshadowing by the author.[93] His own death by typhoid fever, the last in the book, is described in terms of the classical medical symptoms of, and measures against, that disease, impersonally almost. Indeed the other characters only talk "in Andeutungen und halben Worten" about it (773), but it is a form of dying where the tongue of the victim is covered "mit einer schwärzlichen Masse, . . . die den Atem verpestet" (767). Before Hanno, however, his father Thomas dies

---

92. The whole room is "filled with the odor of burnt pine needles," and "Hanno enjoys the smells and sounds of Christmas with abandon." In his dead grandmother's room his "mind was all foggy from the smells that rose from the masses of flower arrangements and wreaths and among which was intermingled, hardly perceptible, another smell, strange and yet curiously familiar." "He was breathing slowly and hesitatingly, expecting with every breath that smell, that strange and yet curiously familiar odor that the flowers were not always able to mask. And whenever it appeared, when he smelled it, he knitted his eyebrows, and his lips started to tremble momentarily."

93. For a very different account of death, decomposition, and smells, see David Howes, "Olfaction and Transition: An Essay on the Ritual Uses of Smell," *Canadian Review of Sociology and Anthropology* 24 (1987): 398–416. Howes stresses the olfactory as a liminal and transitional sense very consciously used in rituals by non-Western cultures. The essay allows us a glimpse at a different social encoding of good/bad from our own. In this light, the editor's remark on Fontane's use of the "Immortellen" flowers as "Bilder eines duftlosen, wehmütig kargen Todes" (709) gains additional meaning.

ignobly of a bad tooth. At the dentist's, Thomas and the reader are overwhelmed by smells. In the waiting room, first, he drinks some water, "das nach Chloroform roch und schmeckte" (690), and as the dentist starts his work, his hand "roch nach Mandelseife, sein Atem nach Beefsteak und Blumenkohl" (691). Before the extraction, he treats Thomas's gums "mit einer scharf riechenden Flüßigkeit" (691). After the failed procedure, Thomas sees him leaning against the instrument cabinet, and he "sah aus wie der Tod" (692). On the way home, Thomas collapses in the street, and during the following days the flower shops "machten Geschäfte" (703). His family receives wreaths "aus starkriechenden Blumen" (703), and in the open coffin, Thomas lies "in einem strengen und betäubenden Duftgemisch von Tuberosen, Veilchen und hundert anderen Gewächsen" (703). Such are the deaths of the Buddenbrooks, leaving behind a faint floral aroma.[94]

Before Rilke's *Malte Laurids Brigge* takes us back to Paris, let us briefly stop over in Vienna. For it is in this corner of the German-speaking world rather than in Berlin, where in the late 1880s and 1890s those developments take place, that we are most interested in. If Berlin can be called the capital of naturalism, with the representatives of the movement developing political programs and forging links, at least theoretically, with Social Democracy, Vienna is much more the capital of the fin-de-siècle, precisely because its cultural scene is unpolitical in proportion to its being dominated by the conservative representatives of the respectable, seemingly unchangeable status quo. It is somewhat paradoxical then but constitutes precisely the unique characteristic of Vienna that decadence and fin-de-siècle, the two aesthetic movements that both in Paris and in Berlin grow out of and in opposition to naturalism, should develop here almost completely without this historical predecessor.[95]

---

94. After Thomas's death, the flower shops "did some brisk business." He lies in his coffin "in a severe and narcotic odor mix of tuberoses, violets, and a hundred other plants." The odor of death in European fiction is well worth a topical study. Including works such as Dostoyevsky's, Mann's, and Tolstoy's and linking Baudelaire, Ernst Jünger, and the death-camp survivors' accounts, such an investigation could corroborate on a broad basis a claim made here: that death, Thanatos, is the second primordial, mythological source of odor, the complement and opposite of love, Eros.

95. For a more detailed account of this question, see Jens Rieckmann, *Aufbruch in die Moderne. Die Anfänge des Jungen Wien: Österreichische Literatur und Kritik im Fin de Siècle* (Königstein: Athenäum, 1985). See esp. chapter 1, "Hermann Bahr: 'Bote und Werber einer neuen Kunst,'" 13–42, and 65–66. Bahr is the link to Paris for the Vienna scene, and usually a step ahead of the most recent developments; he is also the only one among the representatives of the *Jung Wien* who actually had studied Marxism seriously.

In the Vienna of the late 1880s and early 1890s nerves begin to vibrate, senses reach out for new and daring stimulation without warning, so to speak, that is, without preparation by naturalism and its represented universe. In this respect, the titles of Felix Dörmann's two volumes of poetry, *Neurotica* and *Sensationen,* are, in Jens Malte Fischer's words, "höchst bezeichnend."[96] In the literature produced in the circle of the *Jung Wiener,* both in prose and poetry, the olfactory element is present everywhere, from the decadent aromas in the poems of Dörmann (emanating from oranges, narcissuses, and tuberoses) to the prose of Hofmannsthal, for instance in his short account of a travel incident, "Das Glück am Weg" from 1893, when he was nineteen years old. In the first paragraph of this lyrical short text, the narrative subject sits on the afterdeck of a ship, and with the land sinking away in the distant haze over the Mediterranean he still fancies "den feinen Duft zu spüren, den doppelten Duft der süßen Rosen und des sandigen, salzigen Strandes." But he realizes that this cannot be, for "der Wind ging ja landwärts.... So war es wohl nur Täuschung, daß ich den Duft zu spüren glaubte."[97] Embedded in this figure of imagined scent is the visual encounter, through the binoculars, with a woman on a passing ship, a woman he has always known, woman as such. Ephemeral like a scent, images flow through the narrator's soul; "alle diese Dinge dachte ich nicht deutlich, ich schaute sie in einer fliegenden, vagen Bildersprache" (9).

Smells are present in Schnitzler's prose, too, not obtrusively, but as a regular accompaniment of people and a permanent element in the description of objects and places. Thus we find them in the first paragraph of "Die Nächste" as "ein leiser Wind, der ihm vom Stadtpark den kühlen Duft der ersten Blüten herauftrug." They last through the very end of this short story, when Gustav kills the prostitute who had reminded him so much of his dead wife Therese.[98] Gustav had been mourning Therese's loss all win-

---

For an account of the Vienna of the turn of the century from a specifically Freudian psychoanalytical perspective, see also Michael Worbs, *Nervenkunst: Literatur und Psychoanalyse im Wien der Jahrhundertwende* (Frankfurt am Main: Europäische Verlagsanstalt, 1983). Pages 17–24 provide a comparison of Vienna and Berlin.

96. A useful introduction to fin-de-siècle Vienna, general in its *Einleitung,* more specific in the second part ("Kommentare zu einzelnen Werken") is Jens Malte Fischer, *Fin de siècle: Kommentar zu einer Epoche* (Munich: Winkler, 1978), 72. See also Carl E. Schorske, *Fin-de-Siècle Vienna: Politics and Culture* (1961; New York: Vintage, 1981).

97. Hugo von Hofmannsthal, *Erzählungen I,* ed. Ellen Ritter, vol. 28 of *Sämtliche Werke, Kritische Ausgabe,* veranstaltet vom freien deutschen Hochstift, ed. Heinz Otto Burger et al. (Frankfurt am Main: S. Fischer, 1975), 7.

98. Arthur Schnitzler, "Die Nächste," vol. 2 of *Das erzählerische Werk,* (Frankfurt am Main: Fischer, 1961), 48.

ter; now spring and the acquaintance with the new woman revive his sexual desire. He dreams of his wife and "fühlte sich wieder von dem Duft ihres Leibes umhüllt" (58). When he accompanies the prostitute home, it is her smell that seduces him as much as her warmth and the gestures so reminiscent of his late wife's. "Wieder stieg der Duft von ihrem Hals empor zu ihm, zugleich fühlte er ihre Lippen heiß auf den seinen" (64). When he wakes up beside her, however, guilt haunts him; he feels disgusted and deceived as if by an impostor and kills her. Then he calls the police. Memory and eroticism are the main realms of that sensory modality in the Viennese circle. This applies to another of Schnitzler's short stories, "Blumen,"[99] to a particular extent. The first-person narrator is haunted by (the smell of) the flowers that are brought to his door on the very day of the month he used to received flowers from his lover. Now, however, his lover is dead. Although the arrival of those flowers can be easily explained as the accidental continuation of her standing order at the flower shop, the narrator is extremely moved and keeps the bunch even long after it has wilted and dried up, and he cannot overcome the memory associated with it. These flowers are "Gespenster," "ghosts," and even after they are reduced to "dry stalks," "dürre[] Stengel im Glas," they are still powerful, "mächtiger als aller Fliederduft und Frühling" (227). It is not until his new lover throws them out that the narrator is free from the spell and able to notice again a fresh smell, the "kühlen weißen Flieder . . . ein so gesunder frischer Duft" (228).

Stefan George, probably the most strictly formalist and aestheticist of all the authors discussed here, uses the olfactory element sparingly, almost by allusion only. In the thirty-one poems of the collection *Das Jahr der Seele* from 1897[100] we find a very subtle discourse on air, wind, and mostly only just hints at scents. All these instances except one refer to nature, but only one of them is of the more robust "the smell of . . . " type: "Die blätter die den boden gilben / verbreiten neuen wohlgeruch" (123). All the others except the lines "Du aber weißt nichts . . . / Von schalen die mit wolkenreinem rauche / Der strengen tempel finsternis erwärmen" (125) are hints like the following, barely odorous: "Ein wind umweht uns frühlingsweich" (122); "Dies leichte duften oder leise wehen" (124); "Du führtest mich zu den verwunschnen talen / Von nackter helle und von blassen düften" (127). Often temperature is implied: "Beim ersten lauen hauche

99. Arthur Schnitzler, "Blumen," vol. 1 of *Das erzählerische Werk*.

100. Stefan George, *Das Jahr der Seele,* vol. 1 of *Werke. Ausgabe in zwei Bänden* (Munich: Helmut Küpper, 1958), 117–35.

wird sie wach" (126), or "Tauwind fährt in ungestümen / Stössen über brache schollen" (130) as well as "der glutwind" (131). Air and wind as carriers of something are also implied in "Der lüfte schaukeln wie von neuen dingen" or in the line "Und laues schmiegen trocknete den tau" (134).

The olfactory element is not missing, but it is present only in its vaguest, most ephemeral form as the medium of air, wind, and breezes that more often than not carry scents by implication and by allusion to the landscape and the objects over which they roam, such as "Der liebe sachten schlaf im blumenfelde" (135). This technique of verbal allusion to the olfactory is structurally a near inversion of what we have encountered so far where the mention of smell broke a memory block, created text, and set free remembrance and association. With George, the hints are so subtle that the reader is tempted to try to recreate the smell itself (rather than have a memory recalled by a smell), which, however, is virtually impossible to achieve for this sensory modality. The reference, therefore, remains almost purely linguistic, and the olfactory does not break out of the verbal form that the poem represents and that is George's ultimate concern. It blends in with the overall imagery and the atmosphere that each piece preciously creates. The poet is toeing a very thin line in his use of the olfactory, risking the imaginative breakup of the carefully wrought formal structure. But the inclusion of this subtle and highly allusive representational medium seems worth the risk.

Before moving on to Rilke let us briefly recapitulate the strands of argument woven so far. We have found the solid bourgeois subject confronting a solid object world, acting in it, and thereby defining and mediating subject and object. With regard to sensory and perceptual acts, this subject with its eighteenth-century heritage of a hermeneutic bent has been moving through the increasingly positivistic nineteenth century, sanitizing its environment and creating space as well as developing the corresponding perceptual subtlety for new sensory experiences. Toward the end of the bourgeois realist epoch we noticed the first ailments of the heart, the central symbolic organ of the bourgeoisie, representing active life, as well as serving as the seat of emotions and perceptions. The respiratory system also became affected, and we had to diagnose frequent nervous attacks.

The new phenomenon has been the increasing role of the olfactory sense in poetry long before its comparable emergence in prose, certainly in German literature. The reason that smell appears in poetry before prose has indirectly to do with the traditional generic perception of prose as object- and action-oriented and rational, poetry as subjective, contemplative, and emotional; prose representing the external world, poetry the internal. But this distinction is called into question by the poets themselves. It is time to elaborate on this categorical model. The true center from which the new developments in perception are radiating is hidden below the generic surface distinction. It is the subject itself and its slipping hold on reality. The modern "I" seems increasingly unable to derive from the concrete phenomenological world the supportive feedback for its own cohesion. No longer driven by the regularly beating heart that powers a closed system of circulatory interaction between subject and object world, it is more and more given to the unpredictable antics of the nervous system with its open, raw surfaces presented to the outside. This subject, as becomes visible in painting, loses its solid contours, receives vague, hazy outlines in impressionism, and dissolves completely in pointillism. Taking distance, stepping back from it, is the only way to put it together again and have it reappear as a whole. What the dot is to painting, the poem is to literature, with memory marking distance. It is the poem, itself reshaped by its (French) practitioners, that for the time being expresses best the new subject's feeling of isolated moments of perception and remembrance, rather than prose with its emphasis on description and action, of production and appropriation. The new, modern subject no longer exists prior to the text. Its self-construction is no longer a simple "I"/not-"I," subject-object relation but is a move from subject to object and back through a text, through forgetting and remembering, through memory. It is in the text that the phenomena and their perception, both past and present, are mediated with the subject. This calls for a concept of the modern subject as process.

The new poem is about a *sujet instantané,* dispersed in moment after moment, disintegrated into perceptual acts and memory, the two essential components of identity. This is what the genre of poetry in its traditional (lyrical) understanding contributes: the moment, the introspection, the personal. What is added by Baudelaire, Rimbaud, and Verlaine is an existential urgency unknown before. And what will be added eventually, when the borderline to prose is broken down, is the temporal dimension and phenomenological and perceptual continuity of narration and description. To use another example from the visual arts, the subject appears more and more in the liquid form of multiexposure photographs. In its realist, naturalist, and ultimately in its decadent form prose goes on to tell the deeds of a subject, however fragile, and its interaction with the world. Poetry by that time has already been probing the subject's borders, its weak spots and its breaking points. As the new medium in which to launch such investigations, the sense of smell has emerged, the transgressive, permeating, elusive trace, binding inside and outside, present event and memory, enclosed space and surface, subject and object. Smell, the processual sense, is becoming the realm in which and through which subject and object meet and mingle.

The epoch of taming by naming is thus coming to its end, historically as well as ontologically. The naming authority, the subject, has organized the world along lines still adhered to on the day-to-day basis of a realism that has become our reality, and of the adult linguistic curtailment of sensory experience that has turned into our everyday iron cage of perception. It has set things and itself in relation to one another, but now begins to lose its identity. De Saussure's name stands for the first linguistic thrust in this direction, probing the margins of language and the object world; and Rilke is the first author in German to compose this new subject in prose.

It is not accidental that *Malte Laurids Brigge,* the first radically modern German novel in this respect, takes place in Paris and is the product of an author who never subscribed to *Lokalkolorit* and *Heimat* in the bourgeois sense so dear to many a German writer during the nineteenth century. Rilke, the embodiment of the polyglot cosmopolitan writer, can only come into his own in Paris. Rilke's novel, published in 1910 after several years of gestation, is a text radically different in its description, or more precisely, in its representation of the modern subject. Compared with *Malte, Buddenbrooks* is a more traditional novel whose subjects are, however problematic, still cohesive social and historical entities and as such form the central theme of the book's narrative. It is the narrator who provides the unifying perspective of the process of decay that takes place over several generations, so that the problematic status of the individual emerges in a slow, supraindividual, sociohistorical, yet almost genetically determined development. *Remembrance of Things Past* on the other hand is an account from much closer up and from within an individual. Both narratives have one thing in common; the subject, however problematic, exists, takes part in social processes and develops over time. It is in novels such as these that the end of the bourgeois realist master plot becomes visible in its most beautiful and most subtle forms. The telltale sign of change is the representation of the subject itself, which is no longer perceived as creator but more and more as created, composed and recomposed, moment after moment, in its interaction with society. In *Malte Laurids Brigge* the subject and the object world are clearly no longer given a priori and independently of each other, with the latter left to the exploration by the former. They have entered a much closer and at the same time a dialectically contrastive relationship. The "I" constitutes itself, both in its phenomenologically concrete aspects, as well as through memory, in interaction with the external world which, however, appears as fragmented, if not altogether the projection of that individual. There is a strong solipsistic touch in the circular structure of such interaction in which thoughts, concepts, and analyses of the subject are backed by and based on subjective, perceptual immediacy rather than intellectual and structural reasoning. In this lies a large part of the seduction of Rilke's prose (and poetry) as well as the reason for its rejection by many. He rewards the reader in a splendid currency that turns out to be nonconvertible. A structural analysis of the novel that fails to take into account its subject-centrism as the overriding paradigm over the present-past structure, cannot adequately explain the fundamental newness of Rilke's work in German literature.[101]

The metaphor of fragmentation is present both in Malte's architectural surrounding and inside the subject. It is present from the opening page in the "hohe[], warme[] Mauer" (709); it runs through those inside out houses that stimulate Malte's imagination (749ff) and the burnt-down castle of the Schulin family (836ff) he remembers from his childhood. But the metaphor is present in his memory, too, where the image of the old family home at Urnekloster seems "aus unendlicher Höhe in mich hineingestürzt und auf meinem Grunde zerschlagen."[102] Malte, this "junge belanglose Ausländer," this "Nichts" (726), this nobody who was "wie eine leere Stelle" (730), has to start writing. Not to name and tame objects, this time, but to circumscribe, to locate himself vis-à-vis his past and the object world, to catch the fleeting moments where perception and memories intersect and yield meaning in a momentary discourse. Malte has to write—but it could be anybody. Names do not matter anymore. Perceiving and remembering are becoming the same activity and olfactory perception emerges as their medium. Smells just barely, in mere traces of matter, re-member and give form and life to memories. Names, indeed, do not

---

101. For a summary of structural approaches throughout the first half of this century, see Walter Seifert, *Das epische Werk Rainer Maria Rilkes* (Bonn: Bouvier, 1969), esp. 195ff.

102. Rainer Maria Rilke, *Die Aufzeichnungen des Malte Laurids Brigge*, vol. 6 of *Sämtliche Werke*, ed. Rilke Archiv with Ruth Sieber-Rilke and Ernst Zinn (Frankfurt am Main: Insel, 1966), 729. All references are to this edition. Pagination for the novel runs from 702–946.

matter anymore as the big cat goes around the second-hand bookstores in the rue de Seine that do not seem to do much business, the cat "die die Stille noch größer macht, indem sie die Bücherreihen entlang streicht, als wischte sie die Namen von den Rücken" (747).

Malte Laurids Brigge: "Ein Duft ohne Rest"

> Ich bin in Paris, die es hören freuen sich, die meisten beneiden mich. Sie haben recht. Es ist eine große Stadt, groß, voll merkwürdiger Versuchungen.... Ich bin diesen Versuchungen erlegen, und das hat gewisse Veränderungen zur Folge gehabt, wenn nicht in meinem Charakter, so doch in meiner Weltanschauung, jedenfalls in meinem Leben. Eine vollkommen andere Auffassung aller Dinge hat sich unter diesen Einflüssen in mir herausgebildet, es sind gewisse Unterschiede da, die mich von den Menschen mehr als alles Bisherige abtrennen. Eine veränderte Welt. Ein neues Leben voll neuer Bedeutungen. Ich habe es augenblicklich etwas schwer, weil alles zu neu ist. Ich bin ein Anfänger in meinen eigenen Verhältnissen. (774–75)[103]

Malte is, like Des Esseintes, the last representative of a noble family, with roots in the Danish countryside and on estates such as Ulsgaard and Urnekloster. Unlike Des Esseintes, however, he is poor. His moving to the big city, as opposed to Des Esseintes's moving away from it, is at least partly motivated by his hope to make a living. He is twenty-eight, a writer who has published a few "Verse" (723) that he now rejects, for they were not written as true *Verse* should be, as "Erfahrungen" (724) that one forgets until they return as *Erinnerungen*. But these are not yet sufficient either. "Die Erinnerungen selbst sind es noch nicht" (724); they have to become flesh and blood first, "nicht mehr zu unterscheiden von uns selbst" (725). Experience and memories that are forgotten while they incorporate themselves in the subject will emerge as text, as the narrated subject, the only one possible.

---

103. I am in Paris. Those who know it are pleased; many envy me. They are right. It is a big city full of strange temptations. . . . I have given in to these temptations, which has produced some changes. Not in my character, but in my worldview, certainly in my life. A completely new understanding of all things has emerged under these influences, and there are now certain distinctions that separate me from other humans more than anything so far. A changed world. A new life full of new meanings. I am currently in a difficult position because everything is too new for me. I am a beginner in my own things.

How does Malte, who feels that he "müßte anfangen, etwas zu arbeiten" (723), put his own prescription for *Verse* into practice? (*Verse* we
will not take literally to mean poetry but the "new" text discussed
above.) He operates, and is operated on, on three levels that can be derived from the opening quote of this chapter. His life in the city brings
with it *Versuchungen*, new experiences, new perceptions. They, in turn,
lead to *Veränderungen*, to a new weltanschauung, to a totally different
Auffassung of all things. We might say, they lead to a disorientation, a
temporary loss of identity, leaving Malte an *Anfänger* in his own affairs.
Out of this experience emerges a life full of new *Bedeutungen*, as he reconstructs his world, a beginner yet, but making progress. This tripartite
move, in which Malte sketches his crisis and the possibility of its overcoming, is paralleled in the context of his age, in psychoanalysis. The historical subject of psychoanalysis from around the turn of the century has
undergone new unsettling perceptions and experiences and has, unable to
deal with them, fixated itself on fragments thereof, instances and moments in the flux of phenomena, which have started to become unstable
with the crumbling of the bourgeois master plot in social reality and its
deconstruction at the hands of the analyst. This historical subject, increasingly hysterical and neurotic as a result, undergoes a three-step recovery
procedure parallel to Malte's, except for its conceptual emphasis on past
events rather than the immediate present: remembering, repeating, and
working through.

Yet a third parallel tripartite process becomes visible in writing itself as
écriture. Malte gives us its model in his comment on *Verse*, which must be
based on experiences that are forgotten and remembered. In a second step
they are encoded. Malte goes so far as to call it incorporation, thereby
explicitly making the link between the body and the text, for only if those
memories become "Blut, . . . Blick und Gebärde" (725) can they, in the last
step, be reconstructed as text. Remembering, encoding, reconstructing:
this is precisely what the novel does.[104] The link between psychoanalysis
and writing has been pointed out by (among many others) Friedrich Kittler, who sees a veritable competition between the two. "Dieselbe Quelle,
dasselbe Objekt, derselbe Ertrag—Schriftsteller und Psychoanalytiker

---

104. On reconstruction see also Schachtel, *Metamorphosis*, 294n. Our concept of reconstruction includes the freeplay of language in relation to its phenomenological and
perceptual base, which is greatest for the olfactory.

rücken in eine Nähe, wie sie enger nicht Dichter und Denker vor 1800 verband."[105]

The following analysis is restricted to the literary three-step and begins with the question of perception (the narrative present, Paris) and remembering (which in itself may include perceptual acts). It is striking from the first page of the novel what an astute observer in terms of sensory perception Malte is. We find touch as well as temperature (the "hohe[], warme[] Mauer"); we find smell ("Die Gasse begann von allen Seiten zu riechen"); there is vision and its opposite, blindness ("Dann habe ich ein eigentümlich starblindes Haus gesehen"); the mouth is mentioned, even if not in gustatory, but in olfactory terms: "Das Kind schlief, der Mund war offen, atmete Jodoform"; and there are sounds, too: "Elektrische Bahnen rasen läutend durch meine Stube," and there is silence, "furchtbarer" than the noise itself (709–10).

The city is for Malte a treasure trove of impressions and furnishes him with a wealth of sensory stimuli that create, as he writes them down, a strangely anthropomorphic quality in the object world: the "starblindes Haus" (709); the breaking, laughing window pane that causes Malte to hear "ihre großen Scherben lachen" while "die kleinen Splitter kichern" (710). The city changes his mode of perception, so that he notes, "Ich lerne sehen" (710). He does not yet have the ability for "Rezeption in der Zerstreuung," the Benjaminian "distracted perception."[106] On the contrary, Malte takes perception seriously and thus marks a historically short-lived position. He is a modernist who is leaving traditional realism and its perceptual and psychological shortchanging behind in a kind of writing that specifically hinges on the perceptual-psychological nexus. Only a few years later, however, as Benjamin makes clear—indeed by referring to Rilke as an author whose poems allow and even require "Zeit zur Sammlung und Stellungnahme" ("Kunstwerk," 391)—Malte's way of perception and writing will be obsolete.[107] The consequence of this kind of perception is

---

105. Friedrich A. Kittler, *Aufschreibesysteme 1800–1900* (Munich: Wilhelm Fink, 1985), 295. For Rilke, see esp. the chapter "Rebus," 271ff. "The same source, the same object, the same result—writers and psychoanalists are as close as were the poets and thinkers before 1800."

106. Benjamin, "Kunstwerk," 393.

107. The consequence for our investigation is that the role established and defined for the olfactory in Rilke's work will have to be redefined and will change even as smell continues to be a tool for literary characterization and seems here to stay. In a more general context, the current renewed interest in the Vienna of the turn of the century, in fin-de-siècle and decadence phenomena, has to to with the central position of perception and psychology in emerging modernism, which has not yet received full attention. The

profound and affects Malte directly. He notices that everything penetrates "tiefer in mich ein und bleibt nicht an der Stelle stehen, wo es sonst immer zu Ende war. Ich habe ein Inneres, von dem ich nichts wußte, alles geht jetzt dorthin. Ich weiß nicht, was dort geschieht" (710–11). This interior space where things disappear is not the psychoanalytical subconscious, the battleground of ego, id, and superego. It is something more basic and almost physical. It is the locus where perception is transformed into subjective experience, into the consciousness of oneself. It is the locus where the various discourses that the individual holds (mostly with him/herself) and that are interpenetrating to form precisely this unique individual touch their physical base, their phenomenological grounding. Although perception itself is partly socially and discursively determined and although Malte notices changes in the structure of the city, in the way people live and die, and although he does deal with forces of the id and the internalized authorities surfacing from childhood, the text he creates is a literary, artistic account, not a psychoanalytical study. It articulates perception and the phenomenological world in an aesthetic framework.

The interpenetration of interior and exterior is sensory in yet another way: it affects the perception of time. Malte becomes aware of this in the act of writing, realizing, "daß ich erst drei Wochen hier bin." In the countryside this often appeared "wie ein Tag, hier sind es Jahre." He decides not to write letters anymore, as there seems to be no need to tell somebody that he is changing. "Wenn ich mich verändere, bleibe ich ja doch nicht der, der ich war, und bin ich etwas anderes als bisher, so ist klar, daß ich keine Bekannten habe" (711).

The insight into the perceptual process and its effects on the subject is frightening. It is the fear that bourgeois realism never let surface. The perceptual experience of being shot through by the object world, the experience of time ticking away in its smallest denomination, is uncanny. Malte admits that he is afraid: "Ich fürchte mich" (712), adding, however, "gegen die Furcht muß man etwas tun, wenn man sie einmal hat" (712). And what there is to do is writing. "Ich habe etwas getan gegen die Furcht. Ich habe die ganze Nacht gesessen und geschrieben" (721). It is writing, the text, in which the subject survives. Survival is indeed the issue, for the fear mentioned above is the fear of death, made unmistakably clear as the passage

---

context is provided by the modernism versus postmodernism debate with its perceived need for checking the accounts of early modernism once again. New (literary) Historicism is but one upshoot.

continues: "Es wäre sehr häßlich, hier krank zu werden, und fiele es jeman-dem ein, mich ins Hôtel Dieu zu schaffen, so würde ich dort gewiß ster-ben" (712–13). With the move toward writing, Malte is taking the next step in the process outlined above: from perception to encoding. Before we look more closely at this encoding process, however, we need to remain on the experiential level just a little longer and illustrate its historical aspect, perception as remembering, remembering as perception.

To remember, to re-member, is to give back a body to one's memories, to recreate them by means of physical, sensory experience, or to recreate them *as* such. When death (the irrevocable dis-membering) approaches Malte's grandmother, the Kammerherrin Brigge, she becomes at first ex-tremely sensitive and claims "das Jodoform" that the cook has put on her hand after she cut herself "im ganzen Hause zu riechen" (822). As she deteriorates, however, she loses her sensory abilities, "ihr Gehör wurde schwierig" (823), and she enters "nur noch selten und für Augenblicke in ihre Sinne, . . . die sie nicht mehr bewohnte" (823). Death confuses the senses, as in the case of the young woman dying on the electric trolley in Naples, with her mother screaming "in diese Augen hinein, die nicht hörten" and finally hitting "das dicke Gesicht, damit es nicht stürbe" (859). This is a moment of *Todesfurcht* for Malte. Remembering, the opposite of death and to some extent even its overcoming, occurs through present or recalled sensory experience and observation. It requires an effort on the writer's part and indeed *leisten* becomes a key term in Malte's process of remembering, encoding, and reconstructing (e.g., 843, 856, 893, 900). His final *Leistung* is the novel itself. In order to be able to write and to live, he realizes on the occasion of his father's death, "Die Kindheit würde also gewissermaßen noch zu leisten sein, wenn man sie nicht für immer verloren geben wollte" (856). The memory required for this effort is not completely reliable, as we all know. With childhood memories in particular we are often not really sure whether we remember them originally or from photos and narrative accounts. The olfactory memory however cannot be fooled; one can only remember through that mode what is truly one's own. When Malte starts burning his father's papers and letters he notices that most of them "hatten einen starken, überzeugenden Duft, der auf mich eindrang, als wollte er auch in mir Erinnerungen aufregen" (857). But Malte "hatte keine" (857). In contrast to this, visual memory lets one appropriate other people's past. The photos depicting "reife, großartige, deutlich schöne Frauen" that burn so slowly among his father's documents bring it home to Malte "daß ich doch nicht ganz ohne Erinnerungen war" (857), and they recall certain looks that he received when walking the streets as a young man with his father.[108]

The letters burnt by Malte are not his own; the past associated with them is not his, and however directly smell is associated with memory here, it is not Malte's memory, and the appeal fails. This is a key passage illustrating the direct phenomenological grounding of memory in sensory perception, which guarantees its authenticity. In one extreme instance even the inversion holds true, as Malte notes. Narrative, true narrative, not only addresses the senses but is capable of creating sensory impressions itself, even for the senses of proximity. He laments "daß man erzählte, wirklich erzählte, das muß vor meiner Zeit gewesen sein. . . . Der alte Graf Brahe soll es noch gekonnt haben" (844). According to Abelone, who tells Malte of one such occasion, Brahe could tell stories of Persia in a way that she felt "[ihr] riechen die Hände davon" (848). Brahe was one of those persons who believed in the past only "wenn sie *in* ihm war" (848).

Narrative and sensory perception stand in a complementary relationship. Perception, present or past, guarantees the narrative; true narrative, in turn, is able to trigger sensory perception, at least imaginatively but *in extremis* even perception of the more difficult kind as associated with the chemical senses. It is able to verify perception. This narrative, historically speaking, has become rare because bourgeois realism has curtailed the ties to its sensory grounding and restricted the sensory appeal of the represented world to the "objective" senses of vision and sound. And it limited and restructured the relation between subject and object. Objects are clearly *outside;* they are available, manageable, and at the disposal of the bourgeois individual who begins to use them as movable, exchangeable commodities. Old Brahe, in contrast, constructs himself through objects inside of him. For him objects have a history only "wenn man damit geboren wird" (848). This is the aristocratic view. In this context let us also bear in mind that the nineteenth century, the bourgeois age, is the age of history, historicism, historiography. History, even story, is no longer given through objects that one owns by inheritance but has to be constructed in

---

108. The claim that the olfactory sense, its capacities and its memory, is the truly personal sense modality is confirmed by the fact that Malte, in contrast to Hanno Buddenbrook, who is destined to die soon, does not understand the smell of the flowers around his father's coffin. "Der Geruch der Blumen war unverständlich wie viele gleichzeitige Stimmen" (851–52) whereas Hanno on a similar occasion clearly recognizes the smell of death in the air.

an object world from which subjects have grown increasingly distant.[109] Collection of objects in museums for the purpose of reconstructing and grounding history is one of the consequences of this state of things. The older pattern reverberates throughout Malte's narrative. He, the last descendent of a noble family, still feels the auratic quality of the object world. Indeed he experiences his environment through immediate sensory-sensual perception—if not extrasensory perception, a concept that in fact only expands the sensory realm by postulating a "sixth sense." To put it in Benjaminian terms, for Malte the object world (not only nature in a pantheistic sense, but even more so the secondary human creation) has retained some of its aura.

Encoding, the second step of the processual triad of writing that consists of remembering, encoding, and reconstructing as text, is clearly based on sensory perception and certain vibrations that ripple through the object world. Reconstruction now, the *Leistung,* is the effort on the narrator's part to bring together past and present as related within the subject in the form of experienced time. The parable of Malte's St. Petersburg neighbor Nikolaj Kusmitsch, who exchanges the years and months of his life for the small change of seconds in order to have more, illustrates this aspect. What happens to him is precisely that time, *Zeit,* the ultimate subjective possession and money, *Geld,* the ultimate exchangeable object, become indistinguishable, and "etwas Eigentümliches" happens to him. "Es wehte plötzlich an seinem Gesicht, es zog ihm an den Ohren vorbei, er fühlte es an den Händen. Er riß die Augen auf," only to realize that "was er verspürte, die wirkliche Zeit sei, die vorbeizog" (868–69).[110] With time, his individual, subjective lifetime rushing by, the object world too, starts dissolving. "Auch unter seinen Füßen war etwas wie eine Bewegung, nicht nur eine, mehrere, merkwürdig durcheinanderschwankende Bewegungen"

109. Malte—but we can extend this statement to Rilke himself—is particularly aware of the changing relationship between subjects and the object world, which for him is strangely alive. The "gothic" strand of this surfaces in the spirits and ghosts that haunt the story. Conceived of as the auratic, personal and historical dimension of the object world, it can be made theoretically fruitful.

110. Following is the translation of the Rilke quotes in this paragraph. "Something peculiar" is happening to Kusmitsch. "All of a sudden there was a wind in his face, blowing past his ears; he felt it on his hands. He opened his eyes" and realizes that "what he felt was real time rushing by."—"Under his feet, too, there was some kind of motion, not only one in fact, but several strangely wavering motions." Reciting poems has a beneficial effect. "If one recited a poem, slowly and with a regular emphasis on the final syllables, one had the feeling of some stability, of something to focus on within oneself, of course. How lucky he was to know all these poems."

(869). As time and space start moving around him, he sees only one escape: into text. He remains in bed and starts reciting poems. "Wenn man so ein Gedicht langsam hersagte, in gleichmäßiger Betonung der Endreime, dann war gewissermaßen etwas Stabiles da, worauf man sehen konnte, innerlich, versteht sich. Ein Glück, daß er all diese Gedichte wußte" (870).

This Nikolaj Kusmitsch is the tragicomic representative of modern man for whom time and space, subject and object have begun to dissolve and interpenetrate each other as processes and whose only refuge is the text as another form of processual cohesion, as literary theory of the past thirty years or so has pointed out. Language and texts function as solidifying agents of sensory impressions. Bergson claims that "nous tendons instinctivement à solidifier nos impressions, pour les exprimer par le langage."[111] The inversion, which is what we are dealing with here, holds true, too. By putting impressions, experiences, sensations into language, we succeed in saving them, giving them a form that allows us to analyze them. We should not, however, underestimate the effect that language itself has on the objects thus preserved. "Cette influence du langage sur la sensation est plus profonde qu'on ne le pense généralement" (Bergson, 87). Whereas Kusmitsch has foreign texts that alleviate, if not stop, the draft that has arisen in his world, Malte writes his own text. He mediates himself qua experience and sensations to himself qua text and narrative, with time enveloping all, even if in two different forms: remembered time, filled with experience and sensations, and the time of remembering, the present, within which the former rises like a building in its scaffolding. Reconstructing oneself as text, then, writing the autobiographical novel, the diary, the disjointed narrative that Malte writes, means to reconstitute a past of forgotten and now remembered sensory immediacy as immediate sensory memory, triggered by some phenomenon in the present.

Sensory perception serves a double role in this context: it triggers memory and it is recalled qua memory. Into a sentence such as "Alle Städte riechen im Sommer" (709) is packed the immediate perception of "Die Gasse begann von allen Seiten zu riechen" (709) as well as the experience and memory of other cities in the past. To re-member is to turn the past into flesh and blood, into the authentic text, the poem, *Verse* (cf. 725). To re-member is to put together what has become disjointed, the house at Urnekloster, the home, which is "ganz aufgeteilt in mir" (729). *Er-innern,*

---

111. Bergson, "Les données immédiates," 86. "We tend instinctively to consolidate our impressions in order to express them in language."—"This influence of language on sensation is more profound than we generally think" (87).

in the same vein, is to search for the past inside oneself, to search for the house that is "in mich hineingestürzt" (729). It means to investigate this "Inneres, von dem ich nichts wußte" (711). These are the places where the processes of reconstruction have to start. The house as home is always already lost.

There are two such attempts at reconstruction of houses, the lost romantic home, both characterized by the presence of smells. The first is the famous description of the dismantled buildings in a Paris street; "es waren Häuser, die nicht mehr da waren" (749). It is their inside out walls that Malte sees and reconstructs as the former rooms with their furniture, even their inhabitants and their life histories. For him "das zähe Leben dieser Zimmer hatte sich nicht zertreten lassen" (750), and he feels

> die zähe, träge, stockige Luft, die kein Wind noch zerstreut hatte... und das Ausgeatmete und der jahrealte Rauch und der Schweiß, der unter den Schultern ausbricht und die Kleider schwer macht, und das Fade aus den Munden und der Fuselgeruch gärender Füße. Da stand das Scharfe vom Urin und das Brennen vom Ruß und grauer Kartoffeldunst und der schwere, glatte Gestank von alterndem Schmalze. Der süße, lange Geruch von vernachlässigten Säuglingen war da und der Angstgeruch der Kinder, die in die Schule gehen, und das Schwüle aus den Betten mannbarer Knaben. Und vieles hatte sich dazugesellt, was von unten gekommen war, aus dem Abgrund der Gasse, die verdunstete, und anderes war von oben herabgesickert mit dem Regen, der über den Städten nicht rein ist. Und manches hatten die schwachen, zahm gewordenen Hauswinde, die immer in derselben Straße bleiben, zugetragen, und es war noch vieles da, wovon man den Ursprung nicht wußte. (750–51)[112]

The frightening thing for Malte is that he recognizes this wall. "Ich erkenne das alles hier, und darum geht es so ohne weiters in mich ein: es ist zu

---

112. "The tough life of these rooms had not been crushed."—There was

the tough, inert, stuffy air that no wind had dispersed yet . . . and the exhalations and the age-old smoke and the sweat from the armpits that makes the clothes heavy; the bad breath and the fetid odor of fermenting feet. There was the sharp stench of urine and the burning sensation of soot and the gray steam of potatoes and the heavy, smooth stench of old lard. The sweet, long odor of neglected babies was there too and the smell of fear of school-children, and the sultry haze from the beds of adolescent boys. And many things had accrued from below, evaporated from the abyss of the street; and other smells had filtered down with the rain, which is not clean over the cities. And many things had been accumulated by the tame house-winds that

Hause in mir" (751). It is not accidental that smell is the medium of reconstruction here (although vision is strongly present, too). It is the sense of the modern age, penetrating, yet without substance, inside as memory, and outside as strong trigger of memory, a sense of proximity, as well as one of (temporal) distance, "ein Geschmack in der Ferne" as Kant puts it,[113] thereby hinting at the ingestion (*er-innern*) necessary and the disgust (*Ekel,* in psychoanalytical terms, resistance) so often associated with it.

The second such scene is a remembered scene from the past. It occurs on the occasion of a visit that Malte and his parents pay the Schulins, an old family whose castle has burnt down, so that they are reduced to living in one of its former wings. For Malte, however, an adolescent at that time, and his mother, the old building is still present. Even their coachman, as they drive up in the early dusk of a Danish winter evening, "hatte ganz vergessen, daß das Haus nicht da war, und für uns alle war es in diesem Augenblick da" (835).[114] In fact, they walk right up the central stairs and have to be called down by the Schulins. "'Aber es war doch eben ein Haus da,' sagte Maman" (838). In the course of the evening, Malte tries to escape, but is caught and brought back by one of the Schulin daughters. "'Das Haus will ich sehen,' sagte ich stolz. Sie begriff nicht. 'Das große Haus draußen an der Treppe.' 'Schaf,' machte sie, . . . 'da ist doch gar kein Haus mehr'" (839). Malte is convinced that "wenn Maman und ich hier wohnten, so wäre es immer da" (840). All of a sudden, however, the adults fall silent

---

always remain in the same streets, and there were many other things of which one did not know the origin.

113. Kant, *Anthropologie,* 52–53. He calls smell a "taste in the distance" or a "far-reaching taste."

114. Following are the translations of the quotes in this paragraph. The coachman himself "had forgotten that the house was not there, and for all of us it existed at that moment." Maman protests that "there was a house there, just now," and Malte sneaks out to look at it: "'I want to see the house,' I said proudly. She did not understand. 'The big house by the stairs.' 'You sheep,' she said, . . . 'there is no house there anymore.'" But Malte is convinced that "if Maman and I were living here it would always be there." In the subsequent hush "the large objects from the old house were crowding in far too closely on the people."—"'Maman is sniffing the air, . . . we all have to be very quiet, she is sniffing with her ears,' she herself was standing there with raised eyebrows, attentive and all nose." In the Schulins's narrow quarters "a smell rose every minute and was investigated and commented on. Zoë worked on the stove, . . . the count was walking around, pausing in the corners, waiting. . . . The countess had gotten up and did not know where to search. My father turned around as if the smell were behind him. The marchesa who had immediately assumed that it was an unpleasant smell, pressed her handkerchief to her face. . . . As far as I am concerned, I had eagerly been sniffing along." "The adults themselves who had been talking and laughing just a minute ago were walking around, stooping, and preoccupied with something invisible; they admitted that

and "hinter den Menschen drängten sich die großen Gegenstände aus dem alten Hause, viel zu nah" (840), and one of the Schulin daughters whispers, "'Mama riecht, . . . da müssen wir immer alle still sein, sie riecht mit den Ohren,' dabei aber stand sie selbst mit hochgezogenen Augenbrauen da, aufmerksam und ganz Nase." By way of an explanation, Malte describes the rooms as cramped and overheated, so that

> jeden Augenblich ein Geruch auf[kam], und dann untersuchte man ihn, und jeder gab seine Meinung ab. Zoë machte sich am Ofen zu tun, . . . der Graf ging umher und stand ein wenig in jeder Ecke und wartete. . . . Die Gräfin war aufgestanden und wußte nicht, wo sie suchen sollte. Mein Vater drehte sich langsam um sich selbst, als hätte er den Geruch hinter sich. Die Marchesin, die sofort angenommen hatte, daß es ein garstiger Geruch sei, hielt ihr Taschentuch vor. . . . Was mich angeht, so hatte ich fleißig mitgerochen,

says Malte of himself, but then realizes that all the

> deutlichen großen Menschen, die eben noch gesprochen und gelacht hatten, gebückt herumgingen und sich mit etwas Unsichtbarem beschäftigten; daß sie zugaben, daß da etwas war, was sie nicht sahen. Und es war schrecklich, daß es stärker war als sie alle. (841)

Malte, scared, seeks refuge with his mother, and only as she holds him and he feels "daß sie innen zitterte, so wußte ich, daß das Haus jetzt erst wieder verging" (842).

Reconstruction in smell, the liminal option among the senses, is what Malte practices here, and the building planned and hoped for is home, always home. But Malte, the poet who says of himself that he has "kein Dach über mir, und es regnet mir in die Augen" (747), is nevertheless scared of the home where everything is fixed and unchangeable, where the love of its inhabitants has determined once and for all the role of the young man.[115] He does not want to be the prodigal son, returning to that home

---

there was something they did not see. And it was frightening that it was stronger than all of them" (841).

115. Following is the translation of the quotes in this paragraph. Malte, the poet, "has no roof over his head, and the rain is falling into his eyes" (747). Yet he does not want a home where one "only had to enter into its full smell in order to know that everything had been decided." In Venice he feels "a continuously expanding spirit that was stronger

where one "mußte nur eintreten in seinen vollen Geruch, schon war das Meiste entschieden" (940). The home and the love he seeks are better described in the song he hears in Venice, the place he loves and reveres, the Venice of a "sich fortwährend erweiternder Geist, der stärker war als der Duft aromatischer Länder" (932). There, on a social occasion, he meets a young singer who walks up to him; and "ihr Kleid schien mich an, der blumige Geruch ihrer Wärme stand um mich" (935). She sings an unknown German love song "wie etwas Notwendiges" (936). She sings of a love that lasts because it is not possessive. "Du machst mich allein. Dich einzig kann ich vertauschen. / Eine Weile bist dus, dann wieder ist es das Rauschen, / oder es ist ein Duft ohne Rest. / Ach, in den Armen hab ich sie alle verloren, / du nur, du wirst immer wieder geboren: / weil ich niemals dich anhielt, halt ich dich fest" (936). The metaphor of the "Duft ohne Rest" captures the essence of this sensory mode, its elusiveness, as well as its unbreakable bonds to one's past, to one's love, to oneself.

With Rilke we have reached a level of sensory acuteness not encountered before in our investigation. *Malte* combines the various strands of writing outlined previously to form a qualitatively new situation for the human subject, this modern alienation, homelessness, *Unbehaustheit*. Not only the situation, however, the subject itself is new. It has become an entity embedded in, and affected by, its environment rather than confronting it, determined by it as much as determining it. This subject is no longer clearly and firmly circumscribed, but has become fuzzy in its contours. It is no longer a static, but rather an interactive entity. This change has affected the senses. No longer are they the faithful hermeneutic instruments applied to an outside object for the purpose of data gathering in visual, aural, or whatever terms and reporting of the findings to the central processing unit. Now they are sensors of *Befindlichkeit*, beingness, in both its subjective and objective orientation. It is with *Malte* eventually, that we have reached what *Against the Grain* seemed to promise, particularly for the sense of smell, but failed to deliver: true refinement not only in perception, but in imagination: the world inside out as much as outside in.

---

than the perfumes of aromatic countries." The woman's dress "was radiating out to me, the flowery smell of her warmth surrounded me." Her song is sung "like something necessary." The song goes like this: "You make me alone. You only I can interchange. / For a while it is you, then it's only a whisper, / or it is a scent without rest. / Alas, in my arms I lost them all, / only you are reborn again and again: / because I never restrained you, I hold you fast."

CHAPTER 4

From Expressionism to the Shoah: Power and Stench

Sagt mir doch, meine Thiere: diese höheren Menschen insgesammt—riechen sie vielleicht nicht gut? Oh reine Gerüche um mich! Jetzo weiss und fühle ich erst, wie ich euch, meine Thiere liebe.
—(Nietzsche, *Zarathustra* IV, "Das Lied der Schwermut")

Our investigation so far has traced the emergence of and interest in odors, revealed nuances and time lags between manifestations of the phenomenon in various nations and cultures, as well as generic correlations and individual preferences and idiosyncrasies of authors. The phases in the literary emergence of olfaction have shown correspondence with, as well as distinctions from, the traditional literary epochal divisions, and an explicitly aesthetic component has become noticeable as well as a growing awareness of smells in psychology.

The core of the material in this chapter does not—and I believe should not—simply be integrated into a literary categorization without some preliminary consideration, and even then only in a formal way. Although dealing with such literary categories as autobiography, diary, documentary literature, drama, and film, the content of these works, the Shoah, stands, and hopefully will remain, outside the routine of categorization. Our own inquiry, brought to bear on the horrors of the Nazi death camps, gains a new dimension and a revelatory function not encountered so far. In the atrocious surroundings of the camps everything we have said about smells—the whole unfolding of modern olfactory history, from its registration of disgust and loathing in the seventeenth and eighteenth centuries, to its philosophical and aesthetic conceptualization in the eighteenth century and its near banishment in the nineteenth, to its libidinal-aesthetic status with hedonistic and individualistic undertones around the turn from the nineteenth to the twentieth century—is thrown into unexpected relief in the horrendous reality of the camps. The momentary breakdown of the teleology of olfaction within the breakdown of the process of civilization lays bare its oldest and deepest roots and reveals the general direction this teleology has been taking, away from its primordial origins and yet always very much in touch with them.

The texts discussed in this chapter fit uneasily into a traditional literary-historical division of epochs or genres. Rather, they have been selected around a topic: fascism, the Shoah, and the lingering of the fascist mentality in the early postwar years in Germany. Our emphasis is thus less on chronology and olfactory historiography than on thematic issues. This allows us to investigate our topic from the angle of political power structures, their textual representation, and the sensory repertory used for that purpose. Despite this thematic rather than historical and categorical frame, we are participating in a historical debate around the issue of the *Stunde Null*, the zero hour in German literature, and we will be able to contribute new aspects to it. There is no *Stunde Null* from our perspective,[1] because texts from both before and after 1945 dealing with fascism stink.

The material in this chapter is presented in terms of a historical break, a rupture caused by a social and political situation that could not have been inferred from the facts and trends previously outlined. This chapter describes a relapse into barbarism, an onslaught against the civilizing process that we have been following on our olfactory trail. By applying a moral standard to the events in question, a challenge is posed to the tentative aesthetic framework we have begun to sketch for the olfactory around a core of individual, hedonistic concerns. The present texts force us to accept moral issues as an essential component in further discussions of olfactory perception. It is true that olfactory standardization has been part of social power structures for a long time, in the sense of Eagleton's mapping of social norms onto the individual by means of aesthetic valuation, for instance. The trend was clear in nineteenth-century bourgeois realism. Now, however, smells appear as a much more serious phenomenon, arising out of unrestrainedly violent power structures. Smells, both good and bad, are now all of a sudden involved in something larger and far more terrible than

---

1. This answer is not new, of course. It has been given based on biographical considerations of authors involved as well as on account of a German literature written in exile.

social or personal gratification. They revert from the civilizational to the primordial realm with its raw immediacy. In the frightening *mise-en-scène* of an extermination program of truly mass-industrial proportions, they shift from the intellectual and aesthetic superstructure into the very base of the power structure.

There are, then, two contrasting positions to be briefly discussed here. The first is to treat the Nazi death camp as incommensurable with anything ever before or since and hence outside an explanatory historicoscientific discourse. In this view the death camp marks a monumental breakdown of any chain of cause and effect in the sense that there *is* no cause that would explain the horrendous results.[2] Much of the research and analysis on the subject, however, tries to do the opposite: to find reasons and explanations for what happened. Inevitably, this approach falls short. As Lifton points out, it runs into the dilemma of wanting to understand, yet by all means to avoid siding with the perpetrators.[3] Yet it is this attitude only that holds forth the promise of a critical working through and possible prevention of a repetition of the events. Explanatory accounts of this kind, whether written by survivors or others, are by their very nature more removed from the events, and differ markedly from the autobiographical narratives by survivors who equally might want to understand what happened, might still want to accuse or justify, but above all want to *tell*. These texts show a tremendous urge to let the world know something that it cannot possibly imagine. Indeed, these accounts often reflect the very process of finding words to overcome a silence about events barely imaginable for people who were not exposed to them. To convey the message, it is necessary to describe, to put into language an experience that nearly defies narratability. These accounts form a literary category, which, in its struggle to communicate, to make known, is at a loss for, and in search of, adequate linguistic means. A stark naturalism with reference to all sensory modes is one textual strategy often pursued, and this is the aspect that concerns us here.

This first group of texts differs from a second, adduced below, the Nazi

2. This is, roughly, one position in the recent *Historikerstreit* in Germany. A lot has been written on this issue. Cf. for instance Charles S. Maier, *The Unmasterable Past: History, Holocaust, and German National Identity* (Cambridge: Harvard University Press, 1988), which Gordon Craig in his review calls "the best book available on the tangled and acrimonious debate among the German historians" (*New York Review of Books* 2 February 1989, 10–15).

3. Robert Jay Lifton, *The Nazi Doctors: Medical Killing and the Psychology of Genocide* (New York: Basic Books, 1986). Cf. both the foreword and the introduction (11).

accounts. The latter display a stance of business as usual, as if nothing out of the ordinary were happening. It is indeed the translation of the horror into the reified and reifying language of Nazi-German bureaucracy that creates on the textual level much of that banality of evil Hannah Arendt talks about.

Our own approach occurs from the safe distance of posteriority and is based on both types of texts just mentioned. In order to understand the role of the olfactory in the survivors' accounts it is necessary to outline briefly what happened to that sensory mode in the early years of the twentieth century after we left it with the aestheticists and Rilke at the height of its sensual and individual potential. We are not, however, constructing for the present purpose an olfactory history or outline of sensory development that leads to, or even culminates in, the Nazi death camps. Rather, the brief spot check of the literary world between aestheticism and symbolism on the one hand and the literary reaction to emerging fascism and its aftermath on the other simply serves the purpose of showing in what context and in whose company we find the olfactory in the years prior to World War II. If this inquiry reveals a trend, it is only recognizable in retrospect, seen through the horror of the death camps.

I will call the genre in which the olfactory unfolds during these intermediate years technofantasy. The examples discussed here take their starting point in the sense of touch, but aim at a total sensory appeal.

From the "Idee vom Ferntaster" to *Brave New World*

The writer and philosopher Salomo Friedlaender (1871–1946, pseudonym Mynona) rises to some prominence in the teens of the century not so much by virtue of his neo-Kantian philosophy but through his sharp and witty short prose satires and grotesque sketches, which he publishes in the various expressionist journals of the day and gathers into a first collection in 1913.[4] From that time dates the "Idee vom Ferntaster."[5] The gadget described in this short story would facilitate the most advanced communication imaginable, the bodily transferral of its user from one place to another, thus making him or her of palpable reality for the receiver. In this ultimate

---

4. Mynona, *Rosa, die schöne Schutzmannsfrau und andere Grotesken,* ed. Ellen Otten (Zürich: Arche, 1965).

5. Mynona, *Der verliebte Leichnam: Grotesken—Erzählungen—Gedichte,* ed. Klaus Konz (Hamburg: Galgenberg, 1985), 34–35.

communicative network, communication would amount to actual transportation by multiplication of "tactile profiles" and thus regain a physical reality and concreteness that it has long lost.

Mein Gesicht reicht milchstraßenweit, mein Gehör unter Unständen meilenweit, mein Geruch unglücklicherweise bis in das W. C. des Lyrikers Erpresber.... Aber schmecken und tasten kann ich all die Lieben nur, wenn ich sie ganz dicht bei mir habe.... Es geht aus allem hervor, wenn mich einer fragt: wo bin ich? daß er dann eigentlich meint: wo bin ich zu tasten. Denn gesehen, gehört, gerochen könnte er auch anderswo werden. (34)[6]

To Mynona, it seems only logical that what is missing in communication equipment is the *Telehaptor:* "So haben wir denn Telegraphie, Telephonie, der Fernseher ist so gut wie fix und fertig. Und nur die Telehaptie, der Telehaptor, der Ferntaster läßt noch auf sich warten" (34). The new technology Mynona envisages is very simple. "Stellen Sie sich einfach nackt...auf eine Art Wagschale, deren Zwilling am Ziel Ihrer Bestimmung schwankt: Im Handumdrehen ist alles, was an Ihnen tastbar, wägbar ist, hindurchtelehaptiert!" (35). The only catch is, at this point, that *Telehaptieren* only works for naked persons; clothes, at this stage of technology, cannot be transferred. This deficiency, the narrator argues, is probably the reason why the process has not caught on more widely yet. The *Ferntaster* includes "selbstverständlich...den Fernriecher, Fernschmecker, Fernwärmer resp. -Kälter usw.," and is therefore, quite obviously, "das Ideal aller Beförderungsmittel." It might cause a true revolution "in Sonderheit auf dem bisher etwas...umständlichen Gebiet der Erotik" (35).

---

6. Following are the translations of the quotes in this paragraph: "My vision reaches as far as the Milky Way, my hearing potentially for miles, my smell unfortunately into the toilet of the lyrical poet Erpresber.... But I can only taste and touch my loved ones when they are in immediate proximity.... When somebody asks me where I am, the implication is that he is really asking where I can be felt. For I could just as well be seen, heard, smelled somewhere else." "Thus we have the telegraph, the telephone, television is almost ready. Only telehaptics, the telehaptor, is slow in coming." "Simply stand naked...on some kind of scales, whose counterpart at the receiving end will react accordingly: at the flick of a switch everything about you that is tactile and can be weighed will be telehaptically transferred!" The telehaptor includes, "naturally...the teleolfactor, the telegustator, the teleheater or telecooler respectively, etc." It is "the ideal of all means of transport" and likely to change everything "particularly in the currently still somewhat clumsy field of the erotic...."

There are three points here with an immediate bearing on our investigation and representative of the *zeitgeist* in general. The first is a fascination with technology to which, among contemporary social and cultural currents, expressionism and its intellectual surrounding are particularly given. Indeed, a number of technological breakthroughs occur around the start of the new century (radio, x-ray, and so forth). The vision of the "new man" is not infrequently associated with a technological (and often totalitarian) revolution. The catastrophe of World War I can be seen as the culmination of a belief in technological feasibility that, combined with a reckless imperialism, spells utter disregard for the individual human being. For the generation of the first two decades of the twentieth century the experience of the war with its mass deaths—due, precisely, to new technologies such as the machine gun, the airplane, or poison gas—becomes a formative psychological experience.

The second point derives from the first. What is occurring is obviously another shift in the understanding of the body and the senses as physiological entities, as well as in the project of their social construction within relational (communicative, administrative, educational, medical) structures. In bourgeois realism the body was somewhat marginal to the textual representation of the subject (although usually fully described in terms of facial features, clothing, and general appearance); representation occurred through textual rhetoric and ideology rather than through its physical or physiological presence. The (generally male) middle-class subject did his work in the warehouse, conquered territory, and tilled the land more by means of the bodies and the labor of servant classes and through grand schemes of colonization than through his own physical involvement. The sensory and sensual were marginal categories for this individual. We saw this attitude toward the body change and more emphasis placed on its sensory-sensual, its erotic and hedonistic potentials, toward the end of the century, culminating in overindulgence and synaesthetic orgies that, in turn, brought to the fore another aspect of the social interaction of the individual body: the dissolution of the subject into sensory processes that open it up to psychological analysis and memory-oriented introspection.

What Mynona describes and satirizes, then, is an individual that has become thoroughly dissected, analyzed, and discussed, and requires for ultimate dispersion in an all-enveloping communicative network nothing further than the elimination of the body as matter, as that last stubborn remnant of the concrete here and now. The *Telehaptor* is the solution to this problem. It disperses the individual bodily into the discourse network, which the narrator sees as universal. There is but one last moment of reluctance that needs to be overcome. "Ein bißchen Selbstüberwindung kostet es schon, ein bißchen momentane Selbstpreisgebung, sich telehaptieren zu lassen" (35). After all, one hands oneself over, body and soul, so to speak—and naked, at the available level of technology, hence most vulnerable—to a system whose participants one does not necessarily know. This, indeed, warrants a certain hesitation.

The third point relevant for us is the conceptualization of smell. Gone is the decadent olfactory pleasure, not only in this text, but equally in the subsequent examples. Dispersed are the heavy, heady, erotic perfumes of the fin-de-siècle. The ego-constituting olfactory epiphanies tapping a long lost past have vanished. Mynona's is no perfume land. The odors he means are part of the bodily realm. This becomes drastically clear in another of his satires in the same volume on "new toys," "Neues Kinderspielzeug" (36–39), where the narrator argues that children should be exposed early and methodically to the "real world out there" with all its atrocities, so that later on they will find it "vor Unschuld duften[d]" (36). He suggests toys for the realistic staging of battles (including blood), model brothels and mini morgues, and, instead of a doll's house, an "Asyl für Obdachlose—das Appetitlichste, das man sich denken kann. Ob man (vermittels Stinkbomben) die kleinen Rotunden und über- wie unterirdischen Bedürfnis-Anstalten auch für die kleinen lieben Näschen überzeugend machen sollte, wage ich nicht zu entscheiden" (39).[7] Smell is bad again. However, it has acquired increased reach and mobility, both in its production (*Stinkbomben,* which allow for its transportation) as well as in its reception. "Das Gesicht, der Geruch, das Gehör," vision, smell, and hearing as refinements of what Mynona calls "das Getast," "haptics," are able to make "ihren freien Ausflug in die Welt" and are included as subcategories in the process of *Telehaptieren* (34).

This New Odor, then, that begins to rise in the early decades of the twentieth century, is at once less "civilized" and aesthetically pleasing than its immediate predecessors. It is more primitive, more directly natural and bodily, yet at the same time it begins to show sociopolitical (as opposed

---

7. The suggested doll's house would be a "homeless shelter—the most appetizing thing imaginable. Whether one ought to reproduce (by means of stink bombs) for the cute little noses the odor of the lavatories, both underground and above, I do not dare to decide."

to individual and aesthetic) characteristics.[8] It appears integrated in general systems (communication, education) rather than representing isolated subjective experiences. Olfactory phenomena became a public, sociopolitical concern in the seventeenth, eighteenth, and early nineteenth centuries. Then they began, as pleasant scents, to turn private, subjective, intimate, and erotic; and now they are emerging in a new light. No longer are smells something to be *eliminated* by the system, but rather something to be *employed*, if not exploited, by it. Indeed they become a tool for the manipulation of the masses. They become agents in the struggle for political control. An elucidating case in point is Aldous Huxley's *Brave New World*, first published in 1932.[9] It is, like Mynona's short prose sketches, another technofantasy with an unmistakable political message.

Into Huxley's strictly dualistic concept with the technofantasy land forming the futuristic fictional standard and the Indian reservation in Arizona representing a backward stage of civilization, the existing world of the 1930s (and still, to some extent at least, that of the 1990s) inserts itself as an intermediate standard by which to gauge both. Here is not the place to discuss Huxley's vision in its historical and political context or to debate the extent to which *Brave New World* has or has not become reality, but rather to take notice of how the two contrasting realms are evoked narratively and descriptively, focusing on olfaction. To put it simply: the old world stinks, the new is full of pleasant scents, and the olfactory is indeed used as a political instrument of control over the individual. In the new world, olfaction has developed its own technological apparatus and can be implemented effectively for political and psychological purposes. It plays a considerable part in the enterprise of creating stability—political, intellectual, psychological—thanks to its various advanced application technologies. The brave new world is thoroughly sanitized and standardized, medi-

---

8. We will return to what appears as an opposition between the "political" and the "aesthetic," as we will notice an increasing convergence of the two. What we have described as a process of aestheticization (the shift from bad to good smells, from involuntary miasmatic emanations to artificially produced pleasant fragrances) seems to come to an end here and even to regress. Mynona's texts reflect an olfactory milieu that is no longer sensually beautiful but rather, bluntly put, politically ugly. My intention is, nevertheless, to come to terms with this trend within the framework of aesthetics. The challenge will be precisely this: to characterize aesthetics as encompassing the new phenomenon, to merge its libidinal-aesthetic component with the ethicopolitical realm in Eagleton's terminology.

9. Aldous Huxley, *Brave New World* (New York: Harper and Row, 1969). All references are to this edition.

cally and hygienically controlled.[10] This extends from drug consumption to pregnancy substitutes, the talcum powder hoses with the eight different scents, and the eau de cologne taps (24) in the women's lounge at the Central London Hatchery where Lenina and the other major characters work. To this ever-pleasant and sensorially stable atmosphere the scent organs, such as the one in use at the "Westminster Abbey Cabaret"— "London's Finest Scent and Colour Organ"—contribute a considerable share (50). The scent organ, or rather the lack thereof at the North Pole vacation facility, helps swing Lenina's opinion in favor of Bernard Marx and his suggested trip with her to North America rather than to Arctica, thus making possible a visit to the Arizona Savages Reservation (55). The trip turns out to be a disaster, not lastly in respect to the olfactory. Their Indian guide smells. In fact everything "primitive" smells, and as they are climbing up the rocky slope to the village perched on top of a mesa, all is "oppressively queer, and the Indian smelt stronger and stronger" (72). Twice Lenina is forced to hold "her handkerchief to her nose" (72, 75). Other scenes are so unbearable or embarrassing for her that she has to turn and look away or cover her face with her hands (74, 77). The unbeautified and non-standardized world has become unacceptable in its physical reality to the new-world inhabitants, the more so, as Lenina leaves her soma pills at the hotel and has to face reality without the protection of the customary drug haze. Linda, the new-world woman, whom Bernard and Lenina find living among the Indians and whom they end up taking back to their civilization, together with her son John, positively reeks of mescal (84, 88).

---

10. Although not a technofantasy, Margaret Atwood's *Handmaid's Tale* is another recent utopian vision that employs the olfactory in a significant way for the switches between the future-present and the past of the 1980s. Her utopian world is sensually repressed, and smell is a means of individual recollection. The author describes, in extrapolating existing antiemancipatory, antifeminist, antiabortion, and general antiliberal movements, a utopian state where women are stripped of all their individual and social rights and liberties that they have gained in past decades. Atwood's is a centralized totalitarian state based on sexual and reproductive control and the subjugation of women (as well as lower-caste men) under strict biblico-moral standards. The account of life in this state is narrated by a woman of the transitional generation who still remembers "our time." Smell (over forty instances in 380 generously printed pages of text) is the essential liminal and transitional sense in her numerous shifts of perspective from present to past. It is the sense of memory and of the erotic, and it brings sensuality to this brave new world of utter sensual starvation where the women's bodies are to be hidden under long robes, combined with a hood that restricts vision. Deprivation of touch is another means of controlling sexuality and the erotic, and the narrator says of herself that she "hunger[s] to commit the act of touch" (14). Margaret Atwood, *The Handmaid's Tale* (1985; New York: Ballantine Books, 1987).

The twilight of her hut "stank" (79), and when she approaches Lenina, she "smelt too horrible, obviously never had a bath, and simply reeked of that beastly stuff that was put into Delta and Epsilon bottles" (79–80). John, who was born and grew up on the Savage Reservation, loves the stories his mother has been telling him all these years of the unattainable new world, of the "pictures that you could hear and feel and smell, as well as see" and of everybody always being happy "and no one ever sad or angry . . . and everything so clean, and no nasty smells, no dirt at all" (86). It is no wonder that he is attracted to Lenina, the dream-come-true girl, and gets into a veritable frenzy over her scents when he breaks into her hotel room to check whether she and Bernard are still there to take him and his mother away to the new world as they had promised.

> A moment later he was inside the room. He opened the green suit-case; and all at once he was breathing Lenina's perfume, filling his lungs with her essential being . . . [he] kissed a perfumed acetate handker-chief. . . . Opening a box, he spilt a cloud of scented powder. His hands were floury with the stuff. He wiped them on his chest, on his shoulders, on his bare arms. Delicious perfume! He shut his eyes; he rubbed his cheek against his own powdered arm. Touch of smooth skin against his face, scent in his nostrils of musky dust—her real presence. "Lenina," he whispered. "Lenina!" (96)

This orgiastic scene is a clever double take. It allows us to see the new world as the scented paradise from the perspective of the (half) savage; and it glaringly highlights the erotic misunderstanding unfolding here. John goes wild over Lenina's scents because for him, they are unique. They mark "her essential being." The reader knows, however, that in the new world the very opposite is true: the standardized scents of the powder hose and scent tap are ubiquitous and designed precisely to eradicate differences, to deconstruct eroticism as the individual and personal. They help preserve the state of institutionalized absence of jealousy, an emotion that has become obsolete in an environment in which erotic attraction has been replaced by the much more convenient psychosexual hygiene.

Huxley's new world is one of sexual promiscuity that is not only desired but virtually required. The artificial scents wafting through this universe function like perfumes in that they refer to nothing but themselves, ultimately (and originally, as we have shown) a reference to sexuality. The difference with perfumes as we still use them in the late twentieth century lies in their public application as *dampers* rather than their personal use as *highlights* of individuality. Only John, the savage, still operates on this older pattern, whereas the citizens of the brave new world have lost that original sense of smell. Their excitement at the feelies (while "the scent organ was playing a delightfully refreshing Herbal Capriccio" as an opener, 112) is a communal turn-on, directed at nobody in particular. John, however, thinks of Lenina still as a unique person, not lastly characterized by her smell, "her essential being," while he, for her, is just another (although in this case somewhat special) object of desire (and desire itself is not exclusive, but indiscriminate and, so to speak, all-embracing).

If Eros is indeed the constructive and binding force of civilization as Freud claims, it is in the scene at Lenina's hotel that we still encounter it as this force of individual attraction between the sexes—and indeed in its oldest, unsublimated medium, the olfactory. This, however, is only true in John's world. Lenina's, and the whole brave new world, has succeeded in the very annihilation of this force through the mass application of deindividualized olfactory standards in the name of maintaining social stability.[11] The olfactory, as we said above, is back in the public sphere, but this time not as a public-health concern as we found it in earlier scientific discourse, nor as an expression of a sensory and perceptual revolution, in which form it found its way into literature, but rather, within literature, as an as yet utopian political instrument.[12]

Later on in Huxley's book, with John living in the brave new world, the Controller agrees with him that *Othello* is "better than those feelies." But he maintains that they are "the price we have to pay for stability. You've got to choose between happiness and what people used to call high art. We've sacrificed the high art. We have the feelies and the scent organ instead" (150). What is considered art in the new world points only to itself; the feelies and the scent organ lack the referential capabilities of the work of art as we know it. They are not products of sublimation, they do not even induce sublimation: they function as the permanently open safety valve of the sensual and erotic plumbing system. This is Freud taken to the

---

11. The most disturbing aspects of *Brave New World* lie in the manner its author handles the psychological and sensory realm rather than in the sci-fi technological gadgetry. The changes described in the former are just too close to home and too seamless a continuation of actual modern social trends to be comfortable. The olfactory that is harnessed to political service is only the most blatant example.

12. In the meantime reality has caught up with utopia. Cf., e.g., *Wall Street Journal*, 13 October 1988.

extreme, to the point of revaluation of all values where, among other things, smell shifts from the individual, erotic and passive to the public, anaesthetic, and aggressive. Smell finds, emotionally engineered, its political application.

Capping the alteration of values depicted in the Huxleyan binary universe is the fact that the concept of what was formerly known as the *home*, the family, the male and female couple caring personally for a number of children, has become anathema and is transferred onto the savage side and depicted as a place of bad odors. "Home, home—a few small rooms, stiflingly overinhabited by a man, by a periodically teeming woman, by a rabble of boys and girls of all ages. No air, no space; an understerilized prison; darkness, disease, and smells" (24). This is the final blow to the (romantic) home as a place of origin and belonging, and the rejection is couched emotionally in a gesture of physical and sensual disgust and in practice finds its expression in hatchery rearing. The home is replaced in Huxley's work by the anonymous industrial process of artificial gestation. This rejection of home, however, is very different from Malte's experience in Paris. He, too, lives outside and beyond the (romantic) home that has disintegrated and whose material shell, the house, has broken open. Malte's gesture, however, is not one of sensory rejection but rather an empathetic longing, an understanding of the remnants of the life that he sees and smells as something still clinging to the inside out walls of the dilapidated house and home.

In olfactory terms the civilization of *Brave New World* has reached a final stage. Its environment is clean and artificial; the sensory spectrum of the atmosphere has shifted to the exclusively pleasant; and what could be offensive exists only in the Savage Reservations. The family home, negatively characterized as a locus of smell, has been overcome; sexuality and placebo-procreation have been made part of the public domain. There is nothing personal, intimate, erotic about them anymore, and odor thus has lost its original sexual connotation. There are, however, characteristic instances where the old sensitivity for smells resurfaces. The political system of *Brave New World* has not quite succeeded in wiping out all the archaic olfactory patterns. It has indeed managed to manipulate technologically and by means of political indoctrination the spectrum generally available to its citizens and their evaluating mechanisms. But everything penetrating from outside (in whatever limited form an outside still exists) is cause for both disgust and alarm. It is revealing that the very act that guarantees the stability of the system, the molding of the bottled embryos into their various castes, is associated with a stink, "a whiff of asafoetida" (18), which is used in the conditioning of the lower castes along with hypnopaedia, to which all castes are exposed. Characteristically, too, when Lenina meets Linda for the first time on the occasion of her visit to the reservation, she "stiffened and shrank" from Linda's "reek of embryo-poison" (81). The political manipulators of *Brave New World* control and manufacture the good part of the olfactory spectrum; the bad part, however, emerges against their will, escapes from acts and processes of an ethically questionable nature. We will encounter the same olfactory constellation again when discussing the Nazi death camps, with the difference that the powers in control there are not manufacturing pleasant smells to control a population, but are clearly aware of the stench generated by eradicating a population.

Before this, however, let us return to Mynona and the year 1911, when he published the truly visionary grotesque sketch "Von der Wollust über Brücken zu gehen."[13] In this story, "Herr Doktor van der Krendelen, ein Mann von hoher Statur, mit mächtigen Augen von sanfter Schärfe, und

---

13. First published in *Die Aktion*, 11 September 1911. All references are to the edition in *Rosa, die schöne Schutzmannsfrau*, 17–22. Following are the translations and paraphrases of the German quotes in the next three paragraphs. The title of the short story is "On the Bliss of Crossing Bridges." "Wollust" ("bliss") has strong sexual connotations; "orgasm" is a possible translation. "Herr Doctor van der Krendelen, a man of tall stature with powerful eyes of gentle sharpness and a light-blond, accurately trimmed goatee, had found the means: air, air." It is a means for the "purification of the whole planetary atmosphere and thereby of the lungs and thus of the blood and of life." In his effort to establish "the paradise of the lungs" he is joined by "monarchs, bankers, poets, and many other existences." "The effects of this hygiene cannot be appropriately described. . . . For bad air is the misfortune of mankind; . . . The improvement of the air is the surest way to improve humanity, better than all philosophical moralizing!" The problem with Krendelen's project lies in the fact that soon "none of the artificially healed participants was able to exist outside without dropping dead." As his clients begin to desert his program, Krendelen decides to go ahead with his grand plan of universal air purification. "Thus he steeled his heart against all corrupting pity and on Thursday carried out his fateful plan for which he was destined—as the great vacuum cleaner of all life." Almost immediately "the great dying" began, with the bodies, however, "burning without a trace of corrupting odor in the delightful air of early spring." "Nothing was left of corruption. Victoriously it was all banished and masked by the scents of fresh purity that now virtually exploded!" The so-called "'healthy average' died off rapidly and the extremes, the overly dull and the overly sensitive amalgamated to a new average of amazing strictness and precision." The "radiating purity of the air" makes it clear just "how much the world had suffered from its bad air." Eventually, the world produced a "golden sound" so that "everything seemed to stand still and to last," and "dying had come to a viable, livable understanding with becoming." Everybody forgot the past "so that Krendelen did not even become famous!"

einem hellblonden exakten Spitzbart—hatte das Mittel gefunden: Luft, Luft" (17). Krendelen is in search of a means of "Reinigung der gesamten planetarischen Atmosphäre; und dadurch der Lungen; und dadurch des Blutes; und dadurch des Lebens" (17). He owns a "Versuchslaboratorium" (17), a research lab, in which he can recreate any climate of any region of the earth. This, however, is not enough; he aims higher, at the climatic revolution of the planet itself ("und wahrlich, das tat [der Erde] not!" 17). He is aware that such a radical atmospheric change would eliminate all life adapted to the present conditions, including his own family (17–18). After some serious thinking while walking up and down in the artificial climate of Nice, which he recreated in his lab, Krendelen finds the way out of his dilemma of aerial purity and ethical qualms: he founds a shareholder company, connects everybody's home to his lab, and provides them with the new purified atmosphere at their own risk and peril. People are thus able to establish "das Paradies der Lungen" (18), and indeed "Monarchen, Bankiers, Poeten und viele andere Existenzen" join the program (19). "Die Wirkung dieser Hygiene läßt sich gar nicht beschreiben. . . . Schlechte Luft ist nämlich das ganze Unglück der Menschen; . . . Luftverbesserung bedeutet die gewisseste Menschenverbesserung, mehr als alle philosophische Moralisterei!" (19). After initial success, Krendelen's enterprise runs into trouble, for, eventually, "keiner der künstlich Gesundeten [konnte sich] mehr nach außen begeben, ohne tot umzufallen" (19). Many of his clients thus start to wean themselves off the pure air and back to the normal atmosphere and begin to turn against Krendelen, who sees himself confronting the greatest decision of his life: should he go ahead and purify the whole terrestrial atmosphere by means of an evaporation process triggered "durch ein elektrisches Verfahren" (20) of a sufficient amount of his purifying chemical, knowing full well that the new atmosphere would only be breathable for "Kerngesunde" (20)—or should he not. His decision is made quickly and in the name of a visionary higher goal. "So machte er denn sein Herz stählern gegen alle auflösende Weichmut, und am Donnerstag vollzog er das Schicksal, zu dem er nun einmal ausersehen war—als der große Vakuumreiniger der Lebendigen" (20).

Immediately diseases spread; "das große Sterben" begins, but fortunately "die Leichen [verbrannten] in der prächtigen Luft—es war Vorfrühling—ohne allen Verwesungsgestank" (20). The catastrophe or, from the opposite perspective, the "final sanitation" runs its course. "Nichts mehr von etwelchem faulen Rest. Sondern sieghaft wurde alles bald vertrieben und überduftet von der jungen Reinheit, welche jetzt förmlich eklatierte!" (20). While the so-called "'gesunde Durchschnitt' aller Orten rasch krepierte, korrigierten sich die Extreme, die Überstumpfen, die Überzarten, die Blöden und die Hypersensiblen zu einem ganz anderen Durchschnitt von ungemeiner Strenge und Präzision" (20). Thanks to the "strahlende Reinheit der Luft" (21) everything begins to look more etherial, and it becomes obvious "wie sehr die Erde an ihrer schlechten Luft gelitten hatte" (21). Finally, "dank Krendelens Kathartikon," the earth produces a "goldenen Klang" and only now "schien alles zu stehen und zu dauern" (21). Death ends its reign, and "das Sterben hatte sich mit dem Werden jetzt lebendig und leibhaftig verständigt," and everybody immediately forgets the past "so daß [Krendelen] nicht einmal berühmt wurde!" (22).

I leave this short story here without further interpretation, simply suggesting that we bear it in mind as a substratum for the following discussion. It contains a number of terms and concepts that ring disturbingly familiar, and while talking about other texts, its uncanny visionary element will undoubtedly reverberate in the reader's mind. Some of the terms to pay special attention to are: *Reinigung,* the "purification" of the whole atmosphere; *Blut* and *Leben; Hygiene,* as well as the *Schicksal*-decision, the "fateful decision," that one individual has to make all by himself; the steeling of his heart in order not to succumb to *auflösende Weichmut;* the *sieghaft,* "victorious," way in which the whole process of purification unfolds; and the complete absence of all "odor of putrefaction," *Verwesungsgestank,* from the burning bodies. The means to achieve all this is a supertechnology of sanitation brought to bear on a people at large. The actual chemical substance used by Krendelen still has a very clumsy name: "Atoxomyolyo mulpollambixohoptotachylamolinovolmanombosusilotanbolin-oxylpyram idolinoferosambulonolasinolins" (19).

The Nazis will call theirs *Zyklon B.*

Let us, however, undertake some further literary and historical transition work from Krendelen's to Höss's "purification," from a literary, imaginative vision, "harmless" as such, to the horrendous reality of the extermination camps thirty years later. The central question to be addressed in the process concerns the role of expressionism as either an emancipatory and progressive or an essentially totalitarian and reactionary movement.[14]

---

14. A discussion with such overtones did in fact take place, in the 1930s in the journal *Das Wort,* triggered by Klaus Mann's and Alfred Kurella's positions vis-à-vis Gottfried Benn and his temporary partisanship for the Nazi state, and it is summed up and commented in Hans Jürgen Schmitt, ed., *Die Expressionismusdebatte: Materialien zu einer*

These valuations are present in the Marxist view of expressionism as bourgeois and decadent and in the Nazis' branding it as degenerate and beginning to eliminate expressionist art. Marxism in the meantime opted for
realism, namely socialist realism, as its official aesthetic. Within expressionism itself it is the controversial figure of Gottfried Benn who personifies
some of the ambivalence inherent in that intellectual movement with its
grand, totalizing (if not totalitarian) gestures on the one hand and its
attention to esoteric cultural and historical detail on the other. As has
already become noticeable in Mynona, sensory perception is constructed
and used along different lines in the expressionist movement from the
preceding epoch of decadence, aestheticism, and symbolism. It appears
more blunt, more graphic, more oriented to application, by which I mean
to say that it is fulfilling an expressive function in the communication with
the reader rather than being intricately involved in constituting the aestheticist subject. Putting (too fine) a point on it: impressionist aesthetics
(decadence, fin-de-siècle, impressionism proper) is the representation or
interpretation of objects as they emerge in the world of a subject that
thereby constitutes itself. Expressionist aesthetics (dadaism, surrealism, expressionism proper) represents the subject in a world of objects and speaks
of the former's alienation. Art deco and *Jugendstil* straddle the two currents
in their attempt at unification, at subjectivizing the object world while
giving objective expression to subjective feelings. Their attempts at integration are most successful in the border area of industrial mass production
and individually crafted aesthetic objects. Expressionist aesthetics is not a
regression, although at first sight it might appear so, for its novel use of
sensory elements relies for its effectiveness and its shock effect precisely on
the preceding fine-tuning of the (literary) senses. Only this, together with
great inventiveness in terms of sensory appeal—mixed media, collage, mon-
tage, V-effect—in fact brings the desired expressive results. The finer sensory nuances, however, get lost, just as in expressionist visual art the print,
the woodcut, the black and white contrast of simple lines become central
elements of its aesthetic. In Benn's case, this grand categorizing takes on
an additional dimension because he casts it in terms of an opposition

---

marxistischen Realismuskonzeption (Frankfurt am Main: Suhrkamp, 1973). For a general
overview, see the introduction. On this topic see also Shattuck, *Innocent Eye*. The first
essay in this collection, "Having Congress: The Shame of the Thirties" gives a close-up
view of the International Writers' Congress from 1935 in Paris and the climate, politics,
and hopes that permeated it. Shattuck considerably deflates the glory of this event of
alleged international intellectual solidarity.

between intellect and emotion, thoughts and feelings, brain and flesh, with a clear privileging of the former, but a secret yearning for the latter. This figure of polarization becomes visible in the expressionist decade, but continues its reign throughout the 1920s and 1930s and becomes, after undergoing revaluation, the dominant principle of order in the increasingly powerful fascist movement. More subtle distinctions are drowned out and driven into exile. What is left in terms of literature is forced underground or is co-opted and turns into propaganda.[15] Without making expressionism directly responsible for the development of fascism, it can still be seen as leaning toward and—given the frenzied publication and vociferous proclamation of its ideas—actually creating intellectual trends conducive to strongly polarized and thus inherently totalitarian models of thinking and behavior.

With these remarks we have not, of course, given a full and fair assessment of expressionism, and neither have we bridged the gap between literary fantasy and political reality. What develops in the following years and "culminates" in the extermination camps is more than a case of life imitating art, because the relationship is not one of imitation but of annihilation. Mynona, for instance, as a Jew, has to flee the Nazis. He survives the war, despite the lack of support from fellow writers and serious health problems, in Paris, where he dies in 1946.[16]

What I do hope to have shown, however, is an intellectual climate of extreme polarity arising with expressionism and lasting through the 1920s and 1930s, a pathos of grand changes on the level of mankind, no less, which at the moment of their designing are already seen as failing over

---

15. For Kurella (pseudonym of Bernhard Ziegler) expressionism necessarily leads into fascism (cf. his essay "'Nun ist dies Erbe zuende . . .'" in Schmitt, *Expressionismusdebatte,* 50–60). Benn, whom Kurella treats very sympathetically, is for him not an exceptional case, but rather the epitome of a certain development: "Es geht bei Gottfried Benn nicht um Gottfried Benn; *es geht um den Expressionismus,* um dessen Herkunft, um dessen Auslauf" (53). Karl Otten, in a historically based argument, postulates World War I as a central psychological experience and arrives at similar findings. "Der Krieg aber erschüttert jede, auch Künstlers Welt! Er erschüttert und verschüttet die Kultur des Impressionismus, die im Expressionismus eine willkommene Variante fand; da sie Gott und Geist vortäuschte, indem sie *erklärte,* was nur zu *erleben* war und so, dem Menschen eine Formel gebend, ihn der Form, des Willens und der Gläubigkeit an die Verantwortung mehr denn je beraubte" (120, emphasis added). Expressionism appears here as a hollowed-out impressionism, not lastly in terms of sensation and experience. Karl Otten, "Adam," in *Theorie des Expressionismus,* ed. Otto F. Best (Stuttgart: Reclam, 1976), 120–24.

16. On Thomas Mann's attitude toward Mynona see the "Nachwort" in Mynona, *Der verliebte Leichnam,* 154–55.

ridiculous individual human frailties. For the individual, the rift runs, most noticeably represented in Benn, between cold, hard, clean intellect and warm, soft, somehow soiled and swamplike feelings and emotions. These latently existing structures of polarized thought are taken up by the Nazis and revalued in their own terms: here the *Volk* and its leaders, there the individual, standing to the former in a relationship of subordination and obedience; here the "visionary intellects," there the followers as a malleable mass; here the far-reaching, "rational" aims, there the manpower to carry out the work; here the emerging legalization and institutionalization of those grand aims, there the abandoning of reason and responsibility to the increasingly totalitarian system. Fascist politics is, among other things, politics of the body, most noticeably in the rhetoric of health, contagion, and disease of the *Volk,* in the medicalization of genocidal practices, and most dramatically in the power structures of the concentration and extermination camps that bear down directly on the bodies of the prisoners, aiming at their destruction.

The texts discussed in the following belong essentially in three groups, the first two comprising survivors' accounts and notes by perpetrators respectively. These are texts of a more autobiographical and documentary nature. The third group includes writings by people who were neither victims, at least not directly, nor perpetrators but who write about the events out of a historical, psychological, or scientific interest. Such texts can vary widely, from Robert J. Lifton's sociopsychological investigation to Peter Weiss's *Die Ermittlung.* The former focuses on the German medical profession and its shift toward the eventual adoption of fully genocidal structures and is based on archival research as well as numerous interviews with surviving Nazi doctors; the latter is a drama with an explicitly literary and aesthetic bent, using documentary materials as a source.

In all three groups of texts the human body has a central position but is represented from various angles. In the survivors' accounts it appears as the target that the camp structures are set up ultimately to destroy. It is, often literally, the naked, physical, physiological body. For the perpetrators, the body of their prisoners is caught between two conflicting demands: its value as an economic resource to be optimally exploited (lowest possible maintenance, highest possible labor output) and its destruction. As the war progresses, destruction becomes the primary goal. In both scenarios the body becomes an economic and systemic burden once it is dead and has to be disposed of. Indeed, extensive thought and consideration is given to this problem of disposal. In addition, in a gray zone outside this nexus of economy and extermination, the body occasionally becomes the target of explicitly sexual, sadistic destruction, aimed with a horrible insistence at both male and female prisoners' reproductive organs.[17]

The body is present too in the third group of texts, as the object of scientific investigation, even if, for obvious reasons, it is more the intellect, the psyche, the emotions of both victims and perpetrators that are at the center. Both are reconstructed from interviews, in texts and documents, and insofar as they can be deduced from archival work, from finds, and eyewitness accounts. These scientific and historical texts deal with a body that is turning abstract, turning into text in the absence of and as a replacement for the annihilated physical body.

The three groups of sources use different strategies to come to terms with their specific concerns. We will refer to the third group to gain a historical and theoretical framework, even though the phenomenon that we are pursuing first and foremost, smell, is to be found more in the first two, above all the survivors' accounts. It is in the attempts to describe both the physical and the emotional reality of the camp experience that the olfactory fulfills new functions not hitherto discussed.

The Stench of Power

Fascism, be it said in passing, will arise in Europe out of this obsession: loathing for what is unclean, hatred for what is impure.
—(Michel Serres, *Stanford Italian Review* 1–2 [1986])

One major difference needs to be pointed out here between Mynona's and Huxley's texts on the one hand and the two texts discussed in the following. The former are fiction, the latter are fact. From the viewpoint of poststructuralism and deconstructivism such a distinction may appear old-fashioned and indeed problematic. Recent literary investigation following these approaches has exhibited a tendency to dissolve the socially responsible (or irresponsible) subject into a web of texts and discourses. Yet, there seems to exist a difference not only in degree but in principle between Mynona's stories and the accounts of survivors of the Shoah. The former is the

---

17. Cf. Claude J. Letulle, *Nightmare Memoir: Four Years as a Prisoner of the Nazis* (Baton Rouge: Louisiana State University Press, 1987), esp. 49–69. Letulle was a French soldier, captured by the Germans in 1940 and kept as a prisoner of war until 1943. He describes his experience in the torture chambers of a prison camp at Bartoszyce, Poland.

fictional liquidation of the world population on pages coming from a writer's desk; the latter are accounts of some of the atrocities committed in the process of actually methodically exterminating 6 million human beings, as described in the pages of Lengyel, Levi, and many others.[18] Yet, beneath this difference lies an existential commonality, the human body, sensory perception. However wild the imagination runs, however sensorially distorted the fictionally created universe—or indeed reality itself—may be, the original point of reference is always human sensory perception as we know it. Perception is, short of paraphysical and parapsychological phenomena, our only access to what we take to be the world. Regardless of the technological gadgets in use throughout the fantastic worlds of the imagination, they infallibly turn out to be extensions or distortions of the five senses by which we live in our everyday world. The same sensory grounding underlies the terminology of science, where the persistent need for modeling, for analogies and similes in research on the tiniest microlevel of matter as well as along the frontiers of the endlessly expanding universe (if this is indeed what it does), testifies to our eternal desire to be able to grasp (*be-greifen*), to visualize (in its generic as well as its specific meaning) the new concepts and structures through our senses. It is on this common phenomenological ground of sensory perception that we are able to approach and compare the categorically different texts in this chapter. It is the sense of smell that will validate an experience, fictional or real, as authentic and human. This is a grand claim for the humble sensory mode at the center of this inquiry. It will be modified as it takes shape in our move from one interpretation to the next. Important verification will come from the juxtaposition of two texts by Auschwitz survivors with those written by Nazis directly involved in the running of that camp.

Five Chimneys[19] is the harrowing account of a woman from Transylvania, married to a surgeon and in the medical profession herself, who follows her husband, together with her children and her parents, unsuspectingly to Auschwitz/Birkenau, to which he is deported in 1944. She is the sole survivor of the family and publishes her book in 1947. The family is carted away in a cattle car, crammed with ninety-six passengers, into the unknown. This "wooden gehenna" (10) is almost surreal, and during the

18. How problematic the distinction is, and also how fundamental, becomes tragically clear in Primo Levi's suicide over, as far as we understand, the existential incommunicability of the Auschwitz experience, and the fictionalization inevitably involved in writing.

19. Olga Lengyel, *Five Chimneys: The Story of Auschwitz* (Chicago: Ziff-Davies Publishing, 1947). Subsequent references are to this edition.

journey to the hell of the camp she tries "to forget reality, the dead, the dying, the stench, and the horrors" (10). When the train stops, the odors of the dead bodies "in various stages of decomposition" are "so nauseating that thousands of flies had been attracted" (14). The entrance into the camp is marked by a "cool wind [that] carried to us a peculiar, sweetish odor, much like that of burning flesh, although we did not identify it as that. This odor greeted us upon our arrival and stayed with us always" (16). The emphatic end position of "always" helps to mark off the camp as the territory of the "sweetish odor," the stench of death. As the newly arrived are marched off to their dwellings, "the strange, sickening, sweetish odor which had greeted us upon our arrival, attacked us even more powerfully now" (22), but the guide tells them that it "is a camp 'bakery'" (22). One of the witnesses in Peter Weiss' play *Die Ermittlung* rationalizes the smoke/smell in the same way: "ich sah Rauch / . . . ich dachte mir / das sind die Bäckereien."[20] Smell is enveloping the camp. Just as there is no smoke without fire, there is no smell without a source. The naive search by the new arrivals for a source and explanation of the odor, and their tracing it to "the bakery" is particularly gripping because it is so tragically ironic. Olfactory conceptualization, always linking the phenomenon to a source, is fooled here because the atrocity of the truth is as yet beyond the grasp of the prisoners, whose encoding mechanism is civilian and human and does not, in any case, include burning human bodies as the source of the smell they notice.

In the life of the camp it is the contrast between the actual smell of things and normal social, civilian associations and encodings that creates permanent alienation: soup normally has a pleasant aroma; in the camp, however, its "odor was sickening" (Lengyel, 27); it is an "evil-smelling liquid" (29). As olfactory, gustatory, and tactile perceptions are senses of proximity and do not allow for even limited distancing, they are the source of constant revulsion. Taste is much less commented on than smell or used to describe the atmosphere of the camp. The reason seems to lie in the two senses' respective importance for survival: in this world of starvation, to eat, regardless of the taste, becomes a more urgent necessity than to smell or to avoid smells.

Because of its relative unimportance in the struggle for survival and because of its strong evocative and associative powers and its memory-

---

20. Peter Weiss, *Die Ermittlung: Oratorium in 11 Gesängen* (1965; Reinbek bei Hamburg: Rowohlt, 1969), 12.

triggering function,[21] smell retains a degree of freedom and can be used by the writer to stress the outrageousness of the prisoners' situation, the incredible discrepancy with "normal" civilized life. With (bad) smell is clearly associated the feeling of inferiority vis-à-vis the outside world in whatever limited form it is present. "The herd of dirty, evil-smelling women inspired a profound disgust in their companions and even in themselves" (45). When Primo Levi, the second principal author discussed here, and two fellow prisoners are allowed to work in the Buna laboratories and are confronted with the regular employees, Levi notices how badly he compares with them: "We are ridiculous and repugnant." But above all he notices how badly he and his companions smell: "We are accustomed to our smell, but the girls [at the lab] are not and never miss a chance of showing it" (142).[22]

Two elements are mixed here: the contrast of the camp and civilization, and the awkwardness of meetings with the opposite sex. Whereas the impressions of the other senses fuse into the overall reality of the camp and create this world of its own beyond which an outside hardly seems to exist anymore and within which sensory experience has turned into pain, smell with its strong memory component continues to hint at a civilized life, an outside. The most striking example is Lengyel's account of one of the appearances of the feared Irma Griese, the "blond angel," an "exceptionally beautiful" SS woman (147). "Her beauty was so effective that even though her daily visits meant roll call and selections for the gas chambers, the internees were completely entranced, gazing at her and murmuring, 'How beautiful she is'" (147). It is in this "aesthetic torture," degrading the prisoners by hinting at the world outside, that smell plays an explicit role and in fact comes very close to being used actively as an "instrument of torture" and being perceived as such.

Wherever she went she brought the scent of rare perfume. Her hair was sprayed with a complete range of tantalizing odors: sometimes she blended her own concoctions. Her immodest use of perfume was perhaps the supreme refinement of her cruelty. The internees who had fallen to a state of physical degradation, inhaled these fragrances joyfully. By contrast, when she left us and the stale, sickening odor of burnt

---

21. Cf., e.g., Engen, *Perception of Odors;* and Carterette and Friedman, *Tasting and Smelling.*

22. Primo Levi, *Survival in Auschwitz* and *The Reawakening,* trans. Stuart Woolf (New York: Summit Books, 1986), 142. (Italian originals 1958 and 1963 respectively).

human flesh, which covered the camp like a blanket, crept over us again, the atmosphere became even more unbearable. (147–48)

The "refinement" of perfume versus the "sickening odor of burnt human flesh," the luxury product of an advanced society versus the olfactory trace of its uttermost degradation: this is the span within which the aesthetically or hedonistically defined good and bad smells of normal life take on an ethical and moral dimension. And it is here that the silent truce of power with olfactory aesthetics is laid open to criticism.

Primo Levi's account in *Survival in Auschwitz* and the story of his liberation, followed by his tortuous journey home to Italy through parts of Russia, Rumania, and Hungary in *The Reawakening,* are of a less immediate nature, focusing less on explicit cruelty and atrocities than on incidents of a more intimate and individual kind, both positive and negative, thereby creating a more subtle, almost laconic horror, but also leaving room for hope. His first experience after crossing through the gate with its ominous "Arbeit macht frei" is of unbearable thirst and of the water he has to spit out because it is "tepid and sweetish, with the smell of a swamp" (22). The first chapter establishes the camp as a system of rigid rules, as a network of structures that are cut off from everything outside and that completely overturn values and perceptions generally held in the world, but soon become the new norm inside the camp. They do not connect with the outside, yet they allow for strange niches of vague anarchism, both of particular brutality and surprising humanity. Inside, this system is complicated by the confusion of languages, which is "a fundamental component of the manner of living here: one is surrounded by a perpetual Babel, in which everyone shouts orders and threats in languages never heard before, and woe betide whoever fails to grasp the meaning" (38). When language breaks down, the body is in jeopardy. In this state of emptied-out normal meaning and forced understanding of new meanings one "learns quickly enough to wipe out the past and the future" (36). Before the chemistry exam that will eventually permit him to work at the Buna factory, smell comes up as a social marker: "we will have to go in front of some blond Aryan doctor . . . and he will certainly smell our odour, to which we are by now accustomed, but which persecuted us during the first days, the odour of turnips and cabbages, raw, cooked and digested" (102–3).

When language fails, and all the senses report pain and degradation, smell remains a clearly understood realm of social signification. Smell arises by necessity in an inhuman system, marking victims, separating them from the perpetrators. At the same time, however, and thanks to its function of triggering memory and because it is not essential for survival, smell can imaginatively break through the barriers of the system. It both rubs in the inferiority of the victims *and* recalls the last remains of imaginative or imagined freedom: "It was warmish outside, the sun drew a faint smell of paint and tar from the greasy earth, which made me think of a holiday beach of my infancy" (III). When Levi enters for the first time the well-equipped Buna chemical labs he exclaims:

> How clean and polished the floor is! . . . The smell makes me start back as if from the blow of a whip: the weak aromatic smell of organic chemistry laboratories. For a moment the large semidark room at the university, my fourth year, the mild air of May in Italy comes back to me with brutal violence and immediately vanishes. (139)

After he returns to civilization, his experience changes, but "a dream full of horror has still not ceased to visit [him]" (373), ending not with a sensory perception or image but with language, a word: "the dawn command of Auschwitz, a foreign word, feared and expected: get up, 'Wstawàch!'" (374). During the ordeal of the camp, language is reduced to commands, degenerates into an incomprehensible Babel, dissolves as a text in whose place is set the body, the physical, sensory experience: "woe betide whoever fails to grasp the meaning. . . . [W]e later arrivals instinctively collect in the corners, against the walls, afraid of being beaten" (38). Failure to grasp the meaning of the rudiments of text inevitably results in bodily pain. Outside, after the camp, language is restored, the text replaces the body, the written account assures the survival of the message, ineradicably, beyond the death of the victim, the author, the body. In the meantime the olfactory both stresses the alienation from and the memory of civilization.

Levi emphasizes cleanliness, an issue with which smell is closely associated. In particular he talks about the bathing and cleaning rituals that he undergoes as he passes through the hands of various authorities after the liberation, and he particularly remembers the American procedure: "The only efficient equipment [at the transit camp of St. Valentin in Austria] was in the baths and the disinfection room, the West took possession of us by this form of purification and exorcism. . . . [T]here were about twenty wooden cabins, with lukewarm showers and bath wraps, a luxury never seen again" (368). There are two earlier accounts of bathing, particularly memorable the one after the prisoners passed into Russian hands:

Here too, as at every turn of our long itinerary, we were surprised to be greeted with a bath. . . . I am not questioning that a bath was opportune for us . . . But in that bath, and at each of those three memorable christenings, it was easy to perceive behind the concrete and literal aspect a great symbolic shadow, the unconscious desire of the new authorities, who absorbed us in turn within their own sphere, to strip us of the vestiges of our former life. (188)

Bathing and cleaning, the unquestionably necessary medical and hygienic procedure, constitutes a symbolic act. The eradication of the olfactory trace and the restoration of hygiene is a ritual for returning into civilization.[23] One cannot help but think of the perversion of this ritual used by the Nazis at the prisoners' entry into the camps, the promise of a shower, disinfection, and fresh clothes.

Smell, with its free play of meaning, becomes invested with the significance of civilization in the prisoners' self-perception. It marks most clearly the borderline of the camp and the world outside in terms of sensory perception. It denounces the abuse of power on the human body. Smell plays an essential role in an *aesthetics of resistance*.[24] *Because* it is passive, it is always only reflecting existing power structures, denouncing them.

In support of the claims made for the extraordinary representational role of the olfactory sense in the survivors' accounts (and we will add

---

23. There exists, as Lifton convincingly shows, a careful emphasis on sanitary and medical rhetoric and practice during German fascism. While the practice almost immediately after the Nazi takeover begins to hollow out the Hippocratic principles and perverts them into their opposite, official rhetoric as well as some deceptive ploys—such as a bureaucracy issuing false death-certificates, and doctors' presence at selections at concentration camps—are kept up. Lifton argues that the "medicalization of killing" was an essential step in the move from healing to killing (*Nazi Doctors*, 14) and it served the double function of easing the conscience of the perpetrators on the one hand while keeping up for the population and for the victims in the camps, up to their last steps, a spurious disguise of what was really going on. Lifton shows the following process: from racial and social biology to scientific racism in the 1920s and 1930s (17) and to the 1935 Nuremberg Laws; from eugenics to euthanasia to phenol injections in the camps; from the declaration of "life unworthy of life" via the children euthanasia programs to the "T4" program aimed at eliminating adult chronic patients at the six killing centers used for that purpose (cf. 71) where the first gassings take place; and from the "T4" to the "14f13" program, aimed at political prisoners and generally socially undesirable elements (137). Overall, Lifton characterizes the Nazi attempt as bringing "the greatest degree of medical legitimation to the widest range of killing." Auschwitz, finally, means "the racial cure" (145).

24. Peter Weiss, *Ästhetik des Widerstands* (Franfurt am Main: Suhrkamp, 1975).

corroboration of this phenomenon from two somewhat more removed sources, Peter Weiss's *Ermittlung* and Barbara Hyett's *In Evidence*), we need to investigate the other side, the people directly involved in the operation of the death camps and the textual strategies employed by them in their dealing with the experience. *KL Auschwitz Seen by the SS* unites three firsthand accounts by Rudolf Höss, Johann Paul Kremer, and Pery Broad.[25] As Jerzy Rawicz points out in the foreword, Kremer's account differs from the other two in that it "is not a diary written ex post, like the others, but noted day by day" (28). While Höss's notes, coming from the longtime commandant of the camp, represent in some way an authoritative account and shed much light on the mentality, the administrative structure, and the decision making behind the whole extermination project, Kremer's is the more candid, personally revealing narrative, revealing in its laconic tone, in what it does *not* say. It permits some immediate insight into a man who, with both a medical and a philosophical doctoral degree, belongs to the intellectual elite of the Third Reich. In subject matter, this diary is a mixed bag, ranging from Kremer's summons to Dachau in 1941 for a first short stint, and advice given to him on how to treat his new riding boots ("linseed oil for the soles and light or yellow leather oil for the upper leather," 14 October 1941); to the entry on the publication of his paper on "Hereditariness of Traumatic Deformations" (21 January 1942)[26] and the treatment and death of his sick canary (23 March 1942). The diary includes numerous accounts of food and eating (e.g., 23 August 1941, 4 September 1941, before he came to Auschwitz; 5 September 1942, 31 August 1942). These entries are placed side by side with comments such as: "Quarantine in camp on account of numerous contagious diseases (typhus, malaria,

---

25. Jadwiga Bezwinska, ed., *KL Auschwitz Seen by the SS: Höss, Broad, Kremer* (New York: Howard Fertig, 1984). For publishing, editing, and translating details, see the prefatory material of the book. References to Kremer's notes are made by the date of the entries. For short biographical accounts, see 5–10; for an evaluation of the three documents, see 14–15. Höss's account takes up ca. 100 pages. This is roughly half of his total autobiography and leaves out the first part leading up to his involvement with Auschwitz. Kremer's diary is also shortened to ca. 80 pages; of those only about 20 deal with his short (three months) stay at Auschwitz. Broad's reminiscences are complete; they amount to ca. 60 pages. The book includes a very informative foreword by Jerzy Rawicz, as well as a biographical appendix of Nazi figures mentioned in the three accounts as involved in Auschwitz.

26. Cf. Jerzy Rawicz's comment on Kremer's scientific work, which could only be taken seriously in the warped system of Nazi medicine. "[H]e would have become the laughing-stock of his learned colleagues" under normal circumstances (Bezwinska, *Auschwitz*, 32).

diarrhoea). Received top secret instruction order . . . and got accommodation in a room . . . in the *Waffen SS* club-house" (30 August 1942, the day of his arrival at Auschwitz). For the following day we read: "Tropical climate with 28 centigrades in shade, dust and innumerable flies! Excellent food in the Home," followed by a detailed description of the meal: "This evening, for instance, we had sour duck livers for 0,40 mark, with stuffed tomatoes, tomato salad, etc. Water is infected. So we drink seltzer water which is served free." On 2 September, Kremer is "present for first time at special action at 3 a. m. In comparison with it Dante's Inferno seems to be almost a comedy." For the next day we read that he "was for the first time taken ill with the diarrhoea which attacks everybody in the camp here. Vomiting and colic-like paroxysmal pains. . . . Most probably it is the unhealthy continental climate, very dry and tropically hot, with clouds of dust and insects (flies)." On the fourth he takes "against diarrhoea—1 day gruel and mint tea, then on diet for a week. Took charcoal tablets and tannalbin. On the way to recovery." While thus recovering, he is present on the following day "at a special action in the women's camp ('Moslems')—the most horrible of all horrors." For the next day, the sixth, he records "an excellent Sunday dinner: tomato soup, one half of chicken with potatoes and red cabbage (20 grammes of fat), dessert and magnificent vanilla ice-cream." Further in the same entry he complains about the "fleas in my room in spite of using all kinds of insecticides, such as Flit (*Cuprex*) etc." Three days later, on the ninth, he is "as surgeon . . . present at the flogging of 8 camp inmates and at one execution by shooting with small caliber gun," for which he receives as a special compensation "soap flakes and 2 cakes of soap." He has himself inoculated against typhus, orders a "casual coat" to measure: "down to the waist 48, whole length 133, half of the back 22, down to the elbow 51, whole length of sleeve 81, chest measurement 107, waist 100, seat 124" (17 September 1942) and takes part in a "truly festive meal" with "*Obergruppenführer* Pohl." "We had baked pike, as much of it as we wanted, real coffee, excellent beer and sandwiches" (23 September 1942).

These few excerpts from Kremer's early days at Auschwitz—the selections from his diary reprinted in Bezwinska's book run from 26 November 1940 through 11 August 1945—suffice to give us an impression of his *modus operandi*. He is clearly aware of the unsanitary conditions around him, the dirt, dust, the flies, as he is aware of the health risks involved. While he takes appropriate measures for his own person, which is really the only focus of his interest, the prisoners inside the camp, for whom he technically has the medical responsibility, do not even enter his thoughts. Yet he must be aware of their situation, too. He has learned the camp-slang term *Muselmann* (he says "Moslem") for those victims suffering from the most acute effects of starvation, who are in fact reduced to nothing more than wandering skeletons—while he himself is obsessed with food. The reality of others, the prisoners above all, simply does not register with him, and he is capable of noting on 20 September 1942 that he "listened from 3 p. m. till 6 p. m. to a concert of the prisoners' band in glorious sunshine" only to continue that he then had "roast pork for dinner, baked tench for supper." Three days later, that is, six lines further down on the printed page, he is "present at 6th and 7th special actions" (23 September 1942). Reading Kremer's entries against each other and his whole account against Lengyel's and Levi's reveals a serious disturbance of his perceptive capacities, showing his complete obtuseness toward a large part of the reality surrounding him.

It is this utter disregard for the suffering fellow human beings that is the most striking aspect of this account. The psychological defense mechanism of the Nazi personality takes the form of blocking out the victims' reality and in compensation focusing on one's own bodily and physical reality (or as in Höss's case, on the purely administrative and technical aspects of the camp operation). A truly personal and private diary is, of course, always psychologically revealing precisely for not consciously pursuing an explicit agenda and narrative strategy and therefore listing facts and events in the piecemeal fashion in which they occur in real life. The specific crucial revelation from Kremer's account is the clear awareness of three basic physiological facts (food, cleanliness, and health) on the writer's part and for his own person, while the same three issues are blocked out when he talks about the camp inmates. Kremer's concern with his diarrhea, the "colic-like paroxysmal pains" (3 September 1942), cannot but appear cynical in the face of mass deaths among the prisoners due to typhus and other intestinal diseases. Completely in line with, in fact an integral part of, the defense mechanism to shut out parts of reality, is the absence of olfactory impressions from Kremer's notes. Smells, with their strong memory component would threaten the psychological closeout mechanism. They would imply participation, involvement, being part of the same reality as the prisoners—and precisely this is to be avoided. It is also noticeable how short and tersely worded Kremer's entries are for the time at Auschwitz from August to November 1942, with only a minimum of factual adjectives, and how much longer and more chatty they become after that, while also, however, less frequent. While smells (breathing) are completely absent from his account, eating assumes a central position in his entries during the Auschwitz period, and it becomes the most powerful means of distancing, because it is the most important of the sensory and vital activities, and the one where the distinction between the prisoners and their henchmen is greatest. It is through food and eating that Kremer is most obviously able to set himself apart from the prisoners, who have literally nothing in this respect. Kremer's surroundings in no way diminish his appetite. In addition to the instances quoted, he mentions food and eating also on 5 September, 27 September, and 11 October. There is a hint at plum brandy on 25 October; he sends "apple-compote" to Mrs. Wizemann in one of his numerous parcels, and mentions a "first-class meal . . . with lots of meat" on 2 November; he drinks Bulgarian wine also on the second, eats "as much as I wanted" on the sixth, drinks some more "Bulgarian red wine and plum brandy" on the eighth, and mentions several other meals in passing. The actual contacts with victims on the other hand take the barest verbal expression "was present at special action."[27] Only on very few occasions does Kremer betray some emotion. One is the literary comparison of such a "special action" with Dante's *Inferno*, above. The second occurs on 12 October: "Horrible scenes in front of the last bunker!" And the third is mentioned on 18 October: "Terrible scenes when 3 women begged to have their bare lives spared." Horrendous as these remarks are in the face of the reality as it is known from survivors' accounts, they become particularly heartless and psychologically revealing in the juxtapositions in which they occur in the diary. Furthermore, however, between food and special actions we find repeatedly interspersed the remark on "living-fresh material of liver, spleen and pancreas" that was removed from victims who had just been murdered. Kremer used such tissue in his spurious research on starvation effects (Cf., e.g., 3, 10, 15, 17 October).[28] Moreover, his diary contains records of numerous parcels and their approximate value. They contain soap and other daily household necessities and are addressed to his housekeeper, Mrs. Wizemann, in his hometown Münster. He returns there after his time of service at Auschwitz. (See esp. 17 October

27. All entries for 1942. Special action, in German *Sonderaktion,* was the term used to describe gassings of newly arrived prisoners. Kremer has nothing to do on these occasions except, indeed, to be present, in order to keep up the "medical" disguise of the whole extermination enterprise (cf. Lifton, *Nazi Doctors,* on this point, above). Occasionally, however, he performs the selection at the ramp himself. (For more information on this point, see Bezwinska, *Auschwitz,* 26 and 29, as well as footnotes 50 and 51 on p. 214f).

28. Cf. Kremer's explanation, given at the Cracow trial 1947; Bezwinska, *Auschwitz,* 221f., footnote 71.

1942, the day before his departure from the camp).[29] It is the outrageous "banality of evil" that strikes one in this diary, the ruthless juxtaposition of comments on the weather, on food, on coat measurements, with gassings and shootings of hundreds of people at a time. It is a psychological and emotional depravity of stunning proportions.

For our purpose, the fact that there are no smells mentioned is significant, and we will return to this point. "Smell no evil, know no evil," seems to be Kremer's motto. In his case, it is the other sense of proximity, taste, or at least the activity associated with it, eating, that serves as a means of distancing.

Pery Broad's account of his involvement with Auschwitz is drastically different from Kremer's, first and foremost in its form and author-reader relationship. It is a longer and coherent text, written specifically for the British authorities by whom he was arrested after the liquidation of the camp. It is a factually accurate description of the general procedures and daily atrocities of the SS, and it often shows a stance of indignation, criticism, and implicit distancing. It must also be noted that while Kremer is almost sixty at the time of his service at Auschwitz, Broad is just barely over twenty when he joins the SS in 1941 and is sent to Auschwitz the following year, serving first as a guard, then in the Political Section. He stays at Auschwitz until the collapse of the Reich.[30] Despite the commonalities between the two accounts that set them apart from Höss's—the relatively "minor" role their writers play at Auschwitz, due to the short duration of his direct involvement in Kremer's case, the somewhat subordinate function in Broad's—they differ vastly in their textual strategies.[31] For the three months at Auschwitz, Kremer's diary reports just the barest of facts. It is addressed at nobody in particular and the intention of that text emerges against the grain, so to speak, as an involuntary revelation of the author's psychological defense mechanisms. Broad's account is much more novelistic. To an unwary reader it might at first sight even appear as a camp inmate's story, for it takes a seemingly critical position vis-à-vis the SS. It does so, however, by completely omitting the role and the place of the

29. Cf. Bezwinska, *Auschwitz*, 231, footnote 97, for further information about the origin of the content of the parcels.

30. Jerzy Rawicz points out the fact that the three men represent three different generations, for Höss is forty when his involvement with the extermination project begins in 1940 (Bezwinska, *Auschwitz*, 10).

31. I am aware that *minor* is a term in no way appropriate in the face of the monstrosities these men committed or tacitly tolerated. It can only be justified in terms of the Nazi death machine where there indeed existed worse criminals.

"I"-narrator in the events described: he is simply not present as a person in his own narrative. His stance is that of the classical omniscient narrator who is removed, yet, of course, constantly within observable distance of the events he relates. At the Frankfurt trial, "there existed a strong suspicion that Broad had killed people during the interrogatory, but final evidence was lacking."[32] The text is addressed to a specific readership, and it covers a considerable time period from the early days of Auschwitz to its end.

It is interesting to observe how this man, living at Auschwitz and taking part in the operations of the camp, employs smell in an open and truthful text that at the same time serves to create distance between its author and the events he relates. The dominant means to this end is the narrative stance. As a part of that strategy the text abounds with passive constructions, administrative agencies and impersonal expressions as subjects ("it had partly transpired," "it often happened that"), and constructions using "one" or the general "you" as a subject. The sentence "It was only too easy to become suspected of having wanted to get in touch with the prisoners in some way or other, or of being a spy, and then the suspects [Broad is talking about civilians shunning the camp area] would be spirited away into the camp" (142) spirits away its own human subject, Pery Broad, who knows about these things from having witnessed them. Broad joined the SS in 1941 out of his own free will after his return from Brazil and some time spent in the *Hitlerjugend*. While Broad's narrative stance is misleading in its intended distancing effect, it is again at the perceptual level that it becomes clear beyond doubt on which side the narrator really stands. In contrast to Kremer, Broad does mention smells while leaving out all references to food, eating, and taste. In the opening pages he describes the living conditions at Birkenau as "considerably worse than in Auschwitz where they were bad enough" and mentions the "sticky bog" and the "mire underfoot" (141) everywhere in the camp and particularly bothersome in "wet and cold weather." In addition to that, "there was nearly no washing water" (141), and "barbarous hygienic conditions, insufficient food rations and hard work, together with other torments" (142) led to innumerable deaths among prisoners after only a short time in the camp. Broad's tone of near-reproach, which he maintains over the next few pages, is put to the test when he uses smell as a descriptive device. He levels direct accusations against Aumeier, the camp manager, and Grabner, the head of the Political

---

32. Cf. Bezwinska, *Auschwitz*, 27; from the "Foreword."

Section, where Broad works.[33] The following scene takes place on the occasion of one of Aumeier's periodic actions of "dusting out" the prison cells in the basement of Block 11.

> The air in these underground corridors was so stifling that breathing seemed almost impossible. The weird atmosphere was enhanced by the suppressed whisperings behind the cell doors, the glaring light of the bulbs, the sharply contrasting consisted of the warder of the prison and some blockleaders and finally by the death's heads glittering upon the caps of the SS men. (146, sentence structure is defective in the original)[34]

This is a scene of truly Gothic proportions, and it is seen from close up. Although not grammatically marked, the narrator gives away his presence in the sensory detail, "the death's heads glittering" and by his breathing the stifling air. "A prison warder opened the first cell door. . . . A choking stench issued from the crowded, narrow cell" (146). That he is not inside the cell, but rather with the SS men in the corridor is indicated by the "issuing" of the stench. For the next moment, the narrator steps back a little when he notices that "some of those walking skeletons had spent months in the stinking cells, where animals would hardly be kept" (149), but he closes in again for the description of the shooting that is now to take place and for which the helpless prisoners are led out into the yard between Block 10 and 11. "They felt, [*sic*] the cold, bloody muzzle of the gun against their necks, they heard the pulling of the trigger" (150). Grabner, Broad adds with the intention of revealing the former's cruelty and brutal unconcern, "could enjoy a substantial breakfast" (150) after a series of such executions.

Having previously shown the importance of the olfactory in the survivors' accounts, and knowing from other witnesses' testimonies that Broad's is a factual and faithful report of camp life, we may safely claim that he must have been present at the events he describes, and we can even determine with considerable certainty on the basis of this evidence which side he was on. Further clues in this olfactory criminal investigation help us solve the question. We find one when Broad describes in some detail the first crematorium, and then talks about problems with its exhaust system.

---

33. Grabner was sentenced by the Nazis themselves to twelve years imprisonment for corruption, which says something about his personality.

34. The book unfortunately abounds with misprints, grammatically questionable constructions, and awkward English expressions.

The smoke did not always rise above the chimney in transparent, bluish clouds. It was sometimes pressed down to the ground by the wind. And then one could notice the unmistakable, penetrating stench of burnt hair and burnt flesh, a stench that spread over many kilometers. When the ovens, in which four of [*sic*] six bodies were burnt at the same time, were just heated, a dense, pitch-black smoke coiled upwards from the chimney then there was no doubt as to the purpose of that mound. (159)

The spreading of the smoke or stench over a great distance into the world outside the camp makes the crematorium a focal point of his perspective. He anxiously follows on its escape the trace of the crime that ought to be kept secret. This is unmistakably the perpetrator's perspective. The underlying fear of the spreading of the stench—a fear the victims do not share, while they do notice the stench, as we have shown above—becomes more nagging in the following passage, describing the olfactory emissions after the mass graves of Russian prisoners begin to leak. "The sun shone hotly that summer [1942] upon Birkenau, the only partially decomposed bodies began to fester and a dark red mass poured out from gaps in the ground. The resulting stench was indescribable. Something had to be done about it and quickly" (170–71). The concern about the stench becomes even more urgent when the corpses are exhumed and then burned, with Jewish prisoners doing that horrible work and the SS men supervising them receiving extra food and vodka rations in compensation for their unpleasant job (171). "One could, for long weeks, see dense, whitish smoke clouds rising toward the sky from several spots. Nobody was allowed to come near those places without a special pass, but the stench betrayed the truth about which people round Birkenau had begun to whisper" (171). This is, in spite of the grammatically and lexically neutral construction ("one could see . . ."; "nobody was allowed . . . ") clearly the SS perspective, the viewpoint of those in the know about the origin of the stench and aware that it should be prevented from spreading. Broad never talks about the smell of everyday objects, of food, for instance; and smell never occurs as an associative stimulus of memory. This would have established him as an individual in his own narrative, a concrete person, which is precisely what he tries to avoid in his choice of narrative stance. It is nevertheless revealed in the perspective and the reference to the stench of the burning bodies. The point is further illustrated in the following scene: "One night the wind drove the unbearably stinking smoke low to the ground. No guard could bear to stay there. That fact was used by two prisoners who knew they had nothing to lose, if they did not gain something, by escaping, and so they made their get away from the spot under cover of the smoke" (171). Although the prisoners escape "under cover of the smoke," which implies *visual* cover, it is the *stench* of the smoke that drove the guards away in the first place. The lurking fear associated with this incident has its roots in the threatening revelation of the secret of Auschwitz. "What would happen, if the fugitives, one a French and the other a Greek Jew, managed to get abroad or started to tell the German population about the happenings at Birkenau? It was unthinkable!" (172). Broad's concept of revelation seems somewhat naive in its immediacy. Rumors and proofs were already at that time spreading far beyond the neighborhood of Auschwitz, and they were traveling along channels other than smoke signals. As a symbol, however, the events described and Broad's attitude toward them are striking: how the smoke escapes from the place of the crime; how it transforms itself into words in people's whispering; how it materializes in the two fugitives, confirming the rumors, giving substance to the smoke and stench; how the crime, in short, translates into text across the medium of stench. According to Broad, another such incident occurred, and again stench is at its origin. A "guard got sleepy due to the heat and the stunning smell of the smoke. Two prisoners ran away" (172). They are recaptured, and Broad mentions specifically how much "the SS-*Schütze* Strutz [the failing guard] felt relieved" about it (172).

The stench of Auschwitz is a Nazi obsession.[35] It is the unmistakable symbol of their abuse of power, of a power that has degenerated into violence and is aimed directly at the annihilation of its subjects, who are reduced to victims. The obsession with the stench is, in a certain way, the

---

35. This preoccupation with stench surfaces indeed long before Auschwitz, as Lifton points out in the account of the earlier "T4" program, which still tried to keep up appearances, using a "bureaucracy of medical deception" (*Nazi Doctors,* 72) that invented suitable death dates and causes, sent fake death certificates to families, as well as urns containing the ashes of patients who had just been murdered. "Inevitably, there were slip-ups in the bureaucracy of deception," but also people working at killing centers would "sometimes reveal aspects of what they were doing" at local bars. Above all, however,

> there was direct sensory evidence of the killing that no bureaucratic deception would eliminate: "The heavy smoke from the crematory building is said to be visible over Hadamar every day." And: "At full capacity . . . [the chimneys at Hartheim] smoked day and night. Locks of hair went up through the chimneys and landed in the streets." These bureaucratic oversights were mentioned in Nazi documents critical of the way the program was run and urging that "more sensitivity be exercised in carrying out these activities." (75; the inserted quotes are documented by Lifton on 512, footnote 70)

last remnant of bad conscience that the Nazi death machine still reveals.[36] Höss, the ultimate technocrat of that machine, its most diligent and creative administrator, is busily working toward eliminating that bad conscience by eliminating the stench. Höss is a monster of technology, but even he fears the stench escaping from the chimneys of Auschwitz.

Höss's autobiography, written while he was in Polish custody after serving as a witness at the Nuremberg trials, is the most detailed of the three accounts; it is also the most technical and administrative. It reads in part like an annual corporate report written by an overwrought CEO who is unable to delegate tasks to his incapable and recalcitrant employees. Höss appears, although he is in charge of the whole operation, as the one most removed from its sordid everyday details. Like Kremer, he is a master at blocking out certain aspects of his surrounding reality. At the same time— the fact is emphasized by Rawicz—he does not personally involve himself in dealing with prisoners. He "would never stoop to do such things [beatings, torture]. He had more important and more general duties to perform" (25). Unlike Broad's report, Höss's is all in the first person, resembling Kremer's diary in this respect but written in very different circumstances and clearly in full awareness of his readers. The factual, businesslike tone aiming at explaining technical and administrative details, discussing personnel problems, and giving approximate "production" figures breaks down only in a few places to give way to more human emotions and feelings, some personal worries and complaints. It is these passages that afford us some insight into the psychological and perceptual makeup of the man Höss.[37]

His account opens by emphasizing the difficulties and the adverse conditions at Auschwitz, which originally was designed as a transit camp. "My task was not an easy one" (33). The existing buildings "were swarming with

---

36. Another highly revealing aspect, directly linked to the gas-killings, is the fact that the olfactory irritant was removed from the Zyklon-B gas. Lifton discusses this in the framework of his argument of the medicalization of killing. "Given its [Zyklon-B's] extensive prior use [i.e., before it was used as the killing-gas] against rodent and insect spreaders of disease, we might say that Zyklon-B was always considered a form of medical equipment. . . . Sometime in 1943, the gas began to be distributed to Auschwitz without the irritant, and bore the warning: 'Attention! No irritant!'" (161). In a footnote Lifton states that "the manufacturer opposed the removal of the irritant because its patent had been on this irritant addition, rather than on the gas itself" (161). This point is also mentioned in Peter Weiss' *Die Ermittlung*, 121.

37. In writing about Höss and his writing about Auschwitz one is constantly reminded of the inadequacy and the distortions of language in connection with such monstrous events.

vermin. From the point of view of hygiene, practically everything was lacking" (34). He realizes that he has to set an example. "In order to harness all the available man-power to this task, . . . I had to set them a good example. . . . Before they had started their day's work, I had already begun mine. It was late at night before I finished" (35).[38] For obtaining the full cooperation of the personnel, however, his "good intentions were in vain" (35). The "old hands" thus take the blame for the mismanagement, the abuses, the brutality in the camp, which in Höss's disciplinarian view is a cathartic place for every individual.

> In no place is the real "Adam" so apparent as in prison. All the characteristics that a prisoner has acquired or affected are stripped from him, everything that is not an essential part of his real being. Prison in the long run compels him to discard all simulation and pretense. He stands naked, as he really is, for better or for worse. (49)

Höss is fully aware of the physical and psychological situation of his inmates, and he is completely matter-of-fact about it, as the following passage on Polish prisoners shows.

> They all knew that they would remain in the concentration camp at least for the duration of the war. . . . The only question was: which prisoners would have the luck to survive their imprisonment? It was this uncertainty and fear which, psychologically speaking, made imprisonment so hard for the Pole. He lived in a perpetual state of anxiety as to what might befall him each day. . . . He might suddenly be shot or hanged as a hostage. He might also be unexpectedly brought before a drum-head court-martial in connection with a resistance movement, and condemned to death. He might be shot as a reprisal. . . . To this must be added perpetual worry about his family and dependants. . . . Were they indeed still alive? (50–52)

One notices the randomness of threats lurking in the passive constructions without agent, the ubiquity of fear as a matter of course. The following description of a visit by Himmler in July 1942 makes the same point: perfect

---

38. An aside: one remembers at this point Gustav Freytag's declaration of intent, to show the German bourgeoisie at work. Here we see the German Nazis at work, in Poland, moreover, against which Freytag's colonial efforts were already aimed in the 1850s. The "job description" and the attitude, down to the linguistic formulation of it, is much the same—and the goal of that work obviously does not matter.

openness and frankness about the living conditions—and it suggests a way of solving them.

> [Himmler] made a most thorough inspection of everything, noting the overcrowded barrack-huts, the unhygienic conditions, the crammed hospital building. He saw those who were sick with infectious diseases, and the children suffering from *Noma,* which always made me shudder, since it reminded me of leprosy . . . their little bodies wasted away, with gaping holes in their cheeks big enough for a man to see through, a slow putrefaction of the living body. . . . He saw it all, in detail, as it really was—and he ordered me to destroy them. (65–66)

Ten lines further down he comments that "it was not easy to drive them into the gas chambers" (66–67), adding that "I myself did not see it" (67). Höss is perfectly aware of the horrendous conditions and events but, as with Kremer, it does not register with him on an emotional or moral scale. After a series of laments about the hardships of his own position, the pressures on him, the "perpetual rush in which I lived . . . [h]arrassed . . . by circumstances" (88), he notes the consequences he has to draw for himself. "I had to become harder, colder and even more merciless in my attitude towards the needs of the prisoners. I saw it all very clearly, often far too clearly, but I knew that I must not let it get me down. I dared not let my feelings get the better of me" (89). He even admits to doubts about the mass executions, doubts that seemed widespread among the camp personnel. "Many of the men involved approached me as I went my rounds through the extermination buildings, and poured out their anxieties and impressions to me" (103). He himself, however,

> dared not admit to such doubts. In order to make my subordinates carry on with their task, it was psychologically essential that I myself appear convinced of the necessity for this gruesomely harsh order. Everybody watched me. . . . I had to appear cold and indifferent to events that must have wrung the heart of anyone possessed of human feelings. I might not even look away when afraid lest my natural emotions got the upper hand. I had to watch coldly. . . . I had to see everything. I had to watch hour after hour, by day and by night . . . I had to stand for hours on end in the ghastly stench, while the mass graves were being opened and the bodies dragged out and burned. I had to look through the peep-hole

of the gas-chambers and watch the process of death itself. . . . I was forced to bury all my human considerations as deeply as possible. (103–5)

This is Höss the loyal subject, the cog in a command structure that must inexorably function, Höss the victim, the martyr. These, we must not forget, are the words of the man who is directly responsible for the scenes he describes. "If I was deeply affected by some incident, I found it impossible to go back to my home and my family. I would mount my horse and ride, until I had chased the terrible pictures away" (106). He was, however, "no longer happy in Auschwitz once the mass exterminations had begun" (106) although his family had, as he admits, everything necessary for a comfortable life, and his "wife's garden was a paradise of flowers" (106–7). Paradise in Auschwitz! Höss, like other Nazis, tries to achieve consciously a state of desensitized experience, of psychic numbing, of closing-off, and he seems to succeed in this by emphasizing above all his position in the Nazi power structure as a recipient of orders, a faithful performer of a hard duty with which he completely identifies. Desensitizing, psychic numbing, closing-off are mechanisms also found among Nazi victims and survivors of massive catastrophes, and studies among death-camp survivors first led to the discovery of these psychic phenomena. For such people these mechanisms are an essential tool of survival, whereas for Höss they are the condition allowing him to continue his grisly tasks. In the moment of breakdown, he becomes full of self-pity, describing himself in terms of a victim.[39]

In Höss's overall more technical and in that respect nonsensory account, vision is the sense that still conveys some emotions. He has to "watch," to "see everything" (103), and there are pictures that haunt him, images that he has to "chase away" (106). On just one occasion (cf. 104 above) the olfactory is involved, indicating his presence, despite his repulsion, at such a scene of horror. Smell expresses proximity and involvement, and it marks the inescapability of his task and his loyalty to it and to those carrying it out (the guards, I should add, not the Jewish prisoners specially detailed to do the most bestial work), as well as to those who gave the orders. The images, obviously, he is able to chase away whereas about the memory of the stench we do not know. But it is interesting that in the following it is again vision, the sense of distance, and smell, the sense of proximity, that are combined in the descriptive makeup of the scene. In 1942, as larger and

---

39. Robert Jay Lifton in *Death in Life: Survivors of Hiroshima* (New York: Vintage, 1969) points out parallels in the behavior of survivors of the Shoah and the catastrophe of the Hiroshima A-bomb. Cf. esp. chapter 12, "The Survivor."

larger contingents of Jews were beginning to arrive at Auschwitz, it became evident that their dead bodies could no longer simply be burned in the open air.

> During bad weather or when a strong wind was blowing, the stench of burning flesh was carried for many miles and caused the whole neighbourhood to talk about the burning of Jews, despite official counterpropaganda. . . . Moreover the air defence services protested against the fires which could be seen from great distances at night. Nevertheless, the burnings had to go on, even at night, unless further transports were to be refused. (122)

Immediately, Höss begins to look for a technical solution and leads "the energetic planning and eventual construction of the two large crematoria, and in 1943 . . . the building of two further smaller installations. Yet another was planned, which would far exceed the others in size, but it was never completed" (122).

Here we have it again, the Nazi concern with the fire that can be seen and the stench that can be smelled and is stronger than the official propaganda. Fire and death, the flame and the dead body, two of the most powerful and archaic human symbols, signifiers of two of the deepest human fears as well as fascinations, known and commented on for a long time.[40] What has received much less attention is the action of the former on the latter, the fire on the corpse, which is not simply its clean and traceless destruction, but the production of a stench, horrible and loathsome, settling in the olfactory memory indelibly. The ashes are no cause for concern, neither in the real world of things nor in the world of memory. They "fell through the grates . . . and were taken in lorries to the Vistula, where they immediately drifted away and dissolved" (Bezwinska, 136), out of sight, out of mind. This is not so for smell, however, and the odorless burning of the corpses remains an eternal utopia of the perpetrators of evil. We encountered it in Mynona's grotesque sketch almost thirty years before the Nazi horrors; we have revealed it in two of the three accounts by perpetrators just discussed; and the concept is present in a Japanese officer's account about his experience after the Hiroshima bomb, quoted by Lifton:

---

40. One of the profoundest and most original accounts is undoubtedly Canetti, *Masse und Macht*.

Everything at that time was part of an extraordinary situation. . . . For instance, I remember that on the ninth or tenth of August, it was an extremely dark night. . . . I saw blue phosphorescent flames rising from the dead bodies—and there were plenty of them. . . . And yet, at that time I had no sense of fear, not a bit, but merely thought, "Those dead bodies are still burning." (31)

A similar notion with an impossible aesthetic twist to it is found in Marinetti's futurist manifesto on the occasion of the Italian war in Ethiopia.

Der Krieg ist schön, weil er das Gewehrfeuer, die Kanonaden, die Feuerpausen, die Parfums und Verwesungsgerüche zu einer Symphonie vereinigt. . . . Dichter und Künstler des Futurismus . . . erinnert Euch dieser Grundsätze einer Ästhetik des Krieges, damit Euer Ringen um eine neue Poesie und eine neue Plastik . . . von ihnen erleuchtet werde![41]

Marinetti's fascist aesthetic program takes the olfactory one step beyond the level at which fascist practice is affected by it. He removes the ancient stigma from the stench of death. He drags it out into the open and makes it part of an aesthetics whose highest goal is the aestheticization of war.

The preceding chapters highlighted the role of the olfactory in the emergence of the modern subject, and the growing role played by smell as the most adequate sensory medium of expression for those liquefied perceptual and cognitive processes that, for a historical moment, hold in balance sensory-hermeneutic construction and deconstruction, present and past, intellect and intuition, brain and memory, sense and the sensual. For a moment, as in Rilke, modernity seems to reconcile the contradictory elements of past, present, and future, and hold in balance the reflection on the conditions of human existence, in fact living these conditions through narrative. The deeply romantic question of "Where are we going?" that ties these elements together and found its quintessentially romantic answer in Novalis's "Always home," seems to have found a momentary and quix-

---

41. Quoted in Walter Benjamin, *Gesammelte Schriften*, ed. Rolf Tiedemann and Hermann Schweppenhäuser (Frankfurt am Main: Suhrkamp, 1974), vol. 1, 2:468. "War is beautiful because it unites gunfire, cannonades, ceasefires, and the perfumes and odors of corruption into a symphony. . . . Poets and artists of futurism . . . remember these principles of an aesthetics of war so that your struggle for a new poetics and a new sculpture . . . may be enlightened from within!"

otic modern reply in its deflection toward another question: "Where are you coming from?" Malte keeps both questions in balance while writing, *through* writing. But this modernist magic crumbles. Cracks open up, and the true modern and postmodern challenge has been to live with these gaps, smooth them over, and fill them in by all means. In this endeavor the senses, as the phenomenological underpinning of both life and narrative, take sides. Vision is forging ahead, olfaction lagging behind, carrying past and longing with it, memories and old fears and desires. We have seen smell being dragged out and utilized, fictionally and optimistically in the context of technical and political utopias. For this purpose it had to be stripped of its essential qualities. Yet it could not be entirely prevented from insisting on, at least hinting at, past and archetypal worlds. We have seen the olfactory used by victims of inhumanity, for whom it pointed to an outside, a world beyond their misery, a past world of civilization. And we have seen it employed by the rulers themselves of this inhuman universe. For them, too, it marked an outside—an outside to be feared. Olfaction is the archetypal precivilized as well as the ultimately civilized sensory mode in our day and age. Marinetti claims it explicitly for an aesthetics of war. This, however, is a role the olfactory cannot play.

As the stench of death and decomposing bodies, smell will always cut across the necessary, but necessarily threadbare, rational motivation required for war and killing and will instead hint at the primal fear of war and death itself. There are few things so unbearable to the human senses and so lasting in memory as the stench of death, and one must indeed not underestimate its force in an aesthetic framework. So far, no politicization of aesthetics has been able to uncouple the olfactory from its phenomenological origin, from its immediate root in the body. No discursive revaluation has been capable of severing the link of this sense with its most archaic origins in sexuality and death. Discourses and politics are able to bury those links under norms and standards and a lot of verbiage in civilized times. The play on the erotic nexus is, as we pointed out earlier, one of the very markers of civilization. The good part of the olfactory spectrum seems under control. But as soon as human existence is driven to an extreme, for instance in war, the old links resurface and assert their hold. And the stench of death will not cease to horrify, but it will also not cease to fascinate people. Marinetti, with his program, walks a very thin line between horror and fascination. As far as we know, however, horror and disgust prevail. Until this changes, Marinetti's manifesto will remain what it once was, futuristic.

We are now in a position to offer a preliminary conclusion. Olfactory phenomena in both their materializations, the good and pleasurable on the one hand and the bad, revolting on the other, have their origin in the body. Both originally and ultimately relate to fundamental categories of human existence, sexuality and death. The ultimate reference point for bad smells is the rotting human body; the ultimate reference for good smells are sexual odors. Smells cannot be taught to speak of lofty ideals, nor will they carry abstract messages. They may play on those things—as they are made to do on a large scale in perfumery—but their last words will always be sexuality and death.[42] This is why there is no art of smells. There is craft and, yes, artifice, even craftiness behind a lot of smells and scents, and a whole industry has developed around them, but there is no olfactory art *per se*. This does not exclude this sense from participating in aesthetic contexts, as for instance in literature. Indeed literary aesthetics will not be complete without taking into account smells and probing their role within representational structures.

The following two texts take us back to Auschwitz once more. They are not written by survivors, but they do take the victims' side. They are one step removed from the events, and raise questions of an explicitly aesthetic nature.

In Barbara Hyett's case the narrated experience is not even of camp prisoners but of soldiers present at the liberation of the camps, eyewitnesses of the moment when the gates were opened. "In spite of what preparation their soldiering might have provided, those who entered the camps could

---

42. Freud's drive-based model of culture postulates Eros and Thanatos as opposing forces. From an olfactory viewpoint (a mixed metaphor, unfortunately) this clearcut opposition is called into question by the fact that both types of smell, the erotic as well as that of the corpse, are culturally constructed as bad. Both are masked, suppressed by means of deodorants and perfumes, refrigeration and "starkriechende Blumen" (*Buddenbrooks*). But whereas the smells of the dead body have unfailingly marked the bad pole of the olfactory spectrum throughout history, those of the living body have undergone considerable cultural shaping and become the objects of constant vigilance. Good and bad—as well as the various fashions the good smells have undergone—have been (re)defined over time without, however, changing their ultimate reference points. One difference in dealing with smells from opposite ends of the spectrum is evident, though: the corpse and its (offensive) smell is a momentary event. By disposing of the body, the smell disappears too. The living human body, on the other hand, requires constant attention, and it has become a territory on which the lines of olfactory demarcation are mapped and remapped. Thanatos is olfactorily fixed; Eros has to be worked out in cultural practice. Its bad strand might in fact be the truly erotic—to which, however, we only dare to own up *privatissime*.

not believe what they saw there,"[43] she says in the preface, where she also briefly outlines her work, which consists of interviews with veterans. Her attempt to put these statements into an adequate form for publication results in turning them into poems. The passage is worth quoting fully:

> Two years after the first interview, I began the poems about the liberation. At first, I tried to write as a child on the train to Dachau, but I could not speak for the victims. Then, I wrote as an observer, but these poems were faceless. So I listened to all the tapes again, and this time heard the music in the words. I selected details from the accounts, maintaining the language as it was spoken, changing very few words, and then only for the sake of clarity. I arranged the poems to create a narrative sequence, imagining a voice—a young soldier who is there, watching, not necessarily comprehending, letting the horror wash over him. (xii)

There is a new and explicitly aesthetic transformation involved here. The horrible, though for these soldiers (as opposed to the prisoners) not actually life-threatening physical experience is converted into poems, the linguistic art form par excellence. Despite (or because of?) "the music" present in the original words there is insecurity both for the interviewees and the interviewer about the responsibility of the poetic form, the work of art.

> Later, when I showed the manuscript to three of the liberators I had interviewed, and thanked them for the poems, each one told me not to thank them, that the poems were mine. Now I wonder: whose responsibility is it to document history? I did not write these poems, I found them. (xiii–xiv)

The perceptual comments by the liberators in their accounts show how much smell marks the world of horror they encounter and to what degree it infiltrates their own reality as an inescapable trace.

The ovens,
the stench,

---

43. Barbara Helfgott Hyett, *In Evidence: Poems of the Liberation of Nazi Concentration Camps* (Pittsburgh: University of Pittsburgh Press, 1986), xii.

> I couldn't repeat
> the stench. You
> have to breathe.
> You can wipe out
> what you don't want
> to see. Close your
> eyes. You don't want
> to hear, don't want
> to taste. You can
> block out all senses
> except smell.

(8)

They stress the gulf between the two worlds:

> But your clean American hands
> don't want to touch them,
> alive with lice. Stinking.

(56)

Even for the liberators smell is the experience that marks most clearly the borderline between the camp and the world outside. For one of the soldiers, the stench makes it altogether impossible to exercise other forms of perception:

> And I went in
> to take a picture
> and the stench was so much
> I couldn't.

(83)

Or:

> A sour, putrid
> smell that
> left you ready
> to throw up.

(44)

Smell, from whichever perspective, denounces the abuse of power on the human body. Its construction within an aesthetic frame means the organization of sensory perception not in terms of beauty but of the power structures that underlie the phenomenological and perceptual experience on which the artwork draws. Because the olfactory is a registering rather than a productive device, it does not itself shape symbolic, representational structures; but it infallibly reveals and highlights them.

The play *Die Ermittlung* puts the Auschwitz experience in the context of a legal investigation. The trial is the place of discursive reconstruction of experience, and it turns out to be the locus of two antithetical rhetorical strategies, of distancing and of closeness. The defendants at the postwar Nazi trials naturally stress their "not-being-there." The witnesses as victims cannot help but having been there, as witnesses they *have* to have been there in order to be able to support the truth of their statements. In this dichotomy both sides are asked to report where they were, what they saw, what they heard. Smell does not play a role as it cannot be structured into meaning other than in the indexical pairing of cause and effect. That is why it is only alluded to by the victims, not as their proof of having been there, but as the trace of experience that is uniquely theirs.

Throughout the play the burden of proof rests with the survivors, now witnesses; and often it is they who are questioned and doubted. Consequently their argument is having seen, heard, smelled, felt something: in short, emphasizing their presence there. The defendants on the other hand typically claim the opposite: "Ich habe nie auf der Rampe / ausgesondert" (15);[44] "Ich hatte nie etwas damit zu tun" (25); "Ich habe meinen Fuss nie in das Lager gesetzt" (70). Or they claim to have been there only occasionally or in a single, exceptional case: "Ich habe das vielleicht einmal / vertretungsweise unterschreiben müssen" (9); "Das war ein Einzelfall" (120); "Nur in einigen Fällen / hatte ich Abspritzungen zu überwachen" (127).

---

44. Following are the translations of the quotes in this and the next paragraph. "I never made decisions at the platforms"; "I never had anything to do with it"; "I never set foot in the camp." "I may have had to sign this maybe once, as a substitute"; "That was an exceptional case"; "Only in a few cases did I have to supervise injections." "Did you not hear anything of what happened below / They were screaming / . . . / Who opened the room / A paramedic / What did you see / I didn't look closely." In the following paragraph: "The air was full of smoke / The smoke smelled sweetish and burnt / This was the smoke / that remained from now on." "The stench of the latrines / mingled with the smell / of the smoke." Transports arrived "like hot cakes." In the standing cells, "the odors / that the suffocating humans emitted / mingled with the stench / from the pot."

When they actually admit to having been present they express it in terms of seeing and hearing, the senses of distancing: "Haben Sie nichts gehört von dem / was sich da unten abspielte [the judge is referring to the victims in the gas chamber] / Die haben geschrien / . . . / Wer hat den Raum geöffnet / Ein Sanitäter / Was haben Sie da gesehen / Ich habe nicht genau hingesehen" (109). They use the senses of distance which are the senses of power.[45] In contrast to this stands the survivors' experience, which is recalled by drawing on the vocabulary of all the human senses to express their feelings of physical and emotional pain. This is the world of their experience, of their horrors described in visual, aural, olfactory and on one occasion in gustatory terms, "the taste of the camp-soup" (37).

The mentioning of smells on the witnesses' side—despite the fact and their knowledge of it that smell is not legally conclusive evidence—marks this form of perception as special. It cannot reveal anything new; and it cannot serve as evidence for intentional acts by the perpetrators. It is the surplus perception, the highly volatile, yet ineradicable (memory) trace that betrays the abuse of power, its degeneration into violence. We already mentioned the "bakery." Like Lengyel in her account, a witness here describes the camp in terms of its smell: "Die Luft war voll Rauch / Der Rauch roch süsslich und versengt / Dies war der Rauch / der fortan blieb" (14). Another witness alludes to the stench of the latrines: "Der Gestank der Latrinen / vermischte sich mit dem Geruch / des Rauchs" (32). One of the defendants, as if in a monumental Freudian slip, harks back to the positive explanatory image of a bakery with its pleasant smells and says that at times of full capacity the transports arrived "wie warme Brötchen" (43). In the standing cells, however, where prisoners were crammed in far too little space, reigns the stench of death: "Die Gerüche / die die erstickenden Menschen von sich gaben / vermischten sich mit dem Gestank / aus dem Kübel" (152).

Like Hyett's poems, *Die Ermittlung* cannot simply be read as the documentary account of a trial but must also be regarded as an aesthetic product, with aesthetics understood not as the theory of the beautiful, but rather as the representational organization of any sensory perception for the purpose of creating and conveying meaning. As a play explicitly placed in a musical context by its subtitle "Oratorium in 11 Gesängen" and with structural parallels to Dante's *Divine Comedy, Die Ermittlung* is an aesthetic

---

45. Cf. Kamper and Wulf, *Das Schwinden der Sinne,* esp. the essay "Blickwende. Die Sinne des Körpers im Konkurs der Geschichte," 9–45.

product. However, in an account of a topic as powerful and emotionally disturbing as Auschwitz, aesthetics must be defined in such a way as to include the organization, structuring, or theory of human sensory perception as representation. By including the lower senses, such a view transcends Kant's realm of the disinterestedly beautiful. Kant, as we recall, excluded those senses from his aesthetic project with the argument that they are too corporeal, too immediately affecting of the organic level and thus unsuited for distanced and disinterested contemplation. For him the senses of touch, taste, and smell reveal more about the perceiving subject than about the perceived object, which is precisely why we want to include them in our present aesthetic project, where the subjective state of being is as important as the objective moment of appearance. For this refiguring it is necessary to insist on the phenomenological and sensory base of aesthetics, in both its pleasurable and unpleasant aspects. Applied to the play, such an aesthetics takes on new meaning. From the point of view of the ex-guards, the defendants of 1965, aesthetics turns out to be the organization of sensory perception as denial. From the point of view of the survivors, the witnesses of 1965 who face a wall of solidarity among both the defendants and the defense lawyers representing a system that has switched back to normal, aesthetics serves the purpose of revelation. The implicit imbalance of power makes this aesthetics a highly political issue. As the transformation of sensory perception into meaning by the victims of a given social system, such an aesthetics turns into an aesthetics of resistance.

The Smell Lingers On: "Der vertraute Brodem"

Wolfgang Koeppen's three novels, written in the early 1950s, add up to a deeply pessimistic portrait of postwar German society.[46] His aesthetics is one of rejection and disgust rather than of resistance, but has its biographical roots in his own resistance to fascist co-optation while staying in Germany during the war.[47] The author's disgust over the persistence and

---

46. The novels discussed here are *Tauben im Gras* (1951); *Das Treibhaus* (1953); and *Der Tod in Rom* (1954), all in Wolfgang Koeppen, vol. 2 of *Gesammelte Werke in sechs Bänden*, ed. Marcel Reich-Ranicki (Frankfurt am Main: Suhrkamp, 1986).

47. For a recent, brief, and informative account of the author and his work, cf. Martin Hielscher, *Wolfgang Koeppen*, Beck'sche Reihe Autorenbücher (Munich: C. H. Beck, 1988). Hielscher deals with the novels under discussion here in chapter 3, 1, "Die Romane der fünfziger Jahre," 75ff.

reemergence of fascist structures, fascist modes of thinking, and fascist rhetoric has an additional level beyond the intellectual attitude presented in the novels' main characters. Koeppen grounds it, tangibly, visibly, and in olfactory terms, in the concrete world he represents and which his characters inhabit. It is a sleazy, shabby, dirty world, and the same qualities are found in the people themselves. Their world is full of odors, and they themselves are aware of and influenced by them.

The novels have several features in common. They are relatively short, around 200 pages each; all three cover, in terms of actual plot, a very short time (one day in *Tauben im Gras,* and just a couple of days in the other two); but they develop from there, by means of flashbacks and retrospective individual accounts, a much broader picture, the picture of the immediate postwar years, the restoration that, for Koeppen, is still deeply permeated by fascism. The three novels portray and re-create this world for the reader's senses, among them most noticeably, the olfactory. The stench of fascism at its utmost extreme, the rotting and burning human bodies in the death camps, is still lingering on. The skeletons in the cupboards of postwar Germany have not yet been picked clean by time and a thorough political working through and have thus not yet become harmless anatomical, historical showpieces. They are still decomposing and festering—and Koeppen lets out into the open the stench that others among his contemporaries are only too eager to keep a lid on. No wonder that Keetenheuve, the protagonist of *Das Treibhaus,* notices on the occasion of a committee meeting the smell of sweat and lavender emanating from the men in the room and thinks that "immer verweste etwas, und immer wieder versuchte man, mit Duftwasser den Geruch der Verwesung zu verstecken" (311).[48]

The density of olfactory instances is high in all three novels, one occurrence about every four or five pages, even higher in *Das Treibhaus,* where the whole atmosphere, the air itself, seems charged, sultry, and of an almost tangible heaviness. In all three novels the bulk of olfactory occurrences is on the level of discourse and representation between the narrator and the reader rather than on the level of plot among the characters. Although they are aware of the olfactory elements of their surroundings, they do not generally perceive each other, recognize each other, or interact with each other on an olfactory basis. This constellation is different from the one found in turn-of-the-century literature, from Des Esseintes to Hanno Bud-

---

48. "There was always something decomposing, and over and over again they tried to mask with perfumes this odor of corruption."

denbrook and Malte Laurids Brigge. Koeppen does not describe individuals of the same sophisticated perceptual awareness and acuteness, of that high-strung perceptual sensitivity, as do Huysmans, Mann, or Rilke, or as we encountered first in French symbolist poetry. But then also, Koeppen's characters live in a world very different from that of the declining aristocracy or the rising bourgeoisie. They have just survived a war and live as if the next one were immediately impending. It is in the olfactory aftermath of this war that Koeppen's figures are located. Yet Koeppen does use smells to characterize groups of people and occasionally even individuals above and beyond the all-enveloping olfaction of atmospherics.

The city in *Tauben im Gras* is the immediate postwar Munich, occupied by the Americans. The novel picks up a number of individuals, follows them through their day, puts some of them in touch with each other as if by chance, has them meet in the "Bräuhaus" or the pub at the "Heiliggeist-platz," and eventually brings together the most important ones for the speech by the famous American author Edwin at the "Amerikahaus." A recurring feature of the novel is its real-life-sounding newspaper headlines summing up or confirming a point the narrator has just made. The media, both the press and the radio, play an important role in the structure of the narrative. We see the newspaper agents as a group in the early morning hours "mit klammen Händen, mißmutig, fluchend, windgeschüttelt, regennaß, bierdumpf, tabakverbeizt, unausgeschlafen, alpgequält, auf der Haut noch den Hauch des Nachtgenossen, des Lebensgefährten, Reißen in der Schulter, Rheuma im Knie" receive the "druckfrische Ware" (11).[49] This bunch of people can well stand for the population of Koeppen's novels at large; they just happen to be the first recipients of (the bad) news. They are ill-prepared to deal with a world that is shifting gears so fast that "das Zeitungspapier roch nach heißgelaufenen Maschinen, nach Unglücksbotschaften, gewaltsamem Tod, falschen Urteilen, zynischen Bankrotten, nach Lüge, Ketten und Schmutz" (12). It is understandable as a defense-mechanism, then, that these people love the Bräuhaus and the "vertrauten Brodem" (27), the "homey reek" of places like the Bräuhaus, where it is warm, where there is company, community, and camaraderie

---

49. The newspaper vendors sit there "with cold hands, grouchy, cursing, shaken by the wind, rainsoaked, dull with beer, impregnated with tobacco, after a bad night's sleep, haunted by nightmares, on their skin still the scent of their night's companion, their life partner, a twinge in their shoulders, rheumatism in their knees," and are handed out their wares, "hot off the press." "The papers still smell of the presses running hot, of bad news, violent death, judicial errors, cynical bankruptcies, of lies, chains, and smut" (12).

in the macho sense of male bonding in Hitler's Reich, and where "in der Ausdünstung der Menschen und des Bieres," in the "haze of sweat and beer," things become fuzzy, lose their sharp contours "wie in einem Nebel" (196). It does not matter, that it "[dunstete] nach Erbrochenem." They barely notice the "Hauch und Staub der Nacht, de[n] schale[n], tote[n] Abfall der Lust," the odors and the garbage of the night that are enveloping them (18).

These are the two main ingredients of Koeppen's olfactory universe, the almost tangible stench of humans, composed of beer, tobacco, sweat, and a general unpleasant and stale haziness of the air; and the more abstract smell of the "system overheating," the general stink rising from too rapid a reconstruction process on foundations that have not been properly checked for their soundness—the stench, in other words, of "something rotten in the state of Germany." Only the narrator with his relentless adjectival and attributive criticism, and Edwin, the foreigner, in thinking about his speech, are aware that the "Geruch dieser zugeschütteten Keller" still hangs over the city. "Niemand schien es zu bemerken. Vielleicht vergaß man die Grüfte ganz. Sollte Edwin erinnern?" (107). Edwin wonders why nobody seems to be aware of the "odor of the filled-in basements" and is not sure whether he "should remind people of it" in his speech. For him the olfactorily charged atmosphere is almost palpable in which the population resettles, moving back to the city after the "Zuzugsperre" (24), the ban on returning, has been lifted. The city fills up, gets crowded, dense, and thick with teeming, reeking, sleazy life. The narrator notices this.

Sie waren wieder zu Hause, reihten sich ein, rieben sich aneinander, übervorteilten einander, handelten, schufen, bauten, gründeten, zeugten, saßen in der alten Kneipe, atmeten den vertrauten Brodem, beobachteten das Revier, den Paarungsplatz, den Nachwuchs der Asphaltgassen, Gelächter und Zank und das Radio der Nachbarn, sie starben im Städtischen Krankenhaus, wurden vom Bestattungsamt hinausgefahren, lagen auf dem Friedhof an der Ost-Süd-Kreuzung, von Straßenbahnen umbimmelt, benzindunstumschwelt, glücklich in der Heimat. (27)[50]

---

50. "They were back home again, getting in line, grating on each other, cheating each other, dealing, working, building, founding, copulating, sitting in the old dives, breathing the homey reek, checking out the neighborhood, the nest, the asphalt brood, the laughter and quarrels and the radio blare of their neighbors; they were dying at the municipal hospital, were shipped out by the funerary office, and came to rest in the

Smell is an essential part of Koeppen's city and the whole of his postwar Germany. Into this world have entered the American soldiers. When they landed, the earth

roch feucht. Der Flughafen roch nach Gras, nach Benzin, Auspuffgasen, Metall und nach etwas Neuem, nach der Fremde, es war ein Backgeruch, ein Brotteiggeruch nach Gärung, Hefe und Alkohol, appetitanregend und animierend, es dunstete nach Biermaische aus den großen Brauereien der Stadt. (40)[51]

This instance of focused olfactory perception describes the foreigners "sniffing out" Germany. The following represents the inverse, the black American soldier perceived by the Germans.

Odysseus Cotton verließ den Bahnhof. Am schlenkernden Arm, in der braunen Hand baumelte ein Köfferchen. Odysseus Cotton war nicht allein. Eine Stimme begleitete ihn. Aus dem Koffer kam die Stimme, sanft, warm, weich, eine tiefe Stimme, wohlige Atmung, ein Hauch wie Samt, heiße Haut unter einer alten zerrissenen Autodecke in einer Wellblechhütte, Schreie, Brüllen der Riesenfrösche, Nacht am Mississippi. (27)[52]

Those "Neger" appear sensual, animal, erotic and exotic, alluring and repulsive. In any case, the native racketeers and pimps, the small-time wheelers and dealers welcome them into the teeming hothouse of their postwar city. They can be catered to; they can be exploited; money can be made off them; and they can provide access to goods and luxuries still in short supply for the general public. The two central and complementary figures in this respect are Washington Price, the family man, fighting for his relationship

---

cemetery at the intersection of East and South streets, surrounded by the bells of the tramways, the exhaust gases, happy to be back home."

51. The earth "smelled humid. The airport smelled of grass, gasoline, exhausts, metal, and of something new, of a foreign country; it was a smell of baking, an odor of bread dough and fermentation, yeast and alcohol, appetizing and animating; it was the smell of mash from the large breweries of the town."

52. "Odysseus Cotton left the station. From his dangling arm, from his brown hand hung a small box. Odysseus Cotton was not alone. He was accompanied by a voice. The voice came from the box, a soft, warm, gentle, low voice; a pleasurable breathing, a touch of velvet, hot skin under an old, torn blanket in a corrugated iron shack; screams, the noise of giant bullfrogs, night on the Mississippi."

and his child with Carla, his German lover, providing goods and bringing presents to her and her friends; and Odysseus Cotton, "der große listen-reiche Odysseus" (196), "resourceful Odysseus," the sexual animal and pos-sible, if unintended, murderer of the old porter Josef. "Die Schlepper, die Wechsler, die Schnapper" throw themselves at Odysseus, together with their girls, "die Ware," sitting "bei Limonade, Coca-Cola, schlechtem Kaf-fee, stinkender Brühe, den Bettdunst, den Geruch der Umarmungen von gestern noch nicht abgewaschen, die Hautflecken überpudert" (41).[53] That night Odysseus will end up in bed with Susanne, who applied too much of the "Guerlain" she took from Messalina, the wife of her lover from the previous night (14) and thus trails a cloud of scent behind her. At the pub at the Heiliggeistplatz, in the unsavory "Dunst, in d[er] stinkende[n] grau-same[n] Magie des Lokals" (156); in the "Schweiß, Pisse, Zwiebel, Wurstbrühe, . . . Bierdunst und Tabakrauch" (157) of the place two clouds of the same perfume, "Guerlain, Paris" will briefly mingle, Messalina and Susanne momentarily enter each other's olfactory spheres—and drift away from each other as Susanne follows Odysseus, who flees the pub after a brawl. In the no less hazy air full of unpleasant odors at the Bräuhaus, it is easy to get the band to play the "Badenweiler Marsch, den Lieblingsmarsch des toten Führers" (192), Hitler's favorite marching tune. It is an atmo-sphere of unholy, unnatural fraternization, as the Americans, too, become infected, "von der Stimmung mitgerissen" (193). Nobody is a Nazi, God forbid; they are "Biertrinker" (193). They unite, and they simply feel at home in the unsavory atmosphere of stale fascism, racism, xenophobia, and mutual exploitation.

For Koeppen, smells are an essential sensory and aesthetic element for atmospheric characterization.[54] Even where a person seems to stand out by virtue of her individual scent, the "Guerlain," for instance, it turns out to be borrowed from someone else and both together, lender and bor-rower, become submerged in the general olfactory cesspool of the public sphere. The olfactory has lost its individualizing power, and even good smells carry an undertone of sleaze. This comes as no surprise in a public

---

53. "The pimps, the money changers, the crooks" are after him, offering their girls, "their wares," sitting "over a lemonade, a coke, bad coffee, a stinking brew, without having washed off the smell of sleep, the odor of last night's embraces, powder on their skin sores."

54. I am talking about Koeppen the author rather than the narrator, in view of the fact that what is said about the olfactory in *Tauben im Gras* applies equally to the other two novels. Searching awareness of the olfactory seems a concern of the author, beyond the scope of any single narrator in his works.

realm that has lost its earlier cleanliness and odorlessness and is no longer the neutral background on which individual olfactory display can unfold. The overall level of olfactory phenomena, amounting to a veritable stench, is so high that it sucks everything into its hazy abyss of exhalations, of the big bad breath of the community of humans.

Sexuality too is connotated with uncleanliness, unpleasantness; and it smells of cheap perfumes. The whores who live at Frau Welz's place "wedelten Duftwolken aus dem gefärbten Haar" (84).[55] Emilia, the unfortunate lover of the eternally blocked writer Philipp, pawning her heirlooms to the ever-horny Unverlacht, gets sick from the "Gewölbedunst" of his basement store, which "benahm ihr den Atem" (92) while he pats her behind. And among the crowd at Edwin's lecture we find "Modeschöpfer, feminine wohlriechende Herren" with their "Vorführpuppen, . . . die man ihnen unbesorgt anvertrauen durfte" (182). Kay, the American teacher from Massachusetts, is the only exception. With her green eyes, she seems "so unbefangen, so frisch, . . . sie kam aus anderer Luft, aus herber und reiner Luft" (97); and she "duftete nach Reseda" (98). This scent reminds Philipp, from whose perspective Kay is seen, of his own youth.

In certain ways we are back in the seventeenth- and eighteenth-century city full of odors and stenches and unsavory occurrences. In other respects, of course, we are not, and it is precisely the difference that allows us at this point to trace briefly the road of olfactory progress that we have been following so far and to point out the landmarks along the course. In that earlier epoch and into the nineteenth century (bad) smells were emerging not only as actual physical facts, but for the first time as topics of discourse in the public sphere. Now they are reemerging in an atmosphere that seemed to have become quite clean and salubrious in the nineteenth and early twentieth centuries. Their reappearance, however, both factually and discursively, occurs in a new medium. We will spare ourselves the phenomenological details and focus on the discursive realm instead. Whereas the first time around, the evolving discourse was scientific and practical, this time it is literary and aesthetic. The first surfacing occurred

---

55. Following are the translations of German quotes in this paragraph. The whores "were shaking clouds of scent from their hair." Emilia feels sick in the "basement reek," which "takes her breath away." The "fashion designers [are] feminine, well-scented gentlemen" with their "models [more accurately, "mannequins"], . . . whom one could entrust to them unhesitatingly." Kay, in contrast, seems "so unrestrained, so fresh, . . . she came from a different climate [actually, "air"], a sharper, purer climate"; and she "smelled of reseda."

in the framework of civilizational developments as a clear and unmistakable example of progress, whereas Koeppen describes the impact of a moment of regression in the aftermath of a historical breakdown of that progress. Accordingly, the approaches and remedies suggested and undertaken are of a different nature: sanitary, hygienic, and technical in the earlier epoch; psychological and moral at the present moment. Civilizational forces at large are at work in the former; cultural and educational forces in the narrower sense of the term are to deal with the latter. Precisely this, however, as we will see, turns out to be a problem, because these forces are out of touch with reality. Culture, certainly high culture, has no hold on the postwar underground as Koeppen describes it. The high-culture communication system does not carry down into the interstices of a bombed-out city; it does not even carry over to the audience in the lecture hall where Edwin is giving his speech.

Edwin wollte mit der griechischen und lateinischen Antike beginnen, er wollte die Christenheit erwähnen, die Verbindung biblischer Tradition mit der Klassik, . . . aber leider drang statt der Worte nur Geräusch zu seinen Zuhörern, ein Gurgeln und Knacken und Raspeln . . . Edwin, am Lesepult, merkte zunächst nicht, daß die Lautsprecheranlage des Saales in Unfunktion geraten war. . . . Die Technik rebellierte gegen den Geist. . . . "Ich bin hilflos," dachte Edwin, "wir sind hilflos, ich habe mich auf diesen dummen und bösen Sprechtrichter verlassen, hätte ich ohne diese Erfindung die mich nun lächerlich macht vor sie hintreten können? nein, ich hätte es nicht gewagt, wir sind keine Menschen mehr, keine ganzen Menschen." (184–85)[56]

Edwin's audience is asleep anyway (202). Philipp too, who is among the listeners, feels that they cannot understand each other. The medium itself has taken over; "nicht Edwin redet, der Lautsprecher spricht, . . . die Lautsprecher, diese gefährlichen Roboter, halten auch Edwin gefangen: sein Wort wird durch ihren blechernen Mund gepreßt, es wird zur Lautsprech-

---

56. "Edwin wanted to begin with Greek and Latin antiquity, wanted to mention Christianity, the connection of the biblical tradition with classicism, . . . but unfortunately, instead of words, only noise reached his listeners, a gargle and crackle and rasping . . . Edwin, at the lectern, did initially not notice that the speaker system in the hall was malfunctioning. . . . Technology was rebelling against the spirit. . . . 'I am helpless,' Edwin thought, 'we are helpless. I have counted on these stupid and mean speakers. Could I have come before the people without this invention that now ridicules me? No, I wouldn't have dared, we are no longer human beings, no complete human beings.'"

ersprache, zu dem Weltidiom, das jeder kennt und niemand versteht" (202).[57]

This example of a failed oral-aural communication has first of all a metaphoric meaning. An analogous shift in representational function can be observed for the olfactory. No longer is its main concern with actual smells (although the semidestroyed postwar cities certainly do stink) but with the metaphoric level of signification. Just as the true reason for the communication problem described by Koeppen lies hardly in the malfunctioning speaker system but must be sought in an increasingly difficult cultural communication, the olfactory discourse has shifted from phenomenological, factual, scientific "hardware" issues to discussions in metaphoric and aesthetic terms. What we are concerned with is the conceptual understanding of the olfactory, the oral-aural, the visual, and so forth within a literary frame. We have followed smell in its evolution and revolutions over time, starting from the general stink to be gotten rid of. We have noticed the allusive lure that needed to be repressed and the anarchic uncontrollability to be evaded in bourgeois realism; the awakening and honing of individual skills and subtleties in olfactory perception in turn-of-the-century literature; the trace to be feared for its revelation of immoral acts; and are now dealing with the metaphoric web for something rotten in the system. Smell has evolved into a metaphor to be dealt with in the cultural, semiotic superstructure rather than, as was the case in the olden days, at the base of civilizational hardware. This is the situation we encounter, with variations, also in the following two novels.

Das Treibhaus is different from *Tauben im Gras* in that its narrative perspective is more directly that of its central character, Keetenheuve, a member of the new parliament in Bonn. He was outside Germany during the Nazi years, returned after the war with high hopes for a new political beginning and a clean working-through of the fascist past, but now finds himself again in the opposition and fighting against bureaucratic and procedural obstacles, feels himself bogged down in compromises and concessions that he cannot accept. The political idealist realizes that the new Germany carries on with the same personnel that already ran the Reich and that a clean break with the past is impossible. The unmistakable evidence of this is the

---

57. "It is not Edwin speaking, it's the speaker, . . . the speakers, these dangerous robots, are holding Edwin prisoner: his word is being squeezed through their metallic mouth, thus turning into loudspeaker-speak, the worldwide idiom that everybody knows and nobody understands."

representative Dörflich, evicted from his party's committee for his involvement in an "einträgliche Affäre" (356). He now runs a dairy store in the "politicians' ghetto," thus forcing everybody who buys his daily necessities from him to acknowledge his presence. *Non olet,* may be the general opinion about such behavior, and indeed "bei Dörflich stank merkbar nur der Käse"; but Keetenheuve nevertheless notices "an odor of corruption," believes "einen aasigen Geruch, der nicht aus der Käseglocke kam, in Dörflichs Nähe zu spüren" (357). Keetenheuve dislikes this man who smells "nach altem Nazismus" (358) and seems to be headed for a new fascism. The general climate of the novel, always seen through Keetenheuve, is of architectural, political, and economic reconstruction and restoration, and the central metaphor for the busy, even hectic activities is the hothouse, the *Treibhaus* of the title. Heavy, humid, sultry air; plant imagery, often in terms of decay and decomposition; and remarks on the weather and temperature, often in combination with one another, are central elements in the characterization of that climate of the *Wirtschaftswunder,* the "economic miracle" in Germany.[58] More and more, as the novel progresses, the stench of decomposition, of rot, of *Verwesung,* wafts through Keetenheuve's perceptual universe. The consular post that the governing party offers him in Guatemala in order to be rid of him is associated with stink, too, "nach Benzin und nach Verwesung" (298). Keetenheuve is not going to take it, but his own world on the Rhine stinks just as much. At a party meeting everybody is sweating, and through the scent of lavender from the men's cologne, Keetenheuve notices that "immer verweste etwas" (311). He has the same sensation of ubiquitous decomposition and rot when he walks across the market square that is being cleaned for the evening: "Fauliges, Stinkendes, Verwesendes, Ranziges, Verdorbenes lag unter seinen Füßen" (327), and along the Rhine, there is the stench of "Schlick, Verwesung und künstlicher Erhaltung eines Leichnams" (378).

The Federal Republic, in its parliamentary activity, its hustle and bustle of talks and meetings and industrial reconstruction, is in fact, through Koeppen's textual strategies, already being deconstructed. The medium in

---

58. A few examples will suffice here: "Es roch intensiv nach Feuchtigkeit, Erde und Blumen" (264); "Durch das Fenster drang wieder feuchtwarm Erddunst und Pflanzengeruch eines botanischen Gartens" (281–82). Outside his window Keetenheuve sees "Wolken geladen mit Elektrizität, beladen mit dem Auspuff der Essen des Ruhrgebiets, dampfende trächtige Schleier, gasig, giftig, schwefelfarben" (284); and thinking of his wife Elke, who died far too young, he smells again "den Geruch der modrig feuchten Buchsbaumhecken, die süße Verwesung der verfaulten Rosen in den Totenkränzen" (353).

which this is most prominently noticeable, is the olfactory, the climatic and atmospheric. The sense of smell betrays the seamy, corrupt underbelly of the Leviathan (378), and the sense of touch tells Keetenheuve that the bridge from which he will eventually throw himself into the Rhine "bebte unter der Fahrt der unwirklich aussehenden Straßenbahnen" (389). There is a "Zittern im Stahl" (390), "a shiver running through the steel," that he feels as his last sensation before he jumps.

We discussed German bourgeois realist texts from a predominantly sociohistorical viewpoint, as reflections of a social and psychological reality, rather than as purely aesthetic texts; our focus on the turn-of-the-century material was from the angle of a psychological and perceptual revolution for the individual and its corresponding literary expression. In the present chapter we turned, for the death-camp accounts, to the documentary aspects of the material and its psychological and aesthetic consequences; and Koeppen's novels can be read in yet a different, more strictly "literary," way. There exists beyond and in addition to these novels plenty of material in extraliterary discourses about the events described by Koeppen. For the newly founded Federal Republic, a predominant public discourse topic is restoration, progress, *Wirtschaftswunder,* the regained acceptance of the new state in the world's political arena. Koeppen's texts, outside this official *Aufbau*-rhetoric of directed utility, tell their critical version of the events in the literary and aesthetic realm—and it turns out to be a different story indeed. Free from propaganda duties, these novels, qua literature, are at liberty to choose their means of representation. As it happens, the olfactory is selected as an important phenomenological tool to carry the tenor of Koeppen's countermessage. Smell plays a role that by now begins to appear familiar: it tells a truth that official rhetoric prefers to suppress. It tells of an unpleasant, seedy, corrupt reality that the official high-gloss aestheticization of politics would much prefer to have painted over.

Der Tod in Rom is another such story. A German family meets in the eternal city, each person arriving with a different agenda. The mayor Friedrich Wilhelm Pfaffrath and his wife Anna, together with their son Dietrich, plan to meet with Pfaffrath's brother-in-law Gottlieb Judejahn to talk about his return to Germany, which seems safe now for ex-Nazis; and all three of them plan to visit the Monte Cassino battlefield. Travelling and staying with them at the hotel is Pfaffrath's sister Eva. She has been and still is married to Judejahn, the former SS general who escaped denazification and is now a military adviser and arms dealer for an Arab nation. The two have not seen each other for years. Both are characterized as relentless, incorrigible Nazis. There is also Pfaffrath's other son, Siegfried, a musician whose symphony is to be performed at an international competition. The conductor of the performance is his friend Kürenberg whose wife Ilse, née Aufhäuser, is of Jewish descent. Her father was killed by the Nazis, and Pfaffrath, already then mayor of the town, failed to intervene on his behalf, despite Kürenberg's pleading. Finally, there is Adolf Judejahn, Eva's and Gottlieb's son, who is going through the consecration ceremonies of a Catholic dean. Thus the two sons of the two Nazi fathers both go their own ways of overcoming the past, one through art, the other through religion. Yet despite this common trait they are unable to understand each other.

This constellation of characters with their stories and interconnections allows for an effective portrayal of recent German history in a series of encounters ironically to be played out in Rome, the eternal city. Immediately we are steeped in the smells of Rome, which appears as the city of eternal stench. The reader's nostrils are assailed, for instance, in the story of an old woman who brings food to the innumerable stray cats around the Pantheon.

> Eine eklig durchfeuchtete Zeitung umschließt den Fraß. Fischköpfe sind es. Auf blutbesudeltem Druckbild reichen sich der amerikanische Staatssekretär und der russische Außenminister die Hände.... Die Katzen knurren und fauchen sich an. Die alte Frau wirft das Papier in den Graben. Abgemesserte Häupter der Meerleichen, gebrochene Augen, verfärbte Kiemen, opalisierende Schuppen stürzen unter die schweifschlagende maunzende Meute. Aas, ein scharfer Geruch von Ausscheidungen, von Sekret, von Fortpflanzungsgier, ein süßer von Altersfäulnis und Eiter steigt in die Luft und vermischt sich mit den Benzindünsten der Straße und dem frischen anregenden Kaffeeduft aus der Espressobar an der Ecke der Piazza della Rotonda. (397)[59]

---

59. A disgusting, soaked newspaper is wrapped around the feed of fish heads. On the bloody picture the American secretary of state and the Russian foreign minister are shaking hands.... The cats are growling and hissing. The old woman throws the paper into the ditch. The severed heads of the oceanic brood, broken eyes, discolored gills, opalescent scales are thrown among the tail-whipping, meowing pack. Cadavers, a sharp reek of excretion, secretion, copulation, a sweet smell of old rot and pus mounts in the air and mingles with the exhausts of the street and the fresh, stimulating smell of coffee from the espresso bars on the corner of the Piazza della Rotonda.

The characters themselves, above all Judejahn, the Nazi mass murderer, are also marked by smell. About him we are informed at the outset that "Aasgeruch umwehte ihn" (410)[60] as well as the stench of a buck in heat, which he tries to cover up. "Er war weltmännisch geworden, parfümierte sich sogar, bevor er ins Bordell ging." On the way to meeting his family, however, he feels he should not scent himself. "Man stank nicht nach Moschus, wo er hinging. Man verbarg den Bock" (408).[61] With Judejahn are also associated the smells of the military, the stench of power that, at bottom, is the stench of fear.

Er roch den Kasernenmief aus Gefangenschaft, Knechtung, Lederfett, Waffenöl, scharfer Seife, süßer Pomade, saurem Schweiß, Kaffee, heißem Aluminiumgeschirr und Urin. Es war der Geruch der Angst;

---

60. Following are the translations of the German quotes in this paragraph. "A stench of cadaver hung about him" although "he had become cosmopolitan, even put on some perfume before going to the brothel. . . . " Perfume, however, seems inappropriate for the family reunion; "where he was going one did not put on musk. One played down the buck." Judejahn is associated with military odors:

He smelled the stuffiness of the barracks, composed of imprisonment, subjugation, leather grease, gun oil, cheap soap, sweet pomade, sour sweat, coffee, hot aluminum plates and urine. It was the smell of fear; but Judejahn did not know that it was the smell of fear, as he was unaware of fear.

However, "He is afraid of Eva, without makeup, but with her hair tied up; Eva the women's group member and believer in final victory; she was all right, certainly, but nothing attracted him to her." In the brothel "one let off steam, snapped up some women's smell, sprinkled with perfumes, but one remained aware of the carnal aspect of the procedure.

[Judejahn] had gone far beyond the bourgeois in the lobby, yet it was they who had permitted him to go so far . . . they had called out for the Reich and accepted murder and beatings and the smoke of burning bodies for Germany, but themselves had remained at their tables in their old German pubs.

Judejahn bought a ticket. . . . He walked along corridors, mounted some stairs. Nothing but naked people were standing in a red fog. It must be a brothel. Or he was in a gas chamber. That explained the red fog. He was in a large gas chamber with naked people who were to be liquidated; but in this case he had to get out. He was not meant to be liquidated. . . . He was the commandant. (577)

Siegfried loves "the pious smell of incense, melting wax, dust, varnish, old robes, old women, and old fear, so magnanimous and straitlaced" (481). He notices how the irremovable "Judejahn-Pfaffrath-Klingsor-stuffiness" clings to Adolf (502). And he himself longs for the "odor of big dormitories, naked boys' bodies . . . the world of male bonding" (505).

61. Laura, the cashier at the bar, nevertheless notices his stink on the occasion of their sexual encounter toward the end of the novel (574).

aber Judejahn wußte nicht, daß es der Geruch der Angst war. Er kannte
ja die Furcht nicht. (410)

Now, however, he hesitates to enter "Heimatenge und Familiendunst"
(413), the claustrophobic family smells. "Er fürchtete sich vor Eva, der
ungeschminkten und haargeknoteten, dem Frauenschaftsweib, der End-
sieggläubigen; sie war in Ordnung, gewiß, aber nichts zog ihn zu ihr"
(412). He hates women in general, and only accepts them as "Kriegsbeute"
and "im Puff." There, "man ließ Gier ab, schnappte Weibsdunst ein, duft-
wasserüberspritzt, doch blieb man sich der Fleischlichkeit des Vorgangs
bewußt" (521). Judejahn is the prototypical Nazi personality, basically
weak—bear in mind his name change from Gottlieb to the much more
martial Götz (416)—but a monster once in power. He secretly despises all
the fascist petit-bourgeois, such as Pfaffrath, who never fought and killed
and murdered.

Er war weiter gegangen als die Bürger in der Halle [of the hotel where
Judejahn hesitates to proceed further and meet his family], aber sie
waren es, die ihm erlaubt hatten, so weit zu gehen . . . [S]ie hatten "das
Reich" gerufen und Mord und Schlag und Leichenrauch für Deutschland hingenommen, doch selber waren sie an ihren Stammtischen
geblieben in altdeutscher Bierstube. (441)

This combination of *Leichenrauch* and *Bierstube* is what Koeppen really
writes against and what he already described in *Tauben im Gras*. It is the
atmosphere surrounding the small fry, the "petit Nazis," the hangers-on,
the followers whom Judejahn with his grand genocidal perspective feels
justified to despise. It is precisely they who made it all possible, a fact that
Judejahn recognizes and Koeppen, with a view to the future, fears. It is
not accidental that Judejahn's last vision before his death of a heart attack
in the museum is of a gas chamber.

Judejahn zahlte den Eintritt. . . . Er ging durch Gänge, ging eine Treppe
hoch. Lauter Nackte standen im roten Nebel. Es war wohl ein Puff.
Oder es war eine Gaskammer. Das erklärte auch den roten Nebel. Er
war in einer großen Gaskammer mit nackten Menschen, die liquidiert
werden sollten, aber dann mußte er hier nun 'rausgehen. Er sollte ja
nicht liquidiert werden. . . . Er war der Kommandeur. (577)

Siegfried, the artist, is the other person characterized in terms of, and susceptible to, smells. He loves the smell of churches, "den frommen Geruch aus Weihrauch, schmelzendem Wachs, Staub, Firnis, alten Gewändern, alten Frauen und alter Angst, so groß- und so engherzig" (481). He notices about Adolf how "die Familie ihm [anhaftete], ewig wie ein nicht zu beseitigender Geruch, . . . der Judejahn-Pfaffrath-Klingspor-Mief" (502). He himself, the pederast artist, the outsider, longs for the "Herden- und Stallgeruch, nach einer Welt leiblicher Gemeinschaft." He longs for the "Geruch der großen Schlafsäle, die nackten Knabenkörper . . . die Welt der Männerbünde" (505). And from his brief homosexual encounter down by the Tiber, which flows "wie das stinkende Waschwasser einer alten Vettel" (503), he wants to take "etwas Tibergeruch mit in das weiße Hemd" (528), which he puts on for his concert.

Similar to Edwin's lecture in *Tauben im Gras*, the concert here functions as the high-cultural event that draws all the main characters together, and just as in the former novel, it is not able to bring about a discussion among them. They disperse without having understood or even liked the music (cf. 403, 538). While we can read Koeppen's novels as a critique of elitist and ineffective high culture, the question arises whether they offer—from the position of literature as an institution—an alternative model. If popular success were the yardstick, Koeppen could hardly be called overly successful. His novels were never best-sellers. His innovation from our perspective lies in a new aesthetic and representational strategy applied to politically critical writing. But his accomplishment resides in building a sticky, erotically charged, olfactorily rich atmosphere that reveals a malaise. The sense of smell thus employed, expresses criticism, although it does not assure literary success. That the latter can be achieved by foregrounding the olfactory, even if at the expense of criticism, will be seen in the next chapter. The world depicted, however, is no longer a postwar Germany contemporaneous with the moment of writing, but France in the eighteenth century, as perceived in the postmodern 1980s amidst a raging debate about high and low culture and questions of representation.

CHAPTER 5

In Search of the Ultimate Scents

Mein Genie ist in meinen Nüstern
— (Nietzsche, *Ecce Homo*, "Warum ich ein Schicksal bin")

The three great stimulants
Of the exhausted ones
Artifice, brutality and innocence
— (Joni Mitchell)

Smells have come a long way—and they will go even further.

La disqualification de l'odorat, sens de l'animalité selon Buffon, exclu par Kant du champ de l'esthétique, considéré plus tard par les physiologistes comme un simple résidu de l'évolution, affecté par Freud à l'analité, a jeté l'interdit sur le discours que tiennent les odeurs. Cependant, il n'est plus possible de taire la révolution perceptive, préhistoire du silence olfactif de notre environnement.[1]

---

1. Corbin, *Le miasme*, 267. "The disqualification of the sense of smell—called the animal sense by Buffon, excluded from the aesthetic realm by Kant, later considered by the physiologists as a simple evolutionary residue, and by Freud associated with anality— has imposed a silence on olfactory discourses. However, it is no longer possible to hush up the perceptual revolution, the prehistory of the olfactory silence of our environment." For Buffon, see: Buffon, *De l'Homme* (Paris: François Maspero, 1971), 217–18. Buffon uses the fiction of the first human being, waking up and acquiring the use of his senses, first vision, then hearing, followed by smell and touch, and finally taste, in combination with smell ("je sentis que je possédois un odorat intérieur"). After eating some fruit, falling asleep, waking up again, and finding "à mes côtés une forme semblable à la mienne," our ancestor "acheva [s]on existence, je sentis naître un sixième sens," sexuality. At that point of the charming history of creation, the sun goes down and Buffon draws the curtain on this paradise of sensory awakening.

This olfactory silence that blanketed the literature of German bourgeois realism while it was already broken in many places in French literature has been replaced by a veritable cacophony of scents in our time. Thus Corbin's statement above needs complementing: the general background of our everyday lives has become olfactorily quiet, but on this clean canvas new, deliberate, focused, and purposeful as well as playful and experimental scent trails are being sketched, both as actual scents and as textual imaginations. All that is required for the sense of smell to really take off is an invention of similar cultural magnitude as the movie camera or sound recording and replay systems. Imagine the possibilities this could open up! Mynona and Huxley would turn out as no more than a fictional foretaste.

The truth is that olfaction is well on its way toward a new cultural role. Not only literature but chemistry and psychology, the fragrance and flavor industry, perfumery, business, and marketing are all hard at work. "Perfume is a $4-billion-a-year industry trafficking in sexuality and fantasy," says a bold inset in a longer article in a weekend supplement.[2] "Aromatherapy" is a possibility the article talks about, "the idea that scents can stimulate or tranquilize human beings." This has been ancient knowledge and practice in China. According to another article in the *New York Times* aroma therapists see a silver lining on their olfactory horizon, for while they "concede the absence of hard scientific research proving the medicinal powers of natural scents," they are nevertheless convinced that their "day is coming soon."[3] But the fragrance industry's heavyweights harbor much further-reaching plans, called "environmental fragrancing systems" whose "dark side is mind control" as some voices are already warning, as if they were quoting Mustapha Moon in one of his more jovial moments. Let us not be naive. The fact that early childhood exposure to certain odors forms "attachments that go on forever"[4] is already built into profit calculations, and fragrances for babies are put on the market "at prices like $30 for 3.3 ounces. . . . Don't grown-ups know better?" the journalist admonishes the reader, "Don't manufacturers know that there is no smell as appealing as that of a freshly bathed and powdered baby? The real money would be in capturing that scent and selling it to adults."[5] Manufacturers do know this,

---

2. William Ecenbarger, "What the Nose Knows: The Scent of Things to Come," *San Francisco Chronicle*, 20 September 1987, This World section. This article touches on and confirms many of the findings we have been establishing in our detailed literary-historical inquiry.

3. *New York Times*, 8 November 1988, sec. A.

4. *Wall Street Journal*, 13 October 1988, sec. B.

5. *New York Times*, 17 May 1988, sec. A.

of course, selling us precisely those baby shampoos and powders that we have long come to take for the real thing. Throwing out the bathwater has become a hazard to the baby. Our tour through scents and nonsense of the 1980s reveals further tidbits, such as the news that "with the perfume, the pet products industry has taken Americans' taste for pet indulgence to a new extreme." It manufactures, among other things, a line that "offers a cologne for male dogs ($18) and shampoo for each sex ($8.50)."[6] This is the return of Des Esseintes's jewel-studded turtle in its postmodern any-thing-goes guise; nobody cares whether the scent "might cause the animal to paw, scratch, and lick to remove the odor." But humans and pets are by no means the only creatures affected by the latter-day invasion of smells; it is affecting cars too. The Jaguar XJ-6 "is much sexier than the Mercedes. It's more elegant than the BMW. . . . It treats all your senses well. It smells great, that fresh leather smell" says Broderick Perkins in the *San Jose Mercury News* of 30 January 1987. The German weekly *Der Spiegel* has a similar contribution on that topic. Under the heading "Der Nase nach," "follow-ing your nose," is revealed that "die altehrwürdige Firma Rolls Royce sucht ihre modernisierten Typen neuerdings mit einer in der Branche un-bekannten Werbe-Variante zu vermarkten—sie reizt den Geruchssinn." The gadgets are "Duftstreifen," scent strips, which are steeped in an es-sence "die Leder und Luxus vorgaukeln soll."[7] Another article in *Der Spiegel* claims that researchers have called the coming century "das Jahrhundert des Geruchs." After an initial bow to Süskind, whose novel *Das Parfum*[8] has by that date been heading the best-seller lists for months, and to Grenouille, its hero, said to live on "in Gestalt riesiger Duftkonzerne," the report surveys the general trends on the fragrance front, announcing an "olfactory attack," a "Duft-Angriff auf die mensch-liche Psyche" and quoting "William Cain, Psychobiologe an der Yale Uni-versity" as prophesying: "Das 21. Jahrhundert wird das Zeitalter des Geruchs sein." "Duft- oder Aromatherapie," already familiar to us, are mentioned again; and so are experiments relating smell and memory; stud-ies about human pheromones synchronizing women's menstruation cycles; as well as Friedrich Schiller's apples, rotting in his desk drawer and produc-ing the aroma that he liked so much for inspiration.[9] Later that year *Der*

---

6. Olive Evans, "Coping," *New York Times,* 3 December 1988, sec. A.

7. *Der Spiegel,* 6 July 1987, 168.

8. Patrick Süskind, *Das Parfum* (Zurich: Diogenes, 1985). All subsequent references are to this edition. (English: *Perfume,* trans. John E. Woods [New York: Knopf, 1986].)

9. All quotes in this passage from *Der Spiegel,* 30 March 1987, 250–53.

Spiegel follows up on smells once again. A "gnadenloser Ver-drängungswettbewerb," "merciless elimination," is said to be going on in the "knallharten Markt" for perfumes and fragrances. Figures follow: "75 Millionen Mark gaben allein Westdeutschlands Parfümhersteller voriges Jahr für Werbung aus." Dior, the report claims, will have sunk "40 Millionen Dollar in die Promotion ihres Duftkrachers 'Poison.'" Moreover, "im eher prüden Amerika sorgte die Anzeigeserie [for Calvin Klein's 'Obsession'] mit verschlungenen Liebespaaren für Empörung und allein im ersten Verkaufsjahr für 30 Millionen Dollar Umsatz." The article's claim that "eine 'Identitätskrise,' ausgelöst durch die Frauenbewegung, habe die Männer den Wohlgerüchen zugetrieben"[10] seems to find corroboration in a longer *Weltwoche* report on the topic "Wie Dior im überfüllten Parfummarkt für seinen neusten Herrenduft Platz schafft: beispiellose Werbekampagne."[11] The difficulty of creating the perfect advertisement lies, according to the article's analysis, in the fact that so many images have become clichés, "der Mann als Playboy, Macho, Muskelprotz oder Rambo zieht nur noch im Vorstadtkino. Der harte Intellektuelle mit dem sensiblen Blick? Der smarte Yuppie? Beide schon viel zu stereotyp. . . . Was also bleibt dem armen Mann der achtziger Jahre?" Maurice Roger, CEO of Dior, on the occasion of a stroll through New York has an idea: "Da war ihm klar, was den Mann von heute ausmacht: der Übergang. Der moderne Mann hebt sich, auf der Suche nach neuen Werten, von der Vergangenheit ab und strebt der Zukunft, dem 21. Jahrhundert, dem Zeitalter des kollektiven Mystizismus, entgegen. Folglich befindet er sich im Übergang zwi-

---

10. All quotes in this passage from *Der Spiegel*, 14 December 1987, 194–96. Dior is said to have sunk $40 million into their new "Poison"; and "in the rather prudish America, the advertisement series [for Calvin Klein's "Obsession"] featuring entangled couples of lovers has caused an outcry, but also triggered sales of $30 million in the first year alone." An "'identity crisis,' caused by women's emancipation, has pushed men into the field of pleasant odors."

11. Sigrid Tahri, "Die Zeichen leuchteten auf wie Lichter in der Nacht," *Weltwoche*, 15 September 1988, 83. Following is the translation of passages from this article. "How Dior creates space for his new men's fragrance in an already overcrowded market: exceptional ad campaign." Dior found that many of the advertising stereotypes do not work anymore: "man as a playboy, a macho, a hulk or a Rambo only works in the small-town movie theater. The tough intellectual with the sensitive look? The smart yuppie? Both far too stereotypical. . . . What, then, remains for the poor man of the eighties?" The CEO of Dior, Roger, finds the answer:

It became clear to him what characterizes today's man: transition. Modern man, in search of new values, lifts off from the past and heads toward the future, the twenty-first century, the age of collective mysticism. Ergo, he is in transition between yesterday and tomorrow. Now.

schen Gestern und Morgen. Im Jetzt." Whether this is deep or simply
"Hip-Deep in Post-modernism," as Todd Gitlin calls the contemporary
state of affairs, can remain open at this point.[12] We will tackle the question
later. In any case, it yields the advertising image of a man walking out on
a weatherbeaten, pierlike wooden structure into the golden sands of the
Australian desert—produced at an astronomical price after moving tons of
sand to the advertiser's liking.

Perfumes are the junk bonds of postmodern aesthetics, the means of
borrowing aura against an image they themselves are designed to create.
But this burst of interest in and fascination with smells in areas ranging
from the solemn to the ludicrous and involving lots of media and money
explodes against the background of serious scientific olfactory research, and
even as staid a journal as *The Economist* seems to feel the pressure to carry
an article on smell, opening with the lament that "man was given five senses
and all too few clues to understand them with" and pointing out that
among them "smell has proved to be one of the most recalcitrant."[13] The
Wall Street Journal carries a front-page article about a flavor analyst, which
points out that taste is really smell. "The tongue, which registers four or
five basic tastes, is much less important to the flavorist than the nose, which
can differentiate thousands of odors and provides most flavor sensations."[14] Only a day before, the *Journal* reported on Western puzzlement
over Eastern resistance to scents. "Japan is the No. 2 market for cosmetics
in the world, but when it comes to perfume, women refuse to buy." The
brief article concludes on a cultural explanation about the French perfume
industry's coordinated marketing effort in Japan, where "most find fragrance at dinner offensive . . . and men associate it with 'the night-club
business. It's more for the bar girls.'"[15] In its September 1986 issue the
National Geographic Magazine runs a thirty-seven-page scientific, cultural,
and historical account on "The Intimate Sense of Smell," including a

---

12. Todd Gitlin, "Hip-Deep in Post-modernism," *New York Times Book Review*, 6
November 1988. His is a short, lucid no-frills description of postmodernism as something
much more comprehensive than literature or the arts, rather as "the creature of our recent
social and political moment."

13. *The Economist*, 28 January 1989, 82–83. The journal follows up on this theme with
a report on nose simulators. See "A nose by any other name," *The Economist*, 28 September 1991, 97.

14. David Stipp, "A Flavor Analyst should never ask, 'What's for lunch?'" *Wall Street
Journal*, 3 August 1988, 1.

15. *Wall Street Journal*, 2 August 1988, 21.

questionnaire with scratch-and-sniff samples.[16] This feat is closely matched in April 1987 by *National Geographic*'s German counterpart *Geo*, which presents "Die Partitur der Düfte," a twenty-page article including a double page of scratch-and-sniff patches, and asking the question: "Wann kommt ein Picasso der Parfümerie?"[17] The results of the *National Geographic* questionaire, which turned out to be "the world's largest smell quiz ever[,] attract[ing] 1.5 million people," are made public in September 1987 with the press quickly picking up on the more alluring findings, such as the already quoted "4-billion-a-year industry trafficking in sexuality and fantasy" as well as the bold statement that "throughout history, there's been an association between smell and sex."[18] This, of course, is no surprise to us, since we have established, even if along different lines, sexuality as a preferred locus of olfactory phenomena. And neither ought the following account to astonish us, describing smell as a social demarcation line. A student reports about her

> first visit to a Rescue Mission on skid row. The sermon began. The room was stuffy and smelly. The mixture of body odors and cooking was nauseating. I remember thinking: How can these people share this facility? They must be repulsed by each other. They had strange habits and dispositions. They were a group of dirty, dishonored, weird people to me. When it was over I ran to my car, went home and took a shower. I felt extremely dirty. Through the day I would get flashes of that disgusting smell.[19]

In contrast to this, but on the same note of social demarcation, Lady Di, on the occasion of a recent visit to New York and her stopping at the Henry Street Settlement on the Lower East Side of Manhattan "'left the smell of perfume on my hand,' said a beaming Josephine Coll, who lives in a housing project near the settlement."[20]

---

16. Boyd Gibbons, "The Intimate Sense of Smell," *National Geographic Magazine*, September 1986, 324–61.

17. Franz Mechsner and Wolfgang Volz, "Immer der Nase nach," *Geo*, April 1987, 14–34.

18. Ellen Warren, "Nose knows—but not always, test shows," *San Jose Mercury News*, 11 September 1987, sec. A.

19. Peter Marin and Anna Quindlen, "Helping and Hating the Homeless," *San Francisco Chronicle*, 25 January 1987, This World section. Notice also the ritual of cleansing (a shower, a bath) as a condition for the student's "return to civilization," just as it was the case for Primo Levi after his imprisonment in Auschwitz.

20. Georgia Dullea, "A Royal Night at the Opera, a Day on the Town," *New York Times*, 3 February 1989, sec. B.

It is undeniable: the olfactory has made it. It has shed its bad reputation and is now stepping out of the odorless halls of the public sphere to seize the day. The bad has been marginalized, both reduced as a perceptual phenomenon and decentered in its human carriers, homeless people, for instance. Good smell has arrived not in museums or galleries, art institutes or academic lectures, but it is here with the power of industry, the tenacity of scientific research, and the shrewdness of marketing behind it. It is present in our everyday lives; and it has arrived with its own powerful PR machine with vested interests and with fortunes at stake. The olfactory as an institution has gained a formidable presence in its oldest form, perfumery, the form in which it has accompanied humankind for thousands of years.

Has anything changed, then, since the perfume industry of Mycenaean Pylos,[21] since the scented Spanish leathers of Elizabeth I of England and the perfumed gloves of Napoleon? Yes and no. What has remained and in fact become more marked over time, is the binary opposition between good and bad. We live with and take for granted the current standards, enjoying some and suffering from others according to our own dispositions. We have mapped out a short stretch of the olfactory road through recent history, the varying intensity with which (Western) societies have focused on one or the other aspect of the spectrum at various times. The civilizational forces have been pushing the budding awareness of the bad toward masking it with the good; from direct sanitary attacks on the bad as noxious and dangerous, to the exclusive aesthetic focus and propagation of the good and pleasurable. Epochal shifts within the good half of the spectrum have taken place too, from the once-favored heavy animal aromas to lighter floral notes, from a craze for musk to the success of eau de cologne. The good, originating and engaged in cultic and religious ceremonies, in the embalming of the dead in ancient times, and in masking bad odors in postmedieval centuries, is now preoccupied with pleasure more than anything else.

Despite their varied instantiations good and bad remain constant as essential olfactory categories. And constant remains also the human body as an olfactory battlefield. Here, nothing has changed. Following our earlier theorizing that all olfactory concern is ultimately with sexuality or death, nothing *can* change. The olfactory battles in the process of civilization have always been fought along the demarcation line between good and bad that cuts across the body. Areas claimed for the good side, appropriated by

---

21. Cf. Shelmerdine, *Perfume Industry of Mycenaen Pylos.*

civilization, were immediately subjected to social standards and reopened as new battle zones where shame and fear threatened those who did not conform to these standards. From the mouth to the armpits, the crotch, and down to the feet, the modern body is divided into neighborhoods of olfactive vigilance. For sexuality and sexual odors, this coercive force has been "die Ästhetik in ihrer auf den Körper einwirkenden Form der Hygiene," requiring the upkeep of good smells and thus serving as a new inhibition of the "direkte[] Lust am Körper."[22] All these long-term changes and constants form the background of our inquiry into the postmodern literary fate of the olfactory.

Bad smells, as we noted earlier, signify repulsion, corruption, decay, and ultimately death. Good smells, on the other hand, mean attraction, the creation of bonds, sexuality, birth, life. The mythical forces involved are Thanatos and Eros.[23] Sexuality and its odors—there can be no doubt about it—belong on the side of attraction, but it is precisely sexuality that has been exposed to the most drastic sociocultural pressures over time, and the smells associated with it, the essential body odors, have vacillated in their status. Hardly another aspect of the body has been colonized as much as its odors. The gap between their low public standing and their secret personal appreciation as erotically attractive has been widening. Publicly, odors can cross this gap only in disguise, in the shape of perfume, the *ersatz* body odor.

Life, with erotics and sexuality as its climax, and death—the French reveal the closeness of the two in their expression *la petite mort*—are indeed the salient features of the most successful German novel in decades, Süskind's *Das Parfum*.[24] Before analyzing it, both as a text and as the

22. Rüdiger Stiebitz, "Ästhetik und Erziehung zur Gewalt," 134.

23. Thanatos and Eros are used here again (cf. chap. 2) in analogy to, if not identically with, Freud's usage of these two figures of thought in *Das Unbehagen in der Kultur*. "Birth" has to be understood in a slightly extended sense, meaning the immediate formation of the mother-child dyad (Lacan), in which the baby exists in a complete perceptual unit with his or her mother. That this bond is steeped in smell (and touch and taste) rather than the senses of distance is undisputed. (Cf. the *New York Times* article above on babies' smells, footnote 5; the passage in *Buddenbrooks*, 58–59; as well as Schachtel's remarks in *Metamorphosis*, esp. 298–99, as corroboration.) On the other hand, the near taboo on death in modern Western civilization, and the stepped-up hygiene surrounding it, clearly have an olfactory component to it, remarkably present in Hanno Buddenbrook, who, through the olfactory mask of strong-smelling flowers, is able to pick up the smell of death (cf. *Buddenbrooks*, 599–600).

24. The novel sold over three million copies by summer 1988 and, by that time, had occupied one of the top spots on the literary best-seller lists since winter 1984, when it was published. By summer 1988 it was translated into twenty-five languages.

publishing success that it has turned out to be, there are a few questions that deserve our attention: Why, given the literary-historical background of the past 150 years discussed so far, is it a German author who writes the olfactory smash hit of our time? Why, after Corbin's epochal study of the olfactory background, was there no French writer ready to cash in on that groundwork? Süskind sets his plot precisely in the epoch for which Corbin has provided detailed olfactory data. And what, given the astonishing resemblance of essential plot elements in Roald Dahl's *Bitch*, discussed below, and Süskind's *Das Parfum*, is the nature of their relationship?[25]

It may well be that the first two questions are obsolete. Since World War II, since the 1950s and 1960s at the latest, we have been living more and more in an international Western culture, the global village, dominated by exchange and communication networks that have rendered national origins increasingly unimportant.[26] A more historically oriented inquiry, however, such as ours, still finds the constellation around Süskind's bestseller curious. It suggests the conclusion that French literary culture has moved beyond "practicing" smells and on to the level of historical and theoretical analysis. Süskind indeed acknowledges French olfactory dominance historically by setting his novel in eighteenth-century France, the foremost olfactory power of the time. Beneath this surface gesture of acknowledging cultural indebtedness, however, the plot of *Das Parfum* contains some very German features. It has the form of an *Erziehungsroman*, even a *Künstlerroman*, as much as it is a historical novel and a detective story; and it is also the novel of a fascination, even obsession, similar to the fascist obsession, with charismatic power. Moreover, the book is immediately caught up in the German modernism versus postmodernism debate, in fact it serves as a kind of litmus test of positions on this issue. The emergence of the olfactory as the sense modality of modernity and its prominent stature in postmodern literature can be integrated in a view similar to Huyssen's, who sees in postmodernism the surfacing of a trend inherent in modernism itself, the urge to "close the gap" between high art

---

25. Roald Dahl, *Switch Bitch* (1974?; New York: Ballantine Books, 1983) 151–90. References are to this edition.

26. Current political, ethnical, and nationalist incidents worldwide are either historical aberrations or, from a postmodern perspective, can be viewed as instances of challenge to the modernist, functionalist political master plot. In this sense they are only the beginning of a more general ethnic and national "deregulation" and rearrangement where new political units coalesce around new conceptual centers. On the surface, however, the functional integration along Western rationalist lines will no doubt continue.

and (low) mass culture, to overcome, in his words, the "great divide."[27] For Huyssen, the historical avant-garde movements (dada, surrealism, cubism, futurism) are quintessentially modern, aiming at sublating the high/low dichotomy. Peter Bürger views postmodernism as characterized by the "Einbruch der avantgardistischen Problematik in die Kunst der Moderne."[28] This, together with his emphasis on "das Unreine," on the mixing of references, techniques, and aesthetic means as opposed to the "Reinheit," the "purity," of (high) modernity, puts him close to Huyssen. Even if Bürger is not sure that "der Rede von der postmodernen Kunst auch Kunstwerke entsprechen" (8), he believes that postmodern discourse reflects—if nothing else—"Veränderungen der ästhetischen Sensibilität" (10).

Das Parfum: "Die Überzeugungskraft des Duftes"

The following review of selected critiques of Das Parfum reveals how uneasy this novel sits on its reviewers' ideological scales, leaving them to damn it as an impostoring piece of Trivialliteratur or hailing it as a breakthrough in German novelistic writing. The debate focuses from its very beginning on two issues: the (traditional) form and the (phenomenologically new) content. Reich-Ranicki is one of the first to praise Süskind's traditional narrative as a refreshing change in the German literary fare of the day. Süskind's is "ein vielleicht trotziges Bekenntnis zum traditionellen Erzählen." He goes on, "Ich sage nicht, daß man heute so erzählen soll. Aber ich meine, daß man auch heute so erzählen darf."[29] Wolfram Knorr shortly thereafter stresses the "immense Erzähllust" and the distance this novel keeps from the "'Empfindsamkeits'-, 'Betroffenheits'-, 'Erschrockenheits'- und Ich-Literatur-Eintopf" of the day.[30] He also notices that the

---

27. Huyssen, After the Great Divide. "Close the gap" is Leslie Fiedler's expression.
28. Peter Bürger and Christa Bürger, eds., Die Postmoderne: Alltag, Allegorie und Avantgarde (Frankfurt am Main: Suhrkamp, 1987), 11. Cf. also Hassan "Culture of Postmodernism," who distinguishes "tentatively, among three modes of artistic change in the last hundred years. I call these avantgarde, modern, and postmodern" (311).
29. Marcel Reich-Ranicki, "Des Mörders betörender Duft," Frankfurter Allgemeine Zeitung, 2 March 1985. Süskind's writing is "a perhaps defiant commitment to traditional narrative." Reich-Ranicki does not "demand that one ought to write like this," but he thinks "that even today one may write like this."
30. Wolfram Knorr, "Aus Zwerg Nase wird ein Frankenstein der Düfte," Weltwoche, 21 March 1985. He stresses the "immense narrative drive" and the novel's distance from "the stew of sensibility, perplexity, anxiety and 'I'-concerns" that marks contemporary literature for him. The novel "abducts the reader into a world of adventure uncommon for contemporary authors."

first sentences of the novel "[erinnern] an die grossen Epiker" and "[ziehen] den Leser genüsslich . . . in eine vielversprechende Abenteuerwelt [weg], wie man sie von zeitgenössischen Autoren so nicht mehr kennt." For Joachim Kaiser, whose review is as positive overall as the others, the novel is a "Mischung aus Kolportage, schwarzer Schelmen-Geschichte und fesselndem Künstlerroman"; it displays an "anspielungssatte Phantasie." However, in its exuberance it happens that "die Mythen schnurren zusammen zu Anekdoten. Zwischen konkreten Schilderungen und riesigen Bedeutungen bleiben die Lücken gar zu groß" and "Menschliches oder Verbindliches [wird] immer nur momentweise sichtbar."[31] This critique points out as negative an element that Reich-Ranicki praised unrestrainedly, the (re)turn to traditional readerly narrative; and the critique is based on the discrepancy between the formal smoothness of the novel and the lack of thematic substance. This problem of form and content is, of course, stock-in-trade, but it has emerged, if under different names, as a central issue in the (German) debate surrounding postmodernism. Quote, allusion, playfulness, surface are the terms that have gained wide currency as general characteristics of postmodernism. They reveal the movement's leaning toward form but they strongly imply their own Other as content: quote—the original; allusion—its object; playfulness—the rules of the game; surfaces—depth, volume, the enclosed content. In the more theoretically oriented discussion of the novel that follows the first wave of acclaim, it is such contrastive pairs that become dominant. Wolfram Schütte summarizes the trends:

Keiner seiner Lobredner vergißt, Süskinds "Parfum" von "der gegenwärtigen Produktion" (der deutschsprachigen Literatur) abzuheben und an ihm zu rühmen, daß es eben nicht mit autobiographischer "Authentizität," mit subjektiver "Nabelschau" hausieren gehe, sondern Süskind als klassischer Erzähler auftrete, bei dem die literarische Welt glücklicherweise noch nicht (oder nicht mehr) wie in der Moderne "aus den Fugen" sei.[32]

---

31. Joachim Kaiser, "Viel Flottheit und Phantasie: Patrick Süskinds Geschichte eines Monsters," *Süddeutsche Zeitung*, 28 March 1985. He has some reservations about "myths contracting into anecdotes" and the gaps between "concrete description and deep meaning."

32. Wolfram Schütte, "Parabel und Gedankenspiel," *Frankfurter Rundschau* 5 April 1985; rpt. in *Deutsche Literatur 1985: Ein Jahresüberblick*, ed. Volker Hage (Stuttgart: Reclam, 1986), 239: "None of his advocates forgets to distinguish Süskind's 'Perfume'

For Schütte, the success of the novel rests on a reader's reflex against at least the most recent forms of postmodernism, which he characterizes indirectly in the following remarks explaining Süskind's success:

> Das immer präsente Ressentiment gegen das Riskante, Komplexe, "Esoterische" der Avantgarde geht dabei eine Verbindung mit dem verständlichen Überdruß an einer Literatur von "Verständigungstexten" ein, die immer aufs Neue autobiographische und generationsspezifische Problematiken . . . umwälzen. (239)

For Schütte, it seems, postmodernism—if indeed that is what he describes—is foremost a neoconservative narrative attitude, the representation of a world that is no longer "aus den Fugen" and that deliberately forgoes the challenges of the avant-garde. Such a view of postmodernism clashes sharply with, for instance, Huyssen's or the Bürgers', although Christa Bürger forsees the possibility that "wo der Modernismus zur legitimen Kultur geworden ist, wird 'Tradition' zur Avantgarde."[33] However, Schütte does refer to the innovative psychological and sensual strategy of the novel in order to explain its success. Süskind "[appelliert] mit seinem genialen Riecher an den Schrecken des Ekels, der sich—uns nur zu bewußt—hinter dem Drang nach Sauberkeit und dem Wunsch nach Illusion verbirgt." With this "trifft der Autor einen zentralen Nerv unserer Ängste" (241). Grenouille, the specialist "der Sensualität, der Analyse, der Abstraktion und der Synthese" (a strangely contradictory set of attributes, 244) appears as the "enlightenment's dark shadow," a "dunkler Schatten der Aufklärung" (244), and his medium, perfume, as that which Baudrillard calls "Simulation" (245).

---

from 'the current production' (in German literature) and to praise the fact that it is not peddling autobiographical 'authenticity' and subjective 'solipsism'; but that Süskind appears as a classical narrator whose literary world, fortunately, is not yet (or no longer) 'out of joint' as in modernism."

"The ever-present resentment against risk, complexity, the 'esoteric' of the avant-garde joins the understandable disgust with a literature of 'agreement' that time and again turns up autobiographical and generational problems." For Schütte, Süskind "appeals with his nose of a genius to the fear of disgust that lurks, only too clearly, behind the urge for cleanliness and the desire for illusion." With this "the author hits a central nerve of our anxieties."

33. Christa Bürger, "Das Verschwinden der Kunst: Die Postmoderne-Debatte in den USA," in Bürger and Bürger, *Die Postmoderne*, 39.

Frank Lucht, in a review of *Das Grau der Karolinen* by Klaus Modick, makes reference to Umberto Eco's *The Name of the Rose* and Süskind's *Das Parfum* and expresses the need for a preliminary "Charakterisierung dieser postmodernen Version des historischen Romans."[34] He recognizes "Ironie" (304) as one of the salient features of those novels, together with the fact that their main characters pursue a personal development aimed at "entschiedene Individualisierung. Diese Menschen entdecken über die jeweiligen phänomenologischen Zugangsweisen (. . . Sehen, Riechen, Lesen) die Welt neu" (305). Moreover, in all three novels "findet sich ein mythischer Komplex" largely based on the "magische Anziehungskraft der Dinge selbst (Bild, Schrift, Geruch), der sich niemand soll entziehen können; ein Wissen, das sich nur über die Sinne offenbart; eine Macht, die dadurch wirkt, daß sie ein ungeheures Begehren nach ihr weckt" (306). However, and this is Lucht's criticism, all these novels, intended as an "Antwort auf das Dilemma zwischen einer zum einverständigen Ritual gewordenen Revolte der Avantgarde und einer Tradition, mit der man sich weiterhin auf Kriegsfuß befand" (307), have fallen short. Their use of story as "das Medium, in dem formale Konformität und innovativer bzw. eigensinniger Gehalt keinen Widerspruch mehr bilden" defuses all their critical potential (303–4). They are "heruntergekommen zur kindlichen Freude darüber, wie angenehm es sich doch im Stande der verlorenen Unschuld leben und schreiben läßt." They are "Problemkitsch" (307).

Harry Nutt, staunch defender of postmodernism and answering Lucht directly, lambasts Süskind's (as well as Modick's and Eco's) critics and their

> Lamento . . . gegen den Erfolg der einstmal "anderen" Literatur. Eco, Süskind und nun auch Modick tragen nämlich den Makel des Postmodernen, oder besser gesagt, sie sind so zeitgeistig geschrieben, daß er

---

34. Frank Lucht, "Erkennen Sie die Melodie?" *Merkur* September/October 1986; rpt. in *Deutsche Literatur 1986: Ein Jahresüberblick,* ed. Volker Hage (Stuttgart: Reclam, 1987), 303. For him, the main characters aim at "unambiguous individualization. These people rediscover the world along various phenomenological accesses (. . . seeing, hearing, reading)." Lucht diagnoses "a mythical complex" on the basis of "the magical attraction of objects (image, writing, smell) that nobody can resist; a knowledge that reveals itself only through the senses; a power that manifests itself in creating an incredibly strong desire for itself." However, as an "answer to the dilemma of an avant-garde revolt that has become a ritual of approval and a tradition against which one still fights" these novels have failed. They lose their critical potential by using story "as a means in which formal conformity and innovative or idiosyncratic content are no longer in contradiction." They have "degenerated into the childish joy about the ease of living and writing in the state of lost innocence."

ihnen mit Leichtigkeit nachzusagen ist. Das "Postmoderne" in der Literatur taucht für dessen Kritiker, so möchte ich polemisch notieren, überall dort auf, wo Literatur, die ernstzunehmen ist, die engen Kreise augenzwinkernder Kennerschaft zu verlassen droht. Die Signatur des Postmodernen ist in Kritikerkreisen zu einer undefinierten, aber polemisch wirksamen Kennzeichnung geworden.[35]

A few lines further he notes, "Das 'Postmoderne' schlägt inzwischen beinahe allem kritisch entgegen, was auf ästhetischen Seiten- und Abwegen wandelt und damit auch noch Erfolg hat" (310). If Nutt is right in his assessment of literary review and critical practice on the German scene, then postmodernism has become a term of opprobrium, used by conservatives to discredit commercially successful, aesthetically innovative writing. For Nutt, this attitude is clearly linked with the caste system still very much in place in German literature, and with its critical practice of pitting high, true, elite literature against *Trivialliteratur*. "Wenn es um die deutsche Literatur tatsächlich schlecht steht, dann auch deshalb, weil eine Rasterkritik das Herausfordernde gar nicht erst in sie hineinlassen möchte" (311).[36] Could it be that critics simply did not find anything *Herausforderndes* in Süskind? Nutt is convinced "daß in . . . der Spürnase Jean Baptiste Grenouilles im 'Parfum' . . . etwas zum Vorschein kommt, das außerhalb aller Epochenbegriffe etwas mit den Geschichten zu tun hat, die uns etwas

35. Harry Nutt, "Kürzelkritik und Kritik das Kürzels," *die tageszeitung*, 29 September 1986; rpt. in Hagen, *Deutsche Literatur 1986*, 309. Nutt criticizes antipostmodernists for their "lamentation . . . against the success of an 'other' literature. Eco, Süskind, and now even Modick bear the stigma of postmodernism or, more accurately, they are written so much in tune with the *zeitgeist* that they can easily be taken to task for it. The 'postmodern' in literature, as I am claiming here polemically, appears for its critics everywhere where serious literature threatens to go beyond the narrow circle of its connoisseurs. The stamp of the postmodern has become a badly defined but polemically effective brand among critics." The stigma of "postmodernism meets any successful writing off the beaten aesthetic track."

36. "If things are bad in German literature, part of the reason must be sought in a schematizing criticism that tries to prevent challenges from even occurring" (311). This is, at least for initial reviews of and comments on, *Das Parfum* not true; the novel met with almost unanimous enthusiasm. As to more in-depth critical and theoretical assessments, however, there has not been much to date. This fits in with the prevailing reluctance among the university literary establishment toward anything smacking of the trivial. This reluctance and the strict high-low dichotomy of which it is a reflection, is much less prominent in the American literary context. It is no surprise, then, that the postmodernism debate, which centers precisely around this gap, is seen by its German observers to have originated in the USA. Cf. Ortheil below, as well as the discussion in Bürger, "Das Verschwinden."

angehn," (312) namely "eine Aktivierung der Sinne, des Sehens, des Riechens, des Spurenlesens" (312–13).

Hanns-Josef Ortheil's contribution to this debate is a strong, theoretically and historically well-founded article in defense of postmodernism. He refers to Lucht almost despisingly ("Im 'Merkur' hat ein jugendlicher Witzbold Postmodernes in . . . man darf raten . . . in Süskinds 'Parfum' entdeckt. Süskind! Ausgerechnet. Ich verliere kein Wort darüber," 314).[37] Ortheil's dismissal of *Das Parfum* as serious postmodern writing is, as far as we can establish, based on its lack of "Niveau" (315). His postmodernism is a far cry from the populist anything-goes variety. It is strict, even elitist. His key terms are *play* and *playfulness*, based, however, on an especially close relationship between author and reader. "Der Leser wird zum intellektuellen Komplizen des Autors" (314). In terms of its historical heritage, postmodernism is linked with, and depends on, modernism. Postmodernist literature "verabschiedet nicht die ästhetischen Projekte der Moderne, sondern verfügt über diese als Modelle, die in Spiele höherer Ordnung überführt werden können" (314). With the usual "erheblicher Verzögerung" (322) vis-à-vis the most recent developments, postmodernism has reached the German literary scene, and there is no doubt for Ortheil that "die postmoderne Literatur ist . . . die Literatur der Zukunft" (322).

If one thing becomes clear from the above overview, it is the determination with which review and criticism of Süskind's novel focus on form versus content, and high versus low and wrap this in a third discourse, of modernism versus postmodernism. In the first pair, traditional, historical, grand narrative is stressed, the known, the reliable, the absence of experiments versus a content that is upsetting, disgusting, revolting and in its phenomenological crudeness defies history—or rather: in the phenomenology of a repressed sensory mode reveals the very history of its own repression and disgust. Into the increasingly beautified world of Western (post)modern civilization breaks the anarchy of a sensory phenomenology that is still repressed. This comes in a tamper-proof realist wrapper which allows the titillating yet safe enjoyment of the vicarious experience of that

---

37. Hanns-Josef Ortheil, "Das Lesen—ein Spiel: Postmoderne Literatur? Die Literatur der Zukunft!" *Die Zeit*, 17 April 1987; rpt. in *Deutsche Literatur 1987: Ein Jahresüberblick*, ed. Franz Josef Görtz, Volker Hage, and Uwe Wittstock (Stuttgart: Reclam, 1988). For him, postmodernist literature "does not dismiss modernism's aesthetic projects but rather disposes of them as models to be transformed into games of a higher order" (314).

sensory modality of which the progress of civilization has largely deprived Western man. In this high versus low dichotomy there is clearly a whiff of suspicion that *Das Parfum* is really a piece of *Trivialliteratur*. What makes the judges hesitate in openly pronouncing such a sentence is, it seems, the novel's representational and plot structuring through the sense of smell. No one knows quite what to make of this.

On close reading, a third characteristic of the novel seems to be an issue, its antirational, antienlightenment stance; its regress to atavisms; its playing out the victory of a sensory modality over intellect and reason—and of the lowliest of the senses at that. Whether this is inherently postmodern, linking postmodernism explicitly with antirationality, or whether *Das Parfum* represents a counterenlightenment program of its own, aimed at rehabilitating the world of the senses from the disdain in which enlightenment and by implication, modernism, has held it, can be left open for the moment. Such a clearcut bipolar opposition of the paired concepts of enlightenment and modernism on the one hand and the "end of enlightenment" and postmodernism on the other is not commonly found in present criticism, although Habermas seems to point in this direction.[38] In any case, Süskind's novel celebrates the victory of the gut reaction over brain and concept, the (re)emergence of the "Menschentier" (Süskind, 304) at its most primitive. Never before Süskind has the olfactory been used to such an extent to carry the plot structure of a narrative.[39] The olfactory constitutes a new and still largely untapped realm of signification, precise in its reference structure (the smell of . . .), accurate or at least unhesitating in its binary evaluation (good/bad), but extremely unpredictable in its psychological, associative impact on fictional characters as well as on the reader. The exact description of causes, yet unpredictability of effects, is the novel's greatest allure. Its referentiality is historically clad, yet phenomenologically ahistorical. It thus allows the reader to relish his or her safe distance from the events, yet sends a shiver down everyone's spine when thinking of their physiological closeness. Let us take the very uncertainty surrounding the novel as our starting point to uncover its fundamental structures and layers of meaning, which are by no means all located in the olfactory realm.

---

38. Cf. Andreas Kilb, "Die allegorische Phantasie: Zur Ästhetik der Postmoderne," in Bürger and Bürger, *Die Postmoderne*, 84–113.

39. This holds true even in comparison with *Against the Grain*, with its abundance of smells. The structure of that novel is not olfactorily determined; the olfactory is "only" an important element in its phenomenological surface structure.

Jean-Baptiste Grenouille, the novel's central character, born to an infanticidal fishwife who is executed shortly after his birth, grows up at an orphanage on a starvation diet and in emotionally depraved circumstances. He is slow to speak, but discovers early his olfactive talent, and smells will turn out to be his only interest and passion. Soon he is sent to work for a nearby tanner in hideous and unhealthy conditions, but in his meager free time he strolls about Paris, gaining an olfactory map of the city, down to its streets and squares, its every nook and cranny. Once, when he is ordered to take goathides to Baldini, a perfumer with a somewhat declining business and flagging creative powers, Grenouille seizes like a tick, a simile the narrator invokes several times for him, his chance of coming closer to fulfilling his dream of one day creating the ultimate perfume. He knows what this would be, since he discovered it one night emanating from an adolescent girl in the Rue des Marais. He was attracted from across the river by the barest scent trail escaping from her. Her scent "war die reine Schönheit" (55), and based on the "Prinzip ihres Duftes" (58), Grenouille's whole interior olfactory world fell into place. He kills her, "smells her empty," thus committing his first olfactory rape and murder. Grenouille impresses Baldini so much with his intuitive if uneducated knowledge of aromatics that the perfumer buys him from the tanner and has him work in his perfumery, which soon, thanks to Grenouille's indefatigable creativity, rockets to European prominence. Grenouille learns the basics of the trade, but then falls seriously ill out of frustration at his inability to produce those imaginary smells he has in his head. When Baldini tells him that there are other techniques of scent production, practiced above all in the south of the country, Grenouille recovers and, having received the papers that certify him as a respectable citizen and a member of the perfumers' guild, he leaves for the south of France.

Part two is his journey to Grasse, which takes seven years, as it is interrupted by a solitary sojourn on the Plomb du Cantal, the most remote and atmospherically pure area of France, virtually devoid of human beings. There, Grenouille lives on water, insects, small rodents, roots, and lichens while giving himself over to the most exquisite, imaginative, olfactory orgies in the cave where he lives until he discovers one day that he himself is odorless. This horrifying discovery sends him back into civilization, first into the hands of the Marquis de la Taillade-Espinasse, an enlightened aristocrat whose hobbyhorse is a theory of lethal gas allegedly emanating from everything terrestrial. Grenouille, after seven years of living the life of a troglodyte and looking it every bit, serves as his ideal guinea pig and object of demonstration. In an impressive "before and after" presentation to a large audience, Taillade-Espinasse clearly proves the point of his aerial theory. Grenouille manufactures some human scent for himself and escapes to Grasse.

The third part of the novel describes his life in Grasse; his work for the perfumer Druot; his acquisition of the knowledge of the more sophisticated techniques of scent production; his own experiments and eventually the series of murders of young women whom he kills for the sole purpose of obtaining their body odors. Twenty-four victims already mark the murderer's trail, spreading fear and horror in the hearts of the whole population. Laure Richis, the daughter of the richest citizen in town, is the last, the jewel in Grenouille's string of olfactive pearls. She is the one whom he noticed earliest, upon arriving in town; she is the one who reminded him of the highest principle in scents, as he had experienced it with his first victim in Paris; and she is the only one whose fate is narratively presented in some detail. Her death leads to Grenouille's arrest and death sentence. The execution, however, cannot be carried out because Grenouille, stepping out on the scaffold and wearing just a drop of his "essence of woman," inspires love, desire, and concupiscence in the thousands of spectators to such a degree that the scheduled beheading degenerates into a mass orgy and Richis ends up wanting to adopt Grenouille as his son. This is Grenouille's moment of supreme power. His case is closed. Scentless again and thereby unnoticed, he leaves Grasse and heads for Paris.

Part four is only eight pages long. Grenouille is back in Paris, sprinkles the love scent all over himself and is killed and cannibalized at the Cimetière des Innocents by a group of clochards and criminals who, for the first time, do something "out of love."

Das Parfum abounds with narratively radical solutions. This, one must assume from the critical acclaim, is an essential part of its attraction for the 1980s readership. For instance, all the secondary characters with whom Grenouille ever has anything to do are neatly removed by death after they serve their narrative purpose. This begins with his mother; it applies to Mme. Gaillard, the nursing home operator, to Grimal the tanner, Baldini the perfumer, Taillade-Espinasse, as well as Druot, the Grasse perfumer. The novel does contain, however, a more sophisticated underlying set of "structures of fascination." The first four structures permeate the text as a whole; the next three are characteristics more directly pinned onto the hero.

Structures of Fascination

Allusions and Source Material

"Im achtzehnten Jahrhundert lebte in Frankreich ein Mann, der zu den genialsten und abscheulichsten Gestalten dieser an genialen und abscheulichen Gestalten nicht armen Epoche gehörte" (5). Thus opens the most successful German novel in decades. The following are the opening lines of Kleist's *Michael Kohlhaas* from 1808–10, one of the most famous novellas in the German language: "An den Ufern der Havel lebte, um die Mitte des sechzehnten Jahrhunderts, ein Roßhändler, namens Michael Kohlhaas, Sohn eines Schulmeisters, einer der rechtschaffensten zugleich und entsetzlichsten Menschen seiner Zeit." The world "würde [Kohlhaas's] Andenken haben segnen müssen, wenn er in einer Tugend nicht ausgeschweift hätte. Das Rechtsgefühl aber machte ihn zum Räuber und Mörder." Jean Baptiste Grenouille, Süskind's hero, goes to excess not in an abstract social virtue, but in an individual sensory modality; and he is forgotten today "weil sich sein Genie und sein einziger Ehrgeiz auf ein Gebiet beschränkte, welches in der Geschichte keine Spuren hinterläßt: auf das flüchtige Reich der Gerüche" (5). In both narratives we follow a monomaniacal hero, the one over a shorter period, the other over his entire lifetime. The first, a successful and perfectly integrated member of society, becomes an outsider only after a major breakdown in the legal system makes him take the law into his own hands; the second, however, is both physically—he emits no odor—and socially an outcast from the day he is born. Both heroes are executed at the end of their stories, Kohlhaas after the temporary breakdown of the sociolegal system has been mended and he has been granted full satisfaction. Grenouille's death is more unruly. The legal execution fails, his case is closed, and he finds his death at the hands of the rabble. Both men are heroes of excess, Kohlhaas in a socially and intellectually mediated virtue within a society that is legally more backward than his sensitivities; Grenouille in an individual sensory capability that is far too refined for the society *he* lives in. Both, then, are ahead of their time, but both stories are also set at a historical distance of some 250 years from the moment of their writing. Thus the modernity of both heroes can at least partly be attributed to the *zeitgeist* surrounding their creators. Kleist's society is that of the early nineteenth century with its shift from the feudal and aristocratic to the bourgeois legal system; Süskind's time—our own—is one of considerable and growing olfactory interest and certainly the age of an intense cult of the body, sensuality, and the erotic.

There are further points of comparison between Kohlhaas and Grenouille. Both men are associated with the angelical order, Kohlhaas calling
himself a "Statthalter Michaels, des Erzengels" and Grenouille appearing
as an "Engel," an angel, (302) to the completely entranced bishop at his
execution, as well as an "Engelsmensch[ ]" and again "Engel" (319) to the
rabble that kills him. Whereas Kohlhaas dies completely reconciled with
the law and its authorities, and his execution occurs narratively in a subclause of half a line, Grenouille's death is a much more gruesome and
narratively extensive event, and in its unfolding follows closely the operating patterns that Elias Canetti describes for the *Jagdmeute,* the "baiting
pack."[40] The allusion to Kleist, both in the verbal echo of the opening
sentence and the vague parallelism of the unfolding of the plot, gives
Süskind a veneer of literary respectability among his critics although his
language is far from creating the structural vortexes of Kleist's. Nevertheless, like Kleist, Süskind relentlessly pushes the action forward—and
there *is* action, as opposed to the lamented *Nabelschau* in recent German
literature—a refreshing feature much praised by reviewers. This alone,
however, could not account for the novel's success, not even in combination with the obvious stylistic references to biblical prose in those moments
when Grenouille, the hermit on the mount, indulges in his olfactory fantasies of power, creating the world out of scent: "und er sah, daß es gut
war" (161), and he "sprach: 'Siehe, ich habe ein großes Werk getan'" (162).
Grenouille, or rather his narrator, shifts with the greatest ease from the
biblical to the most colloquial. "Das Doppelamt des Rächers und Welten-
erzeugers strengte nicht schlecht an" (163). But beneath these literary, stylistic allusions that create immediate surface familiarity and a colloquial
undertone, Süskind takes out bigger loans from other sources.[41]

The following is not meant to be a philological study of sources.[42] It is
simply a reminder that "smell is in the air" at the moment when *Das
Parfum* is published in 1985. Corbin's *Le miasme et la jonquille* had appeared
in its French original in 1982, in a German translation in 1984, and in an
American edition in 1986. It cannot but strike one as a true treasure trove
of historical olfactory information essential for Süskind's narrative enter-

---

40. Canetti, *Masse und Macht,* (1:106–8).

41. A discussion of these multiple textual references as "pastiche" and as characteristic
of postmodern textuality is found in Judith Ryan, "The Problem of Pastiche: Patrick
Süskind's *Das Parfum,*" *German Quarterly* 63, no. 3/4 (Summer/Fall 1990): 396–403.

42. If this were intended, a direct question to Patrick Süskind concerning his knowledge of *Le miasme et la jonquille* and *Bitch* could settle the point more easily.

prise. It describes the very epoch in which his story is set; it discusses the city where his hero is born and spends much of his life; and it broaches a number of the topics central to his narrative, in a couple of cases in virtually identical terminology. For the noxious terrestrial emanations, for instance, the "fluidum letale" (Süskind, 179) and the "*Vitalluft*ventilationsapparat" (180, emphasis added) featured so prominently in Taillade-Espinasse's theory, we find a model in Priestley's *air fixé* and *air vitale* (Corbin, 16). But above all, the terrestrial vapors discussed in theories by Ehrard, B. de Sauvages, and Ramazzini seem to have served as models for Süskind's enlightenment critique. One researcher explicitly warns of the dangers "encourus par le paysan qui se penche et approche son visage trop près du sol qu'il remue" (Corbin, 26). Druot's "aura seminalis" (Süskind, 232), his "Wolke von Spermiengeruch" (220), is a concept discussed in some detail by Corbin also (cf. 42, 45, 52). And the Cimetière des Innocents, the scene where Süskind's novel both opens and closes, is described by him as the place "an dem der Gestank ganz besonders infernalisch herrschte" (6). In a historical preview the narrator then goes on to say that only on the eve of the French Revolution was the cemetery closed and its space converted into a "Marktplatz für Viktualien" (7). Grenouille, however, is born before that time, on 17 July 1738, to be exact. Corbin, on the same topic, mentions "les exhalaisons des cadavres empilés dans le cimetière des Innocents" (68), and he too points out the closure of the cemetery as a consequence of the growing public awareness of the air quality and the desire "de désentasser les cadavres... avant même de la Révolution. Exemplaire à ce propos, le grand déménagement des morts empilés dans le cimetière des Innocents, véritable épopée dont Thouret s'est fait le chantre fasciné" (120).

While Corbin thus provides invaluable general as well as specific information on the cultural and historical world in which Süskind's novel is set, Roald Dahl's *Bitch* from 1974 contains essential plot elements that are nearly identical with their counterparts in *Das Parfum*. A short summary of Dahl's story will make this clear. The narrator's uncle Oswald in Dahl's story, a wealthy jet-set philanderer, describes in one of his diaries, which the narrator inherits after Oswald's death, his chance meeting with Henri Biotte and its consequences. Biotte, an olfactory chemist, "a small dark man," "as hairy as a goat" (155), approached him one day and introduced himself as an extraordinarily gifted perfumer who was looking for a sponsor for his project to develop "*the* perfume! The only one that counts!" (157). This perfume would have "the same electrifying effect upon a man as the scent of a bitch in heat has upon a dog! One whiff and that'll be it!" (159).

Biotte gives Oswald an introductory lecture on the history of the sense of smell, assures him that the neurophysiological capacities of modern man are still intact, and that the history of civilization could momentarily be wiped out, provided one had the proper scent. Oswald is fascinated, sets him up financially, and three years later receives a call from the excited perfumer, who tells him that the breakthrough has occurred and that he himself had been the first one to be affected. "My dear fellow, I went completely wild! I was like a wild beast, an animal! I was not human! The civilising influences of centuries simply dropped away! I was Neolithic!" (169). Rape, murder, and general mayhem were only prevented on that occasion thanks to the absence of any female from Henri's immediate surrounding and the relatively short duration of the effect of the perfume. Biotte now devises a more controlled setup for a test in his lab, involving a hired boxer (for his assumed physical fitness) and Henri's secretary, who is ravished in the process when "all hell broke loose" (177). The great discovery is, unfortunately, followed by sad news for uncle Oswald the next morning: Simone, Henri's secretary, that "lecherous little slut" (181), sprayed herself with the rest of the trial batch of "Bitch" (as the two men had decided to call their perfume the previous day in a little champagne celebration) before Henri got to his office. Thus, in the ensuing sexual overexertion, the poor man, who was suffering from a heart condition, is "killed in action as they say" (181). Henri, unfortunately, had not yet written down the formula for the stuff, so that the one cubic centimeter of "Bitch" that Oswald had secured for himself, with the intention of using it in a sneaky little attack on the American president, is the only amount left. Of course, his plan fails too, and instead of driving the president to ravish the incumbent president of the Daughters of the Revolution on live television, thereby assuring his speedy impeachment, Oswald gets to do the ravishing himself, offstage and prematurely, while setting up the whole operation—and the rather distasteful Mrs. Elvira Ponsonby enjoys it thoroughly.

Disregarding the addition of Oswald's planned olfactory attack on the American president and looking at the plot only up to Henri's death, the similarities between *Das Parfum* and *Bitch* are striking, especially if we focus more closely on some details. Like Grenouille, Biotte is a rather unappealing man, "hairy as a goat" (155), with "tufts of hair sprouting from his nostrils" giving him "a pixie look" (164). Just as Grenouille is characterized in terms of a tick, Biotte has "a sting in his tail" (164) very much like a scorpion. There is something nonhuman about both men, although it is explicitly discussed in terms of the diabolical order only in Grenouille's case. His first nurse, in her altercation with father Terrier, insists that the baby "ist vom Teufel besessen" and supports her assertion with the fact that he does not smell (Süskind, 14).[43] The motif reappears; Grenouille is olfactively invisible until he creates his own human scent. It is this olfactory nonexistence, the dis-regard—a wrong metaphor, as we are acutely aware here—by his fellow human beings that drives him to create the scent that "vor den Menschen beliebt macht" (305). Both Grenouille and Biotte are the finest noses of their time. Biotte claims that "'on the Champs-Elysées . . . my nose can identify the precise perfume being used by a woman walking on the other side of the street.' 'With the traffic in between?' 'With heavy traffic in between,' he said" (Dahl, 156). Grenouille finds the way to his first victim from half a mile away, from across the Seine and despite his standing in the middle of a crowd and being shrouded in clouds of gunpowder smoke from a firework (Süskind, 50ff.). And for both men the ultimate scent that they are devising means power, very much so for Biotte, who fantasizes that once he has created it, "I shall rule the world!" (157; also 160, 165). For both, this power is close to God's. Biotte says to Oswald that "we'll be the gods of the earth!" (156), and Grenouille was "in der Tat sein eigener Gott, und ein herrlicherer Gott als jener weihrauchstinkende Gott, der in den Kirchen hauste" (304). Biotte as well as Grenouille are outside the realm of social morality. For Grenouille, in fact, the difficulties with moral concepts begin already in the course of his language acquisition as a child. "Mit Wörtern, die keinen riechenden Gegenstand bezeichneten, mit abstrakten Begriffen also, vor allem ethischer und moralischer Natur, hatte er die größten Schwierigkeiten" (32).[44] The murder in the Rue des Marais "war ihm, wenn überhaupt bewußt, vollkommen gleichgültig" (58). And the priest visiting him before his scheduled execution reports that "der Verurteilte habe ihn bei der Erwähnung des Namens Gottes so absolut verständnislos angeschaut, als höre er diesen Namen soeben zum ersten Mal" (291). For Biotte, Oswald observes that he smiles "a wicked little smile" (Dahl, 165), and he character-

---

43. Father Terrier is quick to refute this argument on the basis of traditional scholastic arguments that associate the devil with stench. The baby, therefore, cannot have any commerce with Satan. "Wenn er vom Teufel besessen wäre, müßte er stinken" (14).

44. "With words that did not denote an olfactory object, especially with terms of an ethical or moral nature, he had serious difficulties" so that the murder was, "if it registered at all, completely meaningless" for him. The priest had reported that "the accused had looked at him with utter incomprehension when he mentioned God's name, as if he heard it for the first time."

izes him as "a totally unmoral man," but also admits that this very feature is attractive for him. "A wicked man has a lustre all his own," and "there was something diabolically splendid" about Biotte's scheme (165). In both narratives, moreover, the moment of transition from the practical laboratory work to the written formula for the olfactory product, the textualization of the phenomenological world, represents a critical passage. Thus Baldini has his moment of triumph over Grenouille, who does not know what a formula is (97–98). A little later, however, he has to slow him down in his mixing and blending, so that he can follow with his note taking (118); and when Grenouille falls ill, Baldini is driven to despair to squeeze the last bit of information out of him, to receive his "parfümistische Beichte," his "perfumer's confession" (134). In *Bitch,* Oswald's urgent question after the laboratory demonstration of the perfume's effectiveness concerns Henri's writing down the formula (178). This is thematized again on the next page, and it comes up once more two pages later, when, alas, it is already too late. For Henri "was just settling himself at his desk to write up his notes" (181) when Simone, dripping with "Bitch," sneaks up from behind, thereby depriving us of "the most important scientific discovery of the century" (180).

The comparison of the two men, however, also reveals their differences, and the different value systems of the two narratives. Henri Biotte is driven by a simple, straightforward lust for power that he hopes to satisfy by exploiting sexual desire. He is a well-informed, smooth-talking, salaried employee with a good idea, for which he seeks a financial sponsor, "a sporty gambler with a very keen appetite for the bizarre" (150). He finds him in uncle Oswald. Biotte is the entrepreneurial type, hardworking, creative, and ruthless. Grenouille on the other hand is an outcast from the day he is born; he receives neither love or care nor education; rather he is exploited all his adolescent life. He needs his inherent toughness and resilience for sheer survival. His obsession with smells is primarily phenomenological and perceptual before three significant olfactory epiphanies help shape his career. The first consists in that overwhelming olfactory experience of a pile of wood in the warm spring sun outside Mme. Gaillard's house. Here smells and speech are connected, and the superiority of the former reference system over the latter is established once and for all for Grenouille. The second is the inhalation of his first victim's aroma. This event, the experience of "die reine Schönheit" (55), the discovery of the highest principle in the olfactory realm, orders and (re)structures Grenouille's total experiential reality and olfactory inventory up to this moment and marks the beginning of his monomaniacal drive to manufacture and possess that ultimate smell, regardless of the costs. The third crucial moment occurs when he actually owns the scent, in the scenes around and following his planned execution. At that moment the fundamental differences between Grenouille and Henri become visible: the latter's urge is a direct application of a scientific product to a political end, power. In the former's story however, three elements come together in those climactic moments: love (acceptance, recognition), beauty, and power, each in its tension with its opposite: hatred (rejection, disregard), ugliness, and impotence. For the first time in his life Grenouille is recognized, even loved—not only by an individual human being, but by the masses—and yet, he feels only hatred for them. His scent represents the highest principle of beauty, the ultimate aesthetic instance, as well as the highest pinnacle of power, the sceptre before which everybody bows, but the crowd's reaction is ugly and base. And Grenouille, the god of scents, is powerless to direct the course of events. In vain does he wait for Richis's dagger; he faints.

At this point also are united two of the three social realms that Eagleton understands as separate and mediated ideologically by the aesthetic: the ethicopolitical merges with the libidinal-aesthetic. It is the cognitive, represented in Grenouille, that remains separate, yet including the other two, with Grenouille emerging as its avatar.

Niemand weiß, wie gut dies Parfum wirklich ist, dachte er. Niemand weiß, wie gut es *gemacht* ist. Die anderen sind nur seiner Wirkung untertan, ja, sie wissen nicht einmal, daß es ein Parfum ist, das auf sie wirkt und sie bezaubert. Der einzige, der es jemals in seiner wirklichen Schönheit erkannt hat, bin ich, weil ich es selbst geschaffen habe. Und zugleich bin ich der einzige, den es nicht bezaubern kann. Ich bin der einzige, für den es sinnlos ist. (316–17)[45]

Grenouille is the god outside his own creation. He has chosen a language for his revelation by which the humans are wildly affected but which they do not understand. His creation as communication fails, however successful it is in its overwhelming effect. In this instance another difference

---

45. Nobody knows how good this perfume really is, he thought. Nobody knows how well it is *made*. The others are only subjected to its effect, they do not even know that it is a perfume that affects and magically touches them. The only one who has ever known it in its true beauty is I, because I myself made it. At the same time I am the only one who is not subjected to its spell. I am the only one for whom it is useless.

between Biotte and Grenouille becomes visible: the former is interested in the effect and efficiency of "Bitch" and the power it bestows on its future manipulators, and he would relish the very moment Grenouille comes to hate. Grenouille is asking for more, for social and emotional acceptance by the community; but his supreme moment is flawed. His knowledge places him outside the trinity of love, beauty, and power. The cognitive realm alienates him from the ethicopolitical and the libidinal-aesthetic. The god's feelings turn into hatred and disgust. At this point it is important to remember that this moment of union is based on the murder of twenty-six women. It is a moment of fake harmony: love is hatred, beauty is murder, power is impotence.[46]

In the climactic moment, archaic and anarchic as it is, there are, however, even darker undercurrents to be singled out in the following.

The Allure of Crowds and Power

Grenouille has survived several critical moments in his life, from the attempts at choking him by his fellow inmates at Mme. Gaillard's orphanage to the usually fatal *Milzbrand*, anthrax (42), and the strange disease that afflicts him when working for Baldini. His execution also fails. A more primitive and in that sense, more radical, event is required to deal with the forces associated with Grenouille in those last scenes of *Das Parfum*.

The setup for his public execution has the fundamental structure of what Canetti in his taxonomy of crowds calls a *Hetzmasse*, a baiting crowd.[47]

Die Hetzmasse bildet sich im Hinblick auf ein rasch erreichbares Ziel. . . . Sie ist aufs Töten aus; . . . es ist unmöglich, sie darum zu be-

---

46. On Hassan's binary chart of modernist and postmodernist features (see "Culture of Postmodernism," 312), *Bitch* appears purely "Genital/Phallic" and is therefore located in the "Modernism" column. *Das Parfum* is "Polymorphous/Androgynous," in fact, as regards its hero, essentially asexual and ranks under "Postmodernism."

47. All page references in the following are to vol. 1 of *Masse and Macht*. "The baiting crowd forms with a view to an easily accessible goal. . . . It aims at killing; . . . it is impossible to deflect the crowd from this goal. . . . An important reason for the rapid growth of the baiting crowd is the dangerlessness of the enterprise. . . . A murder without risk, permitted, even recommended, and shared with many others has an irresistible attraction for the vast majority of humans" (49–50). "The baiting crowd is ancient, it has its roots in the original dynamic unit known among humans, the hunting pack" (50).

trügen.... Ein wichtiger Grund für das rapide Anwachsen der Hetzmasse ist die Gefahrlosigkeit des Unternehmens.... Ein gefahrloser, erlaubter, empfohlener und mit vielen anderen geteilter Mord ist für den weitaus größten Teil der Menschen unwiderstehlich. (49–50)

The crowd has the density that Canetti points out as a central criterion for any mass formations (Canetti, 26). With "wohl an die zehntausend Menschen" (Süskind, 296) there are, in fact, more people present than "jemals zuvor in Grasse," and "sie drängten sich" (Süskind, 296). The *Hetzmasse* thus formed is characterized by "rapide[s] Anwachsen" and "Eile" (Canetti, 50). "Die Hetzmasse ist sehr alt, sie geht auf die ursprünglichste dynamische Einheit zurück, die unter Menschen bekannt ist, die Jagdmeute" (50). Certain elements of another mass type, the *Festmasse,* the festive crowd (49), can be observed too: "man aß, man trank, es summte und brodelte wie bei einem Jahrmarkt" (Süskind, 296).[48] What happens, is a flip-over of the *Hetzmasse* into a *Festmasse.* Despite a significant slowdown of events before Grenouille's appearance, "kam in der Menge nicht Unruhe oder Unmut auf.... Und dann geschah ein Wunder" (Süskind, 297–99). This miracle is the unrecognized *olfactory* appearance of Grenouille. Against the archaic structure of the *Hetzmasse* poised to kill, Grenouille appeals to the equally archaic olfactory sensory modality, which prevails and reveals itself as a truly elemental force. The crowd, upon *seeing* Grenouille—they do not know that they are really *smelling* him—is immediately convinced of his innocence, believing firmly, "der kleine Mann... könne *unmöglich ein Mörder* sein" (299). At this point the *Hetzmasse* begins to break up into a mass orgy, the full-fledged *Festmasse,* of which Canetti says: "Es ist ein Überfluß an Weibern da für die Männer und ein Überfluß an Männern für die Weiber.... ganz ungewohnte Annäherungen werden erlaubt und begünstigt" (Canetti, 65).[49] There is a fundamental difference to the *Festmasse,* however, which "lebt auf diesen Augenblick hin und führt ihn zielbewuß herbei" (Canetti, 66). This is precisely not the case in the crowd gathered at Grasse. Their actions are

48. "People were eating and drinking, there was a hum and commotion just as on a fair," and despite the delay "there was no restlessness or anger among the crowd. . . . And then a miracle happened" (297–99).

49. A festive crowd is characterized, according to Canetti, by the fact that "there is an abundance of women for the men and an abundance of men for the women. . . . Wholly unimaginable overtures are permitted and even promoted." The true festive crowd, however, "lives for this moment and brings it about actively" (66).

nothing they could have prepared for, and they recognize their behavior the next day as a shameful relapse into primitivism. Consequently, the events are repressed. "Vielen erschien dieses Erlebnis so grauenvoll, so vollständig unerklärlich und unvereinbar mit ihren eigentlichen moralischen Vorstellungen, daß sie es buchstäblich im Augenblick seines Stattfindens aus dem Gedächtnis löschten" (Süskind, 312).[50] Whoever, only a short time later, inquires in Grasse about the famous murderer, cannot find "einen einzigen vernünftigen Menschen" willing to give some information (Süskind, 314). "Nur ein paar Narren aus der Charité, notorische Geisteskranke, plapperten noch irgend etwas daher von einem großen Fest auf der Place du Cours" (Süskind, 314).[51] The repression among the mentally sane is successful.

Debunking Enlightenment

What happened? Evidently, one of the oldest human structures, according to Canetti, the *Hetzmasse*, is undermined by an even older nexus: of the olfactory and sexuality. The focus of that mass type on its victim, its prey, is thereby deflected onto its own members, who turn against each other not to kill, but to copulate. The driving mechanism of this deflection, smell, remains unknown to them. Their impressions are visual, not olfactory. Grenouille appears as a "Märchenprinz" (303);[52] he seems to smile most seductively, "mit dem unschuldigsten, liebevollsten, bezauberndsten und zugleich verführerischsten Lächeln der Welt" (304). Richis explicitly and grotesquely *sees*, not smells, his daughter Laure in him. "Du bist ihr ähnlich. Du bist schön wie sie" (309). It is also, as we are reminded here, the "visual fallacy" that led to the failure of his and his daughter's escape from Grasse in the first place. However close Richis came to conceptualizing the murderer's principle of action, he fell short by clinging to the visual realm, the "natural" realm of enlightened man. After twenty-four murders

---

50. "To many this experience appeared so horrifying, so completely inexplicable and incommensurable with their actual moral notions that they literally erased it from their memory at the moment of its occurrence."

51. If we needed a scientific confirmation of the emotional depth and intensity of the events surrounding Grenouille's (failed) execution over and above the fascination with which they have been read by millions of readers and the corroboration they find in Canetti's mass-concepts—here it is: repression, one of the key concepts of psychoanalysis.

52. At this point it is helpful and reveals another layer of allusiveness to translate Grenouille's name: the frog. His enterprise can then be understood as the fairy-tale transformation from the loathsome frog into the attractive *Märchenprinz*. His hidden beauty reveals itself through smell, but is perceived as visual.

already committed and only that of his own daughter left, he recognizes that "der Mörder hatte ihm die Augen geöffnet. Der Mörder besaß einen exquisiten Geschmack. Und er besaß ein System" (258).[53] The narrator, in parentheses, explicitly comments on Richis's thought process: "Wie wir sehen, war Richis ein aufgeklärt denkender Mensch, . . . und wenn er nicht in geruchlichen, sondern in optischen Kategorien dachte, so kam er doch der Wahrheit sehr nahe" (259). The shortcoming, maybe the impossibility, of enlightened visual reasoning in the face of the olfactory emerges in yet another instance, when it is revealed that all those beautiful young women were not sexually abused. This is uncanny. The opposite finding would at least have provided an "enlightened" and "acceptable" motif. "Man hätte dann wenigstens ein Motiv des Mörders gekannt. Nun wußte man nichts mehr, nun war man völlig ratlos" (251). The idea of an "olfactory rape" is beyond the scope of enlightenment. It is the civilized, historical ban of the olfactory on which Süskind is playing here as a pivotal element in the construction of the detective story.

On all counts, Grenouille, the olfactory god revealing himself to mankind, is misunderstood. His kingdom, more accurately, his semiotic system, is not of this world. His appeal comes across distorted as sexual and erotic. "Es war, als besitze der Mann zehntausend unsichtbare Hände und als habe er jedem der zehntausend Menschen, die ihn umgaben, die Hand aufs Geschlecht gelegt und liebkose es auf just jene Weise, die jeder einzelne, ob Mann oder Frau, in seinen geheimsten Phantasien am stärksten begehrte" (202). Grenouille's true project, however, is asexual and invisible. His Eros does not aim at sexual practice, but at the supreme olfactory and aesthetic act.

The Charisma of Leadership

Grenouille's position at his scheduled execution is that of a person who is successful beyond belief, but on the wrong premises. In political categories,

---

53. Following are the translations of the Süskind quotes through the end of this section. "The murderer had opened his eyes. The murderer had exquisite taste. And he had a system." His thought process is "enlightened." "As we can see, Richis was an enlightened man, . . . and even though he was not thinking in olfactory terms but in optical categories, he came very close to the truth." If the women had been sexually abused, "one would at least have known the murderer's motive. As it was, however, one knew nothing, and was at a complete loss." Grenouille's sexual appeal is immediate: "It was as if the man had ten thousand invisible hands and as if he had placed them on the genitals of each of the ten thousand people surrounding him, caressing them in just the way each of them, man or woman, desired most in their most intimate fantasies."

Grenouille is at this moment the supreme leader of a mass that is like putty in his hands. They are liquefied; their hearts are a "haltlose[r] Klumpen in ihrem Innern" (301). He could get them to do anything. "Ein Wink von ihm, und alle würden ihrem Gott abschwören" (305). He is the charismatic leader of a demented herd unable to grasp upon what premise his charisma rests—which is precisely one of the characteristics of a charismatic relationship.[54] If charisma rests more on perception by the followers than on the personality of the leader, as Willner points out, then this is exactly Grenouille's quandary. The crowd loves him, which is what he has struggled for so long, but they do so for reasons unacceptable to him. Disgusted, he turns into the antileader. He throws away the moment Biotte and Oswald would have relished. He does not (ab)use his power that he full well recognizes. He simply abandons it. His disillusion drives him to suicide—with a twist. He has himself butchered by a group of humans even more primordial than the *Hetzmasse* at Grasse, namely by the *Jagdmeute*, the "hunting pack," at the Cimetière des Innocents.[55] Grenouille, odorless, is hardly perceived by the bunch of criminals that gather nightly around a fire by the cemetery. The place is alive with "Gesindel, Dieben, Mördern, Messerstechern, Huren, Deserteuren, jugendlichen Desperados" (318). What they later remember is his sprinkling himself with a liquid that makes him appear "mit einem Mal von Schönheit übergossen . . . wie von strahlendem Feuer" (319).[56] What emanates from him is beyond charisma, it is a *Fluidum*, an aura.[57] At that point the *Meute*-mechanism kicks in.

54. Ann Ruth Willner, *The Spellbinders: Charismatic Political Leadership* (New Haven: Yale University Press, 1984). Willner understands charismatic leadership as resting on the following four properties. "1. The leader is perceived by the followers as somehow superhuman. 2. The followers blindly believe in the leader's statements. 3. The followers unconditionally comply with the leader's directives for action. 4. The followers give the leader unqualified emotional commitment" (8). Grenouille certainly fulfills the first condition; as to the second, the crowd is, indeed, "blinded," and they are ignorant that they are being addressed on a different channel; also, they do act as if under order, but they do not know about it. Grenouille's charisma is of the most sublime kind.

55. The leader here does not turn into the survivor (Canetti). Grenouille's charismatic, auratic leadership lasts only a moment.

56. Grenouille appears "all of a sudden as if covered in radiating fire." In the context of Grenouille's appearance and his impression on the crowd, cf. the use of the term "aura" (239, 278, 304 and 306); cf. also the name Laure, Grenouille's last and supreme victim. *L' aure* is a sixteenth- and seventeenth-century frenchified spelling of *aura*. Etymologically, however, the name means "laurel"—an aromatic plant, as we know.

57. The concept of an "olfactory aura" is close enough to Benjamin's aura to be briefly discussed in its central characteristic here. Like his, it denotes origin—indeed not historical, but more ancient: the primordial origin of all smells in Eros or Thanatos. In Grenouille's last stand, precisely this connection to Eros is played out and takes such immediate

"Die Jagdmeute bewegt sich mit allen Mitteln auf etwas Lebendiges zu, das sie erlegen will, um es sich dann einzuverleiben" (Canetti, 106).[58] Blinded by Grenouille's beauty, "wichen sie zurück.... Aber im selben Moment spürten sie schon, daß das Zurückweichen mehr wie ein Anlaufnehmen war.... Ein rabiater Sog ging von ihm aus.... sie began-nen zu drücken, zu schieben und zu drängeln, jeder wollte dem Zentrum an nächsten sein" (Süskind, 319).[59] "Jeder hat denselben Gegenstand vor Augen, und jeder bewegt sich auf denselben Gegenstand zu" (Canetti, 106). "Sie stürzten sich auf den Engel, fielen über ihn her, rissen ihn zu Boden.... Sie schlugen ihre Krallen und Zähne in sein Fleisch, wie Hyänen fielen sie über ihn her" (Süskind, 319). "Bei vielen Tieren ist es, statt Kralle oder Hand, gleich das bewaffnete Maul, das das Ergreifen besorgt" (Canetti, 225). What occurs after the initial onslaught is the distri-bution of the prey, according to "the oldest law." "Das Gesetz der *Verteilung* ist das *älteste* Gesetz" (Canetti, 107). "In kürzester Zeit war der Engel in dreißig Teile zerlegt [i. e., a piece for each] und ein jedes Mitglied der Rotte grapschte sich ein Stück, zog sich, von wollüstiger Gier ge-trieben, zurück und fraß es auf" (Süskind, 320). "Die Raserei läßt nach im Augenblick der Erlegung. Alle stehen um das gefallenen Opfer herum, plötzlich still" (Canetti, 107). "Als die Kannibalen nach gehabter Mahlzeit wieder am Feuer zusammenfanden, sprach keiner ein Wort" (Süskind, 320). Thus we see the *Jagdmeute* shift into a *Vermehrungsmeute*. "[Meuten] haben alle etwas Fließendes und gehen leicht ineinander über" (Canetti,

---

effect that the group's attraction, its desire for him, becomes so overwhelming that it leads to his death. In this death, then, come together the elements of love, hunger, and violence or, to put it differently: love and death are mediated in the moment of power-as-eating, power-as-engorging. (Cf. on this nexus Canetti 223–48). What is revealed is the essential sameness of *Biss* and *Kuss,* the common element in *la mort* and *la petite mort.*

58. "The hunting pack moves irresistibly toward the living creature that it wants to catch and swallow." And further on: "Everyone has the same object before him, and everyone moves toward this object." (Canetti, *Masse und Macht* 1:106) "For many animals it is not only claws or hands but the armed mouth itself that executes the catch" (1:225). "The frenzy ceases at the moment of capture. All surround the fallen prey, suddenly silent" (1:107).

59. The rabble "retreated.... But at the same moment they felt that their retreat was more a gathering of momentum.... An irresistible attraction emanated from him.... They began to push and shove and press, each one wanted to be closest to the center." And further on: "They fell upon the angel, pulled him to the ground.... They sank their claws and teeth into his flesh, like hyenas they assaulted him" (Süskind, 319). "In no time the angel was torn into thirty pieces and each member of the bunch grabbed a piece and withdrew, driven by voluptuous desire to swallowed it" (Süskind, 320). Later, back at the fire, nobody utters a word about the incident.

103).[60] Its center is the common meal, the communion. "Etwas von *einem* Leib geht in alle ein. . . . Dieser Ritus der gemeinsamen Einverleibung ist die *Kommunion*" (Canetti, 125). Grenouille, the god of smell who relinquishes his power, is consumed, unrecognized in his true essence by man.

These are the dark streaks in Süskind's light and easy-flowing narrative, the traces of primordial and deeply repressed structures of behavior and fears, of anarchy and charisma, which account for the public's fascination with the novel, together with the new medium of smell in which its plot unfolds as a detective story and which allows for titillatingly vicarious feelings of disgust and loathing. Not all of these aspects of the novel surface in the mass readership's consciousness—but this is precisely the author's stroke of genius. Moreover, the combination of artifice, brutality, and innocence in the makeup of Grenouille's character is a further essential constituent of the interest, enthusiasm, and fascination the novel's hero holds for a postmodern readership.

What Nietzsche says of Wagner a century ago, in the explicit context of decadence, can be said of Süskind today: "In seiner Kunst ist auf die verführerischeste Art gemischt, was heute alle Welt am nöthigsten hat,— die drei großen Stimulantia der Erschöpften, das Brutale, das Künstliche und das Unschuldige (Idiotische)."[61] Joni Mitchell takes this up on her album *Dog Eat Dog* (1985) when she sings about "the three great stimulants / Of the exhausted ones / Artifice, brutality and innocence." She leaves out the idiotic, though, as a possible aspect of the innocent; for innocence, too, has become completely instrumentalized since Nietzsche's time. There is nothing idiotic about its use; on the contrary, its application is well-calculated.

The look at Grenouille through these three concepts will reveal him as a postmodern hero, singularly befitting the world of the 1980s.

"Artifice, Brutality, and Innocence"

Artifice, brutality, and innocence are stimulants for Joni Mitchell and our exhausted age as much as they were for Nietzsche. The question is whether the element of decadence Nietzsche was so keenly aware of can be figured

---

60. The "hunting pack" transforms into a "multiplication pack." "[Packs] have something fluid about them and easily transform into each other." "A part of *one* body enters into them all. . . . This rite of common incorporation is the *communion*" (Canetti, *Masse und Macht* 1:125).

61. In *Der Fall Wagner*, part 5.

into this analogy and thereby postmodernism be diagnosed as decadent. If we focus on one aspect of 1970s and 1980s culture, its recycling of earlier styles and movements, its allusions to, and quotations from, previous culture, the reframing of existing material as its essential innovative program, the answer to this question is yes. It can of course be argued that the new context into which (old) elements are placed, represents itself a creative drive—in fact *the* creative drive wholly appropriate for an epoch in which the half-life of the cultural inventory has been rapidly shrinking. The Bürgers' suspicion that there are really no postmodern artworks and that postmodernism is above all a change in aesthetic sensitivities seems justified. Decadence in its postmodern variety, the twentieth-century fin-de-siècle, then, appears as a shift of creativity from text to context, from the canvas to the frame, from the object to its spatiotemporal surroundings as well as the reinvocation, through contextualization, of an auratic quality. Smell appears as the ultimate aura, surface and depth simultaneously, denoting as well as hiding its double origin in love and death.[62] If we accept this general argument, the question arises in what sense artifice could serve as a stimulant and the question will also have to be answered for brutality and innocence.

One of the key concepts of our time is *challenge,* a strictly formalistic and empty notion of a demand, real or perceived, objective or subjective, to which an individual reacts. More often than not such a challenge is self-imposed and serves as a life-structuring device in lieu of true existential demands made on the individual. Anything can constitute a challenge, and there is a certain element of sport, of playfulness involved in accepting a challenge, the notion of taking an activity to its extreme, and of testing its limits. To be famous for fifteen minutes, regardless of the reason, is one such challenge of our time, and activities may range from crossing the Pacific in a rowing boat or freestyle rock climbing to chess against computers or, as in our case, perfume making. Grenouille's challenge, self-imposed

---

62. Baudrillard's concept of "simulation" is helpful here. Perfume is "masking" and perverting (in the literal meaning of *per-vertere,* to turn around, to revaluate) its origin in sexuality. More than that: it tries to cut all its ties with this, its phenomenological root, and reinvent sexuality and erotic attraction out of its own aura. Perfume advertisement does nothing but create the product's appeal by fusing it with an image (an aura) that creates its erotics out of this fusion rather than through emphasis on its descent from real sexual odors. Perfume tiptoes a thin line. While it undeniably has ties to phenomenological reality, it behaves, in the public sphere, as a free and clean simulacrum. See Jean Baudrillard, *Simulations,* trans. Paul Foss, Paul Patton, and Philip Beitchman (New York: Semiotext(e), 1983), esp. 11.

but of a truly existential dimension, is to become the greatest perfumer ever and, above all, to create the absolute scent that he discovered for the first time in the Rue des Marais. This is his (postmodern) calling, and artifice his practical means toward that end.

The term *artifice* covers a wide spectrum of meanings, both in English and German, reaching from the highly positive to the almost criminally negative.[63] It surrounds like an ambivalently shimmering halo its etymological root, *art*. We already briefly touched upon the location of the olfactory in the triangle of art, craft, and artifice. At this point we need to take a closer look. Artifice is skill, workmanship, ingenuity taken to some dishonest extent; to cheat; fraud, and deceit.[64] Artifice derives its attraction from beating the system at its own game, from "living on the edge" of legality. Artifice is the challenge of living dangerously. In artifice the highest standards of professional achievement flip over into ingeniousness, artfulness, and trickery. This is precisely the sphere in which Grenouille operates. The most gifted nose of his time, the supertalent of the olfactory, striving to learn the most subtle professional techniques, and to create the ultimately refined product, spends all his short life learning the ins and outs of his profession, but also all the tricks of the trade. He is patiently distilling, endlessly macerating, carefully enfleuraging—but he is also aware of his ability to deceive people, and he looks down on them for the ease with which this is possible. He consciously and purposefully manufactures a whole set of human scents for himself, each with a different, specific appeal (cf. 231ff.). It was the discovery of his own inodorousness that changed his behavior, the insight (the wrong metaphor, as we notice) that he lacked the essential quality to be perceived as human, even to be perceived in the first place: smell. Grenouille the tick, whose only asset was his inconspicuousness, his tenacity, his *Genügsamkeit*, wakes up to be the animal, the brute that will end up a mass murderer.

Etymologically, there is no moral or ethical undertone to the word, but as with artifice above, brutal, too, is situated in an ambivalent realm, a border area, this time between animal and man. Latin *brutus* means "brute," "animal"; "befitting or resembling a brute or animal"; "based on crude animal

---

63. Its German synonyms and components are terms such as *Kunstfertigkeit* and *Geschicklichkeit* at the positive end of the spectrum, *Schlauheit, List,* and *Verschlagenheit* at the negative, and *Kunstgriff, Kniff,* or *Trick* representing special aspects.

64. All terms as well as the equivalents for "brutal," "brutality" and "innocence," below, are from *Webster's Third New International Dictionary.*

instincts"; "archaic: of, belonging to, or typical of beasts or animals as distinguished from man." This very distinction is called into question. Grenouille the tick, Grenouille the one-track mind, leaves twenty-six women dead in the wake of his quest for the olfactory pinnacle. The meaning of brutal as "devoid of mercy or compassion" applies indeed, but in his case does not carry full moral force. Grenouille's case is also different from Dorian Gray's, whom the narrator describes at one point as looking "on evil simply as a mode through which he could realize his conception of the beautiful" (Wilde, 123). Grenouille is unable to perceive his doings as evil in the first place. His environment, the olfactory, itself a transitional realm between the purely animal and the only just dawning human, is virtually exempt from ethics. But Grenouille's drive is to be loved, an eminently human quest. In his world as well as in that of the whole narrative, love or at least the potential for it rests on the olfactory. Grenouille, born without an odor of his own, without "den göttlichen Funken, den andre Menschen mir nichts, dir nichts in die Wiege gelegt bekommen und der ihm als einzigem vorenthalten worden war" (304)[65] succeeds in the Promethean task of creating his own scent. "Grenouille, der Liebe nie empfunden hatte und Liebe niemals inspirieren konnte" (242), overcomes this natural handicap "durch unendliches Raffinement" (204). Grenouille, the tick who can morally hardly be held responsible, aspires to the human order through the brutal murder of twenty-six women, a truly paradoxical situation.[66] Brutality thus appears located in the transitory area between the animal and the human, and the olfactory serves as the key into the human sphere.[67] Here again, then, are surfacing the links of death, love, and the primordial olfactory. To put it in extreme terms: Grenouille is distilling the essence of love out of death, out of untouched beauty, the

---

65. Grenouille is born without "the divine spark that other people receive naturally at birth and that was withheld from him alone." Grenouille "had never experienced love and could never inspire it" (242); but he overcomes this obstacle "through infinite refinement" (204).

66. A comprehensive interpretation of the novel would have to deal with the striking imbalance between male and female sexuality; to be more precise, the virtual absence of male sexuality versus the auraticization of female sexuality through the most archaic form of sexual attraction, the olfactory. Grenouille's ultimate scent is, to quote the narrator of *Against the Grain,* "the essence of woman." Sexual attraction is thus, as in primordial days, the female characteristic par excellence. Is is also noteworthy that Grenouille's victims are all of the most stereotypically "womanly" body type (cf. 247, 250).

67. This is another paradox, given the general association of smells with the animal realm. It is less paradoxical, however, if we bear in mind that it is precisely to man's "animal instincts" that Grenouille appeals.

concentrated aroma of twenty-five females as their bodies cool off and enter the *rigor mortis*.[68] It is ultimate, lethal brutality which yields the potion of inescapable attraction.

But brutal is also defined as "devoid of mercy or compassion," and indeed, Grenouille does not exhibit either. Where should he have learned those human sentiments? He certainly was never shown the one or the other himself. Within the framework of a theory of the social formation of criminal behavior, he cannot justly be declared guilty. He is the product of an utterly depraved upbringing, and even the narrator exploits him for some cheap shots in a number of instances of moral labeling, such as: "Grenouille, der solitäre Zeck, das Scheusal, der Unmensch" (242); Grenouille, "der Mörder, diese[r] Teufel" (289); Grenouille, "eine[r] der verabscheuungswürdigsten Verbrecher[]] seiner Zeit" (303); Grenouille, "ein Scheusal innen wie außen" (304). This is judging Grenouille unfairly from a human, moral viewpoint by the same narrator who is questioning his human status all along. Is Grenouille, then, innocent? There seems to be a touch of innocence in the scene—the only murder described from close up—of Grenouille's "vigil" after killing Laure Richis, his last victim. He hates noise, such as "das Geräusch des Schlages" caused by his little olive-wood club on his victim's skull "in seinem ansonsten lautlosen Geschäft" (275). But once the blow has been dealt, he wraps the dead but still warm and odorous body into the greased sheet. "Er überprüfte das ganze Paket. Kein Schlitz, kein Löchlein, kein aufgekniffenes Fältlein klaffte mehr, an dem der Duft des Mädchens hätte entweichen können" (276).[69] He is tired but he stays awake out of a strange notion of professional ethics, "denn es gehörte sich nicht, daß man während der Arbeit schlief" (276). He is sure and almost happy that he "hatte sein Bestes gegeben. Er hatte all seine Kunstfertigkeit [art as well as artifice] aufgebracht. Kein Fehler war ihm unterlaufen. Das Werk war einzigartig" (277), and Grenouille feels deeply the peace "dieser Heiligen Nacht" (279).

There is certainly artifice, brutality, and callousness—but innocence?

---

68. From this perspective, Grenouille's doings can be understood as transforming one form of beauty, the visual, into a more archaic form, the olfactory. He thereby strips the former of its whole intellectual and aesthetic superstructure and reduces it to its carnal, behavioral basis.

69. "He checked the whole parcel. There was no gap, no opening, no open fold left for the aroma of the girl to escape." Grenouille thinks "it not right to sleep during one's work" (276). He "had given all he had. He had applied all his artistry. No error had occurred. The work was unique" (277). He feels the peace "of this holy night" (279).

The term "innocence" has three distinct meanings. Whereas morally innocent and legally innocent are clearly associated with the perpetrator, we
arrive via the German term *Unschuld,* which is also a designation of "virginity" and "chastity," as a third concept, linked with the victims. There is
some overlap between the first and the second. Significantly, nowhere in
the narrative is Grenouille "found guilty" (i.e., *wurde schuldig gesprochen*).
Is he therefore innocent in the sense of free from "guilt or sin esp. through
being unaquainted with evil?" This, indeed, seems his situation. He is
disgusted by mankind (305); he despises them (304); he hates them (305)
because of their gullibility, because of the ridiculous ease with which they
let themselves be deceived. But he does not kill *because* he hates. He kills
in the name of a higher principle, which is meant to give him access to
human love. "Innocence" has further meanings, though. "Artlessness" is
one of them, "simplicity" another. On these two counts Grenouille is not
"innocent." We mentioned his art, his artifice; and his whole scheme is far
from "simple." However, in his doings there is a touch of "naïveté," of
"ignorance," two further dictionary entries for "innocence." Both are aspects that help make Grenouille acceptable to the reader.

Is Grenouille, then, innocent in a legal sense? Could he, for instance,
plead insanity at his trial? He is certainly collaborating with the investiga-
tors. "Der Angeklagte [gestand] selbst bei den Vernehmungen ohne Um-
schweife die ihm zur Last gelegten Morde" (290).[70] He is reticent, however, when asked about his motives. "Er habe die Mädchen gebraucht und
sie deshalb erschlagen. Wozu er sie gebraucht habe und was das überhaupt
bedeuten sollte, 'er habe sie gebraucht'—dazu schwieg er" (290), and no
torture can make him speak. The judges, therefore, "hielten ihn für geist-
eskrank" (290). Nevertheless, he is sentenced to death on the basis of
circumstantial evidence.

"Innocence" as "chastity" is the third dimension to be considered here,
as this quality—not Grenouille's, but his victims'—seems to inform his
product, the pure distillate of pure innocence. Noticeable is the link between the olfactory, the artistic, and the erotic. Only women before
defloration—an event strangely similar to the process by means of which
blossoms are robbed of their perfume[71]—yield the scent of ultimate attrac-

---

70. "The accused confessed without hesitation the murders he was charged with" but
declares that "he used the girls and therefore killed them. What he used them for and
what that was supposed to mean in the first place, that 'he used them'—on that point he
was silent." The judges "thought he was insane" (290).

71. Called *enfleurage;* cf., e.g., Süskind 221, 228, 237.

tion. Defloration, it is implied, would destroy that *aura*, as it would destroy the *aroma* for ever.[72] The means of obtaining this aura is enfleurage, the olfactory rape. It is *in essence* the victims' innocence that is released to the crowd as the irresistible—and impossible—promise of sexuality as well as of innocence itself. Artifice as the means to rise to the challenge of producing the perfume to end all perfumes; brutality as the only way of procuring the raw material; and innocence, the last nonexchangeable commodity captured in the product, supremely attractive precisely for its one-time-only value: these are the essential features that go into the makeup of Grenouille's universe.

Smell and Mysticism

We traced the primordial origin of the fundamental binary split in the olfactory universe between "good" and "bad" to the stench of death and the aromas of sexuality. Now, however, the analysis of *Das Parfum* forces us to revise this concept, for here exists an even more primordial human smell, encompassing both Eros and Thanatos as its constituents. Grenouille, himself lacking this very human emanation, distills various surrogates for himself and then aims at producing one of its components, Eros, in pure form. At the very beginning of the production process, however, stands its other component, death. One is not to be had without the other. With Süskind, then, it seems we have entered somewhat ahead of schedule, the twenty-first century, the "Zeitalter des kollektiven Mystizismus," as foreseen by perfumers.[73] We have already marched into the new era, touted as the "Zeitalter des Geruchs" by psychobiology. Perfume is the unity of opposites.

Can we therefore equate *Geruch* and *Mystizismus* or at least claim a strong association between the two? As a test, let us map the one term onto the definition of the other. *Mystizismus* is defined as "eine intuitiv-irrationale Geisteshaltung, die durch unmittelbares Ergreifen einer höheren Wahrheit Erkenntnisse sucht, welche weder in den Bereich religiösen Erlebens . . . gehören noch verstandesmäßiger Prüfung standhalten."[74] The

---

72. The notion of irrecoverability is also part of the traditional Christian valuation of chastity or virginity. It also informs more traditional societies' views, where its loss often means the loss of the social commodity value of the woman.

73. Cf. footnote 11, above.

74. *Brockhaus Enzyklopädie in zwanzig Bänden,* 17th rev. ed. (Wiesbaden: F. A. Brockhaus, 1966–74). "Mysticism [is] an intuitive-irrational intellectual attitude that seeks, through an immediate access to higher truth, a kind of knowledge which is neither part of religious experience . . . nor stands up to intellectual scrutiny."

dawning age of a new mysticism as the age of smell would thus seem to favor an intuitive, irrational attitude; it would seek to grasp higher truths immediately, which cannot be called religious but can neither be rationally verified. Scent would thus become—probably while scientific research into its particularities is continuing and producing further results—the veil coming down over the rational, enlightened worldview. Is the olfactory sense indeed capable of all this? Before giving an answer based on our current account of that sensory mode, let us measure smell by placing it against the *Encyclopedia Americana* (1985) entry for mysticism: "Mysticism is the experience of achieving direct apprehension of a Unity, a oneness, or a One that is without internal multiplicity. . . . Mysticism is no doubt in a broad sense a religious phenomenon, but it does not favor one religion over another." Smell as the experience of oneness and unity? The olfactory as a religious phenomenon?

In the literary and intellectual history of the olfactory sketched so far, the emphasis has been on that sensory mode's potential for rationality and enlightenment. We have witnessed Kant's rejection of it as too organic and not intellectual enough for his hermeneutic and aesthetic project. We have seen it fulfill its enlightenment role in the organic domain of cleaning and sanitizing the Western city and the Western body, thereby sublating its own necessity. Hegel excluded it from his aesthetic universe. We have observed its disappearance as well as reappearance in the literature of the nineteenth century: it disappeared (in Stifter, for instance) because its irrationality was feared; but it reappeared (in French naturalism, for instance) as a rational, descriptive social marker. And it boomed around the turn of the century as a perceptual medium expressive of a newly emerging fluid subjectivity. That was the moment when its irrationality began to be revalued as positive, as adding a phenomenological dimension to modern experience not otherwise to be had of a lost, prelinguistic immediacy. The olfactory remained crucial and served as a highly efficient tool for the description of the experience of fascism; and it has been an accepted device in recent and present literature.

While the history of the olfactory can thus be told as a rational and enlightened, as well as an enlightening account, the sensory modality itself has, indeed, always been distrusted, often been associated with the irrational, and we have unearthed what we believe to be its two deepest roots in love and death, in Eros and Thanatos. With *Das Parfum,* smell now reaches a mass readership for the first time—and with a vengeance. Its impact is unmitigated by a tried and tested vocabulary or discursive strategies, and its effects are undiluted by familiar hermeneutic concepts, psychological mechanisms of coping, or intellectual defenses. It hits home directly by aiming at the oldest parameters of human life. It hits with mystical force, it is intuitively grasped, but hardly rationally understood.

Does *Das Parfum* then, irrational, antienlightenment, and postmodern as it is, ring in the age of mysticism, the century of smell?[75] Calvino, before Süskind, does not seem to foresee a whole century of the olfactory. On the contrary, for him it is over. And yet, his "The Name, the Nose" contains and confirms many of the points made so far in this chapter.[76]

"The Name, the Nose": "The noseless man of the future"

In an artistically superb whisp of a text, Calvino interlaces three narrative voices telling of three olfactory moments, each distinct, yet all speaking of eroticism, attraction, and loss. In the lightest of verbal tones he sets up a memorial triptych to scent, love, and death, a warning to "the noseless man of the future" (67), an epitaph to three unknown women, a monument to the end of olfaction. "Epigraphs in an undecipherable language" (67), the opening words: this is what perfumeries will become, and "perfumes will be left speechless, inarticulate, illegible" (68). Calvino's text, an epigraph to scent, is itself structured like scent, ephemeral, yet lingering; transitional, yet insistent; releasing its meaning through its own dissolution, yet solid and hard, carved into the rock of language.[77]

---

75. Baudrillard's concept of simulation is helpful here once again: as the reverse-angle postmodern analogue to mysticism. It deconstructs the unity, the oneness of image and reality and reveals the absence of reality behind the image.

76. "The Name, the Nose," is the third and last of the stories Calvino wrote for a book on the five senses, as Esther Calvino states in a note at the end of the slim volume. Italo Calvino, *Under the Jaguar Sun*, trans. William Weaver (San Diego: Harcourt, 1988), 65–83. All subsequent references are to this edition.

77. Cynthia Ozick, in a review of *Under the Jaguar Sun* comes to a less favorable opinion on "The Name, the Nose": "The last and shortest tale—'The Name, the Nose'— is not a success, though here as in the others the brilliance of language never falters. Calvino's aim is to juxtapose the primitive and the rococo, the coarse and the highly mannered, in order to reveal their congenital olfactory unity." She is indeed right in saying that "the nose, no matter who is wearing it, is an aboriginal hunter." This is a claim we have been making and proving all along. The story seems "all too artful, too archetypal, too anthropological" for her and "especially too programmed and thematic. No use sniffing here after the primeval mythos." With this statement we have to disagree, but we can join her in the following: "The sophisticated aroma is of Calvino, writing." Cynthia Ozick, "Mouth, Ear, Nose," *New York Times Book Review*, 23 October 1988, 7.

The first narrative voice, revealed only in the pronoun *us*, reads the epigraph, opens the triptych of the following three male voices, from different times each, who tell their story. They are linked among each other by verbal or thematic echoes, by a language particle that is picked up in each segment from the preceding one like a whiff of scent wafting by.

"Epigraphs in an undecipherable language, half the letters rubbed away by the sand-laden wind: this is what you will become, O *parfumeries*, for the noseless man of the future" (67). This opening echoes in the first narrator's text. A "man of the world" (68) he is, living in the Paris of the nineteenth century (where else?) and lamenting the decline of olfaction. "How different were the vibrations a great *parfumerie* could once stir" (68). In his own time now, he has entered the well-known perfume shop of Madame Odile's in order to find the scent worn by a mysterious woman at a masked ball the previous night and thus, with the help of Madame Odile's list of customers, the lady herself. Monsieur is well-known in the store; he is "mon chou!" (69), and he knows the shopgirls by their first name and in more senses than one: Martine, pressing her breast against his side; Charlotte, offering him her arm for a sample sniffing; Sidonie, "whose bites [he] knew so well" (69). But soon he becomes confused by the flood of aromas: "No, it was sharper . . . I mean fresher . . . heavier" (71), and he despairs about how he could "put into words the languid, fierce sensation" (70) of the previous night, which for him "was a complete woman" (71). Here the story breaks, the reader's attention is drawn over to one of the side pieces of the triptych, where the second narrator, primordial man, raises his voice. "And wasn't it, after all, the same thing in the savannah, the forest, the swamp, when they were a network of smells, and we ran along, heads down . . . ?" Everything at that time was "within the nose, the world is the nose" (71). It was a time when there were "no words, there is no information more precise than what the nose receives" (72). And again, the smell of all smells is female: "With my nose I learned that in the herd there is a female not like the others; . . . and I ran, following her trail in the grass, . . . following her love summons" (72). But the herd moves on, separating the two, and "I hunt for her spoor in the dusty, trampled grass" (72)—And now "grass" becomes the link to the third narrator's account, who wakes up "in the smell of grass" (73). He is a twentieth-century man,

---

Ozick, like Ortheil (cf. "Das Lesen") calls Calvino "an authentic post-modernist (despite the clamor, there are not so many of these)." And like Frank Lucht (cf. "Erkennen Sie die Melodie?") she stresses the mythical element (re)surfacing in the storytelling of Calvino.

a drummer in a rock and roll band, waking up heavy-headed after a gig and some booze and some smokes, in a dingy place among a bunch of half-naked people sleeping on the floor, groupies, band members, and the usual hangers-on. He is cold and wants "to put more shillings in the gas stove that's gone out and is making nothing but a stink" (73). So he crawls along the floor, over sprawled-out bodies, suffused in their smells and the smell of stale beer in open cans and the overturned ashtrays. "I'm crossing the room, smelling some of these smells of sleeping girls until at one point I stop" (74). It is the smell of a skin that has hit him, "a skin that breathes the way a leaf's pores breathe the meadows, and all the stink in the room keeps its distance" (75), and the two, without words, "find a way of lying and agree on how I should lie and how she should now beautifully lie" (75). When he returns from eventually putting some coins in the stove, he cannot find her anymore, and "I go from one skin to another hunting for that lost skin that isn't like any other skin" (76).

The cue "skin," heavy with aroma, now takes us back to the center piece and the Parisian *homme du monde,* who knows that "for each woman a perfume exists which enhances the perfume of her own skin" (76). He goes on to describe his previous night, the pangs of desire for the mystery woman under the mask. "As I caressed her, she seemed at times docile, then at times violent, clawing. She allowed me to uncover hidden areas, explore the privacy of her perfume, provided I did not raise the mask from her face" (78). All of a sudden, however, she has to leave, following the ominous "shadow, hooded, in a violet domino" who "had appeared in the Empire mirror" (78). "A terrible secret hangs over [her] life" (78), she lets the narrator know, who immediately concludes that he "shall have no peace until I have found the trail of that hostile odor and the beloved perfume, until one has put me on the trail of the other, until the duel in which I shall kill my enemy " (78). Now we move over again, to the first side panel, where the "hostile odor" hangs heavy too, over the trail of primordial man. It is unmistakable, and "every time I think I've caught the odor of the female I am hunting for on the trail of the herd, a hostile odor also mixed with her odor" (79) strikes his nose, and the fight takes place between the two competitors, and "I swing my club, . . . I batter his skull with flints, shards, elkjaws, bones, daggers, horn harpoons" (79). The narrator survives, of course, in fact he goes a long way, taking the first steps on the prehistoric path sketched by Freud toward upright gait and decreasing olfactory, but increasing visual, power; for "caked with blood and dust, I cannot smell odors very clearly any more, so I might as well stand on my hind legs and walk erect for a while. . . . Of course, by keeping my nose suspended up here in the air, I lose a lot of things" (79–80). But "your nose is drier, so you can pick up distant smells. . . . And your eyes help your nose, they grasp things in space—the sycamore's leaves, the river, the blue stripe of the forest, the clouds" (80).—Now back to London, where the drummer steps outside "to breathe in the morning, the street, the fog" and the river Thames. He bangs his "head against the fog" (80)—and on we move, across the Channel to Paris, where Monsieur "with a splitting headache . . . leave[s] the *parfumerie*" to go to that address at Passy Madame Odile has given him (80). The door of the house there, however, "is half open," and he is "struck by a heavy smell of flowers, as of rotting vegetation" from an open coffin in the hall; from the veiled female corpse comes "the echo of that perfume that resembles no other, merged with the odor of death now as if they had always been inseparable" (81). They have.

And the odor of death also rises from the chasm where the primordial tribe throws down the offal of their prey. "That odor I was following was lost down there, and, depending on how the wind blows, it rises with the stink of the clawed cadavers" (82).

And the odor of death rises once again when the musician comes back to the room, empty now, except for the stove stinking more than ever. When he breaks that door down, now locked, there is nothing inside but "thick, black, disgusting gas from floor to ceiling," and he pulls out "the long, white, outstretched form . . . by her stiffened legs," and he still smells "her odor within the asphyxiating odor," and "the air is impregnated with it." It is present even "among the odors of disinfectant and slime that drips from the marble slates in the morgue, . . . especially when outside the weather is damp" (83).

Three times the game of attraction, copulation, and death. Although each of Calvino's narrative strands is set in a radically different cultural environment, the patterns of pursuit are identical, the patterns of female lure and male desire. The smell of attraction is female. This insight allows us to add another facet to the axioms we have established for the olfactory and its cultural coding: good and bad, love and death, Eros and Thanatos were our first categories. *Das Parfum* led us to the recognition of an even more basic notion: human smell, a combination of both components. It is what Grenouille lacks and what he composes, indeed from both pleasant and attractive as well as disgusting and repulsive ingredients. Calvino underscores another of our findings in Süskind's novel, that the Faustian feminine erotic, "das Ewig-Weibliche," the eternal feminine—as well as female—that attracts "us," the male, is in fact its smell. It is so powerful that it remains perceptible even within its structural opposite, the "bad," in its most potent appearance, the odor of death. The two mingle in Calvino's text, just as they were intricately linked in Süskind's. The scent of attraction is "merged with the odor of death . . . as if they had always been inseparable" (81), which indeed they have been: *la mort—la petite mort*.[78]

While Calvino thus does not add new facts to our findings from Süskind's novel, his is clearly a superior literary achievement. His short text performs, as a literary act and with unsurpassable formal elegance and economy, that which is its content: emanation, dispersion, dissolution. The text *is* a whiff of scent, airborne in the language particles that pass on from one narrative strand to the other, lightly, yet doggedly clinging to objects, to the one object of them all: woman and her smell. Süskind's is a powerful text in its own right, but its most striking features are not formal innovations but rather the clever refilling of forms with new content matter, the historical novel as a pretense for the depiction of olfactory landscape and cityscape; the *bildungsroman* as the biography of a physically and psychologically deviant killer; and the detective novel based on olfactory clues. Süskind's sheer (olfactory) descriptive pluck is admirable, but more heavy-handed than Calvino's technique of just barely sketching the environments of the prairie, the perfumery, and the band's quarters by the London docks.

"The Name, the Nose" is dated January 1972. Esther Calvino, in a note appended to the collection, states that "in 1972 Calvino started writing a book about the five senses" (85). In terms of the history of postmodernism, "The Name, the Nose" is thus an early piece, at least in the European context. Esther Calvino thinks her husband "would have provided a frame" (85) in addition, of course, to the tales of the two missing senses, sight and touch, to complete the whole work. And she adds the following note of

---

78. Our findings seem to hold at least for modern Western civilization, but several questions could be asked concerning a possible wider validity of our findings: Is there such a thing as "olfactory universals?" Is the olfactory realm universally split into good and bad (an instinctive value judgment not found in the realm of colors, for instance)? Are the underlying principles everywhere those of Eros and Thanatos? If so, but even independently of the answer to this question, is the olfactively erotic and attractive universally coded as feminine? And lastly, how do various cultures deal practically with sexual smells and the smell of death? It is such investigations of a more anthropological bent that could provide us with some of the answers. (Cf., e.g., the issue of the removal of menstruating women in certain tribal cultures; the issue of im/purity and cleanliness. Douglas, *Purity and Danger,* touches on such questions, as well as Howes, "Olfaction and Transition," above, chapter 3).

Calvino's on the function of framing: "It is the frame that marks the boundary between the picture and what is outside. . . . I might venture a definition: we consider poetic a production in which each individual experience acquires prominence through its detachment from the general continuum, while it retains a kind of glint of that unlimited vastness" (86). This, precisely, he achieves with "The Name, the Nose," even without an external frame around the complete set of stories, merely through those three strands of narrative providing a frame and continuity for each other.

Smell—the Feminine Mystery

An issue that cannot be dodged, although it can only be dealt with superficially here, is the gender coding of smell. For a simple model, we may draw two intersecting lines across the realm of smell, one dividing good and bad, the other female and male. While the whole male half of the spectrum is only marginally represented in the analyzed texts, it contains the combination of bad-male, which we may call double negative and which we found represented in a figure such as Koeppen's Judejahn. The devil would be the ultimate representative of that pole. Indeed, Judejahn, the buck, is associated with the devil more than once. Examples for the good-male we found for instance in Verlaine's (homo)erotic poetry.[79] It is in the female half of the spectrum where the attraction lies, and even the bad-female combination, as found, for instance, in *Soll und Haben,* in Fink's narrative about Indian women, seems to have a strange allure. But the focus of interest, even fascination, is to be found in the good-female quadrant. It is here that the vast majority of instances of erotic attraction are located, including, of course, *Das Parfum* as its epitome. It is in this quadrant also, especially in the border area toward the bad-female, that the history of the olfactory has left its deepest marks in its unfolding as sexual and aesthetic politics of the body. It is in the female sector that, tendentially, the natural has become the bad and war has been waged against it by whole batteries of artificial cleansers and deodorants, scents and fragrances, perfumes and aromas. But the ultimate stimulus of (male) olfactory fantasy is the purest "essence of woman," the virginal, the innocent, the foremost of "the three great stimulants." Vice, too, and degradation are of great attraction, usually in a dialectical tension with their opposite, innocence.

---

79. In a broadening of the text base of this study, contemporary homosexual literature might yield new and/or different examples of olfactory encoding.

What is the role of literature in the historical process of mapping out the bodily, olfactory realm? We have, by and large, treated our texts as *reflecting* social changes and norms, as being informed by cultural codes and their shifts, rather than *establishing* such norms and codes themselves. In retrospect, we must ask ourselves to what extent this assumption is tenable.[80] Quite obviously, the great works by well-known writers, all male, have contributed to the cultural coding of olfactory perception. Wherever such perception takes place in the field of eroticism, scents are emanating from the female and are perceived by the male. They occur either, though rarely, as the untampered-with animal, more often, however, as the aestheticized, civilized erotic qua perfume. *Das Parfum* brings this fact to a point. It describes the technical, artisanal process for obtaining the purest, most feminine body odors, so ethereal that their powers of attraction become non–gender specific and cause a universal desire even more basic than sexual, a desire for general unification and, ultimately, in Grenouille's own case, for incorporating and merging subject and object in the communionlike meal.

The traditional triangle of male author, male hero, and female object of perception has shaped structures of fantasy, projection, and desire—not only in the olfactory realm. Its very orientation from male subject toward female object has put pressure for standardization on the female-good quadrant of the olfactory spectrum, on the one hand through enforcing cleanliness, on the other through retaining or recreating the female aura. Toiletries promise to fulfill both these demands, although in our day, with cleanliness taken more or less for granted, the emphasis is clearly on aura, the crucial sales argument in perfume advertising from the male viewpoint. A central, if unacknowledged goal of literature has been to describe, if not to explain, the female mystery, to come to terms with the *Ewig-Weibliche*. The olfactory turns out to be an ideal medium for this project: while it does provide an explanatory model—the model of artificial-good versus natural-bad outlined here—it remains vague enough, in fact provides a smoke screen for, the preservation of the mystery itself, which it leaves as a refuge for fantasy, imagination, and desire. From the female viewpoint,

---

80. The choice of canonical texts (and thereby, with one exception, texts by male authors) now turns out to be a limiting decision. What we have observed is the male formulation of olfactory attraction by the female. What about the reverse? Do heroines by female authors discuss smells and erotic attraction? Christa Wolf's text in the following will provide us with partial answers, but partial only. This is one of the directions in which this study needs expansion.

the project exhibits fittingly complementary aspects: the desire to enhance the mystery and to play on olfactory allure. Again, the most striking examples can be found outside literature in (fragrance) advertising.[81] The overall codification, not only of the *literary* olfactory-erotic, has made inodorous men the "smellers" of odorous females.[82] Grenouille, whose olfactory perception is unsurpassed, is himself odorless and thus represents the epitome of this principle. What has remained—and probably will remain—unclear, is the precise nature of those smells of supreme attraction. In this respect even the best of writers run up against the limits of the olfactory vocabulary. This deficiency is reinforced by a readership largely uneducated in olfactory terms. Unlike passages of visual description of recognized brilliance, unlike purple passages of musical principles of composition underlying a text, the olfactory has no recourse to an established and accepted tradition in literature as yet. This lack is, as it turns out, the olfactory's gain in postmodernism. It is unhampered by literary verbal clichés, free from the need to extricate itself from the hegemony of an existing master discourse. Every instance of olfactory description has a potential of uniqueness and freshness. This is what makes Calvino's textualization of the olfactory in "The Name, the Nose" so impressive.

On the other hand is it precisely for these linguistic and literary-historical reasons that in Süskind as well as in Calvino scents of attraction remain qualitatively largely empty in their olfactory reference. That applies to Dahl, too. Grenouille's scent is characterized as "Aura" (Süskind, 304), as "das Parfum, das vor den Menschen beliebt macht" (305), as "zum Vergöttern gut" (306). The little bottle in his pocket smells "very gently," "ganz zart" (316)—but just *how* it smells we never learn. The Paris nobleman in Calvino's story is in a quandary when it comes to describing the perfume he is searching for: "How can I put into words the languid, fierce sensation" (Calvino, 70), and while he is sampling fragrances, he makes

---

81. Cf. Robert Goldman and John Wilson, "Appearance and Essence: The Commodity Form Revealed in Perfume Advertisement," *Current Perspectives in Social Theory* 4 (1983): 119–42. Theirs is a Marxist critique of perfume advertisement as an example of a commodity form that is usurping social relations as simple transactions; the selling of images rather than an actual product. "Observe that perfume advertisements rarely mention the actual smell given off by the product" (123).

82. This has been clearly changing in recent years in perfumery and perfume advertising as the industry has turned to the male body as a hitherto not fully tapped potential for the application of scents. This blurring of gender boundaries is both postmodern-androgynous and primordial. It is the (unconscious?) confirmation of and play on the anthropological concepts underlying the arguments put forward here.

up similes such as "the rippling cloud" that "had assailed [his] nostrils" as if he were "breathing the soul of a tigress" (70). The most precise description is his exclamation to Madame Odile that the perfume he is looking for is "unlike any of those you mention!" (70) and thereby dismisses cinnamon and musk, verbena and amber, and bergamot as well as bitter-almond, the whole traditional inventory. Their literary rendition does not concretize perfumes for our noses to smell.[83] While this statement is equally true for vision and hearing, these senses have recourse to a conceptual history. Centuries of semiotic training are channeling our imaginative responses. The olfactory, on the other hand, encounters the additional obstacles mentioned above, the lack of history, education, and art in its field and thus also the absence of a technical, abstract vocabulary that could facilitate at least a certain degree of hermeneutic consistency or imaginative response. For modern and postmodern literature, however, it is this sense's very representational imprecision that is made use of as an auratic device.

What, then, are we talking about when we talk about smells? Quite obviously, the linguistic structure of the simile, the most frequently used figure in the designation of smells, based on spatiotemporal or metonymic and associative proximity of tenor and vehicle in the speakers' mind, can be understood psychologically: it is the figure of *displacement* built into the very structure of language. It is a "displacement in good faith"—for there *are* no other ways of referencing smells than those indicating origin, and the evaluative categories of good and bad. At the primordial bottom of those two categories are Eros and Thanatos, two of the strongest forces in the human psychological makeup. Our earlier labeling of good and bad smells as socially determined categories must now be modified, for these categories are hardly arbitrary, but are the product of some of the most ancient developments of the individual's psyche, and constitute his or her share in the collective unconscious.

What, then, are we talking about when we refer to origins in the description of smells? Obviously, we can hardly mean qualities of the object, for our perceptual apparatus for the olfactory is, as is generally acknowledged, poorly equipped for recall. For the same reason, we can hardly rely on subjective impressions either, as they are too erratic to generalize. What we are referring to therefore, is an auratic phenomenon, a halo involving

---

83. A loss of concreteness and immediacy is, of course, unavoidable in the very transmission of reality through language. That is why Barthes's dictum, "écrite, la merde ne sent pas" is, although true, in fact quite trivial.

both subject and object. Paradoxically, this phenomenon is almost purely linguistic, despite its evident lack of terminological grounding, in fact precisely because of it. The connectors in the "smell *like...*" or the "smell *of...*" are the true linguistic places of the olfactory, empty of sensual quality themselves, functional particles, providers of linkage, connections, bonds. They are the empty spaces where the auratic resides, at the intersection of perception and object, memory and subject.[84] The originally postulated shortcoming of language for the olfactory thus turns out to be the true reflection of the liminal and transgressive qualities of that sensory mode. This linguistic place can be filled *ad libidem*—and libidinal factors indeed play an essential role in the perceptual and representational model developed here for the olfactory.

What, then, are we talking about when we talk about smells? Seemingly hardly anything in particular, therefore about almost anything. The study of the olfactory is the study of everything else—but we have made progress toward determining just what the essential components of this "anything" are: Eros and Thanatos, attraction and disgust, emotionally expressive of imagination and desire, psychologically manifest as displacement, and linguistically located in similes. It is the *tertium comparationis* indispensable in olfactory references that each time it occurs rips a triangle into the linear thrust of the sentence, an opening for the imagination, for memory, for projection and desire.

Störfall: "Der Geruch der Hybris"

Christa Wolf's short novel *Störfall* provides a new angle for our investigation.[85] A female narrator created by a female author talks in a first-person narrative about herself, but allows her brother, physically absent from the plot, an almost equally strong presence. Much of her interior monologue is addressed to him. Although fiction, the novel has its central focus on an actual event, the meltdown of one of the Chernobyl reactors in April 1986.

---

84. We can disregard most adjectives that are commonly used to qualify smells as they either belong to other sense modalities (a *sweet* smell, an *acrid* smell) or are from outside the sensory realm altogether.

85. Christa Wolf, *Störfall: Nachrichten eines Tages* (Darmstadt: Luchterhand, 1987).

"Accident: A Day's News" unfolds during one day, and it centers on two main events: the protagonist, an East German writer, hears the news of the Chernobyl nuclear disaster; at the same time, her brother is undergoing an intricate brain-tumor operation. . . . What interests her are not the bare events themselves . . . but how they register on our consciousness and imagination, how the deep intrusions of technology into our existence alter the substance of our world, our very sense [we might add: senses] of what it means to be human, of who and what we are.[86]

What is discussed in this book is the ambivalence of technology. "Chernobyl is clearly an example of technology at its most malignant; the brain-tumor operation—we're told early on it will be successful—might be viewed as science at its most benevolent" (Hoffman). However, even this technological benevolence is not without its price. The surgeon, as the narrator knows, "may have to sacrifice her brother's sense of smell; a small, terrifying choice" (Hoffman). This is indeed what happens.

Taken out of its old nexus with desire and sexuality, the sense of smell is placed into the more general sensory and hermeneutic context of our age where all the senses have become somehow inadequate and should be complemented by new forms of perception. "Sehen hören riechen schmecken tasten—das soll alles sein? Wer glaubt denn sowas. So unempfindlich wird man uns einst doch nicht auf den Weg geschickt haben. Wenn auch das Verlangen nach einem eingearbeiteten Geigerzähler eher anmaßend klingen mag, sogar humoristisch" (21).[87] Technology, "the Faustian urge to know the innermost secrets of nature, and to exercise the power of such knowledge" (Hoffman), has produced an environment beyond the grasp of our five senses. The perceptual inadequacy results from the growing discrepancy between the human sensory apparatus, developed over an *evolutionary* time period, and an environment that has been changing at the pace of *historical* time. Both main events of the novel, the brain-tumor operation as well as Chernobyl are seen against this background. We will not concern ourselves so much with their *factual* aspects, but rather with the *symbolism* that is created in the framework of the story. The world,

---

86. Eva Hoffman, "Post-Chernobyl Blues, East German Style," *New York Times,* 12 April 1989, sec. B. Hers is a review of the American edition of the novel.

87. "Seeing, hearing, smelling, tasting, touching—is that supposed to be all? Who would believe it! We cannot possibly have been sent on our journey so insensitively. Nevertheless, the request for a built-in Geiger counter may sound presumptuous, even humorous."

increasingly *unsinnlich,* beyond the grasp of our senses, is also becoming *unsinnig,* absurd. It "does not make sense" anymore. "Direkt dankbar ist man ja gewesen, wenn man sich etwas bildlich hat vorstellen können," the narrator, speaking of herself and her brother as children, says nostalgically (12).

The responsibility for a world that can no longer be conceptualized on the basis of the information received through our five senses lies, according to the narrator, largely with man's, that is, the male's, unquenchable thirst for knowledge and, above all, its reckless application in new technologies regardless of their inherent dangers. Mankind's Faustian pact with science and technology is represented as the *male* pact with these forces. In this regard the narrator's brother, however close the two characters seem to be, comes in for some implicit criticism. While we learn little about his life and work, he appears to be involved in scientific research himself and to have been affected by the fascination with technology.[88] He also strongly defends basic research, the innate drive for knowledge, which the narrator views with increasing skepticism. "Wer dem spaltbaren Atom auf der Spur sei, als Beispiel, der könne seine Versuche einfach nicht mehr abbrechen.— Wie die Ratten, sagte ich, welche unaufhörlich die 'Lusttaste' drücken" (54).[89] The male thirst for knowledge, regardless of possible applications, has the power almost of a primary drive.

The "Livermore National Laboratory, an der Westküste der USA," the home of the "Starwarriors" (71), represents this abstract male universe most poignantly for the narrator. This is a world of "höchstbegabte sehr junge Männer, die sich—getrieben fürchte ich, von der Hyperaktivität bestimmter Zentren ihres Gehirns—nicht dem Teufel verschrieben haben, ... sondern der Faszination durch ein technisches Problem" (69–70).[90] And this world of minimal sensuous quality—"(es gibt dort keine Frauen, Bruderherz! ...) ... was sie kennen, ist ihre Maschine. ... Ernährung: Erdnußbutterbrote. Hamburgers mit Tomatenketchup. Cola

---

88. Cf. 34–35; his use of a computer for the prediction of emission patterns of industrial chimneys.

89. "Those who are tracking down fissionable atoms, for example, cannot simply abandon their research.—Like the rats, I said, that incessantly press the 'pleasure button.'"

90. It is a world of "brilliant, very young men who have, driven by the hyperactivity of certain brain centers, as I suspect, made a pact not with the devil, ... but with the fascination by a technical problem" (69–70). In their world "(there are no women, my brother! ...) ... what they know is their machinery. ... Food: peanut butter sandwiches. Hamburgers and tomato ketchup. Cola from the fridge" (70–71).

aus dem Kühlschrank" (70–71)—threatens the narrator's world. It exudes the "Geruch der Hybris" (93), the "odor of hubris."

The male universe of growing sensory maladjustment is juxtaposed with a description of the narrator's own world, now endangered, that comes alive in the single day described in the story. The critique is formulated in the narrator's presentation of her world as a counterworld. The binary model of an ecological and feminine versus a technological and male space is in its simplicity probably the weakest aspect of the novel. The feminine appears as the truly sensual, even if desexualized, realm with a biologistic bent, drawn against its will into the maelstrom of an equally desexualized male technology.[91] The female represents a backward utopia, deeply romantic in its outlook and on the defensive against the onslaught of the male. In the female world, the senses function "hedonistically," in a down-to-earth hedonism, different from the—erotic—pleasure seeking of Des Esseintes or Dorian Gray. The narrator's is a world of rich, sensuous experience encountered at every turn as she and we move through her day. From breakfast with the smell of coffee, one of the "haltbaren Genüsse" (14), she goes to work in the garden, barehanded, "mit bloßen Händen" (30) at first, but later putting on gloves and weeding out nettles, "mit den rosa Gummihandschuhen an den Händen" (32). She looks forward to the "Mahlzeiten im Freien" with the "panierten, gebratenen, mit Knoblauch-sauce bestrichenen Zucchinischeiben" (40). It is the young zucchini plants with their "bleichgrünen, zusammengerollten Blättern" (40) that have given her "einen freudigen Schrecken" and made her think of the dinners outdoors in the summer. She feels, all of a sudden, an urge to move, a "Bewegungsdrang" (76) that makes her take out her bicycle and ride it over the fields to the next village. She enjoys the sunset, "dessen ich niemals satt werden kann" (94–95) and performs a whole set of practical activities, feeling the urge to do something "mit den Händen," such as "Brot schneiden. Kräuter hacken" (100). Her day is made up of all kinds of sensory experiences, feelings, and emotions.

---

91. The implied concepts of nature and sexuality strongly resemble those (feminist) designs criticized by Camille Paglia. Nature appears as the romantic, benevolent Rousseauist realm, and sexuality as a lukewarm, tameable, and controllable force as which a broad array of feminist theory has cast them. Accordingly, both forces only need to be subjected to proper social discursive scrutiny and arrangement in order to be kept in check. Paglia disagrees with these notions. See Camille Paglia, *Sexual Personae: Art and Decadence From Nefertiti to Emily Dickinson* (1990; New York: Vintage, 1991), esp. chap. 1.

The sharp contrast between "female" and "male" worldview has its phenomenological base in the exclusive female claim to the realm of the senses. Moreover, it is doubled in the use of language by the two sexes (more about this later), and in addition to that, the real world of the novel is duplicated in the fairy-tale motif of "Brüderchen und Schwesterchen" that underlies the day's events as a symbolic subtext.[92] The physical environment of the two children in the Grimm fairy tale, the woods, where they escape from the violent home of their stepmother, is ecologically damaged by her spell on all the water sources. Schwesterchen's female sensitivity vis-à-vis nature lets her hear the waters murmuring their warning that "wer aus mir trinkt, wird ein Tiger" in the first instance, "ein Wolf" in the second, and finally, "ein Reh" (69). In the first two cases, which would have turned out to be immediately life threatening to herself, little sister succeeds in deterring her brother from drinking; the third time, however, the inevitable happens, and Brüderchen, unable to suppress his thirst any longer, drinks and promptly turns into a deer.

In this tale is mirrored what the real-life strand of the narrative also hints at: the female is in closer touch with nature than the male. It is the female who is able to harness her drives, apparently without suffering too much frustration or damage. Yet ultimately, she is unable to restrain the male from what he wants to do. Both in real life and in the fairy tale, this leads to a catastrophe: Chernobyl in one case, Brüderchen's mutation into a deer in the other. In the fairy tale we are informed—and as for reality, we may draw our own conclusions—that even this does not drive home the message. Brüderchen just *has* to follow his own agenda. He has to go out and expose himself to the dangers of the royal hunt—and naturally is wounded in the process. It is the female again who takes care of him. Schwesterchen "wusch ihm das Blut ab, legte Kräuter auf, und sprach 'geh auf dein Lager, lieb Rehchen, daß du wieder heil wirst'" (71).[93]

It is noteworthy that Brüderchen turns into a little deer, the least masculine and threatening of the mutation options open to him (tiger, wolf), in accordance with the overall desexualization tendency on the discourse level of the text. One notices also the absence of the narrator's husband and the intimate, presumably nonsexual relationship between her and her brother.

---

92. *Kinder und Hausmärchen, gesammelt durch die Brüder Grimm,* vollständige Ausgabe auf der Grundlage der dritten Auflage (1837), ed. Heinz Rölleke (Frankfurt am Main: Deutscher Klassiker Verlag, 1985).

93. Little sister "washed off the blood, put on some herbs and said, 'Have some rest, my dear little deer, so that you may recover fully.'"

If the narrator's world, on the defensive against the oppressive and implicitly destructive male, is indeed meant as a model, it is one of desexualized
gender interaction. The loss of the sense of smell in the male, the elimination of what we have come to understand as an important aspect in the
male "happiness of pursuit," appears as another step in this direction.

In the fairy tale, as we would expect, everything ends well, and the
evildoers, not male, indeed, but rather the usual suspects, the stepmother
and her ugly daughter, are duly punished. This is less clear in reality.
Permanent damage is done, both to the environment and to mankind, by
the male love of risk. "Wieder einmal, so ist es mir vorgekommen, hatte
das Zeitalter sich ein Vorher und Nachher geschaffen" (43). In the fairy
tale, the transition from a before to an after is not irreversible; in reality,
however, it often is. The narrative stance emphasizes the breakup of experience in a before and after from its very opening lines. "Eines Tages, über
den ich in der Gegenwartsform nicht schreiben kann, werden die
Kirschbäume aufgeblüht gewesen sein" (9).[94] This temporal double perspective runs through the narrator's whole experience, for instance, when
she makes coffee in the morning. "Gerüche stärker, bewußter
wahrzunehmen als bisher, ist mir noch nicht eingefallen, noch habe ich
nicht gewußt, daß sie dir verlorengehen werden" (14).

Against the background of the gender-coded account of the senses and
sensibility, the outcome of the brain operation can be understood as the
factual result of an indisputable medical decision on the level of the plot.
That the sense of smell is the first to go is nothing but the reflection of the
longstanding hierarchy of the senses, which the human drive for knowledge, the Faustian pact itself, has brought about in the first place, and in
which the olfactory generally ranks lowest. The outcome of the operation
is thus in accordance with the very type of modern instrumental thinking
dominant at least since the eighteenth-century Enlightenment, which developed the values underlying its decision-making strategies in tandem
with the scientific and technological capabilities that demanded decisions
in the first place. The issue of a sensory hierarchy is explicitly raised and
vision established as "unser Leitsinn" (46).[95] It is made clear to the patient

94. "One day, about which I am unable to write in the present tense, the cherry trees
will have blossomed." The narrator realizes: "It has not yet occurred to me to perceive
smells more intensely, more consciously; I did not know yet that you will lose them" (14).

95. Vision is established as "our guiding sense." The patient is assured that "they
would keep a close watch on the visual nerve, which, unfortunately, runs very close to
the immediate field of operation" (20). The narrator ponders the issue herself: "If one

before the operation that "den Sehnerv, . . . der ja leider in unmittelbarer Nähe des Operationsfeldes verlaufe, würden sie die ganze Zeit über gut unter Kontrolle haben" (20). A little later, the narrator rationalizes for herself, in accordance with established convictions, the loss of the olfactory sense.

> Wenn schon einer der Sinne geopfert werden muß, dann, so würde wohl jedermann reden, der Geruchsinn. Aber den Geschmack habe ich Ihnen erhalten können, wird dein Professor dir sagen, und du wirst nicht erfahren, ob er sich, für dich und an deiner Stelle, in einem bestimmten Augenblick entscheiden mußte, zwischen Riechen und Sehen, zum Beispiel. (51)

Vision is the doctors' first concern as the patient emerges from anesthesia. "Sehen Sie mich? Können Sie mich sehen!" (64) are the urgent questions shouted at him.

A careful reading of this passage reveals contradictory layers of meaning. On the level of plot, the loss of the sense of smell is phrased as a decision among brother scientists (the doctor and his patient) to minimize damage: vision, the most male, the most phallic of the senses, can be saved at the expense of the least male, the least functionally important sense, the olfactory. This interpretation seems to contradict our earlier findings according to which the sense of smell is the male sense par excellence. In this first text by a female author and narrator, a different view surfaces, for an understanding of which we have to look to the discursive level of the text. Here man, at the hands of his own technology, and in accordance with its overall tendencies, loses a sensory capacity, a realm marked as essentially female in this text. The male is explicitly desensitized. He has lost his closeness to nature mediated through the senses, together with a sense of time, a sense of memory. All these sensitivities are female and form the underpinning of the narrator's ecological model, in contrast to the male technological life-style. The outcome of the operation turns out to be the symbolic punishment of man for a long history of intellectual haughtiness toward the senses. The two life-styles are also correlated with two means of expression: the female with language, the male with science as their primary

---

of the senses had to be sacrificed, everybody would argue for the sense of smell. The sense of taste I was able to save, your surgeon will tell you, and you will never know whether at one point he had to make the decision on your behalf between smelling and seeing, for instance" (51).

modes of representation.[96] Phrased in Welsch's terms, the constellation is of the aesthetic (female) space pitted against the an(a)esthetic male realm. This mirrors a deep-seated unease in the German (literary) aesthetic debate that recently surfaced.[97] The female, ecological ideology can be understood as a *Gesinnungsästhetik,* an aesthetics with strong ethical, if not moral or moralist, undertones. The male an(a)esthetic view appears in this model as the true hard-nosed functionalist, modernist aesthetic, if not aestheticism, with its undertones of immorality.[98]

While the poetic punishment meted out against the male, the elimination of his olfactory capacity, is obviously designed to be as light as possible, it cuts considerably deeper than the narrator seems to be aware of, a claim we can safely make after the preceding analysis of olfaction. Dispensing with the sense of smell means the severing of essential roots of sexuality as well as the loss of a general erotic aura, the capability to perceive the magical emanation from the object world. Poetic justice is indeed done, but "the noseless man of the future" will now be largely cut off from the *mémoire involontaire,* from the Proustian moment of recollection; and he will be alienated from a significant component of the eroticism of the natural world, of its attractions, bonds, and links. While this fits in with the general direction of the narrative's discourse, the "un-nosing" of man means the end of what we have shown as underlying recent literary patterns of the olfactory. It spells the end of the "happiness of pursuit." The "noseless man of the future" is on his way to becoming the "faultless monster" that appears in the narrator's dream (119). Increasingly faultless, as the superfluous, distracting, subversive sense of smell is finally eliminated, and man fits ever more easily into his sensorily deprived environment. A mon-

---

96. In a reading different from ours, *Störfall* could be understood as a text in search of a feminine aesthetics with strong roots in sensory-sensual perception and nature, and critical of male parameters. Such an inquiry is beyond the scope of this study, but its undertaking would form the necessary critical counterpart to our own, admittedly male-dominated investigation, and it could have serious implications for the theoretization of the olfactory element in gender relations. For an example in the succession of Süskind, see Ulla Hahn, *Ein Mann im Haus* (Stuttgart: Deutsche Verlags-Anstalt, 1991).

97. See Welsch, *Ästhetisches Denken.* For the debate, cf. footnote 111, below.

98. This often unacknowledged implicit moral valuation in aesthetics underlies, I believe, the striking inability of the ecological and "alternative," "green," movements since the 1970s to produce an alternative aesthetic to the dominant modernist concepts. For many observers the choice has thus remained one of high-tech modernism versus the drab style of "eco-terror" (in the USA recently and with a more comprehensive thematic sweep) labeled as "political correctness."

ster, indeed, in the face of what he has been doing to his environment as well as to his sensory perception of it.

Overall, the function of the senses in Christa Wolf's novel is far less obtrusive than for instance in Huysmans or, of course, Süskind. She treats them at a more basic level. For Huysmans they provide pleasure (or disgust); for Wolf they furnish essential environmental information, including the pleasurable, and warn of dangers. However, what appears to be a more basic conceptualization turns out to be a more modern one, reflecting the ultimate concern of our technologically advanced age. Whereas Huysmans took those basic functions for granted, human development in the hundred years since then, generally hailed as progress, has in fact managed to thoroughly jeopardize this assumption. Our most urgent concern must be—again—with the basic connection of the senses to their rapidly changing environment. In the meantime, of course, the more narrowly aesthetic and hedonistic issues—together with their artistic achievements—cannot simply be brushed aside.

The novel contains two passages that deal with the development of the species and refer to the sense of smell. "Bei niederen Tieren, übrigens, sollen ja Geruchs- und Geschmacksinn 'oft gekoppelt' sein" (51).[99] Although man appears only three seconds before midnight on the evolutionary twenty-four-hour clock, far away from the lower orders of species, this link of smell and taste is still intact, despite the narrator's implications to the contrary. She herself in fact emphasizes the connection when consoling her brother that "bestimmte Biersorten in Zukunft ein bißchen seifig schmecken werden. . . . Auf Bier, Bruder, läßt sich verzichten" (51). A longer passage treats the decreasing importance of the sense of smell since the time "als sich mit dem Aussterben der Reptilien die Säuger ausbreiteten und zu landlebenden Tagtieren wurden" (58). To this day, however, there are even among humans "eine gewisse Anzahl von Individuen, bei

---

99. Following are the translations through the end of this section. "In lower animals, by the way, smell and taste are said to be 'often connected.'" "Certain brands of beer will taste a little soapy in the future . . . Beer, my brother, you can do without" (51). Smell lost its importance "when, following the extinction of the reptiles, the mammals spread and became land-dwelling diurnal animals" (58). Yet among humans there are still "a certain number of individuals for whom . . . smell plays a larger role as a trigger or amplifier of sexual excitement than for others" (58). She is convinced that "[t]he sense of smell, brother, is, if I am not mistaken, one of those senses that are declining. It will take days before you will miss it, on the most banal occasion, when you notice that your aftershave has become inodorous" (59). "The wood strongly smelled of spring. You know that one cannot describe odors." She wishes "that the smell of the wood in spring is firmly rooted in your memory" (79).

denen . . . der Geruch als Auslöser oder Verstärker sexueller Erregung eine größere Rolle spiele als bei anderen" (58). This ancient nexus is due to the fact that the olfactory cortex forms part of one of the older components of the human brain. Yet overall, the narrator is convinced that "der Geruch, Bruder, ist, wenn ich das richtig sehe, einer derjenigen Sinne, die sich auf dem Rückzug befinden. Erst nach Tagen wirst du ihn vermissen, bei dem banalsten Anlaß, wenn dein Rasierwasser geruchlos geworden ist" (59).

Such sketchy anthropological aspects of the olfactory are the least convincing part about that sense. They sound conventional, are scientifically superficial, and create the impression as if they had been lifted straight from an encyclopedia. It is only in conjunction with an outline of human cerebral development that they gain some justification. In the sense of smell is represented the vulnerability of the (male) brain that has guided mankind to the present ambivalent modern technologies on the strength of just one of its capacities, abstract reasoning, while other capacities apparently have lost their importance. On the one hand, those technologies have become a threat to man, their creator; on the other, they keep him alive.

Narratively more convincing are those few concrete instances where, in the dichotomy of the before and after that this April day creates, a retrospective importance is bestowed on olfactory impressions: the narrator's wish to become more aware of smells, for instance of the coffee in the morning; her bike trip, when she notices the smell of the woods. "Der Wald hat stark nach Frühling gerochen. Du weißt, daß man Gerüche nicht beschreiben kann." At the same time she wishes for her brother "daß der Duft des Waldes im Frühling fest in deiner Erinnerung verankert ist" (79). The loss of the sense of smell is the impending loss of memory. The olfactory appears as the sensory sacrifice to intellectual progress.

Science and Language

The olfactory male-female dichotomy observed in earlier analyses from an exclusively male perspective, with its tendency toward erotic encoding, appears in a broader context in *Störfall*. In the dichotomy of the male, functional, technical brain and the female senses and sensory awareness established by the narrator, the brain and its creations are under a "Dauererregung" (36). If deprived, even only temporarily, of problems to solve, those young scientists would "suffer immeasurably," would "maßlos unter ihrer überentwickelten Gehirntätigkeit leiden" (36). The narrator imagines a whole list of "Tätigkeiten, die jene Männer der Wissenschaft und Technik

vermutlich nicht ausüben oder die sie, dazu gezwungen, als Zeitvergeu-
dung ansehen würden" (38).[100] This list contains all the traditionally female
chores from "Säugling trockenlegen, Kochen, einkaufen gehen" to "wi-
schen, bohnern, staubsaugen" as well as "Geschirr abwaschen" or "Lieder
singen" for the children (38). A split of the world in a male and a female
realm is clearly implied.

If, then, the male is understood as abstract, rational brain with technology as its product and infinite progress as its destiny, the female appears
as senses and language as its creation, a language that struggles against the
"Unvermögen[], mit den Fortschritten der Wissenschaft sprachlich Schritt
zu halten" (34). Despite their structurally contrastive use here, language
and science, as the narrator clearly feels and as her brother points out to
her, have a common drive mechanism. In defending scientific research as
intrinsically unstoppable, he turns the tables on her:

> Ob ich denn innehalten könnte. Ob ich nicht mal zu ihm gesagt habe,
> Worte könnten treffen, sogar zerstören wie Projektile; ob ich denn
> immer abzuwägen wisse—immer bereit sei, abzuwägen—, wann meine
> Worte verletzend, vielleicht zerstörend würden? Vor welchem Grad von
> Zerstörung ich zurückschrecken würde? Nicht mehr sagen, was ich
> sagen könnte? Lieber in Schweigen verfallen? Das war der Drehpunkt
> des Tages. (55)[101]

There is radicalism both in language and science; and language as well
as science has a cutting edge, pushing further and further the limits of
what can be said. Science too is unlimited. No research is unimaginable;
"brain growth," "das Wuchern des Gehirns," cannot be stopped (78). The
grasp of language as well as science is aimed at nature, which they approach
with equally comprehensive, if different, claims: appropriation of nature

---

100. Following are the translations of the quotes in this paragraph. The narrator
draws up a list of "activities that the men of science and technology would probably not
care for or, if they were forced to, would consider a waste of time." Such activites are
"diapering the baby, cooking, going shopping . . . mopping, shining the floor, vacuum-
ing . . . doing the dishes . . . singing songs" (38).
101. "Whether I could stop. Whether I had not told him once that words could hurt,
even destroy, like projectiles; whether I was always able to decide—always willing to
decide—when my words were hurting, even destructive? What degree of destruction I
would shy from? No longer say what I could say? Rather fall silent? This was the turning
point of the day."

through a romantic drive for origins in the first case, explanation of nature through relentless intellectual hypothesizing in the second.

As much as *Störfall* is a book about science, represented in the two contrasted central events that are shown to grow out of the same roots, it is also a book about language, which is characterized by the narrator in terms strikingly similar to those her brother uses for science (cf. 54–55). "Wenn eine Spezies einmal mit dem Sprechen begonnen hat, kann sie es nicht mehr aufgeben. Die Sprache gehört nicht zu den Gaben, die man nur versuchsweise, auf Probe, annehmen kann" (99).[102] The distinguishing criterion turns out to be the underlying reality of the senses and the different ways in which language and science are connected with it. Science employs the senses for selective data gathering from the environment; language relies on them as essential modes of individual human existence. The senses form part of its referential texture. It is indeed "merkwürdig, daß A-tom auf griechisch das gleiche heißt wie In-dividuum auf lateinisch: unspaltbar" (35). What turns out to be the greatest threat to mankind, nuclear technology in its various applications, is reflected in language as having the same roots as the highest principle of humanist thinking, the individual. But science has long broken the designatory spell put on matter, and invented nuclear fission. The very individual has become a mere atom, and atoms can be split. Science, even in its beneficial form, divides up the individual on the operation table, saving some of his functions, discarding others. History too has mocked the notion of the individual many times over, in the Shoah, for instance; and language itself, the distinctive criterion of the human species, contains its own negation: Babel (cf. 93–94).[103] Nevertheless, it is in language where all these changes are recorded— together with their historical antecedents, "A-tom," "In-dividuum," and it is in the sensory base underlying language where the plea originates for human existence as indivisible.

In the male-dominated world, science has precedence over language. In fact it leaves its own imprint on language. Thus mothers now make

---

102. "Once a species has begun to speak, it cannot give it up. Language is not one of those gifts that one accepts on a trial basis."

103. "Der Geruch der Hybris" (93), that metaphor applied to the Babel construction site, is not perceived by the senses—just as Chernobyl, another Babylonian project, is not. Yet, the sensory soundness of the metaphor is easily understood when we think of another moment of hubris, the Shoah. This "Geruch" is real and perceptible. In the meantime, however, technology, in all its variants, has made progress. (See also Levi's reference to Babel above in chap. 4.)

efforts, "die neuen Wörter zu lernen. Becquerel. . . . Halbwertszeit, lernen die Mütter heute. Jod 131. Caesium" (34).[104] The meaning of old words is changing too: "Daß wir es 'Wolke' nennen, ist ja nur ein Zeichen unseres Unvermögens, mit den Fortschritten der Wissenschaft sprachlich Schritt zu halten" (34). Literature comes to the rescue of the old meanings of words, such as the "cloud," in Brecht's love poem (61). Language with its historical dimension and its phenomenological basis in sensory reality becomes more and more a means of resisting the increasing atomization of reality into its material and temporal components, as created by science and "progress."

Störfall with its female author and female narrator and protagonist claims language as the female realm, yet includes male voices, from Goethe to Brecht, Frisch, and others, and the story ends on the narrator's nightly reading of Conrad's *Heart of Darkness*. It is literature, both past and present, that emerges as the counterlanguage to the newspeak of science. "Die Physiker fahren fort, in ihrer uns unverständlichen Sprache zu uns zu sprechen" (48–49). There still exists a community where language is used as a bond. But it cannot cut itself off from science and *its* terminology. Chernobyl has the effect that "alles, was ich habe denken und empfinden können, ist über den Rand der Prosa hinausgetreten" (66). Thoughts and feelings have moved beyond prose—into poetry? or drama? or beyond language altogether? Can they be linguistically recaptured? Language, writing, and literature are subject to processes of transformation similar to those Lessing describes for painting in *Emilia Galotti*.[105] "So wie unser Gehirn arbeitet, können wir nicht schreiben" (Wolf, 66) because man or woman conceptualizes not by the brain alone. But for a case like Chernobyl with its "extrasensory" touch, even the phenomenological connection of sensory experience and language is out of joint. The narrator notices in her writing a "Verlust an Unmittelbarkeit, Fülle, Genauigkeit, Schärfe und an

---

104. The mothers have "to learn new words. Becquerel. . . . Half life, the mothers learn today. Iodine 131. Caesium." "That we call it a 'cloud' is only the expression of our impotence to keep up linguistically with scientific progress" (34).

105. Conti, the painter, is talking to the prince after observing his sharply contrasting reactions to the two portraits of Orsina and Emilia: "Ha! daß wir nicht unmittelbar mit den Augen malen! Auf dem langen Wege, aus dem Auge durch den Arm in den Pinsel, wieviel geht da verloren!" For the olfactory, the question of what is *added* on the way from the nose through memory into the pen is even more critical. Memory, emotions, individual imponderabilia would have to be taken into account here. See also C. L. Hart Nibbrig, *Ästhetik: Materialien zu ihrer Geschichte. Ein Lesebuch* (Frankfurt am Main: Suhrkamp, 1978), esp. the introductory essay, 10.

einer Reihe von Qualitäten, die ich nicht benennen kann, vielleicht nicht einmal ahne" (66).[106] Her answer is the maintenance of an ideal of a language that comprises the senses, a language of compassion, a language that thematizes the losses of concrete experience.[107]

The postmodern concepts of language and literature as an endless chain of references among signifiers, a ghetto of signification closed off from phenomenological reality, is questioned in the growing interest in corporeal and sensory issues. At the same time, however, by foregrounding the olfactory as the sense of the (post)modern, the attempt at breaking through to the phenomenological level is in itself undercut by the very choice. The olfactory *is* eclectic, allusive as well as elusive; it *is* episodic, liminal, and indeterminate. Calvino plays all this out with aesthetic lightness, Süskind in the form of a solid, gripping narrative, while Christa Wolf puts it, a little heavy-handedly, into a moral tale, so that occasionally the narrator's anger "turns a bit pat or righteous" (Hoffman), and the lines (e. g., male-female) seem drawn too straight.[108]

Like Huxley and Mynona, Wolf's narrator has her moment of technofantasy. One could, for instance, "menschliche Wesen eine gewisse Zeit lang . . . ein normales . . . Leben führen lassen, mit dem Ziel, ihren Erinnerungsspeicher 'bis zum Rand' zu füllen." After that, they could be used for their special, inhuman jobs "in irgendeiner Apparatur, einer unterirdischen Raketenstation, einem Weltraumschiff. Und ein Spezialist würde sie in den ihnen bekömmlichen Intervallen an den Erinnerungsstrom hängen" (67).[109] When she reads an article on "Die Wissenschaftler von 'Star Wars'"

---

106. She notices a "loss of immediacy, fullness, accuracy, sharpness and a whole number of qualities that I cannot name, maybe am not even aware of."

107. It would require a more detailed study than there is room for here to determine whether this concept of language and literature would necessarily result in a "Gesinnungsästhetik" as discussed by Greiner (cf. footnote 111, below). In any case, Greiner reads *Störfall* as just such a text.

108. This leaves her in disbelief when she hears thet Peter Hagelstein, characterized as the Faustian epitomy, has left the Livermore Laboratories, cutting his ties with "mad" scientific progress. And it also leaves her with the burden of explaining where in her sharply divided world of female/the senses and male/the intellect he should now go. Indeed, she must "erneut über die Schicksale und Entscheidungen des modernen Faust nachdenken" (102).

109. Following are the translations for this paragraph. One could "let human beings lead a normal life for a while, with the intent of filling their memory 'to the brim.'" Then send them to their jobs "in some kind of machinery, a subterranean rocket base, a space ship. A specialist would connect them at appropriate intervals to their memory flow" (67). The author realizes that the fantasies "that I had not allowed myself had long been surpassed by reality" (70).

(67) she realizes that her fantasies, "die ich mir vorhin verboten hatte, schon längst von der Wirklichkeit überholt worden waren" (70). Those scientists do live that very life of sensory and emotional deprivation that she would never have permitted herself to let on, even as a fantasy, if she had suspected that it could be realized.

Language and writing are problematic, for "was heißt denn das, was kann irgendeine, auch die gelungenste Formulierung überhaupt noch heißen, soviel ist schon geredet und geschrieben worden" (108). In writing itself, as her brother has pointed out, "im Wesen des Lasters Schreiben," lies an urgency that disregards consideration, "Rücksichten," so that "der eingreifende Schreibvorgang ... doch auch immer Menschen mit greift, Personen, die durch die Beschreibung zu Betroffenen werden" (109).[110] The narrator, realizing the destructive force of writing in a manner analogous to the destructiveness of science, wonders whether "Schreib-Lust und Zerstörung" (109) have to be coupled. Writing, literature, is a "historical science" that reflects on its own doings and consequences. This is its purpose as the narrator of *Störfall* understands it.[111]

Back to the Future

Wolf's novel reverses the male-female olfactory relations encountered and discussed before. This reverse perspective, however, is not one of female smelling male, as one might expect, but of the scientific male being made anosmic at the hands of the literary female. This finding should caution us against considering this chapter a neat closure to our inquiry, for it clearly implies that the analysis of women's writing about female heroines will most likely not produce a simple conceptual complement to the findings

---

110. "The engaged process of writing ... infallibly draws in humans, persons who become victims through their being described."

111. Harsh criticism of *Störfall* is raised by Ulrich Greiner in connection with Christa Wolf's most recent book, *Was bleibt*, which has triggered a heated debate about moral and aesthetic positions in the German literary landscape after unification. Greiner calls *Störfall* "der pure Gesinnungskitsch" and goes on to say: "Da hat es eine Autorin verstanden, diese deutsche Mischung aus Leidenslust, Unheilserwartung und Trostbedürfnis in eine ansprechende Form zu bringen, gegen die man einfach nichts haben kann." Ulrich Greiner, "Die deutsche Gesinnungsästhetik," *Die Zeit*, 9 November 1990, 15f. Greiner, in agreement with Frank Schirrmacher, whom he quotes, sees the connection of "Ästhetik" and "Gesinnung," the "Vernunftsehe" between "Literatur und Moral" (15) as a characteristic feature of German post–World War II literature—indeed in both German states.

and theories put forward here on the basis of samples by male authors writing about male heroes. Although the "noseless man of the future" is as much Wolf's prognosis as it is Calvino's, it is so for different reasons. In any case, the *Jahrhundert des Geruchs,* proclaimed so self-assuredly by the producers of scents, appears from the viewpoint of the literary establishment a much more doubtful concept. But even so, in their loss, smells have become a literary topic of our time, as much as they are a topic of the world of science and technology and of business. The literary as well as some nonliterary manifestations have one element in common, an interest in mysticism and insights that are neither religious nor open to rational inquiry, a craving for a *demimonde* between the hard facts of life and their scientific interpretation on the one hand and pure creaturely, sensual enjoyment on the other; a *demimonde* above all between momentary experience and lasting, if often unconscious, effects. The olfactory, in a mechanism called the "Syndrome de Proust,"[112] can reach this in-between world. Perfumes, the one olfactory manifestation most talked about outside literature, provide just that. They are the soft-focus lense on our rough daily existence. They are the invisible, user-friendly interface in daily human interaction. They are sheer present—yet we have unearthed their primordial past. They seem pure phenomenon—yet they contain memory, erratic and unpredictable. And although they seem to lend themselves so well to the game of pure simulation, they do have dark and uncanny origins.

The surfacing of smells in postmodernism or better, the sustained interest in them since modernism, is not accidental. We established the olfactory as the sense of the modern, but it is postmodernism that brings out fully its potentials. In the former mind-set, on one side of the "great divide," the appeal to and through the olfactory was caused by an existential quest; in the latter, it is playful deliberateness, a game, precisely, on the former strictures of manifestation. Smells are eclectic, random, individual. They are historical only on a strictly personal level, thus anecdotal. Beyond that, they dip immediately into the anthropological abyss, skipping history at large, so that their account can always only be given obliquely, through investigations other than olfactory ones. They are unsystematic, yet basically simple in their structure as we have shown. In philosophical terms, it should not surprise us that Nietzsche, that most nonsystematic thinker whose oeuvre is wholly attached to his personal experience, has had such keen a nose for the olfactory in his day as the mottos for our chapters show.

---

112. Trygg Engen, "La mémoire des odeurs," *La Recherche,* February 1989, 170.

And it is no surprise either that Nietzsche, the critic of modernism *avant la lettre,* is enjoying increased attention at present. There is something postmodern about him, from the high-low dichotomy in the *Genealogy of Morals* to the mythical tone of *Zarathustra.*

It is the producers of scents, though, more than literary authors, that are truly optimistic, and hustling and bustling about fragrance. To wit, the "Fragrance Week in New York, June 5–June 9, 1989."[113] It is a marketing ploy, to be sure, but full of verve and creativity. "Nostalgic sensory events, exhibitions, demonstrations and fragrant surprises will take place each day throughout the week from Noon to 2 P.M." Individual happenings have fancy titles such as "Memories of Love," "Smell of the Future," "Fragrant Jewels," and "Childhood Memories," themes which by now, I hope, have acquired a familiar ring or, better, aroma.

Smells have come a long way. The "noseless man of the future"? On the contrary, it seems that the nose in the years ahead is well provided for.

Looking back on our inquiry I see five main components that went into its makeup. First, there are sociohistorical and cultural developments. Their sum total can be called the process of civilization. Of these developments and this process we retraced a stretch roughly spanning the past 150 years, and we emphasized aspects of progress and enlightenment.

Second, and in connection with the above, there developed a heightened sensitivity and sensibility, a sentimentality, and a penchant toward emotions and their expression, together with the new scientific tool for dealing with them: psychology, specifically psychoanalysis. I call these aspects the cultural and historical software, as opposed to the hardware, such as, among other things, sanitation, indoors plumbing, sewage treatment, cleaning, disinfecting, and pasteurizing.

Third: against the background of these two developments became visible a phenomenon that remains historically unchanged during the time period considered. Emerging as an anthropological constant, as the dark bottom layer of our inquiry, the insoluble connections of smells with the sexual and erotic and with death were brought to light.

Fourth: our main investigation unfolded around the developments and changes outlined in points one and two, bearing in mind the submerged anthropological links mentioned in three, and discussed these phenomena in their textual, specifically literary form. At this level aesthetic, linguistic,

---

113. *New York Times,* 5 June 1989, sec. A.

347

and semiotic issues become central; questions of literary technique, of literary representation; the problem of literature as reflecting versus shaping reality. While we looked at individual authors and specific works, we were in this main thrust of our research connecting findings diachronically: we were writing a literary history, the narrative of the olfactory in its textual manifestations. The ties of this history are particularly close to the second point, above. The tale goes something like this: there occurs an increase in the use of olfactory instances in a more and more self-conscious aesthetic milieu, countered by a decrease—yet never the complete disappearance—of the simple mimetic-realist or naturalist mode of using smells. The history has national chapters and confirms or modifies traditional literary epochal divisions. It also shows correlations with genre and reflects geographical patterns. On the level of individual authors and texts it provides fresh viewpoints on phenomenological issues and strategies of texts.

Two further strands of inquiry, fascinating in their own right but rather subsidiary to the main thrust of our inquiry, consist, first, in the strictly scientific, physiological, neurological, and medical approaches that form part of the civilizing process and are tied to the development of the psychoanalytic discourse. And second, there is the history of perfumery or, more broadly speaking, the industrial production of artificial fragrances and flavors. This is a hardware strand of increasing importance—and increasingly recognized in its importance. As for perfume: perfume provides its own fascinating cultural and semiotic sideshow in advertising.

These strands combined weave the complex olfactory tapestry that has been unrolling since the beginning of cultured humankind, with some threads stretching even further back into primordial times. This inquiry, I hope, has produced a loose warp so far, and filled in the woof in a number of exemplary instances. The text thus created is still threadbare and in need of work. A lot remains to be done.

Bibliography

Ackerman, Diane. *A Natural History of the Senses.* New York: Random House, 1990.

Adorno, Theodor W. *Gesammelte Schriften.* Ed. Rolf Tiedemann. 20 vols. Frankfurt am Main: Suhrkamp, 1970.

———. *Aesthetic Theory.* Trans. C. Lenhardt. Ed. Gretel Adorno and Rolf Tiedemann. London: Routledge & Kegan Paul, 1984.

Airkem Inc. *Odors and the Sense of Smell: A Bibliography 320 BC–1947.* New York: Airkem, 1952.

Allport, Floyd H. *Theories of Perception and the Concept of Structure: A Review and Critical Analysis with an Introduction to a Dynamic-Structural Theory of Behavior.* New York: John Wiley and Sons, 1955.

Apollinaire, Guillaume. *Calligrammes: Poèmes de la paix et de la guerre (1913–1916).* Paris: Gallimard, 1925.

Ash, Mitchell G., and W. R. Woodward, eds. *The Problematic Science: Psychology in Nineteenth-Century Thought.* New York: Praeger, 1982.

———. *Psychology in Twentieth-Century Thought and Society.* Cambridge: Cambridge University Press, 1987.

Atwood, Margaret. *The Handmaid's Tale.* 1985. New York: Ballantine Books, 1987.

Auerbach, Erich. *Mimesis: Dargestellte Wirklichkeit in der abendländischen Literatur.* Bern: Francke, 1946.

Augustine, Saint. *Confessions.* Trans. R. S. Pine-Coffin. Penguin Classics. Harmondsworth: Penguin, 1961.

Baggesen, Jens. *Das Labyrinth oder Reise durch Deutschland in die Schweiz 1789.* Ed. and trans. Gisela Perlet. Leipzig: Gustav Kiepenheuer, 1985. Munich: Beck, 1986.

Barthes, Roland. *Sade, Fourier, Loyola.* Collection Tel Quel. Paris: Edition du Seuil, 1971.

Baudelaire, Charles. *Les Fleurs du Mal.* Ed. Edouard Maynial. Paris: Société des belles lettres, 1952.

Baudrillard, Jean. *Simulations.* Trans. Paul Foss, Paul Patton, and Philip Beitchman. New York: Semiotext(e), 1983.

Bauer, Arnold. *Rudolf Virchow—der politische Arzt*. Preußische Köpfe. Berlin: Stapp, 1982.

Baumgarten, A. G. *Texte zur Grundlegung der Ästhetik*. Ed. and trans. Hans Rudolf Schweizer. Hamburg: Felix Meiner, 1983.

Bayerl, Günter. "Herrn Pfisters und anderer Leute Mühlen: Das Verhältnis von Mensch, Technik und Umwelt im Spiegel eines literarischen Topos." In *Technik in der Literatur: Ein Forschungsüberblick und zwölf Aufsätze*, ed. Harro Segeberg, 51–101. Frankfurt am Main: Suhrkamp, 1987.

Bechtold, Gerhard. *Sinnliche Wahrnehmung von sozialer Wirklichkeit: Die multimedialen Montage-Texte Alexander Kluges*. Tübingen: Gunter Narr, 1983.

Beckmann, Johann. *A History of Inventions and Discoveries*. 4th ed. Trans. William Johnston. 3 vols. London, 1817.

Benedum, Jost. "Das Riechorgan in der antiken und mittelalterlichen Hirnforschung und die Rezeption durch S. Th. Soemmerring." In *Gehirn—Nerven—Seele: Anatomie und Physiologie im Umfeld S. T. Soemmerrings*, ed. Gunter Mann und Franz Dumont, 11–54. Stuttgart: Gustav Fischer, 1988.

Benjamin, Walter. *Gesammelte Schriften*. Ed. Rolf Tiedemann and Hermann Schweppenhäuser. 6 vols. Frankfurt am Main: Suhrkamp, 1972–.

———. "Das Kunstwerk im Zeitalter seiner technischen Reproduzierbarkeit." Vol. 1 of *Schriften*. Ed. Th. W. Adorno and Gretel Adorno with Friedrich Podszus. Frankfurt am Main: Suhrkamp, 1955.

———. "Paris, die Hauptstadt des XIX. Jahrhunderts." Vol. 1 of *Schriften*. Ed. Th. W. Adorno and Gretel Adorno with Friedrich Podszus. Frankfurt am Main: Suhrkamp, 1955.

———. "Über einige Motive bei Baudelaire." Vol. 1 of *Schriften*. Ed. Th. W. Adorno and Gretel Adorno with Friedrich Podszus. Frankfurt am Main: Suhrkamp, 1955.

Bense, Max. *Aesthetica: Eine Einführung in die neue Ästhetik*. 2d ed. Baden-Baden: Agis, 1982.

———. *Semiotische Prozesse und Systeme in Wissenschaftstheorie und Design, Ästhetik und Mathematik*. Baden-Baden: Agis, 1975.

Bentele, Günter, and Ivan Bystrina. *Semiotik: Grundlagen und Probleme*. Stuttgart: Kohlhammer, 1978.

Bergson, Henri. *Oeuvres*. 3d ed. 1959. Annotated André Robinet. Paris: Presses Universitaires de France, 1970.

Berlin, Brent, and Paul Kay. *Basic Color Terms: Their Universality and Evolution*. Berkeley and Los Angeles: University of California Press, 1969.

Berlin, Isaiah. *Russian Thinkers*. Ed. Henry Hardy and Aileen Kelly. Harmondsworth: Penguin, 1978.

Berman, Russell A. *The Rise of the Modern German Novel: Crisis and Charisma*. Cambridge: Harvard University Press, 1986.

Bernard, Léopold. *Les Odeurs dans les Romans de Zola.* Conférence faite au cercle artistique. Montpellier: Camille Coulet, 1889.

Bernheimer, Charles. "Of Whores and Sewers: Parent-Duchâtelet, Engineer of Abjection." *Raritan* 6, no. 3 (1987): 72–90.

Best, Otto F., ed. *Theorie des Expressionismus.* Stuttgart: Reclam, 1976.

Bezwinska, Jadwiga, ed. *KL Auschwitz Seen by the SS: Höss, Broad, Kremer.* New York: Howard Fertig, 1984.

Bloch, Ivan. *The Sexual Life of Our Time in Its Relation to Modern Civilization.* Trans. M. Eden Paul. 1908. New York: Allied, 1926.

Blonsky, Marshall, ed. *On Signs.* Baltimore: Johns Hopkins University Press, 1985.

Bohrer, Karl Heinz. *Die Ästhetik des Schreckens: Die pessimistische Romantik und Ernst Jüngers Frühwerk.* Munich: Hanser, 1978.

Boring, Edward G. *A History of Experimental Psychology.* New York: Century, 1929.

———. *Sensations and Perception in the History of Experimental Psychology.* New York: Appleton-Century-Crofts, 1942.

Bourke, John G. *Scatological Rites of All Nations.* 1891. New York: Johnson Reprint Corporation, 1968.

Boyle, Nicholas, and Martin Swales, eds. *Realism in European Literature: Essays in Honour of J. B. Stern.* Cambridge: Cambridge University Press, 1986.

Brecht, Walter. *Heinse und der ästhetische Immoralismus: Zur Geschichte der italienischen Renaissance in Deutschland.* Berlin: Weidmannsche Buchhandlung, 1911.

Brentano, Clemens. *Werke.* Ed. Friedhelm Kemp. Darmstadt: Wissenschaftliche Buchgesellschaft; Munich: Hanser, 1963–68.

Brentano, Franz. *Untersuchungen zur Sinnesphysiologie.* Ed. Roderick M. Chisholm and Reinhard Fabian. 1907. Hamburg: Felix Meiner, 1979.

Brockhaus Enzyklopädie in zwanzig Bänden. 17th rev. ed. Wiesbaden: F. A. Brockhaus, 1966–74.

Brown, Norman O. *Life against Death: The Psychoanalytical Meaning of History.* New York: Vintage, 1959.

———. *Love's Body.* New York: Random House, 1966.

Bucher, Max, Werner Hahl, Georg Jäger, and Reinhard Wittmann, eds. *Realismus und Gründerzeit: Manifeste und Dokumente zur deutschen Literatur 1848–1880.* 2 vols. Stuttgart: Metzler, 1975–76.

Büchner, Ludwig. *Kraft und Stoff: Oder Grundzüge der natürlichen Weltordnung.* 1855. Leipzig: T. Thomas, 1904.

Buffon, Georges Louis Leclerc, Comte de. *De l' homme.* Ed. Michèle Duchet. Paris: François Maspero, 1971.

Bunin, Ivan. "Apple Fragrance" ("Antonovski Jabloki"). In *Shadowed Paths,* trans. Olga Schartse, ed. Philippa Mentges, 7–37. Moscow: Foreign Languages Publishing House, n.d.

Bürger, Peter. *Theorie der Avantgarde.* Frankfurt am Main: Suhrkamp, 1974.

Bürger, Christa, and Peter Bürger, eds. *Die Postmoderne: Alltag, Allegorie und Avantgarde*. Frankfurt am Main: Suhrkamp, 1987.

Bürger, Peter, Christa Bürger, and Jochen Schulte-Sasse, eds. *Naturalismus/ Ästhetizismus*. Frankfurt am Main: Suhrkamp, 1979.

Busse, Klaus-Peter, and Hartmut Riemenschneider. *Grundlagen semiotischer Ästhetik*. Düsseldorf: Pädagogischer Verlag Schwann, 1979.

Calvino, Italo. *Under the Jaguar Sun*. Trans. William Weaver. New York: Harcourt, 1988.

Canetti, Elias. *Masse und Macht*. 1960. 2 vols. Munich: Hanser, 1976.

Cargo, Robert T., ed. *A Concordance to Baudelaire's "Les Fleurs du Mal."* Chapel Hill: University of North Carolina Press, 1965.

Carterette, Edward C., and Morton P. Friedman, eds. *Tasting and Smelling*. Vol. 6A of *Handbook of Perception*. New York: Academic Press, 1978.

Chadwick, Edwin. *Report to Her Majesty's Principal Secretary of State for the Home Department from the Poor Law Commission on an Inquiry into the Sanitary Condition of the Labouring Population of Great Britain*. London, 1842. Ed. M. W. Flinn. Edinburgh: Edinburgh University Press. 1965.

Chefdor, Monique, Ricardo Quinones, and Albert Wachtel eds. *Modernism: Challenges and Perspectives*. Urbana: University of Illinois Press, 1986.

Chekhov, Anton. *The Stories of Chekhov*. Ed. Robert N. Linscott. New York: Modern Library, 1923

Cixous, Hélène, and Catherine Clément. *The Newly Born Woman*. Trans. Betsy Wing. 1975. Minneapolis: University of Minnesota Press, 1986.

Clifford, Frank S. *A Romance of Perfume Lands*. Boston, 1881.

Condillac, Etienne Bonnot de. *Essai sur l'origine des connaissances humaines*. Etabli et annoté Charles Porset. Paris: Galilée, 1973.

Copley, Frank O., trans. and introd. *The Nature of Things*, by Lucretius. New York: Norton, 1977.

Corbin, Alain. *Le miasme et la jonquille: L'odorat et l'imaginaire social XVIIIe–XIXe siècles*. Paris: Aubier Montaigne, 1982.

Coren, Stanley, and Lawrence M. Ward. *Sensation and Perception*. 3d ed., 1984. San Diego: Harcourt, 1989.

Cornford, Francis. M. *Plato's Cosmology: The "Timaeus" of Plato with a Running Commentary*. 1937. London: Routledge and Kegan Paul, 1956.

Cox, Gary. *Crime and Punishment: A Mind to Murder*. Boston: Twayne, 1990.

Dahl, Roald. *Switch Bitch*. 1974?. New York: Ballantine Books, 1983.

Demetz, Peter. "Formen des Realismus: Theodor Fontane. Kritische Untersuchungen." In *Theodor Fontane*, ed. Wolfgang Preisendanz. Wege der Forschung, vol. 381. Darmstadt: Wissenschaftliche Buchgesellschaft, 1973.

Denkler, Horst. "Die Antwort literarischer Phantasie auf eine der 'größern Fragen der Zeit': Zu Wilhelm Raabes Erzähltext 'Pfisters Mühle.'" In *Wilhelm Raabe:*

Studien zu seinem Leben und Werk, ed. Leo A. Lensing and Hans-Werner Peter, 234–54. Braunschweig: pp-Verlag, 1981.

———, ed. *Romane und Erzählungen des bürgerlichen Realismus*. Stuttgart: Reclam, 1980.

———. *Wilhelm Raabe. Legende—Leben—Literatur*. Tübingen: Niemeyer, 1989.

Dessoir, Max. *Ästhetik und allgemeine Kunstwissenschaft in den Grundzügen dargestellt*. Stuttgart: F. Enke, 1906.

Dietze, Walter. *Junges Deutschland und deutsche Klassik: Zur Ästhetik und Literaturtheorie des Vormärz*. 1957. Berlin: Rütten and Loening, 1962.

Ditfurth, Hoimar von. *Der Geist fiel nicht vom Himmel: Die Evolution unseres Bewusstseins*. Hamburg: Hoffmann and Campe, 1976.

Dostoevsky, Fyodor. *The Brothers Karamazov*. Ed. Ralph E. Matlaw, trans. Constance Garnett. A Norton Critical Edition. New York: Norton, 1976.

———. *Crime and Punishment*. Ed. George Gibian, trans. Jessie Coulson. A Norton Critical Edition. New York: Norton, 1975.

Dostoievsky F. M. *The Diary of a Writer*. Trans. Boris Brasol. Santa Barbara: Peregrine Smith, 1979.

Douglas, Mary. *Purity and Danger: An Analysis of Concepts of Pollution and Taboo*. London: Routledge and Kegan Paul, 1966.

Dragstra, Rolf. "Der witternde Prophet: Über die Feinsinnigkeit der Nase." In *Das Schwinden der Sinne*, ed. Dieter Kamper and Christoph Wulf. Frankfurt am Main: Suhrkamp, 1984.

Dundes, Alan. *Life Is a Chicken Coop Ladder: A Portrait of German Culture through Folklore*. New York: Columbia University Press, 1984.

Dyos, H. J., and Michael Wolff. *The Victorian City: Images and Realities*. 2 vols. London: Routledge and Kegan Paul, 1973.

Eagleton, Terry. *Criticism and Ideology: A Study in Marxist Literary Theory*. London: NLB, 1976.

———. "The Ideology of the Aesthetic." *Times Literary Supplement* 22 January 1988, 84 +.

———. *The Ideology of the Aesthetic*. Oxford: Basil Blackwell, 1990.

Ebbinghaus, Hermann. *Memory: A Contribution to Experimental Psychology*. Leipzig, 1885. New York: Dover, 1964.

Eckardt, Wolf von, Sander Gilman, and J. Edward Chamberlin. *Oscar Wilde's London: A Scrapbook of Vices and Virtues, 1880–1900*. New York: Doubleday, 1987.

Elias, Norbert. *Über den Prozess der Zivilisation: Soziogenetische und Psychogenetische Untersuchungen*. 2d ed. 1936. 2 vols. Bern: Francke, 1969.

Ellis, Havelock. *The Psychology of Sex: A Manual for Students*. New York: Emerson Books, 1935.

———. *Sexual Selection in Man*. Philadelphia: F. A. Davis, 1905.

Engelsing, Rolf. *Analphabetentum und Lektüre: Zur Sozialgeschichte des Lesers in*

Deutschland zwischen feudaler und industrieller Gesellschaft. Stuttgart: Metzler, 1973.

Engen, Trygg. "La mémoire des odeurs." *La Recherche,* February 1989, 170–77.

———. *Odor Perception and Memory.* New York: Praeger, 1991.

———. *The Perception of Odors.* Academic Press Series in Cognition and Perception. New York: Academic Press, 1982.

Erman, Adolf. *The Ancient Egyptians: A Sourcebook of Their Writings.* Trans. Aylward M. Blackman. New York: Harper and Row, 1966.

Evans, Richard J. *Death in Hamburg: Society and Politics in the Cholera Years, 1830–1910.* Oxford: Oxford University Press, 1987.

Fenaux, Jean-Paul. "Spleen et Idéal: Lexique et Thématique." In *Analyse et Réflexions sur Baudelaire "Spleen et Idéal."* Paris: Edition Marketing, 1984.

Fetzer, John F. *Romantic Orpheus: Profiles of Clemens Brentano.* Berkeley and Los Angeles: University of California Press, 1974.

Fischer, Jens Malte. *Fin de siècle: Kommentar zu einer Epoche.* Munich: Winkler, 1978.

Fliess, Wilhelm. *Die Beziehungen zwischen Nase und weiblichen Geschlechtsorganen in ihrer biologischen Bedeutung dargestellt.* Leipzig: Franz Deuticke, 1897.

Fontane, Theodor. *Effi Briest.* Vol. 4 of *Sämtliche Werke.* Ed. Walter Keitel. Munich: Hanser, 1962–.

———. *Frau Jenny Treibel.* Vol. 4 of *Sämtliche Werke.* Ed. Walter Keitel. Munich: Hanser, 1962–.

Forster, Elborg, trans. *A Woman's Life in the Court of the Sun King: Letters of Liselotte von der Pfalz, 1652–1722, Elizabeth Charlotte, Duchesse d'Orléans.* Baltimore: Johns Hopkins University Press, 1984.

Foucault, Michel. *Discipline and Punish: The Birth of the Prison.* Trans. Alan Sheridan. New York: Vintage, 1979.

Freud, Sigmund. "Das Unbehagen in der Kultur." Vol. 14 of *Gesammelte Werke: Chronologisch geordnet.* Ed. Anna Freud et al. 1948. London: Imago, 1955.

———. "Die 'kulturelle' Sexualmoral und die moderne Nervosität." Vol. 7 of *Gesammelte Werke: Chronologisch geordnet.* Ed. Anna Freud et al. 1948. London: Imago, 1955.

Freytag, Gustav. *Soll und Haben.* Leipzig, 1855. Munich: Hanser, 1977.

Friedell, Egon. *Kulturgeschichte der Neuzeit.* 3 vols. Munich: Beck, 1927–31.

Garland, Henry and Mary. *The Oxford Companion to German Literature.* Oxford: Clarendon, 1976.

Gay, Peter. *The Bourgeois Experience: Victoria to Freud.* 2 vols. Oxford: Oxford University Press, 1984–86.

———. *Freud: A Life for Our Time.* New York: Norton, 1988.

Geertz, Clifford. *The Interpretation of Cultures: Selected Essays.* New York: Basic Books, 1973.

George, Stefan. *Werke: Ausgabe in zwei Bänden.* Munich: Helmut Küpper, 1958.

Gervinus, G. G. *Geschichte der deutschen Dichtung.* 5 vols. Leipzig: Engelmann Verlag, 1871–74.

———. *Geschichte der poetischen Nationalliteratur der Deutschen.* Leipzig, 1835–42.

———. *Leben: Von ihm selbst.* Leipzig: Engelmann, 1893.

———. *Schriften zur Literatur.* East Berlin: Aufbau-Verlag, 1962.

Gibbons, Boyd. "The Intimate Sense of Smell." *National Geographic Magazine,* September 1986, 324–61.

Gitlin, Todd. "Hip-Deep in Post-modernism." *New York Times Book Review,* 6 November 1988: 1+.

The Givaudan-Index. 1949. New York: Givaudan-Delawanna, 1962.

Godefroid, Susanne, et al. *Bürgerliche Ideologie und Bildungspolitik: Das Bildungswesen in Preußen vom Ausgang des 18. Jahrhunderts bis zur bürgerlichen Revolution 1848/49. Eine historisch-materialistische Analyse seiner Entstehungsbedingungen.* Edition 2000. Theorie und praktische Kritik 14. Giessen: Andreas Achenbach, 1974.

Gogol, Nikolai. *Dead Souls.* Trans. David Magarshack. Penguin Classics. Harmondsworth: Penguin, 1961.

Goldman, Robert, and John Wilson. "Appearance and Essence: The Commodity Form Revealed in Perfume Advertisement." *Current Perspectives in Social Theory* 4 (1983): 119–42.

Greenberg, Valerie. "The Resistance of Effi Briest: An (Un)told Tale." *PMLA* 106, no. 5 (1988): 770–82.

Greiner, Ulrich. "Die deutsche Gesinnungsästhetik." *Die Zeit,* 9 November 1990.

Grimm, Brüder. *Kinder und Hausmärchen, gesammelt durch die Brüder Grimm.* Vollständige Ausgabe auf der Grundlage der dritten Auflage (1837). Ed. Heinz Rölleke. Frankfurt am Main: Deutscher Klassiker Verlag, 1985.

Grimmelshausen, Hans Jakob Christopher von. *Der abenteuerliche Simplicissimus.* 1668. Munich: Winkler, 1956.

Gutzkow, Karl. *Wally, die Zweiflerin.* Ed. Walther Killy. Texte des 19. Jahrhunderts. Göttingen: Vandenhoeck and Ruprecht, 1965.

Habermas, Jürgen. *Strukturwandel der Öffentlichkeit. Untersuchungen zu einer Kategorie der bürgerlichen Gesellschaft.* Neuwied: Luchterhand, 1962.

Hage, Volker, ed. *Deutsche Literatur: Ein Jahresüberblick.* 9 vols. to date. Stuttgart: Reclam, 1982–.

Hahn, Ulla. *Ein Mann im Haus.* Stuttgart: Deutsche Verlags-Anstalt, 1991.

Hanson, Lawrence and Elizabeth. *Verlaine: Fool of God.* New York: Random House, 1957.

Harris, John. "Oral and Olfactory Art." *Journal of Aesthetic Education* 13, no. 4 (1979): 5–15.

Hart, Gail K. "The Functions of Fiction: Imagination and Socialization in Both Versions of Keller's *Der grüne Heinrich.*" *German Quarterly* 59, no. 4 (1986): 595–610.

Hart Nibbrig, Christiaan L. *Ästhetik: Materialien zu ihrer Geschichte. Ein Lesebuch.* Frankfurt am Main: Suhrkamp, 1978.

———. *Ästhetik der letzten Dinge.* Frankfurt am Main: Suhrkamp, 1989.

Hauff, Wilhelm. *Sämtliche Werke.* Ed. Sibylle v. Steinsdorff. 3 vols. Munich: Winkler, 1970.

Hauptmann, Gerhart. *Das gesammelte Werk. Ausgabe letzter Hand. Zum 80. Geburtstag des Dichters am 15. November 1942.* 17 vols. Berlin: Suhrkamp, 1943.

Hegel, G. F. W. *Ästhetik.* Ed. Friedrich Bassenge. 2 vols. Berlin: Das europäische Buch, 1985.

———. *Gesammelte Werke.* Ed. Westfälische Akademie der Wissenschaften. Hamburg: Felix Meiner, 1968–.

Heinse, J. J. Wilhelm. *Ardinghello und Die glückseligen Inseln.* Kritische Studienausgabe. Ed. Max L. Baeumer. 1787. Stuttgart: Reclam, 1975.

Hielscher, Martin. *Wolfgang Koeppen.* Beck'sche Reihe Autorenbücher. Munich: Beck, 1988.

Hildesheimer, Wolfgang. *Tynset.* Frankfurt am Main: Suhrkamp, 1965.

Himmelfarb, Gertrude. *The Idea of Poverty: England in the Early Industrial Age.* New York: Knopf, 1984.

Hoffmann-Axthelm, Dieter. *Sinnesarbeit: Nachdenken über Wahrnehmung.* Frankfurt am Main and New York: Campus Verlag, 1984.

Hofmannsthal, Hugo von. *Sämtliche Werke: Kritische Ausgabe,* veranstaltet vom freien deutschen Hochstift. Ed. Rudolf Hirsch, Clemens Köttelwesch, Heinz Rölleke, and Ernst Zinn. 38 vols. Frankfurt am Main: S. Fischer, 1975–87.

Hohendahl, Peter Uwe. *Literarische Kultur im Zeitalter des Liberalismus 1830–1870.* Munich: Beck, 1985.

Horkheimer, Max and Theodor W. Adorno. *Dialektik der Aufklärung: Philosophische Fragmente.* 1947. Frankfurt am Main: Fischer, 1984.

Howes, David. "Olfaction and Transition: An Essay on the Ritual Uses of Smell." *Canadian Review of Sociology and Anthropology* 24 (1987): 398–416.

Hugo, Victor. *Les Misérables.* Trans. Lee Fahnstock and Norman MacAfee, based on the C. E. Wilbur translation. New York: New American Library, 1987.

Huxley, Aldous. *Brave New World.* New York: Harper and Row, 1969.

Huysmans, J. K. *Against the Grain (A Rebours).* New York: Dover, 1969.

Huyssen, Andreas. *After the Great Divide: Modernism, Mass Culture, Postmodernism.* Bloomington: Indiana University Press 1986.

Hyett, Barbara Helfgott. *In Evidence: Poems of the Liberation of the Nazi Concentration Camps.* Pittsburgh: University of Pittsburgh Press, 1986.

Ihde, Don. *Consequences of Phenomenology.* Albany: State University of New York Press, 1986.

———. *Experimental Phenomenology: An Introduction.* New York: Putnam's, 1977.

———. *Sense and Significance.* Duquesne Studies Philosophical Series. Pittsburgh: Duquesne University Press, 1973.

Im Zeichen der Rose: Leben und Werk Adalbert Stifters. Eine Ausstellung des Adalbert Stifter Vereins. Munich: Adalbert Stifter Verein, 1986.

Jahnn, Hans Henny. *Werke und Tagebücher in sieben Bänden.* Ed. Thomas Freeman and Thomas Scheuffelen. 7 vols. Hamburg: Hoffmann and Campe, 1974.

Johnson, Paul. *Enemies of Society.* New York: Atheneum, 1977.

Joyce, James. *Ulysses.* 1914. New York: Vintage, 1961.

Jünger, Ernst. *In Stahlgewittern.* 1920. Vol. 1 of *Werke.* Klett: Stuttgart, 1978–83.

Jürgens, M., and Wolf Lepenies, eds. *Ästhetik und Gewalt.* Gütersloh: Bertelsmann Kunstverlag, 1970.

Kaes, Anton. "New Historicism and the Study of German Literature." *German Quarterly* 62, no. 2 (1989): 210–19.

Kaiser, Gerhard, and Friedrich A. Kittler. *Dichtung als Sozialisationsspiel: Studien zu Goethe und Gottfried Keller.* Göttingen: Vandenhoeck and Ruprecht, 1978.

Kaiser, Herbert. *Studien zum deutschen Roman nach 1848.* Duisburger Hochschulbeiträge 8. Duisburg: Walter Braun Verlag, 1977.

Kamper, Dietmar, and Christoph Wulf. *Das Schwinden der Sinne.* Frankfurt am Main: Suhrkamp, 1984.

Kant, Immanuel. *Anthropologie in pragmatischer Hinsicht.* Ed. Karl Vorländer. Hamburg: Felix Meiner, 1980.

———. *Kritik der Urteilskraft.* Vol. 10 of *Werkausgabe in zwölf Bänden.* Ed. Wilhelm Weischedel. Frankfurt am Main: Suhrkamp, 1974.

Karl, Frederick R. *Modern and Modernism: The Sovereignty of the Artist 1885–1925.* New York: Atheneum, 1985.

Keller, Gottfried. *Der grüne Heinrich.* Vol. 2 of *Gesammelte Werke.* Ed. Hans Schumacher. Zürich: Büchergilde Gutenberg, 1960.

Kermode, Frank. *The Uses of Error.* Cambridge: Harvard University Press, 1991.

Kern, Stephen. *The Culture of Time and Space 1880–1918.* Cambridge: Harvard University Press, 1983.

———. "Olfactory Ontology and Scented Harmonies: On the History of Smell," *Journal of Popular Culture* 7 (1974): 817–24.

Kielar, Wieslaw. *Anus Mundi: 1500 Days in Auschwitz/Birkenau.* Trans. Susanne Flatauer. New York: Times Books, 1980.

Killy, Walther. "Abschied vom Jahrhundert: Wirklichkeit und Kunstcharakter." In *Theodor Fontane,* ed. Wolfgang Preisendanz. Wege der Forschung, vol. 381. Darmstadt: Wissenschaftliche Buchgesellschaft, 1973.

Kittler, Friedrich A. *Aufschreibesysteme 1800–1900.* Munich: Wilhelm Fink, 1985.

Kluge, Alexander. *Gelegenheitsarbeit einer Sklavin: Zur realistischen Methode.* Frankfurt am Main: Suhrkamp, 1975.

Knorr, Wolfram. "Aus Zwerg Nase wird ein Frankenstein der Düfte." *Weltwoche,* 21 March 1985.

Koeppen, Wolfgang. *Tauben im Gras.* Vol. 2 of *Gesammelte Werke in sechs Bänden.* Ed. Marcel Reich-Ranicki. Frankfurt am Main: Suhrkamp, 1986.

———. *Der Tod in Rom.* Vol. 2 of *Gesammelte Werke in sechs Bänden.* Ed. Marcel Reich-Ranicki. Frankfurt am Main: Suhrkamp, 1986.

———. *Das Treibhaus.* Vol. 2 of *Gesammelte Werke in sechs Bänden.* Ed. Marcel Reich-Ranicki. Frankfurt am Main: Suhrkamp, 1986.

Krafft-Ebing, Richard Freiherr von. *Psychopathia Sexualis: A Medico-Forensic Study.* Trans. Harry E. Wedeck. New York: Putnam, 1965.

———. *Verirrungen des Geschlechtslebens.* Auf Grund der 17. Auflage von *Psychopathia Sexualis.* Frei bearbeitet von Dr. med. Alexander Hartwich. Rüschlikon: Müller, 1937.

Kunz, Joseph, ed. *Novelle.* Wege der Forschung, vol. 55. Darmstadt: Wissenschaftliche Buchgesellschaft, 1973.

Lachinger, Johann, Alexander Stillmark, and Martin Swales. *Adalbert Stifter heute: Londoner Symposium 1983.* Schriftenreihe des Adalbert-Stifer-Institutes des Landes Oberösterreich. Folge 35. Linz, 1985.

Laporte, Dominique. *Historie de la merde (Prologue).* Paris: Christian Bourgois Editeur, 1978.

Lawrence, D. H. *Lady Chatterley's Lover.* New York: Grove Press, 1959.

Lehrer, Adrienne. *Wine and Conversation.* Bloomington: Indiana University Press, 1983.

Lengyel, Olga. *Five Chimneys: The Story of Auschwitz.* Chicago: Ziff-Davis Publishing, 1947.

Lensing, Leo A., and Hans-Werner Peter, eds. *Wilhelm Raabe: Studien zu seinem Leben und Werk.* Braunschweig: pp-Verlag, 1981.

Leroi-Gourhan, André. *Le geste et la parole.* 2 vols. Paris: Edition Albin Michel, 1964.

Letulle, Claude J. *Nightmare Memoir: Four Years as a Prisoner of the Nazis.* Baton Rouge: Louisiana State University Press, 1987.

Levi, Primo. *Survival in Auschwitz* and *The Reawakening.* Trans. Stuart Wolf. 1st Ital. ed. 1958 and 1963. New York: Summit Books, 1986.

Lewes, G. H. "Realism in Art: Modern German Fiction" *Westminster Review* 70 (October 1858): 491ff.

Lifton, Robert Jay. *Death in Life: Survivors of Hiroshima.* New York: Vintage, 1969.

———. *The Nazi Doctors: Medical Killing and the Psychology of Genocide.* New York: Basic Books, 1986.

Lingis, Alphonso. *Libido: The French Existential Theories.* Bloomington: Indiana University Press, 1985.

zur Lippe, Rudolf. *Sinnenbewußtsein: Grundlegung einer anthropologischen Ästhetik.* Reinbek bei Hamburg: Rowohlt, 1987.

Locke, John. *An Essay Concerning Human Understanding.* Ed. Peter H. Nidditch. Oxford: Clarendon, 1975.

Lotze, Hermann. *Geschichte der Ästhetik in Deutschland.* Munich: Cotta, 1868.

———. *Mikrokosmus: Ideen zur Naturgeschichte und Geschichte der Menschheit. Versuch einer Anthropologie.* 3 vols. Leipzig: Hirzel, 1872–78.

Lucht, Frank. "Erkennen Sie die Melodie?" In *Deutsche Literatur 1986: Ein Jahresüberblick,* ed. Volker Hage, 300–308. Stuttgart: Reclam, 1987.

Lucretius. *De Rerum Natura.* In *The Stoic and Epicurean Philosophers: The Complete Extant Writings of Epicurus, Epictetes, Lucretius, Marcus Aurelius,* ed. Whitney J. Oates. New York: Random House, 1940.

Ludel, Jacqueline. *Introduction to Sensory Processes.* San Francisco: Freeman, 1978.

Luhmann, Niklas. *Love as Passion: The Codification of Intimacy.* Trans. Jeremy Gaines and Doris L. Jones. Cambridge: Polity Press, 1986.

Macho, Thomas H. *Todesmetaphern: Zur Logik der Grenzerfahrung.* Frankfurt am Main: Suhrkamp, 1987.

Mahal, Günther. *Naturalismus.* Munich: Fink, 1975.

Maier, Charles S. *The Unmasterable Past: History, Holocaust, and German National Identity.* Cambridge: Harvard University Press, 1988.

Maier, Wolfgang. *Oscar Wilde: The Picture of Dorian Gray. Eine kritische Analyse der anglistischen Forschung von 1962–1982.* Aspekte der englischen Geistes- und Kulturgeschichte, ed. Jürgen Klein. Universität Gesamthochschule Siegen, vol. 1. Frankfurt am Main: Peter Lang, 1984.

Mallarmé, Stéphane. *Oeuvres complètes.* Ed. Henri Mondor and G. Jean-Aubry. Bibliothèque de la Pléiade: Paris: Editions Gallimard, 1945.

Mann, Gunter, and Franz Dumont. *Gehirn—Nerven—Seele: Anatomie und Physiologie im Umfeld S. T. Soemmerrings.* Stuttgart: Gustav Fischer, 1988.

Mann, Thomas. *Buddenbrooks.* Vol. 3 of *Gesammelte Werke in Einzelbänden.* Frankfurter Ausgabe. Ed. Peter de Mendelssohn. Frankfurt am Main: Fischer, 1980–.

Marks, Lawrence E. *The Unity of the Senses: Interrelation Among the Modalities.* New York: Academic Press, 1978.

Martini, Fritz. *Deutsche Literaturgeschichte von den Anfängen bis zur Gegenwart.* 5th ed. Stuttgart: A. Kröner, 1954.

———. *Deutsche Literatur im bürgerlichen Realismus 1848–98.* 4th ed. Stuttgart: Metzler, 1981.

———. *Forschungsbericht zur deutschen Literatur in der Zeit des Realismus.* Stuttgart: Metzler, 1962.

Martino, Alberto, ed. *Literatur in der sozialen Bewegung: Aufsätze und Forschungsberichte zum 19. Jahrhundert.* Tübingen: Niemeyer, 1977.

Mason, Stuart. *Oscar Wilde: Art and Morality. A Record of the Discussion which Followed the Publication of Dorian Gray.* 1907. New York: Haskell House, 1971.

Mechsner, Franz, and Wolfgang Volz. "Immer der Nase nach." *Geo,* April 1987, 14–34.

Merleau-Ponty, Maurice. *Phenomenology of Perception.* Trans. Colin Smith. London: Routledge and Kegan Paul; New York: Humanities Press, 1962.

———. *The Primacy of Perception And Other Essays on Phenomenological Psychology, the Philosophy of Art, History and Politics.* Ed. James M. Edie, trans. William Cobb. Evanston: Northwestern University Press, 1964.

————. *Sense and Non-Sense*. Trans. Hubert L. Dreyfus and Patricia Allen Dreyfus. Evanston: Northwestern University Press, 1964.

Meyers, Jeffrey. "The Duel in Fiction." *North Dakota Quarterly* 51 (Fall 1983): 129–50.

Mirsky, D. S. *A History of Russian Literature*. Ed. and abridged Francis J. Whitfield. 1926. New York: Knopf, 1960.

Mommsen, Katharina. *Gesellschaftskritik bei Fontane und Thomas Mann*. Heidelberg: Lothar Stiehm, 1973.

Monas, Sidney. "St. Petersburg and Moscow as Cultural Symbols." In *Art and Culture in Nineteenth-Century Russia*, ed. Theophanis George Stavrou. Bloomington: Indiana University Press, 1983.

Montaigne, Michel de. *Essais*. 2 vols. Paris: Edition Garnier Frères, 1962.

Muschg, Adolf. *Gottfried Keller*. Munich: Kindler, 1977.

The Museum of the City of New York. "Reflections of Fragrance and Society." (Exhibit handouts). New York, 1988.

Musil, Robert. *Gesammelte Werke in neun Bänden*. Ed. Adolf Frisé. Reinbek bei Hamburg: Rowohlt, 1978.

Mynona [Salomo Friedländer]. *Ich verlange ein Reiterstandbild: Grotesken und Visionen*. Ed. Harmut Geerken. Prosa Band 1. Munich: Text und Kritik, 1980.

————. *Rosa, die schöne Schutzmannsfrau und andere Grotesken*. Ed. Ellen Otten. Zurich: Arche, 1965.

————. *Der verliebte Leichnam: Grotesken—Erzählungen—Gedichte*. Ed. Klaus Konz. Hamburg: Galgenberg, 1985.

————. "Von der Wollust über Brücken zu gehen." *Die Aktion*, 11 September 1911.

Naumann, Ursula. *Adalbert Stifter*. Sammlung Metzler, vol. 186. Realien zur Literatur. Metzler: Stuttgart, 1979.

Nemoianu, Virgil. *The Taming of Romanticism: European Romanticism and the Age of Biedermeier*. Cambridge: Harvard University Press, 1984.

Neugebauer, Klaus. *Selbstentwurf und Verhängnis: Ein Beitrag zu Adalbert Stifters Verständnis von Schicksal und Geschichte*. Tübingen: Stauffenberg Verlag, 1982.

Newman, Charles. *The Post-Modern Aura: The Act of Fiction in an Age of Inflation*. Evanston: Northwestern University Press, 1985.

Nietzsche, Friedrich. *Werke: Kritische Gesamtausgabe*. Ed. Giorgio Colli and Mazzino Montinari. Berlin: De Gruyter, 1967–.

————. *Werke in drei Bänden*. Ed. Karl Schlechta. 3 vols. Munich: Hanser, 1954–56.

Nutt, Harry. "Kürzelkritik und Kritik des Kürzels." In *Deutsche Literatur 1986: Ein Jahresüberblick*, ed. Volker Hage, 308–13. Stuttgart: Reclam, 1987.

Oates, Whitney J., ed. *The Stoic and Epicurean Philosophers: The Complete Extant Writings of Epicurus, Epictetes, Lucretius, Marcus Aurelius*. New York: Random House, 1940.

Obermeier, Renate. *Stadt und Natur: Studie zu Texten von Adalbert Stifter und Gottfried Keller*. Gießener Arbeiten zur neueren deutschen Literatur und Literaturwissenschaft. Frankfurt am Main: Peter Lang, 1985.

Oppenheimer, Paul, trans. *A Pleasant Vintage of Till Eulenspiegel.* Middletown, Conn: Wesleyan University Press, 1972.

Oppermann, Hans. *Wilhelm Raabe in Selbstzeugnissen und Bilddokumenten.* Reinbek bei Hamburg: Rowohlt, 1970.

Ortheil, Hanns-Josef. "Das Lesen—ein Spiel: Postmoderne Literatur? Die Literatur der Zukunft!" In *Deutsche Literatur 1986: Ein Jahresüberblick,* ed. Volker Hage, 313–22. Stuttgart: Reclam, 1987.

Osborne, Harold. "Odours and Appreciation." *British Journal of Aesthetics* 17, no. 1 (1977): 37–48.

Otten, Karl. "Adam." In *Theorie des Expressionismus,* ed. Otto F. Best. Stuttgart: Reclam, 1976.

The Oxford Companion to German Literature. Ed. Henry Garland and Mary Garland. Oxford: Clarendon, 1976.

Ozick, Cynthia. "Mouth, Ear, Nose." *New York Times Book Review,* 23 October 1988, 7.

Paglia, Camille. *Sexual Personae: Art and Decadence from Nefertiti to Emily Dickinson.* 1990. New York: Vintage, 1991.

Palmer, Roy. *The Water Closet: A New History.* Newton Abbot: David and Charles, 1973.

Perkins, David, ed. *Theoretical Issues in Literary History.* Harvard English Studies 16. Cambridge: Harvard University Press, 1991.

Piechowski, Paul. *Friedrich Ludwig Jahn: Vom Turnvater zum Volkserzieher.* Gotha: Leopold Klotz Verlag, 1928.

Piesse, S. *Histoire des parfums et hygiène de la toilette.* Paris, 1905.

Poiret, Paul. *En habillant l'époque.* Paris: Librairie Grasset, 1930.

Popp, Wolfgang, ed. *Die Suche nach dem rechten Mann: Männerfreundschaft im literarischen Werk Hans Henny Jahnns.* Literatur im historischen Prozess. Neue Folge 13. Argument-Sonderband AS 128. Berlin: Argument-Verlag, 1984.

Poppe, Johann H. M. von. *Geschichte aller Erfindungen und Entdeckungen im Bereiche der Gewerbe, Künste und Wissenschaften von der frühesten Zeit bis auf unsere Tage.* 2d ed. Frankfurt am Main: Verlag von Joseph Baer, 1847.

Preisendanz, Wolfgang, ed. *Theodor Fontane.* Wege der Forschung, vol. 381. Darmstadt: Wissenschaftliche Buchgesellschaft, 1973.

Proust, Adrien. *Traité de l'hygiène.* 2d ed. Paris: A. Masson, 1881.

Proust, Marcel. *A la recherche du temps perdu.* Ed. Pierre Clarac and André Ferré. 3 vols. Paris: Gallimard, 1954.

Pütz, Manfred, and Peter Freese. *Postmodernism in American Literature.* Darmstadt: Thesen Verlag, 1984.

Raabe, Wilhelm. *Sämtliche Werke.* Ed. Karl Hoppe. 20 vols. plus 4 vols. supplement. Freiburg and Braunschweig: Klemm, 1951–60; Göttingen: Vandenhoeck and Ruprecht, 1960–.

Radcliffe, Stanley. "Raabe—und kein Ende." *German Life and Letters,* July 1989, 384–93.

Riasanovsky, Nicholas. "Notes on the Emergence and Nature of the Russian Intelligentsia." In *Art and Culture in Nineteenth-Century Russia,* ed. Theophanis George Stavrou. Bloomington: Indiana University Press, 1983.

Rieckmann, Jens. *Aufbruch in die Moderne: Die Anfänge des Jungen Wien. Österreichische Literatur und Kritik im Fin de Siècle.* Königstein: Athenäum, 1985.

Rilke, Rainer Maria. *Sämtliche Werke.* Ed. Rilke Archiv with Ruth Sieber-Rilke and Ernst Zinn. 6 vols. Frankfurt am Main: Insel, 1955–66.

Rimbaud, Arthur. *Complete Works, Selected Letters.* Trans. Wallace Fowlie. Chicago: University of Chicago Press, 1966.

Robbins, Tom. *Jitterbug Perfume.* Toronto: Bantam Books, 1984.

Roch, Herbert. *Fontane, Berlin und das 19. Jahrhundert.* 1962. Düsseldorf: Droste. 1985.

Rodrigues-Lores, Juan, and Gerhard Fehl, eds. *Städtebaureform 1865–1900: Von Licht, Luft und Ordnung in der Stadt der Gründerzeit. Allgemeine Beiträge und Bebauungsplanung.* Hamburg: Christians Verlag, 1985.

Ruckhäberle, Hans-Joachim, and Helmut Widhammer. *Romane und Romantheorie des deutschen Realismus: Darstellung und Dokumente.* Kronberg: Athenäum, 1977.

Ryan, Judith. "The Problem of Pastiche: Patrick Süskind's *Das Parfum.*" *German Quarterly* 63, no. 3/4 (1990): 396–403.

Sagarin, Edward. *The Science and Art of Perfumery.* New York: McGraw-Hill, 1945.

Salloch, Erika. *Peter Weiss, Die Ermittlung: Zur Struktur des Dokumentartheaters.* Frankfurt am Main: Athenäum, 1972.

Sammons, Jeffrey L. "The Mill on the Sewer: Wilhelm Raabe's *Pfister's Mill* and the Present Relevance of Past Literature." *Orbis Litterarum* 40 (1985): 16–32.

———. *Raabe: Pfisters Mühle.* Critical Guides to German Texts. London: Grant and Cutler, 1988.

———. *Wilhelm Raabe: The Fiction of the Alternative Community.* Princeton: Princeton University Press, 1987.

Sawer, J. Ch. *Odorographia: A natural history of raw materials and drugs used in the perfume industry. Intended to serve grower, manufacturer and consumer.* 2 vols. London, 1892.

Schachtel, Ernest G. *Metamorphosis: On the Development of Affects, Perception, Attention, and Memory.* New York: Basic Books, 1959.

Schaffner, Jakob. "Die Geschichte vom Moschus." *Meisternovellen.* Berlin: Zsolnay, 1936.

Schiffman, Harvey Richard. *Sensations and Perception: An Integrated Approach.* New York: Wiley, 1976.

Schiller, Friedrich. *Werke: Nationalausgabe.* Ed. Lieselotte Blumenthal and Benno von Wiese. Im Auftrag der Nationalen Forschungs- und Gedenkstätten der klassischen deutschen Literatur in Weimar und des Schiller-Nationalmuseums in Marbach. Weimar: Hermann Böhlaus Nachfolger, 1943-.

Schlegel, Friedrich. *Friedrich Schlegels Lucinde und Materialien zu einer Theorie des Müssiggangs.* Ed. Gisela Dischner. Hildesheim: Gerstenberg, 1980.

Schleiden, Matthias J. *Die Rose: Geschichte und Symbolik in ethnographischer und kulturhistorischer Beziehung.* Leipzig: Wilhelm Engelmann, 1873.

Schmitt, Hans Jürgen, ed. *Die Expressionismusdebatte: Materialien zu einer marxistischen Realismuskonzeption.* Frankfurt am Main: Suhrkamp, 1973.

Schnitzler, Arthur. *Das erzählerische Werk.* 7 vols. Frankfurt am Main: Fischer, 1961.

Schorske, Carl E. *Fin-de-Siècle Vienna: Politics and Culture.* 1961. New York: Vintage, 1981.

Schütte, Wolfram. "Parabel und Gedankenspiel." In *Deutsche Literatur 1985: Ein Jahresüberblick,* ed. Volker Hage, 237–45. Stuttgart: Reclam, 1986.

Segeberg, Harro, ed. *Technik in der Literatur: Ein Forschungsüberblick und zwölf Aufsätze.* Frankfurt am Main: Suhrkamp, 1987.

Seifert, Walter. *Das epische Werk Rainer Maria Rilkes.* Bonn: Bouvier, 1969.

Sengle, Friedrich. *Biedermeierzeit: Deutsche Literatur im Spannungsfeld zwischen Restauration und Revolution 1815–1848.* 2 vols. Stuttgart: Metzler, 1971.

Serres, Michel. *Les cinq sens.* Grasset: Paris, 1985.

———. "Corruption—*The Antichrist:* A Chemistry of Sensations and Ideas." Trans. Chris Bongie. *Stanford Italian Review* 6, no. 1–2 (1986): 31–52.

Shattuck, Roger. *The Innocent Eye: On Modern Literature and the Arts.* New York: Farrar, Straus, Giroux, 1984.

Sheehan, James J. *Der deutsche Liberalismus: Von den Anfängen im 18. Jahrhundert bis zum Ersten Weltkrieg, 1770–1914.* Trans. Karl Heinz Siber. 1st Engl. ed. 1978. Munich: Beck, 1983.

———. *German History 1770–1866.* Oxford: Clarendon, 1989.

Shelmerdine, Cynthia. *The Perfume Industry of Mycenaean Pylos.* Göteborg: Astroms. 1985.

Siebert, Donald T. "Swift's 'Fiat Odor': The Excremental Re-Vision." *Eighteenth Century Studies* 1 (1985): 21–38.

Sperber, Dan. *Rethinking Symbolism.* Cambridge: Cambridge University Press, 1975.

Stallybrass, Peter, and Allon White. *The Politics and Poetics of Transgression.* Ithaca, New York: Cornell University Press, 1986.

Stavrou, Theophanis George, ed. *Art and Culture in Nineteenth-Century Russia.* Bloomington: Indiana University Press, 1983.

Steinecke, Hartmut. "Gustav Freytag: *Soll und Haben* (1855): Weltbild und Wirkung eines deutschen Bestsellers." In *Romane und Erzählungen des Bürgerlichen Realismus,* ed. Horst Denkler. Stuttgart: Reclam, 1980.

Stephan, Philip. *Paul Verlaine and the Decadence 1882–90.* Manchester: Manchester University Press, 1974.

Stiebitz, Rüdiger. "Ästhetik und Erziehung zur Gewalt." In M. Jürgens and Wolf Lepenies, eds. *Ästhetik und Gewalt*. Gütersloh: Bertelsmann Kunstverlag, 1970.

Stifter, Adalbert. *Der Nachsommer*. Frankfurt am Main: Insel, 1982.

Straus, Erwin. *The Primary World of Senses: A Vindication of Sensory Experience*. Trans. Jacob Needleman. London: Collier-Macmillan, 1963.

Sulloway, Frank J. *Freud, Biologist of the Mind: Beyond the Psychoanalytic Legend*. New York: Basic Books, 1979.

Süskind, Patrick. *Das Parfum*. Zurich: Diogenes, 1985.

Swales, Martin, and Erica Swales. *Adalbert Stifter: A Critical Study*. Anglica Germanica, Series 2. Cambridge: Cambridge University Press, 1984.

Symposium Aristotelicum. *Aristotle on Mind and the Senses*. Cambridge: Cambridge University Press, 1978.

Tahri, Sigrid. "Die Zeichen leuchteten auf wie Lichter in der Nacht." *Weltwoche*, 15 September 1988, 83.

Tellenbach, Hubert. *Geschmack und Atmosphäre: Medien menschlichen Elementarkontaktes*. Salzburg: Otto Müller Verlag, 1968.

Thaden, Edward C. *Russia Since 1801: The Making of a New Society*. New York: Wiley, 1971.

Tolstoy, Leo. *Anna Karenina*. Ed. George Gibian, trans. Louise and Aylmer Maude. A Norton Critical Edition. New York: Norton, 1970.

———. *The Death of Ivan Ilych and Other Stories*. Trans. Aylmer Maude. New York: New American Library, 1960.

Turgenev, Ivan. *Fathers and Sons*. Ed. and trans. Ralph E. Matlaw. A Norton Critical Edition. New York: Norton, 1966.

———. *First Love*. Trans. Isaiah Berlin. Harmondsworth: Penguin, 1988.

Ueberhorst, Horst. *Zurück zu Jahn? Gab es kein besseres Vorwärts?* Bochum: Universitätsverlag Bochum, 1969.

Utitz, Emil. *J. J. W. Heinse und die Ästhetik zur Zeit der deutschen Aufklärung: Eine problemgeschichtliche Studie*. Halle: Niemeyer, 1906.

Verlaine, Paul. *Oeuvres poétiques complètes*. Ed. Y. G. Le Dantec. Bibliothèque de la Pléiade. Paris: Editions de la nouvelle revue française, 1938.

———. *Femmes/Hombres*. Trans. William Packard and John D. Mitchell. Chicago: Chicago Review Press, 1977.

Vigarello, Georges. *Le propre et le sale: L'hygiène du corps depuis le Moyen Age*. Paris: Editions du Seuil. 1985.

Virchow, Rudolf. *Collected Essays on Public Health and Epidemiology*. Ed. L. J. Rather, M.D. 2 vols. Canton, Mass.: Science History Publications USA, 1985.

———. *Die Not im Spessart—Mitteilungen über die in Oberschlesien herrschende Typhus-Epidemie*. Darmstadt: Wissenschaftliche Buchgesellschaft, 1986.

Walder, Ann. "Swinburne's Flowers of Evil: Baudelaire's Influence on Poems and Ballads, First Series." Ph.D. diss., Uppsala University, 1976.

Walkhoff, Monika. *Der Briefwechsel zwischen Paul Heyse und Hermann Kurz in den Jahren 1869–1873, aus Anlaß der Herausgabe des Deutschen Novellenschatzes.* Munich: Foto-Druck Frank, 1967.

Weber, E. H. *The Sense of Touch, (Tastsinn und Gemeingefühl).* 1846. Trans. H. E. Ross and D. J. Murray. Experimental Psychology Society. London: Academic Press, 1978.

Weiss, Peter. *Ästhetik des Widerstands.* Franfurt am Main: Suhrkamp, 1975.

———. *Die Ermittlung: Oratorium in 11 Gesängen.* 1965. Reinbek bei Hamburg: Rowohlt, 1975.

Welsch, Wolfgang. *Ästhetisches Denken.* Stuttgart: Reclam, 1990.

Wilde, Oscar. *The Picture of Dorian Gray (Urfassung 1890).* Ed. Wilfried Edener. Erlanger Beiträge zur Sprach- und Kunstwissenschaft, vol. 18. Nuremberg: Verlag Hans Carl, 1964.

Wildhammer, Helmut. *Die Literaturtheorie des deutschen Realismus 1848–1860.* Sammlung Metzler, vol. 152. Stuttgart: Metzler, 1977.

Wilentz, Joan Steen. *The Senses of Man.* New York: Crowell, 1968.

Wilke, Sabine: "Kreuz- und Wendepunkte unserer Zivilisation. Nach-denken: Christa Wolfs Stellung im Umfeld der zeitgenössischen Mythos-Diskussion." *German Quarterly* 61 (Spring 1988): 213–28.

Willner, Ann Ruth. *The Spellbinders: Charismatic Political Leadership.* New Haven: Yale University Press, 1984.

Winkle, Stefan. *Johann Friedrich Struensee. Arzt, Aufklärer und Staatsmann: Beitrag zur Kultur-, Medizin- und Seuchengeschichte der Aufklärungszeit.* Stuttgart: Gustav Fischer Verlag, 1983.

Winter, Ruth. *The Smell Book.* Philadelphia: Lippincott, 1976.

Winterbourne, A. T. "Is Oral and Olfactory Art Possible?" *Journal of Aesthetic Education* 15, no. 2 (1981): 95–102.

Wittmann, Reinhard. *Buchmarkt und Lektüre im 18. und 19. Jahrhundert: Beiträge zum literarischen Leben 1750–1880.* Studien und Texte zur Sozialgeschichte der Literatur, vol. 12, ed. Wolfgang Frühwald, Georg Jäger, Dieter Langewiesche, Alberto Martino, and Rainer Wohlfeil. Tübingen: Niemeyer, 1982.

Wolf, Christa. *Störfall: Nachrichten eines Tages.* Darmstadt: Luchterhand, 1987.

———. *Was bleibt.* Frankfurt am Main: Luchterhand Literaturverlag, 1990.

Wollstein, Günter. *Das "Grossdeutschland" der Paulskirche: Nationale Ziele in der bürgerlichen Revolution 1848/49.* Düsseldorf: Droste, 1977.

Worbs, Michael. *Nervenkunst: Literatur und Psychoanalyse im Wien der Jahrhundertwende.* Frankfurt am Main: Europäische Verlagsanstalt, 1983.

Zola, Émile. *Oeuvres complètes.* Ed. Henri Mitterand. Paris: Cercle du livre précieux, 1960–67.

Index

DATE DUE

GAYLORD